TOUCHSTONE

THE TWILIGHT
of CAPITALISM

by MICHAEL HARRINGTON

A Touchstone Book
Published by Simon and Schuster

Designed by Irving Perkins
Manufactured in the United States of America

1   2   3   4   5   6   7   8   9   10

Library of Congress Cataloging in Publication Data

Harrington, Michael.
The twilight of capitalism.
Bibliography
Includes index.
1.   Marx, Karl, 1818–1883.   2.   United States—
Economic policy—1961–   3.   United States—Social
policy.   I.   Title.
HX39.5.H28   335.4   75–41465
ISBN 0–671–22196–5
ISBN 0–671–22759–9 pbk.

To the future of an almost forgotten genius:
the foe of every dogma, champion of human
freedom and democratic socialist—KARL MARX

CONTENTS

PART I

The New Karl Marx

CHAPTER 1

ORACLE IN THE RUINS

WESTERN capitalism is in crisis.

During the two decades from 1950 to 1970—from the reconstruction of Europe to the Great Recession-Inflation of recent years—that statement would have been perceived as absurd everywhere but on the socialist left. Conservatives, liberals, even social democrats agreed: capitalism had transformed itself, resolving those of its internal contradictions which had exploded in the catastrophes of the 1930s. For many it had become postcapitalism, a new society, which, though vaguely defined, was supposed to be free from the destructive cycles of boom and bust.

But then, even now, in the tumult of the middle seventies, when a sense of foreboding and fear has seeped through the Western consciousness, it still does not seem that these new troubles are the product of an economic system. Rather, one might blame these things on a remarkable outbreak of bad luck. The Organization of Petroleum Exporting Countries (OPEC) was accidentally unified in response to the Yom Kippur War of 1973 and thereby discovered that it could quadruple the price of oil. Bad weather in Russia and other countries caused prices for agricultural exports to rise on the world market and sent the cost of food soaring. Even the

11

spectacular ineptitude of the economic management in the Nixon and Ford administrations could be understood as a matter of political chance, not of structural necessity. On all these counts, there was no need to have recourse to an outmoded category like capitalism. One simply cursed the accumulation of misfortune and looked for ways to muddle through.

This means that the real history of the crisis of the seventies is still a secret kept from most of the people who must suffer from it. All the explanations to the contrary notwithstanding, it is a crisis of the capitalist system. Outrageous as the truth may seem, those years of prosperity and expansion were preparing the recent calamities even as they gave rise to the understandable illusion that the old problems of capitalism had finally been eliminated. To be sure, the classic contradictions of the system no longer manifested themselves in the traditional ways. Planning and governmental intervention have indeed made a difference. But it turned out that the antagonisms within the system had been postponed, transformed, rechanneled—but not abolished. And ironically, the very process whereby the old devils of the economy were exorcised had given rise to a legion of new devils.

The secret history of our crisis is the subject of Part II of this book. In it, Karl Marx's method is applied to a situation of which Karl Marx never dreamed. But before Marx can be restored to the future, he must be rescued from a murky past. That is the work of Part I.

At first glance, it may seem that this approach results in two books, not one: a scholarly rediscovery of Marx and an analysis of the twilight of welfare capitalism. In fact, Parts I and II are inextricably linked together. If this book's dissection of the current calamities succeeds in what it sets out to do, then the unique signs of its Marxist inspiration will be found in its subtlety and sense of complex social interactions within a massive whole. This is, of course, the exact opposite of the mechanistic explanations that most of the friends and foes of Karl Marx take as his legacy. It is not simply that Marxism is infinitely more supple than is imagined in the Soviet and Chinese catechisms; it is also more open and vital than the contemporary theories of postindustrial society, which contemptuously dismiss it as an obsolete survival from the nineteenth century.

If these things will be demonstrated in the practice of Part II, that is only possible because of the method summarized in Part I. When looking at society, as this chapter will suggest, the eyes must be carefully prepared to see what they see. But this method cannot be presented as if it were an algebra of human history in which one need only fill in the specific quantities of each particular epoch. Its confirmation is, and can only be, found in its application. I go, then, in search of the historical Marx in order to find the future Marx. And that is no easy task.

When the centenary of Marx's death is commemorated, in a few years, it will be widely noted that his thought has been disseminated to every corner of the globe, that it has reached into the minds of scholars and workers and peasants on every continent, into libraries and mud huts. It will probably not be remarked that the ideas which bear his name are at best cheap vulgarizations and at worst outright misstatements of what he said. Yet that is the fact. I therefore propose, first of all, to remove a mountain of rubbish from his tomb, much of it lovingly placed there by those who revere his memory. This cannot be done easily or quickly, yet it is necessary. For I am not concerned with vindicating a ghost; I hope to introduce a living presence into the late-twentieth—and even the twenty-first—century. Let me call him "the new Karl Marx."

I do not pretend to have discovered this authentic Marx on my own. He has been recognized for over fifty years by a sort of Marxian underground, by a handful of political and academic thinkers, all of them on the margin of power, the brilliance of their Marxian theory in an ironically inverse relationship to the impotence of their Marxian politics. Yet, even though others wrote about the new Marx, he is still hardly known; and one must at this very late date summarize those mysterious hieroglyphics, the ABC's of Marxism, for the nonspecialist reader.* (See Appendix A, §1, p. 343.)

---

* Since I want to address myself to the sincere, but often befuddled, scholars as well as to the general reader, I have included in the text references to appendices, which contain more detailed elaboration as well as documentation of points that are not directly or conclusively supportive of

In all of this, I do not make the arrogant claim that mine is the only reading of Marx. I merely, but emphatically, assert that most theories calling themselves Marxism are anti-Marxist, even if they are sometimes murderously effective; and that the new Marx of my explication is located within the range of plausible interpretation—that is, within an area still surrounded by nearly universal ignorance.

I

There are two fundamental objections which must be confronted at the outset of this project, since they suggest, with some apparent reason, that the enterprise should not even be begun. First of all, the non- and anti-Marxist might ask, How can one possibly think that what humankind now needs is another ism? And a resurrected ism at that?

In part, this question rests upon an understandable confusion. What normally passes as Marxism is an ism in the worst sense of the word: dogmatic, rigid, intolerant, dismissing all criticism as the work of a self-interested, though usually unconscious, malice. That "Marxism" and all of the fanatic isms like it deserve to be driven from the face of the earth, which is precisely one of the functions of the Marxism described here. In fact, as a contrast between Marx and Hegel will show shortly, there is an openness, an antidogmatism, at the very center of a genuine Marxism.

But before developing that point, a more sophisticated version of the first objection must be taken up. Confronting it requires that we begin to formulate the uniqueness of Karl Marx, not simply in the past, but in the present and future as well. For there is no justification for even starting this study—other than piety or anti-quarianism—if Marx is not uniquely relevant to the transformation in which we live. The question that forces us to give a preliminary description of his distinctive and ongoing relevance is this: Why

---

the main argument. In addition, numbered notes at the end of each section of a chapter refer to conventional citations of sources for quotations, statistics, et cetera, that may be found starting on p. 343.

not be content with a pragmatic rendering of the facts? Why insist on a world view, on any ism, even an antidogmatic one?

Marx would answer—and in the process differentiate himself from all of contemporary social thought—that social "facts" as we encounter them in the world of daily life are artificial and profoundly conservative products of the status quo, designed and arranged precisely to convince us of its legitimacy. To penetrate these deceptions is, therefore, a task for theory, not for a camera. In part, this response builds upon a commonplace of Western culture that dates back some hundreds of years; in part, it is audaciously and unmistakably Marxist.

At least as far back as John Donne the West had begun to lament the loss of meaning, of a sense of the whole, that accompanied the rise of systematic empirical knowledge. In the "new philosophy" (or science), Donne said, one finds "all coherence gone." In the German classical tradition from which Karl Marx descended, Immanuel Kant brilliantly defined this new and painful consciousness. He said that the very ability of science and industry to transform external reality mocked the philosophers, who could never define that reality as it is in itself. Since we cannot verify the possibility of thought by means of thought, Kant continued, humankind discovers, at the very moment of its greatest triumph over objectivity, that it is locked within its subjectivity, that experience begins, not with the facts, but with the a prioris which permit us to perceive them. The Great Chain of Being, that hierarchy of palpable, known existence, which stretched from the tiniest speck of matter up to God and back, had been sundered. So, that inspired antisocialist, Friedrich Nietzsche, did not simply announce the death of God. He added that God "is my word for the ideal" and prophesied the end of all higher values, of all frameworks.

Max Weber, the great liberal sociologist, said much the same thing in a completely different language: The fate of our times is characterized by rationalization and intellectualization and, above all, by the "disenchantment of the world." Therefore, Weber argued, no one knows "whether at the end of this tremendous development entirely new prophets will arise, or there will be a great rebirth of old ideas and ideals or, if neither, mechanized petrification embellished with a sort of compulsive self-importance." As the world more and more became the product of humanity's mind and hand, it seemed even more opaque than when it had been seen as a blind and mysterious nature.

So there is a most meaningful cliché of some centuries' standing, that the organic wholeness of life was being shattered by the upheavals—religious and cultural as well as political and economic —which accompanied the emergence of the modern world, and some principle was necessary to organize the man-made facts which threaten to overwhelm man. On this count, Marx's insistence upon a theory, a world view, is hardly distinctive. A conservative like Edmund Burke might even share some of his insights (which was indeed the case, as will be seen), much as the workers and the aristocrats sometimes felt a common hatred of the bourgeois in the nineteenth century. But how, precisely, does one explain this sense of lost coherence that brooded within the modern age? Even more to the point, how does one cope with it, both analytically and practically? A contrast between Marx and Weber casts some light on the first part of this problem.

Weber might have concluded that his perception of a disenchanted world demanded that he be a new prophet or a champion of old ideas and ideals. He was fatalistic instead. He fought against the prophetic in politics and in social science, arguing that the "ethic of ultimate responsibility" was fine for those who wanted to save their souls, but irrelevant for the understanding or managing of an imperfect society. The sociologist should make his method value-free; he was chronicler and analyst, not revolutionary. To be sure, Weber never was the political and intellectual neutralist that some of his American disciples made of him in the conservative 1950s, and he always insisted that subjective values influenced the choice of subject matter. Still, he lent the authority of his genius to a certain resigned acceptance of the trends he described. The modern period, Weber had argued, was characterized by "functional rationality"—the progressive application of science to the tasks of the economy and society; only, it lacked "substantive rationality," a sense of the whole. Of critical importance for our purpose, he saw modern technology and bureaucracy, not capitalism, as the cause of this schizophrenia. It was, then, an inherent tendency of contemporary civilization itself, whether it was capitalist or socialist.

Marx had made the identical distinction that Weber did, but with a great difference. The division of labor in the factory, he wrote in *Das Kapital,* is planned in minute detail (it is "functionally rational," in Weber's language), but the division of labor in the society is anarchic (it is not "substantively rational"). "It is quite characteristic," Marx wrote bitterly, "that the most enthusiastic apologist of the factory system does not know anything more vexatious to say against the general organization of social labor [that is, against socialism] than that it will turn the entire society into a factory." For Marx the ingenious incoherence of contemporary life, its scientifically calculated purposelessness, is a function of the social system rather than of its technology.

In other words, the fact of our empirically rich bewilderment is not in doubt. Every thoughtful person for several hundred years has known about that. But the reason for it is a matter of great contention. Is it a consequence of modernity and science themselves, or of the political, economic and social way in which the new forces are organized? For Marx, it was clearly the latter. In a society whose fundamental principle was an antiprinciple of free-market atomism and which, furthermore, did not understand that its own exuberant individualism was the result of the most intricately socialized organization of production in the history of the race, there could be no overarching cohesion. Moreover, Marx argued—rightly as we shall see—that such a system produced not merely goods and services, but a characteristic way of seeing reality as well. There was, then, a capitalist stream of consciousness. *Das Kapital,* the careful reader will note, is among many other things, a psychological analysis of why things *seem* to be a certain way within this particular social formation.

This leads to Marx's response to the second part of the question, How can one cope with these distortions? Marx suggested, in a way that marks him off from all non-Marxists to this very day, that one must understand, and discount for, the systematic bias of what seem to be the unvarnished facts. At first glance, this might appear to be merely a rejection of a naïve empiricism, one which is shared by almost all scholars today. For it is intellectually fashionable in these times to insist that all sciences operate by way of *paradigms* —theories which allow them to order the unruly, infinite data. Marx does indeed make this point, but in a unique way. A brief statement of the current consensus will prepare the way for grasping his inspired departure from it.

Einstein put the matter succinctly with regard to the natural sciences. "It is," he said, "the theory which decides what we can observe." And Raymond Aron responded rather wearily to the insistence of the French Communist philosopher Louis Althusser that a "problematic," a way of organizing the evidence, is a precondition of serious analysis: "That every science implies a conceptual system, a construction of the object, we learned in class from professors of philosophy who themselves learned it, a generation earlier, from their own professors." Aron oversimplifies, as will be seen shortly, but the recent evidence seems to bear out his contemptuous dismissal of this insight as a commonplace. Indeed, in the 1960s and early seventies in the United States, the notion that every science operates on the basis of a "paradigm" became a staple of intellectual discourse.

The vogue of this term dates from a brilliant work by Thomas Kuhn, *The Structure of Scientific Revolutions.* For Kuhn, science does not advance by means of constant confrontations, of counterposed verifications and refutations. In normal periods research is guided by a paradigm, "universally recognized scientific achievements that for a time provide model problems and solutions to a community of practitioners." When some piece of evidence contradicts this model, it is usually taken as an exception to the rule, an anomaly to be solved. But then a genius revises the entire analytic structure, and the science lurches forward to the exploration of a new paradigm. What most of Ptolemy's successors had seen as puzzles within his framework, Copernicus recognized as counterinstances, facts that challenged the very system and required that it be changed.

One of Kuhn's most striking examples is the discovery of oxygen. In 1775, Joseph Priestley isolated the gas, but he interpreted his experiment in terms of the prevailing paradigm and said that he had found "dephlogisticated air." (Phlogiston was supposed to be the element that separated itself from a body in the process of burning, a notion which worked quite well in explaining most of the chemical evidence of the time.) Then, in 1777, Lavoisier realized that what Priestley had produced was a distinct gas, oxygen, and that it had nothing to do with dephlogisticated air. Priestley had made oxygen, but he had not discovered it; Lavoisier had developed a concept adequate to Priestley's experiment. The science of chemistry turned a corner.

Friedrich Engels anticipated Kuhn's basic thesis in the foreword that he wrote for the posthumous publication of the second volume of *Das Kapital* in 1885. His remarkable analysis points the way to a specifically Marxist understanding of the paradigms of social science.

Engels began by emphasizing that the notion that capitalists somehow extract unpaid labor from the workers was widely asserted before Marx. The existence of this surplus labor—surplus value, Marx would say—was known to Adam Smith and David Ricardo, among many others. Indeed, Engels notes, Marx, in Volume I, cited a pamphlet in which one of his precursors had even defined profit in a most Marxist fashion, as surplus labor. If all this had been said before Marx, what was it that made his analysis so distinctive? At this point, Engels recites the history of the discovery of oxygen much in the same manner as Thomas Kuhn, and with a similar interpretation. He then goes on to make a daring analogy: As Lavoisier related to Priestley, so Marx relates to Smith and Ricardo. They had acknowledged the fact of surplus labor, much as Priestley had made oxygen, but like him they did not comprehend their own finding. Marx formulated the new paradigm which permitted it to be understood. (See Appendix A, § 2, p. 353.)

The full import of Engels' claim will not be developed until Chapter 5, for it requires a knowledge of Marxian economics that is not relevant to this Introduction. What is pertinent here is the way in which Engels stressed the uniqueness of paradigms about society. It has been obvious from the beginning of intellectual time that thinkers become so captivated by their conceptual structures that they ignore the meaning of the facts in front of their faces. Kant decisively systematized that insight. It is also true that certain commonplace evidence is not absorbed until there is a theory that permits people to see what they are seeing; bodies fell before Isaac Newton formulated the law of gravity, and everyone knew it, but people did not know what they knew. What is not so obvious is that, in perceiving social, as distinct from natural, reality, problems of vision arise, because the object of study is constructed so as to distort the evidence.

Smith and Ricardo and even the early socialists, Engels argues, "remained trapped in the economic categories which they found before them." For Smith and Ricardo, surplus labor was a "fact," and their task was to quantify it, to determine how it was divided between capitalist and worker; for the socialists, it was also a "fact," an outrageous one, which is in conflict with truth and justice and should be abolished. For Marx, this "fact" was the historically transitory form which surplus labor took in, and only in, capitalist society. By seeing it as Smith, Ricardo and the pre-Marxian socialists did, as a fact, one conferred a kind of eternity, a natural-law objectivity, upon it. When this erroneous conception passed from the theorists into the language of the common men and women, it became a defense mechanism for the status quo. For then the very categories and definitions of the popular consciousness pointed to a single conclusion: that it would be foolish—or, for that matter, blasphemous—to tamper with the "facts" and, therefore, the demand to end the capitalist appropriation of surplus labor was like calling for the suspension of the law of gravity.

The Marxist concept of capital (which will be treated at much greater length in Chapter 5) should help to illuminate this distinctive analysis of the social paradigm. The very notion of capital appears to describe an undeniable, and immemorial, fact of productive life. From the moment primitive man began to claw his way toward civilization, tools have been a crucial means for human advancement. The machine in a factory, like the rock that became the first hammer, is a perennial, natural and necessary factor of all economic life. Yet, Marx argues in one of the central insights of *Das Kapital,* it is not the physical reality of the machine that makes it capital, but the mode of production in which it functions. Only under certain very explicit historical circumstances is it assumed that the private owner of a tool is to be compensated for its use, even if he does not work it, according to some measure of its "productivity." And that last point—that a tool is "productive"— contains the fetishistic assumption that inanimate things are creative. Thus the capitalist consciousness eternalizes and objectifies the relationships of a limited place and time and thereby confers upon them the dignity and solidity of a natural force. Under such circumstances to think of the abolition of capital is like thinking of the abolition of the air.

It is not, in Marx's view, an accident that the concepts and categories of capitalist society are rationalizations of its existence. He does not, of course, imagine that there is some kind of semantic conspiracy by which the agents of the bourgeoisie skillfully construct an apologetic vocabulary. Indeed, he insists that honest and sincere capitalists—and even authentic geniuses like Smith and Ricardo—are deluded by the "facts" which they see. Rather, Marx argues—and we will see that he is right—that the economic mechanism does not simply produce goods; it also reproduces society, and an important part of that output is a consciousness that things seem to be right and just and natural.

What Engels is suggesting in his distinctively Marxist version of the methodology of social science is that there are political assumptions and values underlying paradigms about society. As a result, such paradigms are profound only to the extent that they psychoanalyze the economic and social unconscious of a given society, revealing that its "facts" are functional myths, transitory truths. The paradigm that would have allowed Smith and Ricardo to conceptualize their own discovery of surplus labor was anticapitalist, but Smith and Ricardo were not. It is not, then, just a truism of post-Kantian philosophy, as Aron thinks, that there must be concepts to order—to select—the data. For the data of social life are already concepts masquerading as simple facts, and one must begin by unmasking them.

Indeed, one of the reasons why Marxism is so badly understood is that the authorities literally suppressed it for emphasizing precisely this political—and practical, revolutionary—aspect of its paradigm. Jean-Paul Sartre's experience is typical of all but the last generation in the West:

> When I was twenty, in 1925, there was no chair of Marxism at the university, and the Communist students carefully refrained from recourse to Marxism or even to mention it in their dissertations; they would have been turned back from the examinations. The horror of the dialectic was such that Hegel himself was unknown to us. To be sure, one permitted us to read Marx and even told us to do so; it was necessary to know him—"in order to refute him." But without a Hegelian tradition and without Marxist teachers, without program, without instruments of thought, our generation, like the one before and the one after, did not know historical materialism.

This situation, Sartre adds, was in part responsible for the fact that even those who did proclaim themselves Marxists did so in a void and actually embraced a mechanistic materialism.

The conditions that Sartre encountered in France in 1925 existed, with a few exceptions, in the United States until the sixties. And even now (as Chapter 7 will detail) it is not at all certain that the American academy has accepted Marx into the community of scholars. The natural sciences have encountered hostility and skepticism, but not, usually, repression by the forces of law and order. Thus, the history of Marxism itself emphasizes that it is not a paradigm like all the others since Kant, but a most distinctive, and radical, way of investigating the social whole, one which sees a coherence even in its stream of consciousness, a political function in its very habits of speech. This, I will demonstrate throughout this book, is a profound justification for the contemporary and future value of Marx's "ism."

One last point needs to be made on this count. It has to do with Marx's openness. That is not a distinct quality of his; he shares it with the Enlightenment tradition, with liberalism and rationalism. It is emphasized here only because it is so regularly and widely denied as a characteristic of Marxism. I take a somewhat roundabout and difficult way of documenting this fact, proceeding by contrasting Marx and Hegel. That is justified, I think, because it introduces a critical aspect of Marx's thought, one that will weave throughout this book. It also illuminates the openness of his theory and method.[1]

II

Hegel was a man of such complexity that he was claimed by both the radicals and the conservatives. It is said that he continued to drink his annual toast to the French Revolution every Bastille Day, even after he had decided that monarchy was the highest form of government. But for all of Hegel's awesome and intricate intellectuality, his philosophy is extraordinarily dramatic, and its basic categories are tangible, even simple: desire, fighting, work. History begins when man awakes in a hostile world and realizes that his needs are denied. That drives himself out of himself in an attack upon the environment that is counterposed to him. So he objectifies himself—in tools, for instance—in order to gain control over objectivity. This enterprise is, however, ambiguous; it creates new desires on the one hand, and on the other the very structures that man invented to help him control the world become alien powers over him. No matter, in transforming reality, man transforms and creates himself. The human essence, then, is history—that is, the sum total of what man has made of himself. A remarkably concentrated statement of some of these core ideas can be found in a few pages on the process of life, in Hegel's *Logic*.

So desire moves history and propels man into the future and the fashioning of his own essence. The chief instruments of this dynamic process are fighting and work, the prime means for subjecting external reality, including other people, to human control. The protagonists of this drama—we shall meet them again—are the Master, the fighter, the ruler; and the Slave, the worker.* In one of their many symbolic meanings, they stand for theory (the Master, who does not involve himself in the grubby business of trans-

---

* It is often the fashion to capitalize the first letters of Hegel's categories, a device that emphasizes (and sometimes overemphasizes) the abstract character of his thought. In German, however, all nouns are thus capitalized. In this one case I have used capital letters because the Master and the Slave do seem to me to be clearly intended by Hegel as personifications.

forming reality but concerns himself with universals and pleasure) and practice (the Slave, who shapes the world, but does not generalize or taste the fruits of his own labor). It is Hegel's ideal, no less than Marx's, to reconcile theory and practice, Master and Slave.

For Hegel, that reconciliation takes place at the end of human history. Through the often squalid and bloody dialectic of the Master and Slave, a providential purpose is working itself out. In the pursuit of their private interests, the antagonists unwittingly accomplish a grand design. This notion of the cunning of history is obviously related to Adam Smith's doctrine of an "invisible hand" that, through the market, vectors the greeds of independent entrepreneurs into a common good. Indeed, Hegel was influenced by Smith on this count, writing that the English economist had, along with Say and Ricardo, discovered the "simple principle" that effectively ruled the seemingly infinite individual instances of economic life. The Hegelian providence is like Smith's in that the actors who bring it to fruition are unconscious of it. Through the Master and the Slave, mankind collectively expands its dominion over the external world until reality itself becomes so suffused with human purposes and desires that it is no longer object, but subject. Now man can know that world, for in it he contemplates not an alien and external being, but himself. The rationality of history—its idea—has finally worked itself into, and through, men's consciousness; the hidden essence becomes apparent.

Even now, some fifty years after the profoundly Hegelian origins of Marxism began to be recognized, most scholars do not recognize the depth of the continuities which bind the two thinkers together. In an influential, and misleading, interpretation, Lenin wrote that Marx "was the genius who consummated the three main ideological currents of the nineteenth century . . . classical German philosophy, classical English political economy, and French socialism, combined with French revolutionary doctrines in general." But then, in a completely different way, so was Hegel.

It is not just that, as a young man, Hegel was an enthusiast of the French Revolution or that the *Phenomenology* sees Napoleon as the "spirit on horseback." More profoundly, his thought is permeated with the sense of change and the idea of reason as a force in the world which derived from the French Revolution. As early as 1805, he had privately developed a theory of the inevitable misery of the working class under capitalism, a view that he later published in a book upon which Marx wrote a lengthy commentary. And the *Phenomenology* regards work as a crucial force in history, sees alienation as central to social life and argues that idealistic reformers should not address a hollow "should" to a counterposed world in a manner that Marx was to duplicate in his critique of utopian socialism. In recent years, various scholars have recognized these connections between the two thinkers but that news has not traveled very far.

I emphasize what Marx and Hegel share, the better to define the specific difference between them. And that bears particularly on the openness of the Marxist methodology.

Hegel, whose work is suffused with that sense of furious motion of the age of Napoleon and the French Revolution, is ultimately a quietist. His writing, he himself said, was a *theodicy,* "a justification of God in history." The tumult and the turmoil, so magnificently analyzed in mid-motion, turn out to be only emanations of providence. Therefore, the young Marx charged with great insight, Hegel is a "false positivist"; he does not change the world, but only understands the unconscious purpose it has been fulfilling all along. The alienated life that humankind leads in religion and law and politics turns out to have been the true and genuine life in disguise, a disguise that is finally penetrated by Hegel. Thus, at the end of history there is not a revolutionary reshaping of the world, but an understanding of it that leaves the established order intact. Ultimately, Hegel reconciles us to existence.

Hegel himself insisted on this point. Philosophy, he argued in a famous passage, cannot teach us how the world *should* be. The concept of an age emerges only when its process of development is complete. Philosophy paints a "gray upon gray" in depicting the forms of life which are already old. It does not rejuvenate; it only understands. Therefore, the owl of Minerva—wisdom—"begins its flight only when the twilight [of an era] is breaking out." The contrast between Marx and Hegel on this count is not simply that of a contemplative and an activist who see the same reality in different spirits. Because their attitudes toward action were so different, so also were their ideas of the very nature of truth. Hegel's vision did not require or permit verification in practice. The reality he understood looked the same as it had been before he understood it. Therefore he could, and did, claim without fear of contradiction that there was a total identity of his thought and the world. But since Marx demanded that his ideas prove their worth in revolutionary practice, he was always confronted with the gap between intention and accomplishment. So, as a number of scholars have emphasized in recent years, there is a certain indeterminacy, an openness, at the very center of Marxism.

Friedrich Engels, who sometimes forgot this truth, was quite explicit about it in *Anti-Duhring*. A complete theoretical system is impossible, he wrote, because that assumes that "the kingdom of human knowledge is closed." Men must live with a contradiction—"on the one hand, they must know the world system exhaustively in all its interconnections; and on the other, with regard to their own natures as well as that of the world system, they are never able to accomplish the task." This contradiction, he concludes, is not an embarrassment but rather "a prime instrument of human progress . . ."

Perhaps the most dramatic Marxist statement of this point was made by George Lukacs in his seminal book of 1923, *History and Class Consciousness*. One can be an "orthodox Marxist," Lukacs said, and reject all of Marx's specific applications of his theories, as long as one asserts that the Marxist method offers the best way of proceeding and that it can only be deepened in the spirit of its founder. This is not to suggest that Marxism is an algebra that can be abstracted from its original subject matter and applied by thinkers of whatever, or no, point of view. Marx insisted that his method and subject matter were inextricably linked; but neither in theory nor in his analytic practice, did he deny that both could change.

Given this understanding of the openness of the Marxist method, this book will deal with ambiguities in Marx in the opposite way from that of the respectable academicians.

It has long been the practice in academic circles, as I noted in my book *Socialism,* to stipulate "that the proper reading of any passage by Marx is the one which demonstrates he was a blockhead." When I made this comment, I referred to Paul Samuelson, the Nobel laureate, who had reproached Marx for having ignored the "patent fact that natural resources are productive." In fact, Samuelson had casually misunderstood a Marxian ABC—that natural resources create wealth, but not exchange value. It was only after my book was published that I realized how ironic Samuelson's unfairness was. The quotation that he used to summarize the proper doctrine, of which Marx was supposed to be ignorant—Sir William Petty's remark that labor is the father of value and earth the mother—is cited by Marx, to make the very same point, in a not too obscure text, Chapter I of Volume I of *Das Kapital.*

In what follows, I will reverse Samuelson's procedure. Where Marx was clearly wrong, either as to fact or method, that will be noted. But where, after a careful and scholarly consideration of the internal and circumstantial evidence, two or more interpretations of Marx's meaning are possible, I will use the one that makes Marxism the more effective as a tool of analysis, taking every advantage of hindsight in the process. I am concerned with scrupulously establishing the truth about Marxism, but not for the purpose of enshrining it in a mausoleum or a variorum edition. Like C. Wright Mills, I believe that Marxism "certainly does not end with Marx. It begins with him." That is one of the many reasons why the new Marx, who will be recovered from the past in Part I, is turned toward the future in Part II.

There is warrant, then, for the revival of Marxism. The crisis in which we are living is profoundly systemic, as is well known, and it therefore requires a systematic analysis—a fact that is not so widely recognized. Secondly, the Marxian paradigm offers a unique way of organizing and selecting the data, one that sees through the concepts that, in the common consciousness, pretend to be facts. And finally, that paradigm is open to the future, to evidence that Marx never dreamed of. Thus, the possibility that a new and future Marx is needed can be established. It remains to demonstrate that he can exist.[2]

III

The second basic objection to the purposes of this book is Marxist. It could be said that I am turning Marx into Hegel.

Leon Trotsky can serve as a poignant symbol for this charge. In 1917 he seemed the very incarnation of the idea of unity of theory and practice. He was the military leader of the October Revolution, a thinker and literary critic of enormous Marxist culture, a brilliant orator who swayed masses. But then, during the twenties and thirties, Stalin, whom Trotsky thought a "mediocrity," triumphed, using a vulgar, mechanistic "Marxism" as a rationale for exploiting workers and peasants. Trotsky spent the last years of his life in a suburb of Mexico City, in a villa that had been turned into a small fortress—and a prison. He was isolated from the great struggles of his time, hunted by Stalin's assassins, and finally murdered by them.

It is magnificent that even under such appalling circumstances Trotsky's moral courage did not falter. He wrote shortly before his death:

> Hegel was fond of saying: what is rational is real. This means: every idea that corresponds to objective needs of development attains triumph and victory. No intellectually honest individual can deny that the analysis and program made by the Bolshevik Leninists (Fourth Internationalists) during the past fifteen years have met and still meet with confirmation in the events of our time. It is precisely in the certainty of their correctness that the basic sections of the Fourth International are strong and immutable. The catastrophes of European and world capitalism which are hovering over mankind will clear the path before the steeled cadres of the revolutionary Marxists.

Those catastrophes did nothing of the sort: the Trotskyist Fourth International was as impotent after the Second World War as before it. But then, isn't it significant that Trotsky's fantasy was introduced by one of Hegel's most famous—and ambiguous—remarks. For Hegel had not said simply, "What is rational is real." He had immediately added, "and what is real is rational," a proposition that conservatives took as justification of any existing order of things. Indeed, Hegel's quietest remarks about the "owl of Minerva" are introduced and rationalized by that formula. But even leaving aside this complicating factor, what Trotsky seems to have been saying is that the correctness of the Fourth International's program guaranteed its triumph. That turned out to be untrue; but more to the point, it makes the idea decisive in history, it moves from Marx to Hegel.

But isn't this a devastating critique, not simply of Trotsky in his last years, but of the very notion of the new and future Marx? For if the "real" Marxism has been, for almost a century, the province of lonely thinkers, is that not the ultimate rejection of Marxism itself? Marx broke decisively with the philosophers who only observed history; he insisted that his theory must prove itself in the thick of action. How, then, can one possibly argue in the name of Marx that pseudo- and anti-Marxists have been shaping this century while the authentic Marxists have been understanding it? Hegel would not have been bothered by this problem, since he insisted that an age could be understood only after the fact, when the ideas it expressed had worked themselves out in all of its existential richness. But it was precisely that proposition that Marx challenged. Isn't my "new Marx" the old Hegel in a left-wing disguise?

Harold Rosenberg put this basic issue brilliantly, from a slightly different perspective. "At the heart of Marxism," he wrote during the 1950s, "is its contention that its criticism and the revolutionary action of the working class have the identical objective, revolution by the second being the material equivalent of the first and supplying its positive content. This daring conception, whatever be its scientific validity, is a precondition for thinking as a Marxist." Therefore, Marxism "is a philosophy suspended upon an event, a monologue in the drama of history which only the action of its mass hero can save from being a soliloquy."

This is succinctly said, still widely believed and, I think, wrong. Since it is obvious that Marx's proletarian revolution has not taken place, Rosenberg's interpretation questions the very premise of this book: that in spite of the failure of that event, a meaningful Marxism still exists. He would say that the disappointment of this crucial expectation is decisive; that, in my terms, it turns us back from Marx to Hegel. Such a critique deserves to be taken most seriously.

To begin with, there are some Marxian texts that seem to corroborate Rosenberg's view, but only when they are taken out of the context of Marx's life and thought. The classic source is the Introduction to the *Critique of the Hegelian Philosophy of Right,* written in late 1843—that is, when the young Marx was in the process of becoming a Marxist. This is the work in which the astounding claim is made that the proletariat will be the heir of classical German philosophy: "If philosophy finds its material weapon in the proletariat, the proletariat finds its spiritual weapon in philosophy." The great ethical values, which the German intellectuals can only discuss, Marx holds, actually will be realized by the workers —"Philosophy cannot effectuate itself without the abolition of the proletariat," for all those high-sounding assertions about human nature are contradicted by people in actual misery; but "the proletariat cannot abolish itself without the effectuating of philosophy," for it must be possessed of the vision of human emancipation which, until the 1840s, had existed in Germany only in theory.

Two things can be said about these assertions. First, Marx was clearly wrong in making them. Second, as he matured he understood that he had been wrong. The relationship between theory and practice, he realized—and he was right—is much more complex than his youthful simplification of it.

For example, in his Introduction, Marx had spoken of the workers as "a class of civil society with radical chains which is not a class of civil society . . . a sphere which has a universal character because of its universal suffering, which does not take arms for a *particular* right, because it is not a *particular* injustice but injustice *pure and simple* which is done to it . . ." Out of extreme degradation, Marx argues, will come total emancipation. This is a romantic and unrealistic picture of working-class life—even working-class life under the brutalities of early capitalism—and it became progressively less true as the century and capitalism proceeded. Moreover, it has little to do with Marx's own mature description of the working class—organized and schooled by the class struggle in unions, building political parties, winning increments of dignity even within the capitalist order. When Rosenberg says that for Marx the workers are "human nothings" he faithfully captures an attitude that Marx abandoned shortly after he adopted it and one which, in any case, is historically wrong. (An error similar to Rosenberg's was the cause of Herbert Marcuse's abandonment of Marxism in the fifties and sixties. He, too, wrongly thought that Marx regarded the proletariat as "the absolute negation of society," and when it became painfully obvious that this was not the case in the welfare state, he became a kind of Spenglerian anarchist.)

This textual point can be deepened by using a method that will be employed throughout this book—that is, to spell out the theoretical implications of Marx's own practice of Marxism, defining premises which he must have acted upon, but which he sometimes did not explicitly formulate and sometimes, particularly in his youth, even contradicted. In this case, then, what does Marx's own political lifetime tell about the revisions that he made in his early vision of a revolutionary philosophy inspiring a philosophical revolution?

In 1847–48, only three years after he wrote the Introduction, Marx was a champion of united fronts with bourgeois liberals in the battle for democracy. During the 1850s, when he was developing the analysis that would culminate in his masterpiece, *Das Kapital*, he was utterly isolated from the mass movement. In the period of the First International, from 1864 to 1872, he was an active participant in working-class struggles, but his power derived from an alliance with British trade-unionists, who were quite reformist, and French followers of Proudhon, whose theories he despised. The Marxists hardly played a role in the Paris Commune, but Marx's defense of that rising cost him much of his British labor support. Later on, in the 1870s, he wrongly fought against the merger of the Marxist and Lassallean factions of German socialism and was outraged at all the errors in the unification program.

In *Anti-Duhring,* a book made necessary by the growing strength of the anti-Marxists among the German socialists, Engels commented that "most socialist workers in France and England" believed in an "eclectic, leveling socialism," and both Marx and Engels made it clear on a number of occasions that they did not think that American workers were capable of understanding their theory—that is, they knew that most proletarians were hardly the "heirs of German classical philosophy." In 1895, a few months before his death, Engels wrote a famous Introduction to their first reprinting of Marx's *Class Struggles in France*. It was widely regarded as his "testament" at the time, yet it would be hard to imagine a more radical critique of how imperfectly the Marxist theory of the Communist Manifesto was related to political practice.*

> History [Engels wrote] proved us and all who thought like us to be wrong. It has made it clear that the level of economic development on the Continent in that period was not at all ripe for the abolition of the capitalist mode of production. It has shown this by means of the economic revolution which, since 1848, has taken root throughout the entire Continent. . . .

But, then, the tactics of the struggle that Marx and Engels had elaborated in the Manifesto, and that Engels criticized so frankly in 1895, had themselves been an advance over Marx's philosophical generalities about the workers in 1843 and 1844. Not only had the facts disproved their youthful strategies, requiring that they be revised, but Engels had assumed that it was completely in keeping with the Marxist method to analyze the Marxist failure in this area.

The Communist euphoria that followed upon the October Revolution in 1917 reawakened Marx's romantic and youthful expectations that philosophy and history, theory and practice, were to be one. In *History and Class Consciousness,* George Lukacs, a participant in that fervor, quoted from the 1843 Introduction and went on to argue that the proletarians were intellectually superior to the bourgeois, able "to see the totality of society as a concrete totality." A more sober and accurate assessment was made around the same time by Antonio Gramsci, the Communist genius whom Mussolini

---

* This text has been disputed because the German Socialists, fearful of legal reprisal, got Engels to soften some of his formulations. The changes are not involved in the parts cited here; and in any case, the version that I have used restored the edited material.

imprisoned until his death. The oppressed class, Gramsci wrote, does not have the same cultural opportunities as their rulers. Marxism, therefore, comes to them, in the first phase, as a prejudice, a superstition, an aroma of necessity which gives meaning to the struggle for daily bread.

There was a period of about sixty years (from the 1870s to the 1930s) when Marxism functioned as the integrating ideology of a mass workers' movement in Central Europe. But that was, ironically enough, in a time when the proletariat was struggling mainly to gain bourgeois rights—to vote, to organize, to be a part of the society—not to create a revolution. In those battles, it was hardly a "sphere of universal suffering," and it was very concerned about particular and limited gains.

If, then, one judges the project of this book by the standards of the Karl Marx of 1843, it should not be written. In the oversimplified world of that young radical, it would be preposterous to talk of a "Marxism" which in fact survived mainly among a remnant of intellectuals and gifted workers. But Marx changed his mind on this count when reality forced him to do so; and Marx was right the second time around. More to the point, his own life is a magnificent demonstration of how a profound theory can develop on the margin of mass movements and even under conditions of political isolation. Judged by his absolutist standards of 1843, Marx should have given up by 1849 or 1850, when the defeat of his first revolutionary perspective became painfully apparent to him. He did not, and neither will I.

And even if one were to make an ultimate admission and conclude that socialism and Marxism had turned out to be a noble illusion, Marx would still have a certain relevance. As George Lichtheim understood the consequences of the total failure of Marx's hoped-for revolution, "there is no reason why his theoretical discoveries should not survive the termination of the attempt to construct a 'world view' which would at the same time serve as the instrument of a revolutionary movement." In other words, even if Marx became a kind of Hegelian figure, useful for the comprehension, if not the creation, of history, he is a giant of our culture.

But Marx has not turned into Hegel. Rather, he is an oracle in the ruins in two meanings of that phrase. He is the oracle who has survived in the ruins of Marxism itself, those ruins which people calling themselves Marxists did so much to create. And he is the oracle in the ruins of the bourgeois order, which, even as it recovers from the inflation-depression of the 1970s, is heading inexorably toward a final collapse, as this book will demonstrate. His writings are not, of course, a mystic text in which one deciphers predictions of events to come; they contain an applied methodology that permits us to analyze and hopefully to shape the future whose alternatives are being prepared within the history we live and make.

And perhaps the most profound witness to the vitality, the newness, of this Karl Marx is that his very existence is denied by those who preside over the ruins in which he survives, by the official Marxists as well as by the capitalists. His specter still haunts our world.[3]

CHAPTER 2

MARXISM MISUNDERSTANDS ITSELF

AT the end of W. H. Auden's *Dance of Death,* Karl Marx appears on the stage with the members of the Young Communist League, as Death (capitalism) dies, leaving all his wealth to the people. The masses sing, to the tune of Mendelssohn's "Wedding March,"

> O Mr. Marx, you've gathered
> All the material facts,
> You know the economic
> Reason for our acts.

With all of its preciousness, this passage summarizes the teaching of the very popular, very familiar and very misleading Karl Marx. He knows "the economic reasons for our acts." In the vision of this familiar Marx, history develops according to laws as inexorable as those discovered by the physical sciences. The dynamic principle of this process is an economic base, the means of production, which determines a political and cultural superstructure. Thus, the laws and art of an age, and particularly its political conflicts, are to be understood as masquerade in which the real actors are the economic forces.

All this takes place, the familiar Marx continues, according to the rhythms of a dialectical thesis, antithesis and synthesis. A new, and revolutionary mode of production triumphs and itself becomes the status quo (the thesis). Its economic development engenders a social class that is hostile to the established order (the antithesis), and the latter's struggle eventually prevails, thus creating a new mode of production (the synthesis, which is then the thesis of the new cycle). In this way, the bourgeoisie emerged within the feudal system, overthrew it and created capitalism, which in turn gives birth to a working class destined to carry through the socialist synthesis, the first synthesis in human history that is not self-contradictory, and therefore the final synthesis. Thus, history has followed a progression, from primitive communism, through ancient (Roman and Greek) society, to feudalism, capitalism and then to socialism and communism.

So goes a summary of the familiar Marx. Only, the statements in it are, at the very best, the half-truths of Marxism; at the worst, they are caricatures and outright falsifications. And yet, it is precisely this pseudo Marxism, so misshapen and vulgarized, that has taken hold in the minds of millions and helped to change reality. What must be explained is not simply that there has been a degradation of authentic Marxism, but why it became a powerful historical force and the authentic Marxism did not.

The answer to that outrageous paradox is, of course, quite complex. It begins with a seemingly scandalous assertion: that Marx and Engels on occasion seriously misrepresented Marxism. The particular misstatements that they made then lent themselves to the purposes of new elites. These elites were not, to be sure, the products of Marx's thought, or even of his erroneous version of it. They were the men and women of new social structures who, sincerely deluded for the most part, seized on Marx's distortion of his own ideas because it articulated an important truth for them. Once pseudo Marxism had thus become a major historical power, it duped most academics as well as its political adepts and became, for most people, the only Marxism they knew. Destroying it is the first step in bringing to life the new Karl Marx.*

* A somewhat similar argument has recently been made with regard to the philosophy of Ludwig Wittgenstein. In a brilliant study, Alan Janik and

I

First of all, there is Karl Marx's signal contribution to the misunderstanding of Marxism.

The most influential case in point is Marx's *Forward to the Critique of Political Economy* of 1859, perhaps the best known, and certainly the most unfortunate, statement of what Marxism is. This text is, of course, a favorite of the catechists of Marxism and of students cramming for exams. Here, in just a few pages, one can get a succinct statement of his doctrine from Marx himself. But then, even a sophisticated scholar like C. Wright Mills puts it first in his anthology of Marxist writings. And Joseph Stalin, who had very good political reasons for wanting a deterministic Marx, proclaimed the *Forward* "the brilliant formulation of the essence of historical materialism." In fact, it is either so compressed as to guarantee that most readers will miss its subtleties, or else, when it is straightforward and clear, it gives an inaccurate—and unMarxist —description of social reality.

These flaws and errors of fact and analysis all have the same import. They make Marxism into an account of how the base, which is material, determines the superstructure, which is intellectual, cultural and political. That is, of course, the very essence of vulgar Marxism; it is also an ideological foundation of Stalinism. In the course of this brief critical reading of the *Forward,* I will take up only a few, symptomatic instances and make no attempt to refute, with appropriate evidence from his other books, the vio-

---

Stephen Toulmin argue that Wittgenstein wanted to carefully delimit and define the possibilities of language in order to make it clear that the most important issues—ethical values, beauty, et cetera—had to be treated by means of a different mode of communication, by aesthetic representation, example and even silence. The positivists read him, Janik and Toulmin demonstrate, in an exactly opposite sense: that the important things are those of which we can speak in a precise, linguistic style, while all other matters are "pseudo questions." I am not competent to judge whether they are right or wrong in their scholarly interpretation, but I find it fascinating, and even supportive, to discover that others feel that a major thinker can be turned upside down by his enthusiastic, but quite errant, disciples.

lence that Marx does to his own thought. That will be done in the five chapters that follow. For now, I will simply call attention to Marx's garbled version of himself.

"The mode of production of material life," Marx writes in the *Forward,* "determines the social, political and spiritual life process in general." Nothing, it would seem, could be simpler: on the one side there is "material" life and its "mode of production" (that is, machines and markets); on the other side social, political and spiritual life (that is, the conscious existence of human beings). And the former determines the latter. The only problem is that, even in this text, this satisfying simplification is much more complex than it seems. Understanding this fact requires a scrupulous, even scholarly, attention to precisely what Marx is saying; and militants, dictators and students, for their own reasons, don't indulge in close textual explications.

Shortly before that lapidary statement about the mode of production, Marx comments that his researches in 1843–1844 led him to the conclusion that

> legal relations as well as the form of states are not to be conceptualized [*begreifen*] on their own terms or on the basis of the so-called general development of the human spirit, but rather are rooted in the material relations of life, whose totality Hegel summed up under the term "civil society," following the French and English of the eighteenth century. The anatomy of civil society is to be sought in its political economy.

In part, this is clear enough, and unexceptionable. When the French Revolution proclaims that its principle is "liberty, fraternity and equality," one is not to accept that on its face value, but to inquire after the social and economic reality behind it.

The complexity arises when one tries to define "the material relations of life." What, exactly, does Marx mean by that obviously key phrase? Does it refer to the inanimate, the "material" in the grossest, nonhuman sense of the term? Pseudo Marxism thinks. Only, Marx himself gives a rather broad hint as to his meaning, one that most readers sluff over because it is obscure. The totality of those "material relations of life," he tells us, is what Hegel, and the French and English of the eighteenth century, called "civil society" (*"bürgerlichen Gesellschaft"*).

Hegel wrote about civil society in a book that Marx had read with extreme care, subjecting part of it to a paragraph-by-paragraph commentary—*Outline of the Philosophy of Law*. It defined the sphere of private rights and economic self-interest, a "system of all-sided dependency." The ancients, with their patriarchal and religious principles and their simpler morality, had regarded such self-seeking as decadent and subversive of community. But the moderns, with their emphasis on the subjective, the individual, the person, values rooted in Christian religion and Roman law, exalted this new area of social life. Its great dynamic principle was that which set man apart from the animals: his drive to go beyond basic survival needs, to create and proliferate new needs.

Civil society, then, defined the whole world of *laissez faire,* its pleasures and poverty, its human interrelationships and its needs, as well as its material goods and machines. It was, even in its greed, suffused with a specific humanity, with precisely that which made man greater than the animals. Now, all this is anything but clear in Marx's very brief allusion to it, and one can understand why people have taken Marx's formulation "mode of production of material life" as describing the crudely economic, the unconscious, even the inanimate. But if one reads this passage carefully, probing its hidden complexity, all of this becomes apparent. More to the point, there are literally hundreds of other occasions on which Marx is much more explicit about the consciousness, the social classes and the human interrelationships which are part of the "economic" factor. Only, most readers, for reasons to be explained shortly, did not read this text carefully or look up Marx's other, and clearer, statements of the same theme.

Marx can hardly be faulted for his reader's intellectual slothfulness. But there are other passages in the *Forward* which are simply, and unambiguously, inaccurate, even given the most careful of interpretations. Marx writes,

A social formation never goes under before all the productive powers are developed which it can possibly contain; and new, higher production relationships never appear in place before all the material conditions of their existence have matured in the womb of the old order. Therefore, mankind only poses itself tasks that it can solve, since, looking at the matter more closely, the task itself emerges only when the material conditions for its solution are already at hand or are at least in the process of development.

This is not simply an appeal to a providence that Marx knew did not exist; it is also a contradiction of facts that Marx insisted on, time and time again. For example, he saw the decline of Roman society as a case in which the material conditions for a new social order seemed to be at hand, but then there was a decadence, not an advance. This instance, which fascinated him all his life, is a clear and convincing demonstration that he did not believe in a linear progress in history. So is his description of Asian (or Oriental) Despotism, a system that prevailed in China and India and that, for Marx, lacked *any* principle of internal change. (Both Roman and Asian cases will be examined more carefully later on.) (See Appendix B, § 1, p. 357.)

No matter. The passage just quoted is a clear Marxist precedent for a simple "progressive" theory of history. To sustain it, Marx's next sentence must be self-contradictory. "In grand outline," he says, "the Asian, ancient, feudal and modern bourgeois modes of production may be characterized as progressive social formations." But again, Marx thought nothing of the kind about Asian Despotism—which he regarded as stagnant, unmoving and anything but progressive—or of feudalism.

Here we have an excellent textual basis for vulgar Marxism from the pen of Karl Marx himself. And ever since the *Forward,* it is this misinterpretation of his thought, for which he bears a certain responsibility, that has stuck people as the very essence of Marxism. The organic interrelationships of a mode of production are reduced to the mechanical model of "base" and "superstructure." The world of ideas is turned into a mere reflex of the world of matter. And a metaphysical design is projected onto human history, which is seen to move majestically upward through the four modes of production that are the way stations to socialism.

Why did Marx do such a disservice to his thought? Since he obviously did not intentionally sit down to write a poor and misleading summary of his ideas, we can only speculate. The *Forward* and the *Critique of Political Economy* itself were written in 1858 and 1859. They were the climax of a period in which Marx was attempting to sort out and order the enormous amount of research he had done in economic theory and data. One explanation, then, is that the *Forward* is the kind of oversimplification even a genius might write when confronted with the problem of summarizing extremely complicated material. The more than one thousand pages of notes and outlines which preceded the *Forward* and the *Critique*—the *"Grundrisse"*—provide some ambiguous evidence on this count. On the one hand, the *Grundrisse* contains some of the most "Hegelian"—and therefore antimechanistic—formulations made by Marx since his youth (and we know that as Marx was writing it, he reread, and was impressed by, Hegel's *Logic*). This reinforces the case for considering the *Forward* a mere aberration, for it suggests that even as he presented his oversimplifications, Marx was aware of the complexities. In this context, the 1859 statement would be subsumed under the famous rule, "Even Homer nods."

On the other hand, Jurgen Habermas, an extremely perceptive Marx scholar, has argued that the fascinating discussion of automatic machinery in the *Grundrisse*—it seems to anticipate the coming of automation—asserts a kind of technological determinism that Marx then abandoned in *Das Kapital*. If so, the *Forward* was simply bad theory, not a slip of the pen. I do not think Habermas is right on this count, for the *Grundrisse* contains several references to the failure of capitalism to develop in Rome, even though the "material conditions," narrowly understood, were present for it. But suppose one concedes that Marx might have been confused at this point. What is indisputable, even if one accepts the proposition (as I do not), is that he was not at all confused when he wrote *Das Kapital*. But, alas, it cannot be denied that Marx, for whatever reason, helped to obfuscate his own ideas in the *Forward*.

Friedrich Engels, the lifelong friend and colleague of Marx, who shared in his intellectual development and sometimes saved him from physical poverty, is the second great figure in the Marxist misunderstanding of Marxism. Marx was unjust to his ideas in a few passages; Engels did much more consistent harm to his mentor's theory although he sometimes was its shrewdest interpreter. He was the inventor of an omniscient theory of society and nature, called *dialectical materialism,* which is not to be found, even as a momentary indiscretion, in the writings of Marx.

There are many reasons why this happened, but it might do well to state the most important at the very outset, for it establishes a context in which all Engels' analyses must be read. He himself defined it poignantly in a letter to Marx. "You can lie in a warm bed," he wrote, "and study Russian land relations in particular and ground rent in general, and nothing interrupts you. But I have to sit on a hard bench, drink cold wine and go after the irksome Dühring." Dühring was an ideological rival of Marx and Engels in the German socialist movement. While Marx went on with his theoretical work, Engels was given the task of dealing with him in a series of newspaper articles which were eventually collected into the famous book *Anti-Dühring.* The point is that Engels was the polemicist, and most of his writings must be read with this in mind. The result, if I am right, was that Marx tolerated a kind of intellectual double standard, allowing his factionalist partner the rhetorical luxury of imprecisions and sweeping generalities, which he himself would never tolerate in his own scientific work. (See Appendix B, § 2, p. 360.)

On at least one occasion, V. I. Lenin, a man of fierce Marxian orthodoxy, adopted this explanation. Noting a sloppy formulation in Engels' writings on philosophy, Lenin commented that he committed it "in the interests of popularization."

Here, for example, is a fairly typical statement from Engels in his simplistic mood:

> The materialist view of history proceeds from the proposition that production, and after production the exchange of products, is the basis of all social orders. It holds that in every historically emerging society the division of products, and with it the social articulation into classes or estates, accordingly bases itself upon what is produced and how the producers exchange it. So the final

causes of all social changes are not to be sought in the minds of
men, in their growing insight into eternal truths and justice, but in
changes in the mode of production and exchange; they are to be
sought, not in the *philosophy* but in the *economics* of the epoch in
question.

But Engels did not always write in this simplistic, polemical
mode, a fact that makes his case complicated. He was a genius—
though not of Marx's rank—who sometimes had brilliant and subtle
perceptions of his friend's theory. Thus a letter to Karl Kautsky
states almost the direct opposite of the schematic determinism just
quoted: "As soon as you speak of 'means of production,' you speak
of society codetermined by those means of production. Means of
production *in themselves,* outside society, without influence upon
it, are just an nonexistent as is capital *in itself."* In this formulation,
the economic base does not unilaterally determine the superstructure, and philosophy is not a mere reflection of economics. Society
is "codetermined" [*mitbestimmte*] by the means of production—
that is, there is a relationship of interaction and reciprocity, and
one cannot speak of an "economic" factor which is not simultaneously a social and political factor.

Engels was not simply wrong; he was right and wrong. This
can be seen even in the book that is certainly his major contribution to the misunderstanding of Marxism, *The Dialectics of Nature.*
It is a posthumous collection of articles and other material, published by the Russians in 1925. In it, Engels argued for a concept
in which the dialectic is universal, operating in nature as well as
society. He wrote, "The fact that our subjective thought and the
objective world are subject to the same laws and therefore also
both in their results cannot finally contradict one another, but must
agree, absolutely dominates all our theoretical thought." This is
the basis for the thesis that dialectical materialism allows one to understand all of reality, that it is the key to the "laws of motion" of
matter itself. It is a claim that cannot be found anywhere in Marx's
writing, either explicitly or implicitly. Above all, it assumes that
there is no essential difference between processes involving human
consciousness and those that are only animal or even inorganic.

And yet, in the very same book, as Lucio Colletti has brilliantly stressed, Engels refutes his own dialectical grand design for all of existence. Engels, writes Colletti,

> puts us in a position to understand that it is meaningless to speak (as he himself does elsewhere) of "motion in the most general sense, conceived as the mode of existence, the inherent attribute of matter [which is] common to all changes and processes occurring in the universe, from mere changes of place right to thinking"; and therefore it is also meaningless to speak of a law of this motion in general, or of any "general laws of development of nature, society and thought."

Toward the end of his life, the complex Engels began to realize the harm that the simplistic Engels had done. In a series of letters, he tried to take back some of his own schematic and overly deterministic formulations. He wrote, for example, to Joseph Bloch:

> According to the materialist conception of history, the production and reproduction of social life is the *ultimately* determining element in history. More than that neither Marx nor I have ever asserted. Hence if somebody twists this into saying that the economic element is the *only* determining one, he transforms that proposition into a meaningless, senseless phrase.

And, lending some support to an argument advanced here, Engels ruefully notes that the exaggerations arose out of a polemical situation and there was, therefore, never "the time, place and opportunity" to give proper play to the reciprocal and interacting elements in history.

This is a serious, even generous, attempt by Engels to make amends for his own exuberant formulations. Unfortunately, as George Lichtheim and Lucio Colletti have pointed out, the self-criticism is a failure. In it, Engels retains the model of the "economic" as some kind of independent factor apart from society. Only, now he admits that at the intermediate range, the social, cultural and political have their role to play; the "economic" is only ultimately decisive. That, however, leaves the basically flawed model intact, even if it greatly improves it. There is still a determinant and a determined. There is not that "codetermination" of which Engels himself spoke in another letter and upon which Marx almost always insisted.

So Engels was contradictory, sometimes profound, sometimes an agitational simplifier. But then the question arises: Why, during his lifetime did Marx allow his friend to misinterpret his theory? A good number of Engels' crudities, along with some of his penetrating insights, appeared in *Anti-Dühring,* a book that Marx not only read in advance but to which he contributed a section. Therefore he was perfectly aware of what his friend was doing, yet there is no sign that he ever protested, either publicly or privately. Why?

The only answer that even begins to respond to that question (and it is put forth here in precisely that tentative fashion) has already been noted: that Marx allowed Engels to exaggerate because he felt that was necessary in a factional struggle which involved many uneducated people. If that was the reason for Marx's silence when his own ideas were distorted, he paid a very high price for the tactical advantage that he gained. He acquiesced in formulations which were to play a major role in the full-scale vulgarization of his theory.

There is another, related aspect to this story, one that was a factor before Marx died and even more so afterward. The second half of the nineteenth century was very much under the spell of Darwin's triumph, and there was a general search for universal laws of development that would be similar to the theory of evolution. In the Afterword to the second German edition of *Kapital,* Marx delighted in a positivistic and utterly inadequate summary of his theory, and he quoted it at length. As Raymond Aron, a shrewd critic of Marx, correctly describes the incident, "In 1874, philosophers asserted positivism, scientism, evolutionism. Marx congratulated himself on an interpretation conforming to the style of the epoch."

After Marx's death, Engels was bent on making the Darwinian parallel. One might say that the project of turning Marx into a dialectical positivist—which is to say, into a contradiction in terms —was announced at the great man's funeral in 1883. At the graveside Engels proclaimed that "as Darwin discovered the law of development of organic nature, so Marx discovered the developmental laws of human history." When the Darwinist temptation thus entered into a mind that had been influenced by Hegel—that is, by a philosopher who saw all of reality as the emanation of a universal reason—it was only a short step to the idea that Marxism is a universal guide to all modes of being, whether natural or social. (See Appendix B, § 3, p. 360.)

Yet, at the same time that Engels was under the spell of the age and its intellectual fashions, he was immersed in Marx's writing, bringing together and sorting out the various manuscripts that were published as Volume II and Volume III of *Das Kapital* (and preparing the material for Volume IV, *The Theories of Surplus Value,* which was published after his own death). In those twelve years allotted to him after Marx's death, Engels was beset by a cacophony of influences: by his friend's theories, the scientist temper of the times, the political task of winning for Marxism some of the enormous prestige enjoyed by Darwinism, and so on. And although he was a man of great erudition and brilliance, Engels was not capable, like Marx, of establishing or maintaining a unique and implacable synthesis. His writings of this period are contradictory and filled with references conducive to a creative misunderstanding of Marxism.

Both Marx and Engels, then, contributed to the distortion of Marxism, the former on occasion, the latter more systematically. But if these misstatements were, particularly in the case of Marx, only episodic and counterbalanced by a huge corpus of intellectual work that put matters rightly, why was the false coin of Marxism so widely accepted and the genuine treasure all but ignored?[1]

II

The answer to that question requires the description of two distinct trends in the vulgarization, and later the totalitarianization, of Marxism. One involves the working class, the other a socialist bureaucracy and then an antisocialist ruling class. Each of these social formations had its own, and quite different, reasons for misunderstanding Marx.

The basis for the workers' acceptance of pseudo Marxism was

suggested in the previous chapter, in the analysis of Marx's abandonment of his youthful, romantic vision of a philosophic proletariat. Engels, it will be remembered, even publicly admitted that the French and British workers thought of socialism eclectically, as a leveling of society; and Gramsci rightly pointed out that those denied access to bourgeois culture, but struggling for their rights, would first see in Marxism a view of historic necessity that would confer dignity and hope upon the battle for daily bread. This is not to say that workers were, or are, stupid. Moreover, as Gramsci stressed, unlike the popular, superstitious Catholicism he saw in Italy, Marxism "does not maintain the 'simple people' at the level of their own primitive philosophy of common sense, but on the contrary leads them to a higher conception of life." Still, the masses were not and are not capable of the intellectual subtlety required to fathom authentic Marxism on the theoretical level. They veered instead toward a vulgar Marxism that corresponded to their needs in capitalist society.

A different and more complex dialectic was at work in the tendency of socialist bureaucrats, and then of antisocialist bureaucratic collectivists, to embrace pseudo Marxism. Marx himself anticipated an important aspect of this process in one of his briefest and most important philosophical statements, his *Theses on Ludwig Feuerbach*.

Thesis 3 asserts:

> The materialist doctrine of the changing of circumstances and of education forgets that the circumstances are changed by men and that the educator must himself be educated. This doctrine must therefore split society into two parts, of which the one is raised above the other. The coinciding of the changing of the circumstances and human practice, or self-changing, can only be conceptualized and rationally understood as *revolutionary* praxis.

Marx did not, of course, address this reproach to social-democratic functionaries or Stalinist officials, none of whom existed in 1843 when he wrote the *Theses*. He had in mind all those philanthropic radicals who, basing themselves on an eighteenth-century materialism, proposed to graciously transform reality so as to per-

mit the people to become better human beings under changed circumstances. But the central point of the Thesis applies to twentieth-
century phenomena that Marx did not imagine. Whenever the
subjective element, the creative role of consciousness—the function
of *self*-changing—is taken out of socialist theory and it becomes
deterministic, then the ideological foundations are laid for one part
of society raising itself above the other. Vulgar Marxism is, in
short, a perfect ideology for dynamic bureaucracies that are going
to save the workers from themselves.

This proposition can be seen clearly in the history of two dissim-
ilar, indeed basically antagonistic, movements, the social-democratic and the Communist.*

In the 1880s and 1890s, two things influenced the German socialists to declare themselves Marxists. From 1873 to 1895 there
was a "Great Depression." (Actually there were also two mild
recoveries, but the dominant fact of those years was capitalist
failure.) In this period, Colletti notes,

> all the fundamental categories of Marx's analysis came into full
> play: the tendency for the rate of profit to fall, due to the in-
> creased "organic composition" of capital; stagnation and partial
> saturation of outlets for investment; unimpeded action of compe-
> tition, which, apart from affecting profit margins, resulted in a
> spectacular fall in prices.

It seemed written on the very surface of reality that a final breakdown of the system was at hand.

During part of that troubled time, between 1878 and 1890, the
German Socialist Party was outlawed by Bismarck. It could not
function as an open political organization, and its leaders were
driven into exile, but its candidates could, and did, run for office
with increasing success. Bismarck's action seemed to confirm yet
another Marxist tenet: that the bourgeois state was inherently and
implacably hostile to the aspirations of the workers. Both eco-

---

* Throughout this book, Communist with a capital *C* refers to the individuals and movements supporting the existing Communist states, like
Russia and China. When communism is spelled with a small *c,* I am talking
of the ideal defined by Marx, which is denied in the daily practice of the
Communist governments.

nomic and political realities seemed to conspire to prove Marxism valid. The German Socialists declared themselves Marxist.

And yet, by one of those ironies of history, at the very moment when the party took this step, the objective reality shifted. The anti-Socialist laws were repealed, and both the party and the unions grew impressively. Simultaneously, capitalism itself began to change, moving from *laissez-faire* competition to trusts and monopolies and, in Germany, toward the welfare state. From the middle of the 1890s until the outbreak of World War I, living standards for the masses were rising. So the party's basic political posture, that of a Marxist organization of an outcast proletariat, had to be applied under circumstances which were almost the exact opposite of those that had caused it to be adopted. Instead of the revolutionary self-change of the workers, of upheaval from below, there was now a perspective of orderly, gradual change under the sponsorship of a benign bureaucracy. An "inevitablist," scientistic Marxism of the kind that Marx rejected in Thesis 3 and throughout his life, now seemed to be both an accurate description of life and a proper ideology for the movement.

Engels himself stated the key thought in 1895 (even though he did not accept the bureaucratic conclusions that followed from it):

> We can count even today on two and a quarter million voters. If these things continue in this way, by the end of the century we shall conquer the greater part of the middle strata of the society, petty bourgeois and small peasants, and grow into a decisive power before which all other powers will have to bow, whether they like it or not. To keep this growth going without interruption until it of itself gets beyond the control of the prevailing government system, that is our main task.

A mechanistic Marxism that interpreted this process as a necessary consequence of developments in the economic base transforming the political superstructure was thus an eminently functioning—if transient—truth even though it was a Marxist falsehood.

In August 1914, the underpinnings of this theory were shattered. With the outbreak of a savage civil war within European civilization, the notion of a pacific, gradual and harmonious progress, of a capitalism—and a socialism—without contradictions and discontinuities was a casualty of the hostilities. And when the Second International utterly failed in its antiwar objectives and the national proletariats of Europe began to slaughter one another, the whole structure of vulgar Marxism came tumbling down. Then, in October 1917, Lenin led the Bolsheviks to power, and it seemed that there was a new alternative, a new Marxism. The Bolsheviks had, after all, proved that political militancy was at least as important as economic evolution. Their socialist opponents, the Mensheviks, had expected to be the left wing of a capitalist revolution in Russia. Capitalism, they said, was what Marxism placed upon the agenda. (It was this thesis that caused Gramsci to refer to *Das Kapital* as "the book of the bourgeoisie" in countries like Russia and Italy.) But Lenin and his comrades, many Marxists felt, had applied their theory in a creative and revolutionary fashion.

Those hopes were utterly disappointed. If Lenin himself emphasized the subjective and even called for a Marxist society of the Friends of the Hegelian Dialectic, his successors were bureaucratic collectivists who sponsored an utterly mechanistic Marxism for the very elitist reasons that Marx had described in Thesis 3.

I will not attempt to make a documented analysis of Stalinism here. I have already done so in *Socialism,* and in any case I only raise the issue in terms of the Marxist misunderstanding of Marx. Let me simply summarize from my earlier study. Communism in all its existing forms (and there are obviously differences of a considerable, and even murderously antagonistic, significance among them) is a system of bureaucratic collectivism in which the state owns the means of production and a party bureaucracy owns the state by means of a totalitarian monopoly of political power. It is exploitative in the exact sense that Marx gave that term—the workers and peasants are forced to surrender a surplus to the bureaucracy; a portion of their working day is a "free" gift to the rulers.

Within this context, Marxism functions as an ideology—that is, as the very opposite of the revolutionary theory that Marx intended —as a tool for mystifying the relations of power in the minds of the masses. Marx had talked of a society in which the means of production are in the hands of the producers. For him, socialized property was the means whereby the true end of socialism, the domination of the masses over the social conditions of their existence, could be achieved. Stalinism took the form of socialized property, but filled it with a new, totalitarian content. It then stressed the formal similarity of its institutions to those proposed by Marx and cited this as the living proof that Soviet (or Chinese or whatever) Communist practice was the incarnation of Marxism.

So a doctrine that seemed quite similar to the vulgar Marxism of the Second International became functional under Communism. Stalin was the supreme scientist who deciphered the inexorable laws of history. Therefore, what he decided to do for the masses was right, even if he did it literally over their dead bodies. A typical example of this kind of thinking is found in Stalin's last essay, *Economic Problems of Socialism in the U.S.S.R.*

First, there is the general statement of an all-embracing dialectic to be found throughout reality: "Marxism regards laws of science —whether they be laws of natural science or of political economy —as the reflection of objective processes which take place independently of the will of man." Then comes a deduction in a characteristically nonempirical and catechetical style:

> [The Soviet government] relied on the economic laws that the relations of production *must necessarily* conform with the character of the productive forces. The productive forces of our country, especially in industry, were social in character, the form of ownership, on the other hand was private, capitalistic. Relying on the economic law that the relations of production must necessarily conform with the character of the productive forces, the Soviet government socialized the means of production, made them the property of the whole people, and thereby abolished the exploiting system and created socialist forms of economy.

There are a number of revealing aspects to this quotation. First of all, it implies that the Soviets made history in an utterly rational fashion. They surveyed reality, noted the appropriate law (which is supposed to operate independently of human will) and they enacted it (that is, they *willed* it). For a Marxist to suggest such a picture of the revolutionary process is preposterous on the face of it. Secondly, it is the Soviet *government* that is the agency of this transformation. The working class is not mentioned. Thirdly, Stalin does not determine that Soviet society is socialist by examining the actual, existential conditions of the people. That, among other things, would prove to be embarrassing. Instead, he makes a scientific syllogism based on a sham law: Where the means of production are socialized, there is socialism, and the people rule; but in the Soviet Union the means of production are socialized; therefore in the Soviet Union there is socialism and the people rule. With such a methodology Stalin did not have to bother about facts or 180-degree turns in the party line. A law could be found, or invented, to justify anything the master scientist did.

At first glance, it might seem that Stalin's scientistic, deductive Marxism is the same as Engels' or that of the Second International before World War I. That, however, misses an important distinction. The dominant Marxism of the Second International served as the integrative ideology of a genuine workers movement, particularly in Central Europe. It was an ideology that for all its flaws, allowed the masses who believed in it to make real gains in freedom and dignity. It was liberating and enlightening, even with all its simplifications and errors. It was, if you will, a sincere, honest distortion of Marx. Soviet Marxism, at least after the triumph of Stalinism, was the ideology of a state that stood over the workers. It had lost all contact with the most essential single postulate of Marxism: an identification with the proletariat. Soviet leaders, to be sure, felt that they were building "socialism," just as American businessmen genuinely believe that capitalism and democracy are synonymous. But the intentions of the Communist bureaucracy have nothing to do with the objective function of its ideology, or with its position as a ruling class.

The Communist interpretation of Marxism is not a misunderstanding of it, but rather a transformation into its opposite. And this fact enormously complicates the task of persuading people of the existence of a new Marx, for the Communists have changed the very content of the original Marxist vocabulary. When the misunderstood Marxism of the Second International said "working class," its definition may have been schematic and flawed, yet it was trying to talk about a working-class reality. But when Soviet Marxism says "working class," it refers, like Stalin, to an abstraction whose role it is to endorse anything the dictatorship says or does.

The Communist vocabulary, then, is a mystification, and it must be approached with great care. When the medieval Church could not break a dissident, it would turn him over to the secular arm with the prayer that the Church abhors bloodshed and begs for mercy. That meant, kill or maim him. Communist Marxism is similarly a language of power in which the most virtuous—"Marxist"—assertions are a cover for ruling-class policy. Thus it was that the corruption of Marx became a nationalized industry.[2]

III

After such events within the main movement calling itself Marxist, it is hardly surprising that non- and anti-Marxists consider the degraded Marx to be the only Marx.

For some, there is an immediate polemical purpose. Opponents of socialism, they want the most simple-minded of Marxes to refute, and the vulgar version of him is all but designed to invite contemptuous dismissal. This is the "Marxism" that is defined by the House Un-American Activities Committee and the Federal Bureau of Investigation, and it is obviously without any serious content (though it is interesting as a symptom of American political pathology). It will not be discussed here. Neither will the "Marxism" articulated by pedestrian scholars, most of whom content themselves with repeating the errors and slanders that have accumulated in the course of more than a century of misinterpretation.

I am concerned, rather, with the "strong" cases, with thinkers who are sympathetic to Marx, cannot be dismissed as mere polemicists, and yet perpetuate a shoddy Marx, sometimes with great sophistication and erudition. Perhaps the most surprising thing about these eminent misreadings of Marxism is that they often fall into mistakes which, even with charity, can only be described as silly.

For instance, take this passage from Edmund Wilson's *To the*

Finland Station, a book by a distinguished critic, written with style and grace. Wilson is speaking of Marx:

> He still believed in the triad of Hegel: the *These, Antithese* and the *Synthese;* and the triad was simply the old Trinity, taken over from the Christian theology, as the Christians had taken it over from Plato. It was the mythical and magical triangle which, from the time of Pythagoras and before, had stood as a symbol for creativity and power and which probably derived its significance from its correspondence to the male sex organs . . . Certainly the one-in-three, three-in-one of the *Thesis,* the *Antithesis* and the *Synthesis* has had upon Marxists a compelling effect which it would be impossible to justify through reason.

There are a number of spectacular problems with these statements. First of all, Hegel himself hardly ever used the expressions "Thesis," "Antithesis" and "Synthesis" in his writings. (His most characteristic dialectical expressions are "immediacy," "mediation" and "overcoming.") Secondly, Marx himself used these terms only on a very few occasions—and then as a joke. He talks with disdain of "wooden trichotomies" and calls their use "speaking Greek." And he excoriated Ferdinand Lassalle for trying to apply the Hegelian dialectic as "an abstract, finished system" to social analysis. Thirdly, the most significant point (among a very few instances) when Marx did speak in Hegelian, is to be found in the famous chapter on the "Historical Trend of Capitalist Accumulation" in Volume I of *Das Kapital.* "The capitalist production process," Marx writes there, "produces its own negation with the necessity of a natural process. It is the negation of the negation." But Engels, who was much more enamored of references to the Hegelian dialectic than Marx, pointed out in *Anti-Dühring* that this is not to imply that Marx deduced the event from the "law" of the negation of the negation. He first proved the fact, Engels writes; he then characterized it according to the negation of the negation. And Marx's critique of Lassalle made this very same point.

It turns out that Wilson's scholarly gloss on the triad in Hegel and Marx rests squarely on a careless reading of both. But how is it that a man of his learning and culture could make such elementary mistakes?

James Joyce provides an answer. In speaking of his incredibly intricate book, *Finnegans Wake,* Joyce commented that all he asked from the reader was his lifetime. In the case of Marx (or Hegel, or any thinker of the first rank), Joyce's outrageous demand applies. The Marxian canon is so huge and complex—the incomplete *Marx-Engels Werke* is in some forty-three volumes; a projected complete edition will be in one hundred volumes—that it is impossible for even a genius to simply drop in on Marxism and produce something of real value. "A halfway complete knowledge of Marxism," Bertolt Brecht said, "today costs, a colleague has assured me, twenty thousand to twenty-five thousand Goldmarks, and that is not counting the aggravation." So it is that when writers of enormous and unquestioned ability—Wilson, or a Nobel laureate like Paul Samuelson—take some time off, even several years, to deal with Marx, they are capable of almost laughable mistakes.

Karl Popper is an excellent case in point. As a philosopher of science and epistemologist he is a man of great accomplishment and influence. And yet his *The Open Society and Its Enemies,* a book which is highly regarded by many serious liberals, is a shocking compendium of traditional misinterpretations, a scholarly monument to the familiar Karl Marx who never existed.

Part of the problem is that Popper does not give the slightest indication that he is even aware of the authentic Marxian tradition. It is clear from *The Open Society* and other writings that the only Marx he has ever encountered is in the dogmatic, Stalinist and utterly false persona. Though he sometimes indicates that he knows that there is a vulgar Marxism, he himself unconsciously reads Marx through its eyes.

Here, for example, is a crucial judgment of Marx:

> Owing to his Hegelian upbringing, he was influenced by the ancient distinction between "reality" and "appearance," and by the corresponding distinction between what is "essential" and what is "accidental." His own improvement upon Hegel (and Kant) he was inclined to see in the identification of "reality" with the material world (including man's metabolism), and of "appearance" with the world of thought or ideas. Thus, all thoughts and ideas would have to be explained by reducing them to the underlying es-

sential reality, i.e., to economic conditions. This philosophical view is certainly not much better than any other form of essentialism. And its repercussions in the field of method must result in an over-emphasis upon economics. For *although the general importance of Marx's economics (ism?) can hardly be overrated, it is very easy to overrate the importance of the economic conditions in any particular case.* Some knowledge of economic conditions may contribute considerably, for example, to a knowledge of mathematics, but a knowledge of mathematics themselves is much more important for that purpose; and it is even possible to write a very good history of mathematical problems without referring at all to their "economic background."

All of this is very poor and very wrong, and very typical of the level of honest and reputable academic treatment of Marx. To begin with, Popper is scandalously unfair to Hegel throughout his book, even referring to him at one point as a "clown." This is particularly embarrassing when one considers that Hegel taught something quite close to the exact opposite of what Popper attributes to him. For him, reality and appearance, the essential and the accidental, interpenetrated each other, and it was precisely on these grounds that he rejected the "ancient distinction" that Popper says he held. One reason for the incredible failure of scholarship in all of this has been suggested in a devastating essay by Walter Kaufmann: that Popper based himself primarily on a little student anthology of Hegel which does not contain a single work of that philosopher in its entirety.

The point at issue here is not a textual quibble, however, for an understanding of this aspect of Hegel's thought is crucial to a central Marxist point. One of the basic criticisms which Marx addressed to the classical political economists was that they did not define the necessary links between the *form* which the value of a commodity takes, and the essence of that value, human labor. The form, the appearance, the accident, Marx holds, is related to the essential, to commodity production. This perception, as will be seen, is crucial to Marxism. It inspired, among many other things, the whole first half of Marx's *Grundrisse,* as well as major sections and the underlying logic of *Das Kapital.* With regard to this extremely important question Popper has both Marx and Hegel turned neatly upside down. (See Appendix B, § 4, p. 361.)

Secondly, Popper proceeds from this misreading to a proposition that Engels, even in his most positivist mood, would have rejected: that Marxism explains all thoughts and ideas "by reducing them to their underlying economic reality." From there it is but one step to the absurdity of implying that Marx would have denied that "it is even possible to write a very good history of mathematical problems without referring at all to their 'economic background.' " These things, as the rest of this book should make clear, are nonsense.

Given this basic methodological misunderstanding of what Marxism is about, it is not surprising that Popper makes similar errors when he tries to grasp Marx's politics. For he is dealing, not with the actual Karl Marx but with an essentialist, historicist Marx, who, had he ever existed, should indeed have been as simple-minded as Popper says he is. For example, Popper says of Marx's allegedly essentialist viewpoint:

> What are the consequences of this theory of the state? The most important consequences is that all politics, all legal and political institutions as well as political struggles, can never be of primary importance. Politics are impotent. They can never alter decisively economic reality. . . . Or, in other words, political developments are either superficial, unconditioned by the deeper reality of the social system, in which case they are doomed to be unimportant and can never be of real help to the suppressed and exploited, or else they give expression to a change in the economic background and the class situation, in which case they are volcanic eruptions.

There are two rather obvious problems with this characterization. First of all, Marx never developed such an essentialist theory; secondly, and more obviously, Marx's own political practice completely contradicts what Popper says it must be. Even in the early, militant period, in the Communist Manifesto, Marx was arguing that the first decisive step in the socialist revolution was the conquest of political power by the working class. Then, in the years of his maturity, he was even more explicit. The British Ten Hours

Law, limiting the length of the work day, was, Marx told the founding Congress of the First International, a "triumph of the political
economy of the working class over the political economy of the
middle class." And this was not, as some have said, an opportu-
nistic remark made to curry favor with the reformists who co-
operated with Marx in the First International. For Marx devoted a
considerable portion of Volume I of *Das Kapital* to an account of
the process that led to the Ten Hours Law.

Indeed, if Popper had noticed Marx's analysis of Ten Hours
Law in *Das Kapital*—it is part of a rather large chapter, ninety
pages long, on the struggle over the lengths of the working day in
capitalism—he would have found further evidence to disturb his
own preconceptions. Marx points out that the right wing of the
ruling class, the landed aristocracy, supported the Ten Hours Law
—they were furious at the industrial capitalists who had stopped
protecting them from foreign corn producers—and that a portion
of the working class fought the law, because it believed the capitalist
propaganda that it would cause unemployment. And Popper would
be astounded to learn that Engels, very accurately summarizing
Marx's analysis of events in Britain, France and Germany, noted
that in bourgeois society the bourgeoisie only rarely exercised political power in its own name. Such subtleties have no place in the
determinist Marx for whom the economic is determinant in every
instant; they do play a prominent role in the real Marx.

It would be easy to go on and on documenting the most remarkable lapses of scholarship. Popper, to take one last example, believes that Marx had a doctrine of "starvation wages" and indeed
that "the *law* of increasing misery" is the "doctrine of Marx on
which the whole prophetic argument hinges" (his emphasis). There
are some ambiguities on this subject in Marx, but they are clearly
resolved by a chapter in Volume I of *Das Kapital,* wherein Marx
points out that rising wages are a characteristic of one period of
capitalist existence, and the entire analysis of Volume III, which
makes higher living standards a necessary stage in the preparation
of capitalist crisis. (This point will be elaborated in Chapter 5.)

But how is it, then, that such a reputable and serious thinker can make such mistakes.* In part, the factors already listed are clearly at work: the inability of a liberal reformer to come to grips with a revolutionary critique of the system; the fact that Popper obviously devoted less than a lifetime to his study. But now, another element should be added. The familiar Marx acts as a kind of negative paradigm, a guide to the themes in Marxism, but a guide that points in all the wrong directions. Most people, including most scholars, ignorant of authentic Marxism, see Marx through the lens of vulgar Marxism. That converts some and repels others but serves the truth in neither case.

Therefore, one of the very important functions of debunking the familiar Marx is to make it possible for readers to see Marx's pages as they are. This work, however, is made tremendously difficult, because of the history described in this chapter. Marx made his own contribution to vulgar Marxism, and Engels helped to codify it. The two most massive movements calling themselves Marxist were actually proponents, for utterly different reasons, of the misunderstood Marx. Communist nations have placed their totalitarian power in the service of the cult of the familiar Marx (or, more precisely, put him in their service), and decent and liberal scholars commit gaucheries in this area which they would not tolerate for a moment in the fields of their own specialization.

For most people the first step in grasping the new and future Marx is to forget everything they have heard or read about the familiar Marx. At the same time, they must accept one of history's strangest ironies: that Marx and the Marxists made a major contribution to the misunderstanding of Marxism.[3]

---

* In a note to the 1965 edition, Popper tells us that his basic sympathy for Marx was shaken by the "shattering" evidence he found in Leopold Schwartzschild's *The Red Prussian*. Schwartzschild's book is utterly undistinguished in its scholarship, completely polemical in form, and without any of the "new" evidence that Popper finds in it. It is a measure of the confusion in Popper's image of Marx that it could be disturbed by such a mediocre volume.

CHAPTER 3

THE PERVASIVE LIGHT, THE
SPECIAL ATMOSPHERE

THE fundamental Marxian concept of society is not that of an economic base determining a political and cultural superstructure, even though Marx sometimes carelessly implied that it was, as in the 1859 *Forward*. It is rather the image of an organic whole filled with internal movement, of a "rich totality of many determinations and relationships."

So, for example, Marx conceives of capitalism as a system in which the economic, political and social interact reciprocally upon one another. The relationships arising out of production are dominant in the very simple sense that they are the primordial precondition of the life of the species and in the complex sense that they provide a society with its pervasive lighting, its special atmosphere. These production relationships are not economic in the technological or material meaning of the term; they are, rather, human relationships which have been turned into things. Moreover, the production relationships do not infuse every aspect of cultural and political life with a single, underlying content. They bathe the superstructure in that pervasive light, they touch and color the totality, but that leaves room for relative autonomies. Art, science and politics all have their own rhythms.

All this is incalculably distant from the vulgar mechanistic notion that Marxism is a universal, deterministic key to the linear evolution of human society. More to the point, it provides a first step toward methodology that can help in the understanding of the late twentieth century. In short, the new Karl Marx, announced in the first chapter and contradicted by the familiar Karl Marx in the second, now begins to emerge in his own right.

I

First, there is Marx's description of society as an organic whole.

The strange thing about one of Marx's earliest statements of this theme is that it is immediately preceded by one of his most mechanistic remarks. It is typical of the state of Marxist scholarship that his neat but misleading aphorism has been all but graven in stone, while the brilliant complexity that follows usually is ignored. Both passages occur in Marx's *Poverty of Philosophy,* a polemic against his onetime friend Proudhon, which appeared in 1847. The deterministic and famous formulation is that "The hand mill gives you society with a feudal lord; the steam mill, society with the industrial capitalist." So, obviously Marx believed that technology decides the shape of society. One of the many difficulties with this proposition is that the four volumes of *Das Kapital* are, among other things, a sustained attack upon it.

Right after this false simplification comes an extraordinarily rich and precise analysis. Marx writes:

> The relations of every society form a whole. M. Proudhon considers the economic relations as so many social phases, engendering one another, the result of one another, as the antithesis of the thesis, and realizing in their logical succession the impersonal reason of humanity.

The reader will note that the theory which Marx condemns here is the one that most people think he holds.

The only problem in this method [Marx continues] is that, in taking up the examination of just one of these phases, M. Proudhon cannot explain it without recourse to all the other relations of the society, relations which, however, he has not yet engendered by his dialectical movement.

There is no linear explanation for society. There is not a foundation that is put in place and upon which a superstructure is constructed, because the foundation and superstructure have a simultaneous and mutual existence. Marx uses another metaphor:

When M. Proudhon then passes, by means of pure reason, to the birth of the other phases [of the society], he acts as if they were newborn infants, forgetting that they are the same age as the first. . . . How, in effect, can the sole logical form of movement, of succession, of time, explain the body of a society in which the relations coexist simultaneously and support one another?

This is, I think, clear enough. But there is a much more sustained statement of the same theme, which Marx originally wrote as an Introduction for the *Critique of Political Economy,* but then scrapped, unfortunately substituting the celebrated *Forward* for it. But why, it might be fairly asked, take a document that Marx himself decided not to publish and give it greater weight than the one that he actually presented to the public? The answer was suggested in the last chapter: Marx's actual analyses, above all *Das Kapital,* conform much more to the method of the unpublished Introduction than to that of the published *Forward.* However, I ask only provisional acceptance of the assertion that the 1857 Introduction is the most important methodological statement in all of Marxism. The demonstration of this claim waits upon the proof that will be supplied from Marx's mature writings throughout the next four chapters. They will show that the 1857 Introduction is not only a fine statement of what Marx intended to do; it is an accurate anticipation of what he actually did and as such has a compelling authority.

In the 1857 Introduction, Marx takes up the relationship between production, consumption, distribution and exchange, or circulation. In the process of an intricate analysis he develops his own

THE PERVASIVE LIGHT . . .

point of view as against three other theories. One, associated with Jean Baptiste Say, argues that production and consumption are identical. In this thesis, people consume in order to produce, and produce in order to consume. A second holds that it is force that is decisive in the economy, seeing conquest, revolt and political power as primary, and production, consumption and the rest as secondary. The third argues that production is eternal and unchanging, but that societies differ from one another in the way that they distribute their goods.

In each case, Marx answers that it is how a society produces that is decisive. Under capitalism, individuals do not work to fulfill one another's needs; they participate in a complex process, which produces capital goods as well as consumer items, and there is production for production's sake. Force has its functions, Marx concedes, but they are conditioned by the means of production—that is, both the form and the content of robbery in a modern nation are different from theft in a society of cowherders. And finally, the distribution of goods of a society is determined by the distribution of its members in the productive process. It is that process that defines social structure, not social structure that defines itself.

But isn't this just another statement of a proposition dear to the familiar Marx—that the mode of production is basic and everything else derivative? At the end of this section, Marx explicitly explodes that myth.

The result at which we have arrived [he writes] is not that production, distribution, exchange and consumption are identical, but that they all constitute the members of a totality, the differences inside a unity. Production predominates [*übergreift*] . . . The process always departs anew from it. . . . A specific production thus determines a specific consumption, distribution and exchange, *the specific relations of these various aspects to one another*. But of course, production, *in its one-sided form*, is also on its side determined by the other aspects. For example, when the market expands itself (that is, the sphere of exchange expands), production grows in like volume and is subdivided to a greater extent. With changes in distribution, production changes itself—for example, with the concentration of capital, a different distribution of the people in the city and in the countryside, etc. There is a reciprocal interaction between the various aspects. This is the case in each organic whole. (See Appendix C, § 1, p. 363.)

So, production predominates within the organic whole. (Exactly what that "predominance" means will be made clear shortly.) Yet, even so, it exists in a reciprocal relationship with all the other elements. It cannot, therefore, be taken "in its one-sided form,"— that is, as a mere technology or even as the entire complex of production relationships abstracted from social and political structure. Therefore, one must always consider the system of production "in its specific social articulation." If the economic is primary, it is not independent; it is part of an "organic whole."

The notion of the "organic whole" has an exceedingly complex intellectual history. It was, for instance, one of the chief ideological weapons in Burke's attack on the French Revolution; it is a central category for Hegel, who used it to critique democracy, with its individualistic head counting, and who counterposed the organic "spirit of the people" (*Volksgeist*) to it. It has been employed for conservative and, later on, for Fascist purposes; but in Marx's hands it becomes a tool of revolutionary analysis (which is another, striking example of how it is impossible to draw necessary links between theoretical premises and political conclusions). In the form in which Marx took the idea from Hegel, it was directly pitted against the mechanistic, merely statistical, understanding of living reality—that is, to the base-superstructure model, among other things. (See Appendix C, § 2, p. 366.)

It might seem that all this has a nineteenth-century air about it, that organic models of society borrowed from Hegel have no place in the age of the computer. Yet, ironically, there is a clear relationship between this Marxist concept and the notion of a "system" so much in technocratic vogue today. Here, for example, is a 1973 definition of the latter term:

A system . . . is any set of reciprocal relationships in which a variation in the character (or numerical value) of one of the elements will have a determinate—and possibly measurable—consequence for all the others in the system. A human organism is a determinate system; a work-group whose members are engaged in specialized tasks for a common objective is a goal-steering system; a pattern of bombers and bases forms a variable system; the economy as a whole is a loose system.

Clearly, the idea of a reciprocally interacting causation, which is so central to the Marxist method on this count, plays a major role in the intellectual technology of the defense planners and crisis managers of contemporary society.

Moreover, the concept of the organic whole played a central role in an extremely sophisticated dispute over social analysis in West Germany during the last fifteen-or-so years. It was hotly debated during the *"Positivismusstreit,"* the quarrel over positivism, which pitted Adorno and Habermas against scholars like Karl Popper and Ralf Dahrendorf. And it was critical to both sides of a fascinating debate between Habermas and Niklas Luhman over the application of systems theory to the study of society. Marx's concept of an organic whole in which the economic is "predominant" is thus pertinent to computerized sociology as well as to Hegelian philosophy. (See Appendix C, § 3, p. 368.)

And yet, doesn't this notion of reciprocal causation subvert the whole idea of the dominance of one factor of the mode of production? Alexander Gershenkron, the distinguished economic historian, made that point with regard to those letters of Engels in the 1890s in which he tried to take back his own mechanistic interpretation of Marxism. Engels, Gershenkron argues,

> admitted the interaction between economic and noneconomic factors and asserted that the materialist conception of history claimed only "in the last analysis" it was the economic element that determined the course of events. This was hardly a tenable position. Once the existence of circular effects was granted so that, say, economic factors influence political factors and the latter in turn affected the economic, the assertion of "last analysis" or "last instance" becomes impossible. There is no "first" and "last" in a circle.

Engels' formulations in those letters, as the last chapter noted, were indeed faulty. Still, Gershenkron's complaint would seem to be valid against Marx's more sophisticated analysis. How can production be determinant in an organic whole? How can there be a last instance in a circle? The issue, it should be noted, is quite contemporary. For example, Daniel Bell accuses present-day sociological theorists of a procedure very much like the one imputed by Gershenkron to Engels: "One posits a set of subsystems—the educational, the occupational, the political, the religious, the socialization—which influence one another, yet there are no clues as to which is the most important, or why. Everything is dissolved into interacting forces." Doesn't this apply to Marx's notion of the organic whole?

Here again, Hegel is surprisingly relevant. Anticipating Bell by almost a century and a half, he contemptuously dismissed those people who explained a country's mores by its laws and its laws by its mores, then concluding that the two interacted reciprocally. This was, he said, a relationship without a concept—that is, without any notion of the totality in which the mores and laws influenced one another. Marx assimilated this approach in his own way. The social, economic, political and cultural cannot be understood apart from their mutual interpenetration; but that interpenetration takes place in a context in which the economic has a unique, and often quite subtle, role.

On this last count, Marx wrote in the 1857 Introduction,

> In all societal formations, there is a specific production which allocates rank and influence to all the other productions and whose relationships therefore assign all the others their rank and influence. It is a pervasive lighting [*eine allgemeine Beleuchtung*] in which all the other colors are bathed, and which modifies them in their particularity. It is a special atmosphere [*ein besonder Aether*] which determines the specific gravity of every being that arises out of it.

Two aspects of this passage are particularly relevant to understanding how Marx regarded the economic as both determinant and part of an organic whole. First of all, it is clear that the economic is not conceived of as a material, or technological, factor. This is plain enough from Marx's language—a machine hardly gives off a pervasive lighting that illuminates the entire society. It is also made specific in some examples which follow the remarks just quoted. Under feudalism, Marx notes, industry and even the property forms which correspond to it take on an agricultural cast. Even capital itself is dominated and defined by the social relations of the countryside. And conversely, under capitalism the fields are organized like a factory. A plow under feudalism and a plow under capitalism might be physically identical, but they exist in different and special atmospheres.

Secondly, Marx says that the specific production (or mode of production) "allocates rank and influence to all the other productions. . . ." This requires a first approximation of a complex Marxian truth, whose full meaning will be apparent in the next chapter. Some comments from Volume I of *Das Kapital* provide a point of departure.

In the text, Marx is attacking the classical political economists for assuming that capitalist forms are "natural," for not seeing them as historically specific—that is, as functioning within an organic whole, with its own pervasive lighting. In a footnote he goes on to defend himself against the charge, made in a German-American paper, that his method applies to capitalism but not to feudalism or ancient society. In the latter cases, his critic says, either Catholicism was dominant (feudalism) or politics (Greece and Rome). "It is clear," Marx replies, "that the Middle Ages could not live on Catholicism nor the ancient world on politics. The way and mode in which they gained their living explains why in the one place politics played the decisive role [*Hauptrolle*], and in the other, Catholicism."

Marx is saying here, in concrete and specific form, exactly what he generalizes in the 1857 Introduction. On the one hand, production was basic to Rome, Greece and the Middle Ages, since it was the precondition for their very existence; but on the other hand, how production was organized explains why the decisive role was played by noneconomic—political and religious—factors. This focuses upon an extremely important Marxian thesis, which will be explored at greater length in the next chapter: *it is only under capitalism that economics as such plays the leading social part in its own name.* The economic is basic to every society, but it does not function in the same way in each society. Since Marx's masterpiece concerned capitalism, and careless scholars and politicians tried to generalize a universal key to history from it, it has been generally assumed that Marx makes an "economic" interpretation of every social structure.

In fact, Marx understood that the very pervasiveness of the economic factor in history means that it explains very little in and of itself. As he wrote to his friend Dr. Kugelman:

> Every child knows that any nation that stopped working, I will not say for a year, but for two weeks, would die. He also knows that the mass of products corresponding to the different needs require different and quantitatively determined masses of labor time. He knows that the *necessity* of dividing up social labor in certain proportions cannot be transcended by the *specific form of* social production but only *in the mode of that necessity's phenomenal appearance.* . . . . What can change in different historical circumstances is the *form* in which this law asserts itself.

It is, of course, precisely the analysis of the changing forms—the different modes of production—that concerns Marx, not the repetition of a truth known to children. It is, unfortunately, the latter that has often passed itself off as Marxism.

A distinction developed by Louis Althusser and his colleagues aptly expresses this Marxist complexity. For Marx, they rightly argue, the economic is "determinant in the last instance"—that is, it is that precondition and pervasive element of life about which every school child should know. But the economic necessity does not necesarily assert itself in a specifically economic form. The economic is ultimately "determinant," but it need not be "dominant" in a given economic social formation. The Catholicism of the Middle Ages and the politics of the ancient world, just as Marx says, could not have existed unless there was first provision for food, clothing, shelter and the other necessities; but in these societies that basic and primordial fact was mediated by religion and politics rather than by economic forces acting in their own name. In capitalism, the society of *homo economicus,* one has the unusual situation in which the economic is both determinant and dominant. Most interpreters of Marx, his friends and foes, have unfortunately taken this historically unique case as valid for all times and places.

We can return now to Gershenkron's question. How can there be a "last instance" in a system of circular effects? If one concedes the terms in which Gershenkron poses the problem, there is no answer to it. Obviously, as Engels failed to realize when he tried to correct his earlier simplifications of Marx's theory, there can't be a "circular" base and superstructure. What Marx did, in the 1857 Introduction, in the *Grundrisse* and in *Das Kapital,* was to abandon, not simply the geometric and spatial imagery, but the flawed methodology that lies just behind it. Unlike circles, organic wholes, be they human bodies or human societies, can have determinant preconditions and dominant functions—and a pervasive lighting and special atmosphere.

Strangely enough, the work of a prominent contemporary econometrician bears out this Marxist point. Oskar Morgenstern developed a theory of the "compressibility" of an economic system, a theory that dealt with a very practical question: in event of war, how many economic functions could be sluffed off in a society? Is there a core, a kernel, of the economic system that, if destroyed, would necessarily lead to the end of all the rest of the system? Morgenstern asserted that this is indeed the case, and went on to comment that therefore "in organizations and systems possessing kernels there exist *several kinds and degrees of interdependence."* This notion, arrived at in a completely non-Marxist fashion, corroborates, I would suggest, the basic Marxist conception defined here.

But even though econometrics can thus be used to bolster the Marxist theory, a very chastening thought must be stated at once. As a generality, that theory is quite imprecise, literary rather than analytic. It could not be otherwise, as Marx pointed out in the 1857 Introduction. As long as one stays in the realm of general propositions about all societies, there is not very much that can be said. Some children's truths can be emphasized, particularly since learned scholars often deny them; some broad guidelines can be established, but that is all. It is, Marx comments sarcastically, the "wisdom of classical economics" to abstract from the differences and to stress those continuities which prove that the existing social relations are really eternal. For example, "there is no production possible without an instrument of production, even if this instrument is only a hand." It is a central thrust of Marxism to mistrust any grand historical models and to stress that each mode of production, each epoch of social history, has its own atmosphere. The theory that social facts must always be understood in the context of a specific organic whole—of a mode of production—is thus the very opposite of a universal key to history.

I do not claim for a moment that the Marxian concept of society as an organic whole is a *passe partout* that is simply to be substituted for the now discredited image of base-superstructure. It is a paradigm, a suggestion, a perspective, a program of questions; it is not an answer. For that, one must be historically and analytically specific. Two cases in point might help to illustrate this Marxian truth. The one has to do with art, the other with economics. In each case one gets a sense of the complex interactions which take place within the organic whole.[1]

II

If the base determined the superstructure, then art would progress along with everything else and the best artists would be, by definition, those who expressed the "progressive" point of view in a given age. It was just such a vulgar reading of Marx that Joseph Stalin used to rationalize the antiaesthetic called "socialist realism."

Marx had nothing to do with such nonsense. At the end of the 1857 Introduction he commented that "it is well known in the case of art that its specific periods of blooming do not in any way stand in a relationship to the general development of society, and thus also to the material base and likewise to the skeleton of its organization. For example, Greek art or Shakespeare compared to modern art." And a little later on, "The difficulty is not in understanding that Greek art and epic are bound up with certain forms of societal development. The difficulty is that it still provides artistic pleasure for us and serves in a certain way as a norm, an unsurpassable model."

Marx's own personal tastes testify to the complexity of his sensibility. He regarded Balzac, a reactionary, monarchist foe of the French Revolution, as an infinitely greater novelist than various socialist writers; and, his son-in-law reported, he intended to write a book on *La Comédie humaine* after he finished his economic labors. He even argued that it was because Balzac was a reactionary that he was able to write his incomparable masterwork. As Engels put their common view:

> Well, Balzac was politically a Legitimist; his great work is a constant elegy on the irretrievable decay of good society; his sympathies are with the class doomed to distinction. But for all that, his satire is never keener, his irony never more bitter than when he sets in motion the very men and women with whom he sympathizes most deeply—the nobles.

Indeed, at the very beginning of the 1857 Introduction, Marx applies his Balzac analysis to political economy itself. Sir James Steuart, he notes, did not confuse the eighteenth-century individualist with an ideal human type located in the past, as Adam Smith and Ricardo did. As an aristocrat—and here the Balzac parallel surfaces—he stood more firmly on historic ground than the economists of rising capitalism. So even in economic theory, but much more so in art, there is no simple, deterministic relationship between society and its intellectual creations. Reactionaries and aristocrats sometimes see more deeply than revolutionaries.

Given these complexities of the Marxist model, Louis Althusser is quite right in asserting that Marx does not describe society as an "expressive totality"—that is, as a whole that in every one of its parts articulates some single and central principle. (Althusser is, however, wrong to attribute such a theory to Hegel.) (See Appendix C, § 4, p. 373.) There is not in Marx some essence of the system that informs every aspect of it. It is possible, as we have just seen, to have ancient Greek works as standards of excellence in modern capitalist societies. You cannot, therefore take a random "slice" of the social whole and consider it as representative of the totality. That would be true if the base-superstructure theory held —if Greek art flourished only in Greek society—but it does not work in the infinitely more intricate reality that Marx describes.

Althusser explains this in an image that derives in part from Freud and which he finds in Marx. There are, he says, various "times" within a society. For Freud, the chronology of the conscious and unconscious are quite different, though interrelated in the same person. It is possible to be both sixty years old and a child, in Althusser's description; biological and psychological time do not always coincide. Marx has a similar attitude. Philosophy has its history, art has its history, the means of production have their history. All are interacting parts of the same organic whole, but "each one of these histories is scanned according to its own rhythms . . ." And this, of course, is precisely what Marx was noting when he described the divergence between economic and aesthetic history in the 1857 Introduction.

These convolutions do not exist simply as between the various "levels" of the organic whole—say, as between the economic and the cultural. They have their analogue in our perception of even one isolated aspect of this rich totality, a point that Bertel Ollman has made with particular clarity. This is demonstrated at length in *Das Kapital,* Volume II, where Marx takes three elements of the same process—the capitalist buys labor power and the material means of production; the labor power and material are then consumed in the production process; the commodities are sold at a profit, thus enabling the capitalist to begin anew on an expanded basis. These aspects of a single process are then examined in different sequences. If you begin with the capitalist and his money, pass through production and sale and end with the capitalist having more money than at the beginning, that emphasizes the old truism that "it takes money to make money." It is a perspective congenial to the socialist, since it stresses that profits are the purpose of the system.

But if you begin with production and end with expanded reproduction, then one is made particularly conscious of capital's role in developing society's wealth and creating work through the reinvestment of profit. This is the sequence favored by the *Wall Street Journal*. (It is also, interestingly enough, the sequence of Volumes I and II of *Das Kapital;* Marx was always concerned with analyzing the "strong" case.) Finally, if one begins and ends with a sale, that highlights the mercantile character of the whole enterprise; it is the shopkeeper's version of capitalism.

John Kenneth Galbraith made a brilliant statement of a similar point in *Economics and the Public Purpose*. He wrote that

> all social life is a fabric of tightly woven threads. The change of which the corporation is the driving force is a complex process in which many things are altered at the same time and in which cause becomes consequence and cause again. No description is uniquely correct; much depends on where one breaks into the matrix.

Even a single social fact, then, exists in a web of relationships. It cannot be pictured as the "expression" of an essence. And art cannot either. In the organic whole there are relative autonomies, different historical "times"; and the reactionary Balzac turns out to be the unrivaled chronicler of the revolution he despised. These complexities also present themselves when one turns to what seems to be a simple, basic question: What did Marx mean by the "economic" factor?[2]

III

Engels was particularly good on this point. There was, he said, a fact that bewildered the vulgar economists—"Economics does not deal with things, but with relationships between persons and, in the last instance, between classes; however these relationships are always *bound up with things* and *appear as things*." Other economists, Engels remarked, had glimpsed this or that aspect of this fact; but Marx probed it to its depth. It is the unique vocation of Marxism to perceive the personal relations embedded in things —and not, as so many people (including many Marxists) think, to discover the thing relationship underlying persons. This point will recur in many different contexts throughout this book. For now, it will be seen in terms of the relation between workers and capitalists.

In the process of examining it, a number of the interpretations of Marx just made will become more concrete and clear. One will see that the distinction between the economic as "determinant in the final instance" and "dominant" in a given society does not rest on the authority of a single quotation—and the comments on medieval Catholicism and ancient politics are found in a lowly footnote—but is central to a basic theme of *Das Kapital*. This in turn will show, in rich detail, how historically specific the interrelationships of each organic whole are, and how they must be analyzed as such. As a result, the "economic" factor will emerge in some of its Marxian complexity.

In wage labor, Engels remarks, "the whole capitalist mode of production is found in embryo." It probably comes as a shock to most readers to learn that the notion of "wage labor" has this importance in the Marxist theory. It has been the dominant form of labor in the capitalist West for some centuries, and most people think of it simply as being equal to labor in general (which is to say they make the characteristic error of bourgeois thought, eternalizing the transitory). Yet wage labor is obviously different from slave labor and from the feudal serf's obligation to work for the lord or to deliver him a certain share of the surplus. The difference between these various relationships between exploiters and exploited are at the very heart of Marx's analysis. (See Appendix C, § 5, p. 374.)

Marx makes a sweeping assertion on this count in *Das Kapital*. Wage labor, he says, is a "phenomenal form." That is a Hegelian way of arguing that the immediate, perceivable reality of wage labor disguises its real nature. Upon this phenomenal form, he continues, "rests all the notions of justice of the workers as well as the capitalists, all the mystifications of the capitalist mode of production, all of its illusion about freedom, all of the apologetic nonsense of the vulgar economists." A fuller explanation of this critical passage waits upon Chapter 5; for now, only those aspects of it that are relevant to the present analysis will be treated.

When a worker is paid four dollars an hour, it is obvious that he is being paid four dollars for the value of an hour's work. That is clearly written on the very surface of his bargain with the capitalist, and both of them believe in the essential fairness of the transaction. It is also a mystification. In fact, as Marx analyzes wage labor, the worker receives the exchange value of his labor power, which is four dollars, but the use value of that same labor power for the capitalist is six dollars. Or, to put it another way, one third of the .hour is an unpaid contribution by the worker to his employer; two thirds are paid.

In the course of working that hour, one third of it gratis, the worker makes a useful product that satisfies the need of someone else in the society. He thus enters into a social relationship with that person. But he never knows it; for him the hour is defined as being "worth" four dollars. He does not normally care about the quality of his product or those who enjoy its use. That human interrelationship is expressed only in its cash form. Within the historically specific context of capitalist society, social relationships are thus necessarily turned into things. Everything, even honor itself, is said to have its price.

This is not the case in feudalism; and once again Marx's meaning becomes easier to grasp when it is placed in the context of a comparison of social systems. In feudal society, Marx writes:

> Personal dependence characterizes the social relations of material production just as much as the spheres of life based upon it. But just because relationships of personal dependence form the specific social base, labor and the products of labor need not take on the phantasmagoric form that is different from their reality. In social life they enter as service and payment in kind. The natural form of labor, its particularity, and not as in commodity production, its generality, is here its immediate social form. The compulsory labor is measured by time just like commodity producing labor, but every serf knows that it is a specific quantity of his personal labor power which he expends in the service of the lord.

It is worth while lingering over this comment for a moment. Under one form of feudalism, the serf is required to work a certain period of time on the lord's property; in return he gets the right to work his own property the rest of the time. This relationship is not predicated on an exchange of money, and it does not take place on a free market. It is imposed by tradition, sanctified by religion and enforced by political power. The serf is personally dependent on the lord and owes him fealty. Therefore he must work for him for nothing. The fact that his labor time is divided up into paid and unpaid portions is right there for everyone to see—except that they would not see it, for the very distinction between paid and unpaid time requires a commercial calculus and does not enter into the general consciousness until capitalism emerges. What the serf and the lord saw in their relationship was the will of God.

In capitalism, on the contrary, the economic reality must appear other than it is. Feudalism and all other precapitalist forms present the economic in a noneconomic guise. Since exploitation is the will of God, not of man, the unjust relationship between lord and serf can seem to be what it is. Its sanction is, after all, divine. But capitalism is a secular society of supposedly free agents making contracts on the basis of *quid pro quo*. If the worker were told that he was going to get paid for two thirds of his time, but that he would be required to make a gift of the remaining third to the capitalist, he would reply that he was being cheated precisely according to the bourgeois law of the market. This society has to hide its true character. But note that this fraud is sincere—that is, Marx says that it fools the capitalists (who are sober and upright men, believing in an "hour's work for an hour's pay," and all that) as well as the workers.

So, wage labor is not only a historically specific form of work that becomes general under capitalism. It is also the very secret of the capitalist mode of production, for it is here that the surplus is concealed, that precondition for the accumulation of capital and the growth of the system as a whole. Therefore, wage labor is also the spine of the capitalist class system. Those who contribute the unpaid labor time are in a subordinate position, those who appropriate it are in command. This is the origin of the two distinctive (but not the only) classes of capitalist society, the workers and the *bourgeoisie*.* But, since these production relations are dominant in an organic whole of reciprocal interaction, they do not exist independently of the social relations they call forth. One deals, not

---

* In the United States, the term "bourgeois" usually means middle class. In Marx, it refers to the class of big capitalists.

with the economic "factor" as cause and social class as effect, but
with "modern production in its specific social articulation."

Marx's definition of economics, then, is a function of his subject
matter, not an arbitrary classification external to it. It is only in
bourgeois society that there is a unique mystification of human
relationships that appear as things. In precapitalist mystifications,
those relationships appear as dictates of the supernatural will, and
though they are also exploitative and unjust, their earthly appearance is straightforward. Marxian economics is uniquely an analysis of capitalism, and its method is a necessary response to the
reality being investigated. It is a laying-bare of the human relationships that appear as things in the historically singular, capitalist
form of society. A study of feudalism, then, would not simply concern itself with another mode of production; it would use a method
different from that of *Das Kapital,* one appropriate to its subject
matter.

Capitalist society, then, is based on an illusion peculiar to it: that
the worker is paid for the value of his work. But this deception has
an enormous "objectivity," for it rationalizes the functioning of a
gigantic system which has revolutionized the very face of the earth.
It is a lie, but a lie that informs the most substantial social reality
mankind has ever known. And yet the power of this fraud is provisional; for ultimately it is a fraud. The very categories in which
capitalism thinks of itself will become absurd as the system disappears. They will then seem to the everyday consciousness as
superstitious as the divine right of kings appears to the mind of
modern, capitalist man.

But it is not just machines or work relationships that are bathed
in the pervasive lighting of a given organic whole; so are human
consciousness and its ideas. This is the methodological point of departure for Marx's attack on the classical political economy. In
Marx's analysis, Smith and Ricardo, with their magnificent intellectual accomplishments, remained uncritical of their most basic
assumptions. Even though understanding this requires an anticipation of matters that will be dealt with in Chapter 5—Marx's analysis
of capitalism as such—it is important to take it up now, for it bears

significantly on a critical aspect of the present analysis: that for Marx there is no economic "factor" independent of social structure. Smith and Ricardo did not realize that fact, and could not. That, for Marx, was their central flaw.

For Marx, capitalism is a contradictory system of private social production. It uses all the power of science and technology to bring the remotest corners of the world into contact with one another, but only in the pursuit of profit, not in the name of humanity. Therefore this system cannot express the social sources of its power openly, for that would subvert its private institutional framework. Men do not master the productive process that they themselves have created; they do not impose their priorities upon it. Rather they submit themselves to the laws of a supposedly impersonal market, and periodically the work of their own hands comes crashing down around their ears. In this irrational context of private socialization, the "value" of a product is established deviously and sometimes catastrophically. It is determined by the amount of "socially necessary labor time" that the commodity contains. A carcinogenic cigarette that satisfies an artfully induced demand is "valuable"; a house desperately needed by poor people, but costing more than they can pay, is so valueless that it will not even be built. All of this is justified, because it allows the individual to choose. So, the worker buying potatoes, Marx notes wryly, and the kept woman buying laces are equal, because both are following their opinions. In short, when one says that an item is "worth" such a price, and that it has such and such a "value," an entire framework of anti-human priorities is implied.

Bourgeois economics can understand these things only at the cost of turning into socialist economics. It must, therefore, be unconscious of some of its deepest assumptions—unconscious, that is, of that pervasive capitalist light which bathes its very categories. So it was that Smith and Ricardo formulated the proposition that labor is the basis of economic value but never understood their own discovery. For they never

posed the question of why . . . labor thus presents itself as value . . . It is plainly written on the surface of this formula that it belongs to a social formation in which the productive process is master of men, and men have not yet mastered the productive process. To their bourgeois consciousness, these forms are valid as a self-evident natural necessity, like productive labor itself.

In other words, capitalism exults in the fact that it is not run by conscious, socially motivated human intervention, but by the invisible hand of the market. In such a society, value has to be established surreptitiously. Only, Smith and Ricardo assume that this state of affairs is natural. It is of the essence of their theories—and of bourgeois economics itself—that it treats the "economic" as a perennial factor that can be abstracted from social structure and historic context. They wrench it out of the organic whole which confers upon it its specific meaning.

It is, then, no accident that *Das Kapital* is subtitled *Critique of Political Economy*. In German thought, this term, "critique," harks back, of course, to Kant. It was his great contribution to examine the very possibility and preconditions of knowledge; in him, method becomes critical of itself. So also with Marx. He does not write a *work* of political economy; he produces a *critique* of political economy. In this sense, he did not consider himself an economist at all, since he believed that economic science, which had developed precisely in the course of the revolutionary struggle of the bourgeoisie against feudalism, is, for all that it had done to liberate humanity from the old prejudices, unconscious of its own, new prejudices.

If Smith or Ricardo had asked why labor takes the form of value under capitalism, they would thereby have admitted that it could take another form under some different society. Ricardo, to be sure, had intimations of a capitalist decadence, but no perspective for a socialist future. There were socialists who took over Ricardo's labor theory and tried to give it a radical interpretation—if labor is the source of all value, it should be the beneficiary of all value. But Marx was deeply critical of them too, and for much the same reason that he scored the classical political economy. The Ricardian socialists used concepts that, like "value," were the functional illusions of capitalist society and tried to force them to socialist conclusions. But as long as labor was expressed as "value," and not as a planned expenditure of human effort to meet a social need, that implied a capitalist way of thinking and acting.

Because Marx looked at society from a revolutionary and working-class point of view, he could see things that escaped Smith and Ricardo; indeed he could penetrate to the flawed foundations of political economy as such. That obviously does not mean that anyone who adopted Marx's political point of view would automatically be gifted with his inspired perception. The hearts of the Ricardian socialists were eminently proletarian, but their minds were still imprisoned in capitalist categories. Still, without question, there is a profound link between Marx's political vantage point and the substance of his theories. For the former permitted him to see the latter as having to do, in the most radical fashion, with the revelation, and possible liberation, of the human creativity that capitalism had poured into its unique industrial mold.

So, when Marx says that production relations are dominant within an organic whole, he was suggesting the very opposite of a mechanistic interpretation of societal causation. Not only did art and other aspects of the culture observe their own, proper "times," but also ideas were affected by the atmosphere specific to a given mode of production. In this perspective, it was and is the function of Marxism to make a social order conscious of its own assumptions, of that often elusive lighting that is the setting for the crudest of facts.[3]

IV

Finally, the Marxian concept of the organic whole does have some very specific methodological implications. They are one more reminder that Marxism is open-ended, undogmatic.

Where, Marx asks in the 1857 Introduction, does one begin the analysis of a society? The obvious answer is, With the facts. Only, that is not the case. Marx writes:

> When we observe a given nation from a political-economic point of view, we begin with its population, its division into classes, city, country, sea, the various production departments, exports

and imports, yearly production and consumption, commodity prices, etc. It seems right to begin with the real and concrete, with the actual premises, and thus, in economics to begin with population, which is the basis and subject of the entire societal production.

But, Marx continues, population as a concept is "a chaotic representation of the whole," for it leaves out the classes, the elements upon which the classes rest, like wage labor and capital, and so on. Therefore one must proceed back toward the most simple and fundamental categories. Then, in the possession of basic concepts, one returns to population, but this time not as "a chaotic representation of a whole, but as a rich totality of many determinations and relationships."

This method of first constructing a paradigm, a concept, that organizes the facts is obviously related to the idea of the organic whole. In it, Marx emphasizes the interdependence of all the factors, this time from a methodological point of view—". . . the simplest economic category, say exchange value, presumes population, producing in specific relations, and also certain sorts of families or communities or states. It can never exist except as an abstract, *one-sided* relationship of an already given, concrete and living whole."

Moreover, the categories of economics, like the works of art, do not stand in any neat relationship to their time and place. The most sophisticated economic forms, like cooperation and a developed division of labor, are to be found in a society that does not even have money (the Inca civilization in Peru). And even though money appears very early on in history, in the ancient Mediterranean world it is a dominant element only in certain trading nations (Phoenicians, Carthaginians). Even in Greece and Rome, the most advanced of societies in ancient times, the full development of money appears only at the point of decadence and decline. This is one of the reasons why, in the Marxist view, the economic *as such* did not play the same kind of a role under feudalism and classical antiquity as under capitalism.

As Marx wrote much earlier in the *German Ideology,*

particular individuals who are active within a specific mode [of production] enter into these determined social and political relationships. Empirical observation must in each individual case demonstrate the connection of the social and political articulation with production empirically and without any mystification.

Thus, one must perceive both the organic whole and the intricacy of its interconnections. And, as a Marxist, one must always be wary of those "one-sided" categories which abstract from the living totality. Thus it is that Marxism is always at a beginning, that it proclaims that there can be no definitive methodological statement so long as the living, concrete whole of society is in movement, in change. It is then not a liberal banality to say that Marxism must be constantly revised. That is one of the most fundamental imperatives of the Marxist analysis. It is, so to speak, its pervasive lighting, its special atmosphere.[4]

CHAPTER **4**

THE MODE OF LIFE

KARL Marx worked out his theory of the mode of production by viewing the organic whole of capitalism from the perspective of its economic relationships. His ideas in this area are extremely rich and obviously central to Marxism. By this time it should come as no surprise that they are also widely misunderstood. Indeed, only the simplifications about base and superstructure have done more violence to Marx's meanings than these confusions.

A simple, though somewhat dramatic, example will serve as a first statement of this point. In Marx's analysis, the capitalist mode of production has never existed. Indeed, it could not possibly exist, since it is an abstraction that helps one to understand reality, not a description of reality. There is, as Nicos Poulantzas has brilliantly emphasized, such a thing as the capitalist economic-social formation. It contains economic, political and cultural remnants and anticipations of other modes of production. It is under the domination of the economic relationships that Marx so brilliantly defined in his abstraction the capitalist mode of production, but the latter must never be taken as a depiction of the complexity of the capitalist organic whole.

All this is, I suspect, a shocking revelation to a good many students of Marxism, the Marxists as well as the anti-Marxists. So it is, for instance, that even sophisticated scholars like Raymond Aron and Daniel Bell mistakenly think that the Marxist concept of the mode of production asserts a seamless unity of the economic, political and cultural relationships within that mode. The truth is almost exactly opposite. And yet, here again Marx and Engels must take some slight blame for the misunderstanding of their work. They did change their minds about the significance of the mode of production. Typically, however, both their friends and their foes preferred their youthful sweeping generalizations to the intricate insights of their maturity.

Once that textual problem is cleared up, the authentic Marxist theory of the mode of production will be brought into focus. That will involve some critically important themes: the distinction between historical and dialectical analysis; the uniqueness of the capitalist mode of production; the special problems of dealing with its rise and fall; and so on. These ideas are more than a century old, and for most people they are new. (See Appendix D, § 1, p. 376.)

I

Marx and Engels committed a youthful indiscretion in the *German Ideology*. Their conception of history, they wrote, "is based on analyzing the actual production process, and the forms of exchange which are part of this mode of production and produced by it, and thereby to conceptualize [*aufzufassen*] civil society in its various stages as the basis of all history." In the course of understanding civil society "as the basis of all history," they also promised to unravel "the various theoretical products and forms of consciousness, religion, philosophy, ethics, etc., which are to be explained in terms of it . . ."

It was a staggering task they had set themselves. Where Hegel in the *Phenomenology* had dared to interpret, not only history but the very forms of consciousness to which it gave rise, in terms of spirit, or *Geist,* Marx and Engels were going to do the very same thing, but now in terms of "civil society." It was not very long before they abandoned this project, at least partly because it rested upon what was practically a contradiction in terms. "Civil society," it will be remembered from Chapter 3, explicitly refers to that sphere of private economic life that first became decisive in capitalism. Indeed, Marx makes the same point as Hegel on this count: that precapitalist societies regarded accumulation of wealth as a decadence. But how could one conceptualize all of human history on the basis of a social reality that is primarily capitalist? That was and is impossible.

Marx and Engels never formally retracted their youthful error, probably because they had formulated it in a book that was not published during their lifetime. Yet, as Helmut Reichelt has shown, it is abundantly clear from their later work that they had understood that their dream of a universal key to history had to be surrendered. Marx insisted over and over that the capitalist mode of production was unique, that it represented a break with all forms of precapitalist society. That meant that "civil society" was the clue, not to all of social evolution, but to the construction of a single economic system. One of the most important passages in all of Marx's writing helps in making a preliminary statement of this important point.

This pregnant analysis occurs in a description of labor rent—that is, of that form of feudalism under which the serf is obliged to work on the lord's property in return for the right to till his own land. "Rent and surplus labor," Marx writes, "are identical here. It is rent, not profit, that is the form in which the unpaid surplus labor is expressed." In other words, the underlying substratum of all modes of production is labor, which, at the very least, must produce subsistence for the direct producer plus enough to replace the materials used up (for example, primitive agriculture must yield both food and seed). This is "a natural precondition of all continuing and reproducing labor . . ." But in all but the earliest of societies, there is also a surplus over and above subsistence and depreciation. This surplus can take various "forms"; it can appear as rent, as profit, as a tax paid to the state. Exactly what form it does take will be a key to the very structure of society and will be related as well to its stage of development, its mode of working together and its technology.

In the case of labor rent, unlike profit under capitalism, the reality is not disguised; it appears as unpaid surplus labor which is yielded up to the lord. Then Marx goes on to an important generalization, one that separates many precapitalist modes from the capitalist mode: ". . . in all forms in which the immediate laborer is 'possessor' [*Besitzer*] of the production means and conditions of labor necessary for his own subsistence, the property relationship must at the same time enter in as an immediate relation of lordship and servitude, and the immediate producer must be unfree . . ." This is an extremely clear statement of a point that was made earlier: that the economic, as such, plays a decisive role in its own right and guise in only one mode of production, capitalism. In all other systems, the economic is inextricably and immediately suffused with the political. This applies to postcapitalist planned societies, whether socialist or *bureaucratic collectivist* (the generic term I use for Communism). In them, the economic process is politicized; in mechanistic terms, the superstructure dominates the base. The impossibility of applying the vulgar Marxist theory of the all-determining economic base and the dependent political superstructure to most of recorded history should be quite obvious.

This is spelled out by Marx when he examines three different precapitalist societal types. In feudalism, the immediate producer, the serf, is independent. This is the case, in a different way, in the Indian commune, where the individual is subordinated to the group, but the group itself is independent as against the landlord, the state. "Under these circumstances, the nominal landlord can only pump out the surplus labor through extra-economic force, whatever form this also takes." Slavery is different in that the slave is not independent, like the serf or the commune, but is a possession. But here again personal unfreedom is the basis of the system.

When Marx argues there is no private property, as in Asia, the relationship of lordship and servitude takes on a special quality. Rent and taxes become identical—"the state is here the highest landlord." So, "sovereignty is here concentrated landed property. Therefore there exists no private property but only private and communal possession and use of the land." The individual and the commune have possession, but not ownership of the land; the latter belongs to the sovereign. This case, as one might imagine, was particularly embarrassing to Stalin and his associates, since it provided Marx's own analysis of an exploitative, class society based on state ownership of the means of production. As a result, Stalin forbade discussion of "Asian despotism" in the early 1930s.

Finally Marx generalizes these observations in a passage that concludes with a strong emphasis on how history is not neatly determined by modes of production.

> In every case it is the immediate relationship of the owner of the conditions of production to the immediate producer—a relationship that always conforms naturally to a specific developmental stage of the manner and mode [*Art und Weise*] of labor and thereby to its societal productive power—in which the innermost secret, the hidden basis of the entire societal construction, and therefore of the political forms of sovereignty and dependency relations as well, is found. This does not stop the same economic base—the same in terms of the crucial conditions—from showing infinite variations and gradations in the way it appears as a result of countless different empirical circumstances, natural conditions, racial relations, historical influences working from the outside, etc. These can only be conceptualized [*zu begreifen sind*] through analysis of the empirically given circumstances.

Now these pages on labor rent, and the climactic generalization just quoted, make it very clear that the Marx of *Das Kapital* had abandoned the project he had outlined in the *German Ideology*. He stresses, to be sure, some regularities that are to be observed in history: there is a labor process underlying all societies, and the way in which the surplus labor is pumped out of the direct producers is the "secret" of the societal construction. But he makes it abundantly clear that these propositions are only the most general abstractions, and that it is capitalism, a system qualitatively different from all those that went before, that is the focus of his attention. Clearly, "civil society" functions in ways that are so radically different under feudalism and slavery from those under capitalism— it is subordinate under feudalism and slavery, dominant under capitalism—that there can no longer be any pretense that it offers a universal key to the understanding of all history.

And indeed, the mature Marx was at great pains to point out the uniqueness of capitalism. It "towered beyond comparison above all previous epochs," he said. All the earlier systems are simpler and more transparent than capitalism. They either rest upon tribal and familial relationships or upon immediate relationships of servitude and domination. Engels added that when society is underdeveloped, "the predominant influence of blood relationships seems to rule the social order." And Marx himself commented that "under primitive, little-developed conditions . . . tradition necessarily plays a dominant [*übermachtige*] role" in the mode of production. Even in the *German Ideology,* Marx and Engels insisted that where trade was local, each discovery had to be made anew in each area and that "mere accidents," like barbarian invasions, could force a nation to begin its economy all over again.

This Marxist emphasis on the special characteristics of capitalism is related to one of Marx's most dialectical conceptions: his defense of the progressive role of greed and of production for production's sake in bourgeois society.

In precapitalist societies, where there is no widespread production for the market, the drive for surplus labor is limited by the needs it has to satisfy. For that matter, in the earlier modes of production, as we have seen, the accumulation of great wealth signaled a decadence, not a progress. Moses well understood that the worship of the Golden Calf would corrupt his people. Capitalism, on the contrary, has an insatiable appetite for surplus labor and riches, for if the system does not produce more this year than last, it faces a crisis. This capitalist crisis is itself unprecedented, for it normally breaks out at the high point of a boom and is characterized not by a scarcity of goods as in precapitalist famines, but by an overabundance of goods that cannot find a buyer.

All of these things—the voracious appetite for surplus labor, the treadmill of production for production's sake, the crisis of glut—were regularly denounced by pre-Marxist socialists. Only Marx viewed these evils dialectically. For him they were the horrible, but unavoidable means for the creation of a technology of abundance, which would, in turn, make socialism possible. In the *Grundrisse* he described "the universal tendency of capitalism which differentiates it from all previous productive stages . . . Although capitalism is by its nature limited, it strives for universal development of the productive powers and therefore becomes the precondition for a newer mode of production." Here again, capitalism is clearly presented as being different from "all previous productive stages." It is a discontinuity in history, not the result of an orderly progression.

Thus far, then, there is a serious Marxist theory of only one mode of production, and its concepts cannot be promiscuously applied to the past, present and future. I thus insist on the limits of Marx's work, not simply because he did, but also because this is the only way to protect his achievement against a sloppy, useless universalism. The same point applies to the method that Marx used to analyze that capitalist mode of production.[1]

II

Das Kapital is suffused with history. Indeed, as the last chapter emphasized, Marx's central theoretical critique of the classical political economy was that it was not aware of its historical assumptions, that its categories were presented as timeless. And yet, *Das Kapital* does not begin with the actual capitalism that Marx encountered in history. That, as the 1857 Introduction noted, would be to start with a "chaotic representation of the whole." Instead, Marx's masterpiece opens with an examination of the central relationship of the system in its "pure form," abstracted for all other forms. So, as Roman Rosdolsky has brilliantly demonstrated, Volume I is about "capital in general." (See Appendix D, § 2, p. 378.) Therefore it excludes any data that interfere with that focus. It does not, for instance, discuss competition and credit, but only the way in which a surplus is created and appropriated in the course of capitalist production. The relationship of wage labor and capital is put under a spotlight; everything else is left in shadow.

As a result, Marx puts an enormous amount of reality into parentheses in the early part of his book. He makes the simplifying assumption, for instance, that workers are paid a subsistence wage, not because he believes that this is the case, but because he cannot treat all the factors affecting wages at the very outset. This, as the next chapter will show, has confused many scholars who take this simplifying assumption as if it were a statement by Marx about the real world.

The dialectical method of presentation, then, aims at explicating a historic totality, but it does not follow a historic chronology. This could lead readers to assume that the consciously simplified model of Volume I—in which the mode of production is self-contained and in equilibrium—is Marx's characteristic and definitive statement. They might then even miss a point that Marx insists upon on numerous occasions: that there is, and must be, a contradiction between the actual, unschematic development of the capitalist social formation and the functioning of the capitalist mode of production as it is described in *Kapital*.

Perhaps the most dramatic illustration of this complexity is the fact that the genesis of capitalist society is not explicable in terms of its own laws, since its origins are located in another mode of production. Capitalism, in short, is a contradiction within feudalism before it is capitalism. Thus the historical definition of capitalism is not, and cannot be, the same as the dialectical definition of Volume I, in which a self-contained, self-perpetuating system is assumed and its internal "laws of motion," of change, are analyzed.

The most explicit statement of this point is found in the *Grundrisse*. Its importance cannot be overemphasized. Marx writes:

> That the possessor of money *finds already in existence* labor power on the market as a commodity within the limits of circulation, this precondition, from which we depart here and from which bourgeois society in its production process departs, is obviously the result of a long historical development, the résumé of many economic transformations, and presupposes the downfall of other modes of production (societal production relations) and a specific development of the productive powers of societal labor. This specific, prior historic process, which is given in this precondition, will be yet more specifically formulated by a further observation of the relations. This historic developmental stage of economic production—whose product itself is already *the free laborer*—is, however, the precondition for the emergence and very existence of capital as such. Its existence is the result of a protracted process in the

economic formation of society. *It is clear at this point how the dialectical form of presentation is only correct when it recognizes its own limits.*

In other words, the two basic actors in the most fundamental capitalist relationship—the "free" worker (free in sense that he has only his labor power to sell on the market and has no traditional-legal ties to the land or the guild) and the capitalist—develop prior to the capitalist system itself. They must be in existence before the new mode can begin and they are, originally, not its product but its precondition. Moreover, there are a whole host of historical factors which influence the emergence of the new order. For instance, there are

the discovery of the gold and silver deposits in America, the extermination, enslavement and entombment of the indigenous population in the mines, the beginning of the conquest and plunder of the East Indies, the transformation of Africa into a plantation for the commercial hunting of black skins . . .

This new colonial market could not be satisfied on the basis of the small number of city workers inherited from feudalism, and it becomes a spur to the rise of capitalism.

The sudden expansion of the world market [Marx writes], the variety of the circulating commodities, the competition among the European nations to seize Asian products and treasure, the colonial system, all contributed to the breaking up of the feudal limits of production.

Now, these developments are prior to capitalism, but they are hardly characteristic expressions of feudalism. They are, in short, part of a transition period that cannot be understood on the basis of the normal functioning of either of the modes of production which it bridges. That is why the dialectical presentation "is correct only if it knows its own limits."

Similarly with the agricultural revolution that was another of the capitalist preconditions. "The theft of land of a grand scale, as in England, first created the field of application of great agriculture.

In its beginning, therefore, this transformation of agriculture had more the appearance of a political revolution." So, a political event has enormous economic consequences—which is one more striking example of reciprocal, rather than mechanical, causation.

But, then, does this interpretation of Marx make his method so indeterminate as to be useless? For if there are historical events which can be of enormous, even decisive, importance and yet are not the product of any mode of production or even subject to its laws, doesn't that reduce history to a succession of chance happenings?

First of all, there *is* a considerable amount of indeterminacy within the Marxist system, and it is only because vulgar Marxism dominates our consciousness that this is shocking. For instance, when Marx discusses the role of usury in preparing the way for capitalism (by destroying both rich landowners and small producers), he adds:

> However, the extent to which this process abolishes [*aufhebt*] the old mode of production, how this was the case in modern Europe, and whether this process leads to the capitalist mode of production depends completely upon the historical stage of development and the circumstances which result from it.

Helmut Reichelt is quite right to say that the concept of capitalism—or capitalism in general—does not explain why this system first developed in Europe (or why, to take Marx's own repeated example, it had not emerged earlier in Rome or Byzantium, where the preconditions for it seemed to exist). These things cannot be deduced from the dialectical model of capitalism as a pure case; they have to be observed empirically, historically.

At the same time, the historical "accidents" that happen to capitalism are, in considerable measure, shaped by that mode of production. Thus the great geographical discoveries of the sixteenth and seventeenth centuries and the consequent growth of merchant capital were not fated by either the feudal or the capitalist mode of production; neither were the gold and silver deposits of the New World consequences of the primitive societies that existed there. But how these momentous happenings impinged upon different nations had much to do with their internal structure. Marx's case in point is the contrasts among Portugal, Holland and England during the age of discovery.

In Holland there was already a commercial foundation within the society when the world market began to expand. Therefore it was able to take advantage of the new circumstances: ". . . the modern mode of production only developed (in the sixteenth and seventeenth centuries, when the new possibilities opened up). In its first period, the period of manufacture, where the conditions for it had been produced within the Middle Ages." Holland had undergone sufficient internal transformations to be able to take advantage of the events; Portugal had not (indeed both Portugal and Italy, which had been supreme upon the seas, declined, in part at least, because of the revolution of the world market). But then, as the capitalist mode of production moved to a higher level, it was not trade (at which Holland excelled), but industry (in which England was pre-eminent) that became crucial.

The historical events which led up to the emergence of the capitalist mode of production were not created by it, or even by the normal workings of its predecessor; yet the impact of those events was determined by the differences between the modes of production in various countries. The historical is not merely indeterminant; the structural is not all determining. There is, rather, a complex interaction between the two kinds of causation. This kind of phenomenon will be encountered again in Chapter 9 when the energy crisis of the 1970s in the capitalist nations will be seen as the result of an accident—the cartel of the Organization of Petroleum Exporting Countries—whose possibility and consequences were not at all accidental.

Thus the capitalist economic self-formation is not self-contained, even though the brilliant abstraction which helps us to understand it, the theory of the capitalist mode of production is. With this understood, we can now proceed to that theory itself and confront another proposition that contradicts a widely held version of Marxism: In Marx's conception of the capitalist mode, it is not technology that is the driving force of change. That negative point then leaps to the basic, positive content of this part of his analysis.[2]

III

Capitalism, Marx emphasizes on a number of occasions, does *not* begin with a technological revolution. Rather, the capitalist employs scattered artisans who continue to work as they always have worked. So, "the production mode itself is not determined by capital but is taken over by it, as it is." In the vocabulary of *Das Kapital,* the worker is only "formally" placed under the rule of capital; his work, his tools, his techniques, remain as they were under the conditions of the feudal artisans. Indeed, Marx comments that this situation persisted in the French silk industry and the English hosiery and lace industries into the middle of the nineteenth century.

The revolutionary way out of feudalism into capitalism, Marx argues, would have turned the producer into merchant and capitalist and set him up in opposition to both the natural economy in the countryside and the medieval guilds in the city. On the other hand, the merchant can take over production, and this is what generally happened. When, for example, "the English clothier of the seventeenth century brings the weavers—who, however, remain independent—under his control, he sells them their wool and buys their cloth" and this does not revolutionize the mode of production, "but rather conserves it and keeps it as a precondition." Indeed, this mode of the transition from feudalism to capitalism eventually comes to stand in the way of the development of capitalism itself. It is only when this formal control of the worker by capital is replaced by real control—that is, when the very way in which men and women produce and live is dominated and determined by capital, that the system finally achieves its characteristic form. The worker must be turned into an appendage of the machine before that can happen; the skills of the artisans must be destroyed.

A number of extremely important historical aspects of the Marxist concept of the mode of production should now be apparent. First of all, this analysis should put an end, once and for all, to the interpretation of Marx as a technological determinist. He insists that the transition from feudalism to capitalism—the most momentous change in production modes in the history of mankind—takes place on the basis of a conservative technology that is simply taken over from the old system. In his brilliant, but often ignored, study of the transition from the feudal to the bourgeois world view, Franz Borkenau notes that the inventions which paved the way for early capitalism—gunpowder, the compass, printing—belong to the late Middle Ages. Blast furnaces were developed in the sixteenth century, and the next great wave of discovery took place in the late-eighteenth century (mechanical weaving, steam machines, et cetera). Thus, in Borkenau's analysis the bourgeois consciousness was a product not of technological change but of transformations in social relationships which took place during a period in which invention did not flourish. What is critical in this transformation is not the machine but the fact that a feudal technology is put to a capitalist use. As I have noted earlier, this point that the capitalist relationship is decisive, and not the machine, can be found throughout *Das Kapital*.

Secondly, it should be clear from this part of the analysis that a mode of production is not conceived of as a seamless, motionless whole. That may be the impression received by the casual reader of Volume I's abstractions and functional simplifications, but it is not Marx's intention, as any serious look at the distinction between the formal and real control of the worker by capital will show. That distinction, it should be emphasized, is quite prominent in Volume I itself. I stress this fact, because it is ignored by some of the most influential of the recent misinterpretations of Marx, that of Daniel Bell, Raymond Aron and the other theorists of "postindustrial society."

Before turning to that sophisticated error, however, it is necessary to summarize Marx's own definition of capitalism. The capitalist mode of production, as he sees it, is distinguished by two characteristics. First, it produces its goods and services as commodities. Second, the creation of "surplus value," not the production of those goods and services, is the aim of the system.

A commodity, in Marx's usage, is not simply a good or service, but a good or service produced to be sold for someone else's use. A meal cooked by a member of a family for consumption by the other members is not a commodity; a meal prepared in a restaurant for sale is. With the exception of such familial goods and services, most of the things consumed in present-day capitalism—our clothes, food, housing, et cetera—are commodities. We take this for granted, as part of the human condition. But in Marx's analysis—and he is quite right on this count—the dominance of commodity production is a relatively recent (three- or four-hundred-year-old) phenomenon. Commodities exist in the far reaches of history, but they become predominant only under capitalism.

In this system, the decisive commodity exchange takes place between the capitalist and the worker. The latter is himself or herself a commodity, and that too is something new in history. The slave was the legal possession of the owner; the serf was tied to the feudal lord by bonds of tradition. But the worker under capitalism is "free"—that is, he or she does not own means of production; he must sell his or her labor power. Moreover, he or she does not sell a specific, hand-tailored product, like the artisan of the Middle Ages. He or she sells an abstract "labor power," for the thousands of workers who are now crowded into a single factory are interchangeable parts of a machine. Therefore, the capitalist mode of production is impersonal. Its chief agents, "the capitalist and the wage worker, are . . . only embodiments [*Verkorperungen*], personifications of capital and wage labor; determined social character-types [*bestimmte gesellschaftliche Charactere*] that the social production process stamps upon individuals; products of these specific social relations."

This perception of the depersonalization of a society in which humans sell themselves as commodities provides the basis of the Marxian social psychology (which was developed by Erich Fromm, the early Wilhelm Reich, Theodore Adorno, Max Horkheimer, and others). Moreover, it leads to a deepening of a central Marxian insight that has already been noted: that capitalism is a system of (and I use Max Weber's terms for convenience) functional rationality and substantive irrationality.

Marx writes:

The authority which the capitalist takes on as the personification of capital in the immediate production process, which he wears as the leader and controller of production, is essentially different from the authority on the basis of production with slaves, serfs, etc. On the basis of capitalist production, the mass of the producers confront the social character of their production in the form of a strong, ruling authority and as a hierarchically ordered social mechanism of the labor process—which authority only comes to its bearer as the personification of the conditions of labor as against labor, and not, as in earlier forms of production, as political or theocratic rule. But among the bearers of this authority, the capitalists themselves, they confront one another only as owners of commodities; and therefore, there prevails the most complete anarchy, in which the social interrelationship of production asserts its value only as an all-powerful natural law as over against the individual will. (See Appendix D, § 3, p. 380.)

This passage states that fundamental distinction to which Marx returns on a number of occasions. As a labor process, as a system of production, capitalism is rational, technological, scientific—even though that rationality dominates those who exercise it. Within the factory there is conscious planning, and the workers are ordered around by the capitalists like so many pawns. But within the society itself, and particularly in the market place, there is no plan. So when capitalism does achieve an equilibrium of supply and demand, it does so by means of countless failures, crises, through overproduction and underproduction. And the capitalist himself is victim of this process, for his fate is fixed by a market that he tries to anticipate, but that ultimately seems to him as capricious and mysterious as storms did to primitive peoples.

In other words, the dominance of commodity production is not simply an economic fact. It is psychological and sociological as well; it suffuses—but does not determine—the entire society. The second defining characteristic of capitalism is to be found in the pursuit of surplus value.

Capital produces capital. Or, as that animistic saying of the popular wisdom has it, it takes money to make money. The result—which will be outlined in much greater detail in the next chapter—is, first of all, that capital becomes an independent power that towers over the workers who produce it. And secondly, the antisocial priorities which one encounters so often within the capitalist system are not products of the malevolence of evil and greedy individuals, but essential and structural tendencies of the mode of production. Thus, huge and frivolous luxury industries flourish, while the basic needs of the poor are not met, but the capitalist who would, out of decency, attend to the latter would find himself earning a lower rate of profit than his unscrupulous competitors and would succumb to their pressure.

Finally, the surplus that is the aim of capitalist production is taken from the workers. Marx put it succinctly in Volume IV of *Das Kapital:* "The whole capitalist production rests here: that labor is purchased directly, and in the process of production a portion of this labor is appropriated without compensation, but is then sold in the product. This is the ground of existence, the idea of capital."

So the essential concept of capitalism is of a system dominated by commodity exchange, in which the purchase and sale of free labor power is the crucial economic-social-political relationship, and the purpose is the extraction of more and more surplus labor from the workers. But even in this stark formulation, which abstracts from historical reality to a certain extent, the concept of the mode of production is far from mechanistic. This can be vividly seen in one of the first generalizations of it, found in *The German Ideology,* the very book that contains Marx and Engels' overly ambitious program for deciphering world history in terms of the concept of civil society. Even then, when they had some youthful tendencies toward the simplistic, their idea of the mode of production was much richer than most of their friends and all of their enemies have yet realized.

They wrote that

the mode in which men produce their life depends first of all on the conditions of the means of life which they find before them and which are to be reproduced. This mode of production is to be observed not merely from the standpoint that it is the reproduction of the physical existence of individuals. It is rather a defined kind of activity of these individuals, a definite way of externalizing their life [*ihr Leben aussern*], a definite mode of life.

And a few pages later they remark that

a specific mode of production or industrial stage is always united with a specific mode of working together, or a social stage, and this mode of working together is itself a "productive power" . . .

The result is that

in history at each stage there is a material result, a sum of productive powers, a historically created relation to nature and of individuals to one another, which each generation inherits from its predecessors, a mass of productive powers, of capital and circumstances, which on the one side the new generation modifies, but which on the other side dictates its conditions of life and gives it a specific development, a special character. The circumstances make men just as much as men make circumstances.

There are, in these passages about the mode of production, a number of themes that Marx and Engels were to develop throughout their lives. First, the concept of the mode of production does not deal with the mere physical reproduction of life; it suggests, rather, a mode of life itself. Secondly, among the "productive powers" one finds not technology alone, but the relationships whereby human beings work together as well. This is a clear case of a social "factor" being economic, and vice versa. And thirdly, there is a dialectic of necessity and freedom at work within a mode of production—that is, its circumstances make men—but men modify them and make their own circumstances.

It is this perspective that gives the young Marx a theory of history. Its periods are not arbitrary; they are determined by that dialectic of freedom and necessity within the mode of production. In the first statement of the concept, in *The German Ideology,* it is marred by the excessively high hopes that Marx and Engels had for it. Yet, even then it was extraordinarily complex and profound. As time went on, Marx realized the uniqueness of the capitalist mode, the only mode of production for which he provides a theory. He saw it, not as a deterministic economic construct, but as a mode of life.[3]

IV

Daniel Bell and Raymond Aron, two of the most important proponents of the theory of "postindustrial society," fail to understand
this Marxian concept of the mode of production. I take up their
particular misinterpretation for a number of reasons. It is related to
their thesis that the technological organization of society has now
become the defining factor, a view that will be examined at length
in Chapter 9. As such, it represents a fundamental rejection of the
Marxian analysis. Moreover, theirs is a prestigious misunderstanding of Marx by serious scholars, and in dealing with it one must
confront the sophisticated prejudices of the academy in this area.

For now, the Bell-Aron approach will be seen only in so far as it
touches upon Marx's concept of the mode of production; the more
extensive survey will take place in that later chapter. Typically,
Bell presents Marx in the guise of the simplistic proponent of a
base-superstructure thesis. "Marx," he writes, "set the problem of
how to define society by positing the idea of a substructure based
on economic relations, and a superstructure that was determined
by it." And, in a similar mood, "few societies as distinct political
and historical entities can be defined completely around a single institution as Marx believed, i.e., that one could define a system as
capitalism and that *all other relations,* cultural, religious, political,
derived from that base." So, Bell mistakes the familiar, and erroneous, Marx for the authentic Marx (he also makes a very careless interpretation of Marx's theory of social class in the process,
precisely because he does not understand the relationship between
Volume I's "capitalism in general" and the rest of the analysis).
(See Appendix D, § 4, p. 381.)

After the all but obligatory quotations from the Preface to the
Critique of Political Economy, Marx's succinct contribution to his
own obfuscation, Bell gets down to the interrelationships within a
mode of production. Rather than the presumed Marxian seamless
whole, he argues, there is actually a growing conflict between social structure (the economy, the occupational and stratification
structures) and the culture ("the realm of expressive symbolism

and meanings"). The social structure is characterized by functional rationality, the culture by an "antinomian justification of the en-hancement of self." And this is supposed to refute the Marxian notion of the mode of production in which the base must always be in conformity with, and indeed determine, the cultural superstructure.

Aron makes much the same error in a book, *Marxismes imaginaires,* which is a fair-minded, if flawed, critique of Althusser, Sartre and other French Marxists. He writes that " 'empirically' what characterizes industrial society is prodigious means of production, similar organization of labor in spite of the diversity of the juridical status of the enterprise." Therefore there is no correspondence between the productive powers and the relationships of production. "The process of production and the process of exploitation reveal themselves to be autonomous in their relation to one another." Like Bell, Aron thus assumes a rather simplistic Marx who thought that the productive powers—here perceived as technology—must always be in harmony with the productive relations.

But that is not the Marxist case at all. Indeed, we have just seen that feudal powers of production were the technological basis of the capitalist revolution and that in some instances they persisted into the middle of the nineteenth century! This point, it should be noted, is hardly obscure; the distinction between the "formal" and "real" subordination of the worker to capital occupies a prominent place in Volume I of *Das Kapital.* And the noncorrespondence of culture and economic base is not a charge to be made against Marx, but a phenomenon that he discussed at length—in, for instance, the cases of Shakespeare, Greek art, and Balzac.

Something more than a scholarly quibble over texts is involved here. The Marxian analysis—as Pierre Naville and E. J. Hobsbawm have pointed out—emphasizes the possibility that two contradictory forces are at work in a social economic formation. On the one hand, a society does not simply produce goods; it strives also to reproduce itself. On the other hand, it is possible—not necessary; Indian society, in Marx's view, did not have this quality—that there are destabilizing forces within the system. That was the case with the bourgeoisie within feudalism (and in a cultural, as well as an economic, sense); it was certainly the case with the proletariat in

Europe in the nineteenth century or with the Third World in the colonial system of the twentieth. Indeed, the only situation when there would be the kind of correspondence that Bell and Aron impute to Marx would be on the model of India—that is, a society of stagnation.

Bell is under the mistaken impression that he has confounded Marx when he shows that the social, cultural and political orders are at variance with one another in present-day society. "In the past," he writes, "these three areas were linked by a common value system (and in bourgeois society through a common character structure). But in our times there has been an increasing disjunction of the three . . . and this will widen." But, then, what is that situation but an example of Marx's own theory of what happens when capitalism goes into decline? Far from being unable to cope with such a disjunction, Marx anticipated it and said that the contradiction between economic powers and juridical (and culture) structures was a sign of the end of the system. And since, as Chapters 8 through 13 should show, it is indeed the case that we live in the twilight of the capitalist epoch, Bell has corroborated Marx when he thought he was refuting him.

The concept of the mode of production is, then, quite dialectical. It simultaneously describes the mechanism whereby a society reproduces itself, both materially and physically, and the contrary mechanism that, from time to time, contradicts that equilibrating principle and leads to a revolution. "Such a dialectical model," E. J. Hobsbawm notes, "is difficult to set up and use, for in practice the temptation is great to operate it, according to taste or occasion, either as a model of stable functionalism or as one of revolutionary change; whereas the interesting thing about it is that it is both."

But, then, it might be argued that the interpretation of Marx's concept of the means of production in this chapter robs it of its grandeur and sweep and makes it much more prosaic—empirical— than one usually thinks. In part, that is right, and Marx himself came to the conclusion that he had to abandon the dreams of his youth in which the analysis of "civil society" would lay bare the structure of all of human history. And yet, the more modest version of Marxism (which is both closer to reality and to his thought) still has enormous power. It understands economic-social structure in its complexity, as a mode of life and not just as a "material" process. And the capitalist era is not yet over, and its decline is much more complicated and surprising than Marx ever thought it would be. Therefore the incomparable analysis of that one mode of production—with the appropriate modifications that a century of its existence since Marx's death require—is still enormously relevant to the contemporary predicament.

Moreover, if authentic Marxism has had to learn humility, that does not mean that it cannot grow and develop. Marx did not leave behind a theory of the feudal mode of production, but Marxist scholars might well create one. And, Marx's method can be fruitfully used to probe a mode of production that he never imagined: the bureaucratic-collectivist system of Communism. In other words, the incompleteness of Marxism, upon which I have insisted in this chapter, can be seen as a flaw or as an opportunity. It is obviously the latter interpretation that is central to this book: that Marx's concept of the mode of production provides not a pass key to the ages, but a paradigm that can help us understand the tumultuous transition in which we live.[4]

CHAPTER 5

THE ANTI-ECONOMIST

FOR Karl Marx, economics is, by its very definition, a bourgeois discipline. Therefore his work is a "critique" of political economy in the most profound sense of the word, denying that its subject matter has the right to exist at all. Marx is, one might say, an anti-economist.

Endless confusion could be saved if this basic point were understood. For more than a hundred years, academic economists have fulminated against Marx for not living up to the standards of their science, for not answering the questions they have posed, and so on. They ignored the fact that he thought their science to be a rationalization—sometimes a brilliant, insightful rationalization—of the status quo. They were quite right when they said he gave poor answers to their questions—though one wishes that they might have noticed that he never asked them.

The last two chapters, I hope, will have already suggested why a Marxist "economics" does not and cannot exist. When one conceptualizes society as an organic whole in which the economic, the political, the sociological and the cultural so interpenetrate one another that they cannot be explained in and of themselves, then there is no room for a completely independent discipline of economics or political science or sociology or aesthetics. One can obviously examine the organic whole from some particular perspective, which Marx himself did in *Das Kapital*. But in his method—which in this case I take to be quite right—that procedure is legitimate only if it is explicit and conscious, an abstraction in search of a synthesis.

Marx argued that it was characteristic of bourgeois economics, even at its best, that it did not make such distinctions. Adam Smith and David Ricardo, he felt, were scientists who tried to probe beneath the surface of social reality, to get to its underlying dynamic. But they isolated the "economic" from its social and political interconnections and studied it as if it were a domain apart. For Marx, that was not simply an error; it was an error that necessarily arose in the minds of those who—unconsciously—saw bourgeois behavior as human nature. Given that premise, one could dispense with the examination of the specific, historic institutions of the capitalist era. One was, after all, dealing with invariant relations. So precapitalist formations were not different social systems but only the first, primitive, incomplete approximations of bourgeois human nature. Thus, the stone ax of paleolithic man—or, for that matter, the hand of his even more savage ancestor—was an immature form of "capital."

The geniuses who developed this analysis were not "bourgeois" thinkers because of their class origins, which Marx shared, and not in the crude sense that they had been bought and paid for by the capitalists. More subtly, their genuine, epoch-making discoveries about capitalist man wrongly immortalized him. They could not and did not see that the bourgeois era had a beginning and a middle, because that required that they predict its end. So with fearless honesty and great perception they rationalized the existence of the status quo.

Marx proceeded in a radically different fashion. Each fact, each category, is seen in its historical setting—and it changes as history changes. A most characteristic analysis should help as a preliminary illustration of this point, which is a Leitmotif of his work. Capital, in one of its metamorphoses, is money. But when, precisely, does money become capital? There were, Marx pointed out, all kinds of money, and some of them are to be found in the earliest recesses of time, long before capitalism. But money is not, in and of itself, capital. Something must happen before it is transformed from a medium of exchange into a power that yields a profit. That "something" is the complex historic process noted in the last chapter: the laborer is separated from the means of production and life; the capitalist appears and buys his ability to work; as a result, the capitalist is able to extract surplus labor. In short, a social class relationship—the owner of the means of production on the one side, the seller of labor power on the other—is a precondition for the transformation of money into capital.

If equals were exchanging the products of their labor—if, say, two independent farmers were dealing with each other—then money would function as a means of payment. But it is only when there is an exchange between historically specific kinds of unequals, between capitalists and workers, that the possession of money allows the former to "make" more money from the labor of the latter. So a social class relationship, itself the product of a long history, is the precondition for turning money into capital. "It is not money that posits this relationship," Marx writes; "it is the existence of the relationship that converts a mere money function into a capital function." Thus the emergence of capital is economic, sociological and historical, and those three disciplines can exist properly only if their interconnections are understood.

The accepted academic definition of *economics* is not a mere semantic convention. It arose in the classical political economy at precisely that moment at which the private pursuit of wealth became an honorable, dominant activity—that is, at the moment when "civil society" became a sphere in its own right and needed a discipline to explain and justify itself. That discipline produced not a value-free definition, but an argument, a rationale for the status quo, in the guise of a definition. By imagining an autonomous realm ruled by impersonal, ahistorical laws of the market, it asserted that we are dealing with unchanging realities. And that, of course, is a "scientific" argument against trying to change them.

Sometimes, as Joan Robinson reminded the American Economic Association, this whole process comes to resemble the theater of the absurd:

In 1932 [she recalled] Professor (now Lord) Robbins published his famous essay in which he describes economics as the subject that deals with the allocation of scarce means between alternative uses. No doubt this was the expression of a long tradition, but the date of publication was unlucky. By the time the book came out there were three million workers unemployed in Great Britain and the statistical measure of GNP in U.S.A. had recently fallen to half its former level. It was just a coincidence that the book appeared when means for any end at all had rarely been less scarce.

Hans Albert even goes so far as to describe the current orthodoxy in economics as a kind of "Platonism." Albert is a non-Marxist (he has conducted some spirited polemics against Jurgen Habermas), yet his basic point repeats one of Marx's crucial ideas and applies it to the present intellectual situation. Most current economists, he argues, isolate themselves from the other social sciences. Consequently, they build naïve assumptions about human behavior into their elegant models or else they finesse that troublesome topic altogether by specifying that "all other things," including some of the decisive variables, are to be taken as "equal" —that is, they are to be ignored. So a law is defined and it predicts that demand will decrease as price increases but leaves the economic, social and psychological determinants of that demand outside of the theory. As a result, Albert continues, they often construct ingenious tautologies with "alibis" which immunize them against empirical falsification. Contemporary academic economics, he concludes, does not meet the rigorous methodological standards of the logic of science. This is roughly what Marx said a century ago, and it is, this brilliant critic of Marx testifies, still quite relevant.

One of the best of the liberal economists in America today, Arthur Okun, offers a magnificent example of the phenomenon Albert describes. In a book which analyzes how much equality is compatible with the efficiency necessary in American society, Okun writes, ". . . I, like other economists, accept people's choices as reasonably rational expressions of what makes them better off. To be sure, by a different set of criteria, it is appropriate to ask skeptically whether people are made better off (and thus whether society really becomes more efficient) through the production of more whiskey, more cigarettes and more big cars. That inquiry raises several intriguing further questions. Why do people want the things they buy? How are these choices influenced by education, advertising and the like? Are there criteria by which welfare can be appraised that are superior to the observation of the choices people make? Without defense and without apology, let me simply state, I will not explore these issues despite their importance."

But if the established theorists were and are thus capable of absurdities, it must be freely admitted that Marx, on his side, did not fulfill his own program. Encyclopedic Titan that he was, he could not integrate all the social sciences into a rounded and comprehensive analysis of capitalism. For the rather socialistic fact of the matter is that no one individual could possibly accomplish such a fusion. It is obviously a collective task and one that will, at the very best, approximate its ideal. For, as Marx and Engels themselves understood, there is no final and finished truth about a mankind continuously immersed in time and its changes.

For that reason, among many others, the purpose of this chapter is quite modest.* It does not pretend to be even a full outline of Marx's extraordinarily rich and complex analysis. Rather, I have taken three central Marxist themes—his concepts of the "labor theory of value," of labor, and of capital—and restated them with particular reference to present-day non- and anti-Marxist scholarship. I have also included a brief account of the "War of the Two Cambridges," the academic battle that raged in the sixties between the economists of Cambridge, England, and those of Cambridge, Massachusetts, because it shows how contemporary the perennial Marxist concerns have become.[1]

I

The "labor theory of value" is one of the most spectacularly misunderstood elements of Marx's analysis. Properly grasped, it also

* Chapter 5 of *Socialism* is devoted to an outline of *Das Kapital*. That analysis is complemented, not contradicted, by this chapter. There will be some unavoidable repetitions, but the material here is placed in a different context—that is, it is seen in terms of its relationship to current economic and sociological theories.

offers fundamental and crucial insights into both his meaning and his method. Thus it is a difficult point of departure, but one whose rewards are commensurate with its risks.

It is well known that Marx's labor theory of value argues that commodities exchange at prices proportioned to the socially necessary labor time spent in their production (the "socially necessary" labor time being simply that which corresponds to the average efficiency of work in its particular industry). Labor is thus primarily a measure of value and, in a complex way, the ultimate regulator of prices.

There are a number of things wrong with this summary. First of all, Marx held no such theory. Adam Smith and David Ricardo did have versions of it, but that was one of the reasons for which Marx attacked them. Joseph Schumpeter, one of the few non-Marxists to even begin to understand this point rightly said that, for Marx,

> the labor quantity theory was no mere hypothesis about relative prices (as it had been for Ricardo). The quantity of labor embodied in products did not merely "regulate" their value. It *was* (the "essence" or "substance" of) their value. They *were* congealed labor.

Even a sympathetic writer like Joan Robinson thinks that Volume I of *Das Kapital* is concerned with establishing value as the basis of price, something that Marx explicitly excludes from the analysis. It is small wonder that Mrs. Robinson then asserts that the value theory is "metaphysics." If the theory is so defined—that is, according to the school of Ricardo rather than that of Marx— Marx himself might well agree with her.

The second problem with the labor theory of value as it has just been stated is that it obviously contradicts reality. If socially necessary labor time was the determinant of price, then industries with the highest number of employees and the lowest investment in machines would clearly get the highest return. In present-day terms, this would mean that the most backward, least mechanized (not to say automated or computerized) industry would have the best profit statement in the nation. This, of course, is utterly unreal. A fact of which Marx was perfectly aware.

Most of Marx's critics chose to ignore the embarrassing, and utterly compelling, evidence on this count. For about three quarters of a century, and even up to this very moment, anti-Marxists have repeated Boehm-Bawerk's famous charge that Marx did not discover that real-world profits contradict the assertions about surplus value in Volume I until he got to Volume III and tried to cover up his tracks. Yet long before he wrote Volume I, Marx attacked Ricardo for holding the very view which Boehm-Bawerk and his numerous posterity attributed to Marx! It was so comforting to be able to show that Marx's theories did not take the "facts" into account that scholars apparently felt justified in not taking Marx's theories into account.

But was it, then, simple political perversity that led economists to behave in this scandalous fashion? In part, yes. But in part, it was also a function of honest confusion. The academicians were normally looking for the answers to questions that Marx didn't ask. They assumed that he, like them, was primarily concerned with relative prices, and they tested his analyses according to how well they dealt with that subject. It was then discovered that Volume I does so poorly, which is indeed the case. The scholars thus ignore what Marx himself was trying to do—to analyze the process of capitalist production and, in particular, the formation of surplus value in it. When this is understood, it becomes clear why Marx excluded price movements from the entire volume, which makes it not too surprising that he fails to develop an adequate theory to account for them.

Specifically, the misinterpreters of this rather crucial point ignore Marx's methodological warnings. For instance, in his discussion of the transformation of money into capital, Marx notes that he will not explain capital formation on the basis of a deviation between price and value—that is, the sly practice of charging the buyer more than the product is worth or tricking workers into settling for less pay than they deserve. Ben Franklin's notion that business is cheating is characteristic of merchant capitalism, not industrial capitalism. Marx insists on confronting the difficult case: to demonstrate that capital formation can go forward even if commodities, including labor, are paid for at their value.

If prices actually deviate from values, he goes on (and he knows, of course, that this is the case), we must, nevertheless, assume for the moment that they are equal, in order to have before us a *pure* case of capital formation on the basis of commodity exchange, without the distracting presence of alien and secondary details. This is clear enough, perfectly legitimate and yet unnoticed by most people who read the book. Prices can deviate from values (or, as he has pointed out in the previous chapter, *must* do so) but this fact will be held in parentheses. What Volume I is about is "the phenomenon of capital formation on the basis of commodity exchange"—that is to say, about the relationship between worker and capitalist which gives rise to *surplus value,* the basis of capitalist accumulation.

Marx proceeds to develop this concept by means of a number of abstractions, and they too have usually been ignored. Some scholars have understood his complex theory—the Marxist Ronald Meek and the non-Marxist Thomas Sowell among them—and Marx himself said rather clearly what he was doing in the first chapter of the third volume of *Das Kapital.* But for the most part, the exposition and commentary on the labor theory of value has been a hopeless muddle. In what follows, I have attempted to summarize the main points of Marx's extremely rigorous analysis.

First, it is necessary to state some crucial facts about the Marxist method. The manner in which Marx presents his theory is not the manner in which he worked it out. In fact, he wrote the fourth, and last, volume of *Das Kapital* first and then worked backward to his beginning. He did so for the simple reason that he had to have the whole analysis completed before he could present it in the mode he set for himself in the 1857 Introduction, moving from the simplest, consciously formalized abstractions, which focus on the central themes, through successively more complex approximations until he arrives at the model in Volume III which is much closer to the "real world" (though still an abstraction from it).

At each stage in this analysis, Marx specifies a certain number of economic, social and political conditions. Everything else is then held in abeyance. (But only provisionally, unlike the "all other things being equal" refuge of so many anti-Marxists.) He asks,

What kind of qualitative social relationships arise necessarily out of these conditions? That is the critical question. He also asks, What kind of quantitative relationships also arise from those same conditions? That is the subordinate question. During the past century or so, academic economics has had a reverse set of priorities. Its surliness toward, or ignorance of, Marx can be explained in large measure by that fact.

In Chapter I of Volume I, Marx specifies a very limited—but, for him, crucial—set of conditions. Where private producers work independently of one another to satisfy their reciprocal needs through the agency of a market rather than of a conscious plan, what are the results? Now all these conditions exist in capitalism, but they would also exist where yeoman farmers or hunters and fishermen who hired no labor (and therefore were not capitalists) exchanged their commodities. So, here one is dealing not with the capitalist economic-social formation or even with the capitalist mode of production, but only with a model of commodity production that would be relevant to a number of social systems.

Yet Marx derives a complex number of necessary consequences from these seemingly simple premises. In such an economy commodities would actually exchange in rough proportion to the labor time they contain (a proposition with which Adam Smith and Paul Samuelson would agree). But this statement, which is regularly taken as Marx's basic labor theory of value, applies only in this first, highly simplified, and not even exclusively capitalist model. And at no time does he intend it to function as a quantitative measure of real-world prices. It is designed to illuminate a series of qualitative relationships. Among them is the necessity for having prices rather than the prices themselves. Since the society does not have a conscious plan, it must find some way of allocating its total labor so as to satisfy the needs of its various citizens. Prices, expressing the proportionate value, in labor time, of the different commodities would do that. But those prices would also state an essentially social relationship—that people are working for one another's needs, in a non-, or even anti-social way—that each is "worth" so much per hour. Moreover, the work of the unconscious cooperators in this system would become "abstract." They would toil for one another not in a human relationship, but by means of an impersonal market that would reduce their social interconnections into prices. And since the allocation of labor in such a society is unplanned, it would also be menaced by economic crisis. For one would never know if one had expended the proper amount of labor time on a commodity until it is first offered for sale. At that point, it might turn out that too much labor time had been used up on a particular item, and there could be a glut.

In short, simply by examining the inevitable consequences of those very few specifications in a model of simple commodity production, Marx arrives at a first statement of complex themes. Under such conditions, there would be abstract labor, alienation, crisis, and so on. By now, it should be obvious that Marx chose those first premises in Volume I because he thought that they would reveal the basic mechanism that produces the most fundamental characteristics of a capitalist society. Having done that, he now moves to a second, more complicated model.

All of the conditions of the first model are retained, and two crucial new conditions are added. The producers are now capitalists who employ workers; and there is a labor market as well as a commodity market. But how, under such conditions, is it possible for there to be a surplus, a profit, which motivates the capitalist? It is still assumed that all commodities, including labor power, are purchased at their value. If one rules out chicanery, how can the system operate? We have already anticipated the answer in Chapter 3: the capitalist pays the worker the proper exchange value for his labor power, but he gets a use value from it greater than that exchange value. The crucial point here is that the monopoly of the means of production by the capitalists enables them to strike this bargain, so advantageous to them and so seemingly fair. The economics of capitalism cannot be understood apart from its class structure.

Then Marx develops a third model, which takes into account a number of phenomena excluded from the previous analysis. In the second case, he had assumed that value is determined by labor time. But if that were the case, as has already been noted, the capitalist with the least investment in machines and the greatest outlay in wages would get the greatest surplus (or profit). That is, as Marx knew all along, simply not the case in the actual capitalist system. If it were to happen, then the capitalists from the capital-intensive industries would rush to invest in the labor-intensive industries, and their competition would bid down the profits there. So, the actual system must work on the basis of an average rate of profit that rewards the capitalist, not in proportion to the labor time contained in his products, but according to the average rate of profit in the society. Volume III explores the implications of this model.

But hasn't Marx thereby conceded his whole case? Reality turns out to be reality and the simplifications of the first model do not explain it at all. For all the Hegelian hocus-pocus of Volume I, isn't he forced to be a "sensible" economist in Volume III? Not at all. The economists who began and ended with "reality" wrote idylls in which everyone got paid a fair price for labor power and commodities, there were no class conflicts, and breakdowns in the system were possible only because someone tinkered with it or there were external influences brought to bear upon it.

Marx, who begins his theory with the simple abstractions so distant from the surface of life, is able to analyze that very surface all the more profoundly precisely because of them. He locates the basic tendencies—of crisis, of the domination of production over distribution and exchange, of alienation and the degradation of work, and all the rest—in a "pure" model and then shows how they operate even in that real world whose normal categories describe a happy and productive equilibrium.

But is this intricate procedure justified? Joseph Schumpeter puts the matter quite well: Value theory, he says, "is nothing but a construction devised for purposes of analysis and to be judged in the light of considerations of analytic usefulness and convenience." Using this criterion, the reader will have to judge, on the basis of the evidence of this chapter, whether Marx's abstractions have been helpful for understanding social reality. Paul Samuelson, Nobel laureate and the most influential academic economist of his generation in the United States, answers that the Marxian methodology is really a fraud. I propose to examine his case for a moment, not simply because it deals with a crucial aspect of Marx's critique of political economy, but also because it provides a marvelous demonstration of how sloppy an acknowledged genius can become when he deals with Marxism.*

In his most recent foray into Marxism, Samuelson concerns himself with the "transformation problem"—that is, the connection between the value relationships of Volume I and the prices of Volume III. And he attacks Marx's method with vehemence:

> . . . when you cut through the maze of algebra and come to understand what is going on, you discover that the "transformation algorithm" [the formula which translates values into prices] is precisely of the following form: "Contemplate two alternate and discordant systems. Write one down. Now transform by taking an eraser and rubbing it out. Then fill in the other one. *Voila!* You have completed your transformation algorithm."

The problem with this biting whimsy is that Samuelson's article shows clearly that he is quite confused as to what Marx's theory is. On a number of occasions, for instance, he equates the value theories of Smith and Ricardo with that of Marx. Thus it is that he shows that the hypothesis of a capitalist existing in Adam Smith's "early and rude state" is absurd, and he implies that he has scored a point against Marx in the process. The only problem is that Marx made Samuelson's point against Smith and Ricardo over a hundred years before Samuelson imputed their error to Marx. All of this is not, however, a mere quibble over scholarly sources. For the confusion of Smith-Ricardo and Marx is quite revealing; it is a way of "transforming" the function of Marx's value theory and turning it into a dissection of prices. It is to overlook the qualitative side, which differentiates Marx from Smith and Ricardo, and to focus only on the quantitative, where Marx is not particularly profound,

---

* I would not presume to even write about Samuelson in the area of his specialty, the mathematical exploration of the post-Keynesian synthesis, which he himself did so much to develop. I am simply unqualified to engage in such an enterprise. However when Samuelson reads Marx—and carelessly— he forfeits the respect his accomplishments in other spheres have won for him. Despite his often haughty tone in these matters, he is something of a new boy and a brash one at that.

not least because he didn't try to be. Indeed, if one were given to heavy-handedness, it would be possible to write: "Contemplate Karl Marx's value theory. Write it down. Now transform by taking an eraser and rubbing it out. Then fill in the Smith-Ricardo theory. *Voila!* You have completed Samuelson's transformation algorithm."

But does this all mean that Marx concerned himself with something vague, called the "qualitative" aspect of capitalism, and that he ignored the real world of quantities? The answer is no, in a double sense. First of all, it is quite possible to show that there is a formal consistency between prices and values, and one of Samuelson's colleagues, Martin Bronfenbrenner, has even cited Samuelson himself to make the case. However, it should be quickly added that if one were primarily interested in prices it would be a foolish waste of time to first work out labor values and then transform them. Marx's theory holds up in terms of prices, but it was not designed to explicate them and doesn't do so very well. As Marx himself warned in this regard, "the general law asserts itself as a dominant tendency only in a very complicated and approximate way, as a never attainable average of constant fluctuations." Secondly, and more importantly, Marx's "qualitative" analysis concerns something extremely real: the economic consequences of certain social and historical institutions. It allowed Marx insights into phenomena such as depressions, monopoly, the process of expanded reproduction, and the like. In Schumpeter's terms, it has more than demonstrated its convenience and usefulness as a method.

Thus far we have been concerned primarily with showing what Marx's theory of value is not. But what, then, *is* it?

There is a stunning simplicity to the answer. Value is objectified, or materialized, human labor. As a source of wealth nature is, so to speak, a given, like a deposit of coal; and human labor transforming and shaping that given is, for Karl Marx, the sole source of value. Things can be useful, and an element of wealth, without having value. In a more innocent age, before pollution put a price tag on the atmosphere, Marx cited the air as a case in point. One of the best statements of the positive content of value idea occurs in a passage wherein Marx is summarizing the views of two of his precursors. It applies, I think, to his own key term. In it, the independent, material *stuff* of wealth disappears and it [wealth] appears as merely the activity of men. All that which is not the result of human activity, or labor, is natural and is not social wealth. The phantom of the world of goods dissolves, and it appears as only the constantly disappearing, constantly reproduced objectification of human labor. All materially solid wealth is only a temporary objectification of this social labor whose measure is time, the measure of movement itself.

In their younger years, before their break with Proudhon, Marx and Engels praised him in words that reveal the basic attitude underlying their definition of labor as the substance of value (and not simply as its measure):

In making labor, that is to say direct manifestation of human activity as such the measure of the wage and of the determination of the value of the product, Proudhon makes the human element decisive, while in the previous political economy this role is given to the material power of capital and of landed property.

This is an early anticipation of a fundamental Marxian proposition that is present in his definition of value as objectified human labor: that our concepts are profoundly affected by our social class position.

Throughout *Das Kapital,* for instance, Marx explains that it would never occur to the capitalists to think in terms of labor value. He computes his profits as a percentage of his total investment in men, machines and materials, for that is how surplus value is distributed (but not how it is created). He therefore "knows" from his own experience that machines and raw materials are creative. But then the worker does not instinctively see through this deception. He often thinks that he is paid sixty minutes of every hour and is unaware that he is contributing unpaid labor to his employer part of the time. To be sure, there were, as it has been seen, working-class socialists (the followers of Proudhon among them) who demanded, before Marx, that labor be given the full fruit of its toil. But, more often than not, these were skilled craftsmen who were being crushed down by the rising industrial capitalists and who yearned for the good old days of the Middle Ages when a man was supposed to be paid the "just price" of his labors. And in any case their demand, Marx knew, was impossible, for even the most perfect of societies would have to deduct from current output for depreciation, new investment and the care of dependents (in this case, primarily the aging).

Thus, it was possible to see that human activity was the real content of the huge factories only if one looked at the question from the vantage point of the working class's objective role and interest. Therefore Marx's labor theory is not simply the passive and objective report of a scholar dissecting impersonal laws (which is the posture—or, one should say, masquerade—of most academic economists). His political commitment, his view of the social process from the standpoint of a proletarian rather than of a bourgeois, opens up his eyes to realities the latter cannot even perceive. But then this was true of the bourgeois in his own day, for in the period of his struggle against feudalism, he stood for rationality and against the superstitions of the old order. Indeed, a David Ricardo developed his labor theory of value in part as an attack on parasitic landlords who did nothing but collect rent. It was only when a version of this insight was put to socialist use that bourgeois economics decided to drop the very questions that had inspired it and to concentrate on the "safe" issue of relative prices.

So, Marx's theory is not "value free," even though some of the positivistic Marxists of the Second International thought it was (Rudolf Hilferding, the author of an otherwise brilliant study of finance capital, among them). This can be seen rather vividly when one looks at a surprising error made by Raymond Aron, who is usually a sophisticated and knowledgeable critic of Marx. Aron is attacking the labor theory of value and asks, "By what right do they [the Marxists] assert that the reduction of rent, interest and profit to the unity of surplus value represents a definitive gain for science when Western as well as Soviet practice denies this reduction?"

To say this is to imagine that a status-quo power can use a revolutionary theory for conservative ends. The labor theory and the idea of surplus value show, above all, that accumulation takes place through the appropriation of unpaid labor time. Can one imagine an American or Soviet official economist announcing that the growth in G.N.P. has been higher than usual because we were successful in extracting more unpaid time from the people? Marx's insight, in short, is predicated on a class point of view. That does not, of course, mean that workers are intellectually superior to capitalists as individuals. It means—and I simplify, but not, I think, too violently—that the view from the bottom of society can be much more candid than from the top.

The labor theory of value is not the simplistic statement that most of Marx's critics and many of his disciples imagine. By a conscious initial simplification, which was actually made after the analysis had been completed, Marx isolates the decisive economic-social-political determinants of the capitalist system: that independent producers engage in unplanned social production by means of a market. From this highly abstract model, he develops the necessity of crisis, alienation and the like, and then applies his basic insights to a progressively more "real" world in which the simplifications are removed. The result, as Part II of this book will show, is a method and a set of conclusions that, far from being quaint and outdated, will help us to understand the secret history of the 1970s, events that occur more than one century after the publication of Volume I of *Das Kapital*.[2]

II

Marx was hardly the only person to notice the "dark Satanic mills" of nineteenth-century England. William Blake had unforgettably baptized them before Marx was born. And official government reports had described the degradation of the new urban mass of unskilled workers; Marx himself relied upon them. Here, again, what is remarkable in Marx's theory is not his depiction of the brute *fact,* but his account of why it necessarily had to exist within a system of capitalist commodity production.

The dissection of an unprecedented kind of work—wage labor— is basic to this analysis. What follows will focus upon four aspects of it: the notion of *abstract labor,* as a key to the comprehension of the emergence of the working class; a deepening of the concept of the wage as a *phenomenal form;* an examination of the thesis that it is technology, not human labor, that is decisive in a modern economy; and finally an encounter with that pervasive misstatement of Marx's view, the idea that he argued that capitalism would inevitably and increasingly impoverish the workers.

In developing these Marxist concepts it will sometimes be necessary to enter the abstruse reaches of theory. Yet one should never for a moment forget the purpose of these intricacies: to explain why those "dark Satanic mills" emerged inevitably from the capitalist organization of work.

First, there is use of the idea of *abstract labor* to explain the development of the modern factory system.

In describing that system, Marx relies upon and criticizes the writings of Andrew Ure, "the Pindar of the automatic factory." Ure's definition of factory work is, Marx argues, ambiguous. On the one hand he describes it as the "combined cooperation of many orders of work people, adult and young, in tending with assiduous skill a system of productive machines continuously impelled by a central power"; and on the other hand, he sees the factory as "a vast automaton, composed of various mechanisms and intellectual organs, acting in uninterrupted concert for the production of a common object, all of them [the workers] being subordinate to a self-regulating moving force."

For Marx, it is the second description that begins to suggest the reality of factory work under capitalism: "the automaton itself is the subject and the workers are only coordinated as the conscious organs of an organ without consciousness and subordinated to the same central power source." This is a real-world application of the concept of *abstract labor,* which is one of those simplifications in the first chapter of *Das Kapital.* It is no longer the personal and purposive activity of a shoemaker or a tailor who creates a product for a person he meets face to face. It is, rather, the repetitious, machine-dominated toil of the growing mass of unskilled and semi-skilled workers characteristic of nineteenth-century England. Or, as Marx put the same thought in the *Critique of Political Economy,* "Labor, which is thus measured by time, seems in fact not to be the labor of different subjects, but rather the different laboring individuals seem to be mere organs of *the* labor."

This was written before the development of time and motion study and other refinements of mature capitalism, yet it clearly anticipates what was to come. As Daniel Bell put it, "Modern industry began not with the factory but with the measurement of work. When the worth of the product was defined in production units, the worth of the worker was similarly gauged." Bell's comment, not so incidentally, is a rather precise statement of a central theme of the labor theory of value. And it emphasizes the function of that theory for Marx: to explain why the historical and social facts that he recorded were also the expression of the inherent economic laws of the system.

As labor becomes "abstract" under capitalism, there are many consequences. One of them has to do with how people think. Marx writes: "Since living labor . . . is incorporated into capital, it appears as an activity which belongs to capital, and as soon as the labor process begins, all the productivity of social labor presents itself as the productivity of capital . . ." There were many people who instinctively recognized the horrors of industrial capitalism, but Marx was the first to demonstrate that they were the ineluctable consequence of the capitalist mode of production, turning even our consciousness upside down. In this context, the analysis of labor in *Das Kapital* is an explanation of the phenomenon of alienation which had so concerned the young Marx.

But this does not mean that Marx saw work under capitalism as merely brutalizing. He also spoke of the "civilizing aspects" of the system. It "extorts surplus labor in a manner and under conditions which are more favorable for the development of the productive powers, of societal relations and the creation of elements for a higher and new construction [of society] than were slavery, serfdom, etc." This is a first statement of a theme that contradicts a theory widely imputed to Marx: that he believed that capitalism necessarily held the workers down to a subsistence wage. (That myth will be explored shortly.)

However, even though Marx insists on the progressive role of capitalism—he faults Ricardo for not recognizing the system's drive to shorten the labor time required to produce the necessities of life—he stresses the uniqueness of "abstract" labor. One consequence of it is that this mode of production is utterly unconcerned about the content of its exchange values. Marx quotes the English economist Nicholas Barbon on this count: "One sort of wares is as good as another if the values be equal. There is no difference or distinction in things of equal value. . . . One hundred pounds worth of lead or iron, is of as great a value as one hundred pounds worth of silver and gold."

Marx has a brilliant, dialectical formula that distills this complexity. Under capitalism, he writes in the *Grundrisse,* "the reciprocal and universal dependence of individuals indifferent to one another forms the basis of their social interconnection." The individuals are "indifferent" to one another; their abstract labor is broken down into units of activity without any self-contained meaning, units that create products for strangers. And yet, these strangers are dependent upon one another, caught up in a social relationship that they understand only in inverted terms. They do not even produce things for themselves. They produce commodities for others and they receive, not a share in their actual output, but a wage that allows them to pay for commodities someone else has made.

Under such conditions work must inevitably be abstract and unconcerned with quality or social utility. So, it is wrong to think that the machine develops out of its own functional necessity into an automaton that reduces human labor to a "conscious organ of an unconscious organ." Rather, it is the capitalist mode of production that designs and programs such a technology, not the other way around. This is dramatically demonstrated by a history already noted in the last chapter. Capitalism, it will be remembered, actually began not with a revolutionary technology, but with a new mode of production that took over an existing conservative technology. The process of taking the worker, who is originally only "formally subsumed" under the machine (that is, who retains his old skills but exercises them in a new, capitalist environment), and substantially subsuming him under the machine is thus a product of the system, not of its tools.

In *Labor and Monopoly Capital,* Harvey Braverman brilliantly demonstrated what this meant. The capitalist organization of work not only expropriates the skill of the feudal artisan; it progressively separates the planning of work from its execution and thus digs a political, social and economic chasm between manual and intellectual work. This was done first of all in the factory, but in recent years it has also extended to the organization of office and bureaucratic work. In the "stenographic pool," the typist may spend her entire day transcribing tapes, never once seeing the person for whom she is working. This does not mean, Nicos Poulantzas has rightly pointed out, that this typist has become a proletarian. She is still on the "intellectual" side of the great work divide, even if at the lowest rung; and the typewriter is still at her command, it is not yet an automaton that runs her.

This analysis of how capitalism distinctively organizes work, and not vice versa, leads to a deepening of a second aspect of the Marxist analysis, one that we have already briefly encountered. That is the concept of wage labor as a *phenomenal form* that disguises its true nature. Now it is possible to understand how historically specific—how capitalistically inevitable—this development is.

This phenomenal form, Marx writes in a sweeping indictment, is the source of "all the ideas about rights on the part of workers as well as capitalists, all mystifications of the capitalist mode of production, all its illusions about freedom, all of the apologetic humbug of the vulgar economists."

To understand how the wage form of labor is responsible for such awesome confusion and nonsense, it is necessary to return for a moment to the distinction between capitalism and all precapitalist forms. The earlier modes of production, it will be remembered, rest ultimately upon noneconomic power—that is, the slave produces because he is forced to do so, the serf contributes his surplus labor to the lord because tradition, sanctified by God and upheld by the sword, requires it, and so on. Capitalism disdains these primitive means of exploitation. It proclaims itself a society of freedom, of contract, of equivalent exchange. At the same time, its internal dynamic requires that the owners of the means of production appropriate an increasing surplus. If the workers are paid the "full value" of what they produce, then there will be nothing left over for profit and new investment. The problem, then, is to rationalize a nonequivalent exchange, in which one party to a contract gets more than the other, as an equivalent exchange.

The wage, Marx argues, does this, because it is a "phenomenal form," a reality whose appearance conceals, rather than reveals, its meaning. It defines an "equal" exchange between unequals. The worker is paid for every minute he toils, and under contemporary conditions with strong unions, he even gets a premium for overtime. And yet, during an hour's work, he produces more than he is paid for; there is a surplus left over. Therefore, the wage presents a fundamental inequality as if it were an equal exchange.

Put simply, this insight is a commonplace that had been defined long before Marx. The Ricardian socialists, as Marx himself pointed out, had said that labor was all and that the capitalists were stealing labor time from the workers. On the basis of this radical interpretation of the labor theory of value, they demanded that the producers receive the full fruit of their toil. But the Ricardians never asked the critical question that always drew Marx's attention: Why did this take place?

They could not ask the question, because they had foreclosed the answer to it. For the Ricardians, the capital-labor relationship was the "natural" way for a society to produce. They only wanted, as Marx aptly put it, "capitalism without capitalists." But the fact of the matter, Marx insisted, was that exploitation, the appropriation of an unpaid surplus and the existence of capitalists, were utterly necessary to this mode of production. When a social labor process was owned and directed by private entrepreneurs, they absolutely had to have that surplus in order to invest, to increase jobs, the wealth of the nation, et cetera. Therefore, the only way in which one could call for an end to exploitation would be to transform the economic structure that made exploitation essential to the future of the system.

So the "phenomenal form" of the wage was a complex reality. It did indeed try to falsify the fact that the worker was on the losing end of an unequal exchange, proclaiming that he was paid for every minute he labored. But it also functioned as a truth, for that unequal exchange was the justice and logic of a society of private social labor. Moreover, it presented that truth in a historically specific way. Karl Popper, for instance, wrote of Marx's assertion that the worker does not receive the equivalent of the use value of his labor power—"There appeared what seemed a rather obvious solution of the difficulty. The capitalist possessed a monopoly of the means of production, and thus superior economic power can be used for bullying the worker into an agreement that violates the law of value." But in Marx's analysis, it is precisely capitalism's unique quality that it does not resort, in the first instance at least, to "bullying" of any kind. To be sure, the ultimate sanction of repressive force is always there, as it is in every society; fascism is the monstrous case in point. Yet in the normal, everyday operation of the system, it justifies its exploitation by a wage form in which equivalencies seem to be fairly exchanged by one and all.

What did mainstream economics think of this analysis? Nothing. That is, it regarded Marx's questions as irrelevant and unscientific, and therefore it did not need to bother with his answers. Sometimes there is the glimmer of the idea of a surplus. Samuelson, for instance, reads John Bates Clark to say that a landlord pays a wage equal to the product of the last worker hired—that is, he keeps on adding new hands as long as, but only as long as, an added unit of labor adds more to output than it costs. So, Samuelson notes, the landlord is actually getting the benefits of the higher productivity of the workers hired earlier who are paid the same as the last worker hired. He is getting, in short, an unpaid surplus. But such themes are hardly emphasized, because they conflict with the apologetic function of Clark's theory of the harmony and justice prevailing among all the factors of production.

Again, this is not to treat the academic economists as mercenaries who juggle the truth for pay. In the twentieth century, they have obviously become aware of the historical nature of the capitalist system. Moreover, when they say that their marginal-productivity equations do not define a necessary policy, but simply indicate the most efficient use of resources, they are, in a strict logic, right. Only, for all their newfound historical sophistication about the past, the academic theorists treat the present as if it were a timeless sphere in which perennial rules of economic behavior are at work. And the strict and "impartial" logic of their equations inevitably leads to that supreme capitalist value judgment: what is efficient is good. Two contemporary, and non-Marxist, scholars are witnesses for my point.

Gunnar Myrdal writes:

> When, in my youth, I studied the political element in the development of economic theory along the classical and neoclassical line, I found the whole structure of this theory, as it had evolved over the generations, to be determined by the need of economists to protect themselves from their own radical premises as inherited from the Enlightenment.

Joan Robinson comments in the same vein:

> This shift in argument, from a measure of *value* to a theory of the determination of relative prices, was connected with the shift in interest from Ricardo's problem—the laws which regulate the distribution of the produce of the earth between the classes of the community—to the much less burning question of relative prices.

On another occasion Mrs. Robinson wrote:

> The orthodox economists have been preoccupied with elegant elaboration of minor problems, which distract the attention of their pupils from the uncongenial realities of the modern world, and the development of abstract argument has run far ahead of any possibility of empirical verification. Marx's intellectual tools are far cruder, but his sense of reality is far stronger, and his argument towers above their intricate constructions in rough and gloomy grandeur.

The very fact that Mrs. Robinson—a student of Keynes, the author of a classic book on the economics of imperfect competition—should thus turn back to Marx's concerns (even if critically) is of enormous importance. This will be developed in greater detail shortly, when the War of the Two Cambridges comes into view.

One consequence of Marx's theory in this area is that it emphasizes the decisiveness of the process of production as against that of distribution. The harmonies of the trinitarian formula operate best when one concentrates on market relations. But when the stress is on what takes place as people work, as they sell their labor power to be used in the plant, an entirely different perspective emerges. Then one begins to understand that the demand for goods, which is treated as a "given" in most academic analyses, is determined "by the relationship of the different classes to one another and by their respective positions." So,

> the distribution of the products is obviously only the result of the distribution (of the various members of society as they are assigned—usually by the accident of birth—to a specific function) which is included in the production process itself and which determines the structure of production.[3]

III

Thus, Marx's emphasis on work and the work process has ramifications throughout his entire analysis. One of the most obvious objections to his attitude is that it is not the laborer, but the increasingly sophisticated machine, that is the secret of growing social wealth. As Daniel Bell makes the point, "For Marx, wealth was gained through 'exploitation.' Now we can see that wealth, private corporate wealth and national wealth, increase only through increases in productivity." But this is to make a remarkable assumption about Marx: that he counterposed exploitation to productivity. In fact, he saw them as inseparably united: capitalism's exploitative lust for more and more surplus value drives it to be more productive and innovative. There is one passage that makes this point in a rather striking way. In it, Marx is chiding Ricardo for having slighted "the *historic* justification" of capital.

Since, Marx argues, Ricardo does not clearly grasp the origins of surplus value in the distinction between the paid and unpaid portions of the working day, he does not understand capitalism's enormous stake in reducing the amount of labor time—above all, the labor time required to compensate for the wage paid out. He fails to grasp that it is the *"compulsion for surplus labor"* that makes capitalism try to push productivity to its absolute limit. It is this compulsion for reducing necessary labor time that constitutes capitalism's "historic justification" and ultimately lays the technological basis for socialism. It is also the mechanism that makes the degradation of work an inherent necessity in capitalist society.

This is the case because the increasing productivity takes place within a historically unique framework of private competition and unplanned, but social, production. In an industry, the first capitalist to innovate receives a bonus of surplus labor time for his risk, since he thereby reduces the cost of necessary labor time, of wages, as compared with his competitors. But then the capitalist class as a whole has a stake in new techniques, since they can cheapen the price of the workers' living standard. And the system as a whole must produce more this year than last to provide the funds for new investment, the lifeblood of the capital-goods sector and through it of the entire economy. Under such conditions, any concern for the safety, intelligence or sensibility of the laborer is destructive sentimentality, and machinery must be designed to maximize output, not humanity.

Daniel Bell fails to grasp this dialectical Marxist truth in which productivity and exploitation are seen, not as counterposed explanations of society's growing wealth, but as its inseparably united cause. Since this interconnection is the basic theme of the entire fourth section of Volume I of *Das Kapital*—some two hundred pages of analysis—it is not an unimportant failure on his part. And because of this confusion, Bell also fails to understand that Marx had anticipated his own point on the growing importance of productivity in the domain of capitalist labor.

> To the degree that modern industry [*die grosse industrie*] develops [Marx wrote in the *Grundrisse*], the creation of actual wealth becomes less dependent upon labor time and the quantity of labor applied and more dependent upon the power of instruments [*Agentien*] which are set in motion during the labor period, a period that stands in no relationship to the immediate labor time which the production of these instruments costs. Now the creation of wealth seems rather to be dependent upon the general state of science and

the progress of technology, or the application of science to production. [However,] as soon as labor in an immediate form has
ceased to be the great source of wealth, then labor time ceases, as
it must, to be the measure of wealth.

As Marx developed this analysis in the *Grundrisse,* this growing
productivity was one of the factors which were going to destroy
the capitalist mode of production. There was, he said, a "Contradiction between the basis of bourgeois production [the value measure]
and its very development. Machines, etc." In other words, once
again, it was not simply the technology (or productivity), but the
technology in its institutional setting that was crucial. Bell, writing
in the very book in which he indicted Marx for not understanding
about productivity, repeats the essential point of the passage from
the *Grundrisse* a century later. He writes:

> Modern industry began not with the factory but with the meas-
> urement of work. When the worth of the product was defined in
> production units, the worth of the worker was similarly gauged.
> . . . But under automation, with continuous flow, a worker's
> worth can no longer be evaluated in production units.

Two points should be stressed about this ironic coincidence of
the views of Bell and those of the Marx whom he criticized. First,
although Marx envisions the end of labor time as the measure of
value, he still sees wealth as the product of human activity. Now,
however, that activity is science more than immediate labor. Secondly, Marx makes the institutional setting—the class relationships
—decisive even under this radically new situation. If technology
bursts the bourgeois framework, how will it be controlled in a new
kind of a society? At no point, not even in this futuristic passage
from the *Grundrisse,* did Marx think that there would be an automatic transition to socialism on the basis of technology alone.
Moreover, whatever Marx thought, a present-day Marxist with
much more evidence available can see that the political and social
context (which are class relationships and vice versa) and struggle
are going to be decisive. But this, as will be seen in the analysis of
the welfare state, is what Bell either fudges or denies.[4]

IV

Finally, there is a last, monumental misunderstanding with regard to Marx's analysis of labor. It is said that Marx believed that wages under capitalism necessarily tended to a subsistence level. This is not at all true. Indeed, the evidence for the contrary proposition is so abundant and overwhelming that one must first ask, How can so many people, including some with real intellectual depth, have been so incredibly careless about Marx's meaning?

There are a number of reasons. First of all, if Karl Marx held that a subsistence wage were necessary under capitalism, then that makes it child's play to prove that Karl Marx was wrong. For it is obvious that no such minimal level of pay exists and it is questionable as to whether it ever did. This is the lazy man's key to the refutation of Karl Marx (even though some brilliant people have used it). Secondly, a subsistence wage is assumed in the very first section of *Das Kapital*. Marx did so, as he wrote to Engels, "to avoid having to deal with everything under each particular relation." But why have so many scholars failed to note that Marx openly and loudly abandoned that simplifying assumption? The answer has already been suggested, because they think that the abstractions of Chapter I—and its labor theory of value—are characteristic of Marx's entire economic critique. The misconception about wages reinforces the misconception about value theory. Thirdly, Joseph Stalin and the world movement he led wasted forests of paper to show, not only that Marx had predicted the absolute misery of the working class, but that his prophecy had been fulfilled after World War II. Stalin fired (but for some reason did not shoot) Eugen Varga, the Soviet economist who contradicted this nonsense. And even after Stalin's death, the official Soviet crusade against the Marxist "revisionists" accused the heretics of not believing in the pauperization of the masses—that is, they charged them with having confronted reality.

Finally, there are passages in Marx which either state (in the early years, most prominently in the Communist Manifesto), or could be interpreted to state, that Marx had a subsistence theory.

But Engels remarked on the obvious—that the mature Marx rejected and fought against the notion of an "iron law" of wages—and in any case *Das Kapital* is quite clear on this point. But still the myth persists. Thus, Martin Bronfenbrenner, who is rather sympathetic to the Marxists in their dispute with Paul Samuelson, nevertheless asks, "How seriously did Marx consider the Ricardo-Lassalle 'iron law of wages' as a long-run determinant of the equilibrium wage rate?" Only, Marx did not consider this law to be a determinant of anything. But, then, Bronfenbrenner is not alone in his confusion.

However, Joseph Schumpeter, as is often the case, got Marx's position right. He understood that Marx rejected the "iron law" and developed a wage theory that "forms an extremely complex whole which covers practically all the aspects of the wage phenomenon and includes careful investigation into the deviation of wages from the level determined by the 'value' of labor, especially into the cyclical deviations." The proof of this is overwhelming. Marx wrote two lengthy polemics against the "iron law," both of them significantly dedicated to showing that trade unions could make a difference (the Lassalleans, against whom Marx also fought on this question, did believe in the "iron law" and therefore ignored the wage struggle of the unions and concentrated only on politics). In *Das Kapital,* Marx showed that unions could affect wages, and he argued that under some circumstances the workers could even get a share of their own surplus value!

But then couldn't Mrs. Robinson or Samuelson or any one of the legion of people who have made this error reply that there are ambiguous references on this count in *Das Kapital* itself? For example, Marx does say with regard to the *"absolute, general law of capitalist accumulation"* that "the greater the Lazarus stratum of the working class, the greater the official pauperism." And he also said, "the ultimate cause of all actual crises always remains the poverty and limited consumption of the masses." With such statements from Marx himself, how can one be so intolerant of those who concluded that he thought wages would be at a subsistence level?

In part, the answer is that even these statements do not confirm the idea of a subsistence wage in Marx. The "Lazarus stratum of the working class" is in no way the same as all the poor and is certainly not identical with the working class itself. The employed workers, the temporarily unemployed, the disguised unemployment in agriculture are all above the "Lazarus stratum." Moreover, as Marx insisted on numerous occasions (acknowledging his debt to Ricardo), he was concerned primarily with the relative wage— that is, with the wage as a percentage of total output—than with real wages. For with this focus, Marx remarks, ". . . the worker is seen in his social relationships. The position of classes in relationship to one another is determined more by proportionate wages than by the absolute amount of wages."

But even though the scholars who think Marx held the theory of a subsistence wage should have noticed these texts, that failure is not the real scandal. What is shocking is that anyone who believes that Marx had this position admits thereby that he has not understood the analysis of capitalist crisis that is central to *Das Kapital*. This is not a matter of textual detail; it has to do with a crucial theme of the book itself.

For, as Schumpeter understood, Marx's theory of wages is cyclical—like his theory of capitalism. During the upswing, when there is vigorous capitalist accumulation (that is, much new investment), competition for hands on the labor market bids wages up. Indeed, this is one of the factors that tend to lower the profit rate at the height of a boom and thus to bring on a crisis. With the crisis, there is "overproduction"—that is, overproduction in a society based on a structure of limited consumption for the masses—and unemployment. The growth of joblessness reduces pressure on the capitalist in the labor market, and this is one element that restores profitability and prepares the way for another round of the cycle. "The characteristic life course of modern industry," Marx writes, "which takes the form of a ten-year period of moderate activity, feverish production, crisis and stagnation which is broken up by smaller variations, rests on the constant formation; great or lesser absorption and then reformation of the industrial reserve army."

If Marx had held a thesis of subsistence wages, he could not have developed his theory of capitalist crisis. This is made clear, not in this or that isolated passage of *Das Kapital,* but in the very thrust of the central argument. It confirms one's worst suspicions about the low quality of so much that is written about Marxism to think that serious people could believe that Marx propounded a view that subverted practically all of *Das Kapital.*

But what, then, of Marx's theory of capitalist crisis itself? Couldn't the critics say that it has hardly held up very well?

The central, organizing theme of all Marx's comments on depressions can be put in terms of the basic contradiction defined in Volume I: a system of private producers must act in a social fashion; an unplanned process must somehow achieve integrated and intricate goals. This can miscarry in any number of ways. The frantic expansion of production characteristic of a period of accumulation expands capacity at a much greater rate than consumer demand, and that can lead to a crisis. Or there can be fits and starts due to the fact that capital-goods production grows rapidly during good times but that demand in this case also must inevitably fall off. This is the idea that is central to Marx's theory, alluded to in his comments on the relationship between the reserve army and the industrial cycle, that there is a ten-year rhythm to the boom-and-bust pattern.

These theories in much of the literature have been given second place to Marx's assertion that there is a tendency in capitalism for the rate of profit to fall and that this is a source of crisis. This claim has received great attention, I suspect, because it is fairly easy to question, or even refute, on the basis of the economic facts of the last century. And, as has been said earlier, any reading of Marx that proves that he was egregiously wrong is certain to be popular. The problem is that Marx himself insisted that there were countertendencies of this trend and noted that, in his lifetime, they seemed to be stronger than the trend itself. He noted that "in place of what economics has previously described—namely, the explanation of the fall in the rate of profit—one must tell why, on the contrary, this fall has not been greater and much more precipitous than it has."

One of Marx's most important statements of why the tendency for the rate of profit to fall had not had the predicted impact was that the very same forces that set this trend in motion—the increasing mechanization and even automation of the productive process —also increased the mass of profits. So one can, on this point, agree with Samuelson that the tendency of the falling rate of profit is not at all central to, or inherent in, Marx's analysis. If, however, there is some possible ambiguity and indeterminacy here, on another count there is none: Marx clearly and systematically rejected the thesis of a subsistence wage.

Marx's conception of work, then, like his definition of capital, is complex and rich. He magnificently describes the historically unprecedented kind of human labor that appeared within the capitalism. But, more than that, he explains this degradation of work and anticipates the coming of automation as tendencies inherent in a capitalist society of private, competitive producers within an unconsciously social system that has as its passion the appropriation of more and more surplus labor time and is therefore subject to cyclical crisis. Thus, work and the working class are one set of crucial, complex terms in the Marxist analysis. Capital is the other.[5]

V

What is capital? That is one of those questions that seem innocuous, elementary. And yet the entire economic profession was agitated by it during the 1960s, when it occurred to some theorists that they had neglected to carefully define this central term in their discipline. Karl Marx, dismissed by the mainstream academicians as a musty, obsolete thinker, suddenly seemed relevant, because he had addressed this issue. How, then, did he answer this basic, but by no means simple, question?

For Marx, capital is not money or machines, although both of these may, under certain specific conditions, serve as forms of capital. As we have just seen, when money is simply a means of payment, it is not capital; but when it is invested in the purchase of labor power and thereby enables its owner to appropriate the surplus created by that labor, it is. A tool is not capital when it is used by a peasant to meet his family's needs; but in the hands of a laborer working for an agribusiness, it is. A machine would not be capital when it is employed by a socialist society to satisfy human needs according to a democratic plan; but that same machine under the control of a private corporation is capital.

So, capital is not a thing, but a relationship that determines a particular way of utilizing things. It is also a process. When the individual capitalist begins, his capital takes the form of money. Then he buys labor power, raw materials and machines, and these are now the objectification of his capital. When he has products waiting for market, that inventory is his capital; when he successfully sells it, realizing a profit, the enhanced sum is his capital. These incarnations of capital are, to use one of Marx's persistent images, stages in the "metamorphosis" of capital. The capitalist, Marx writes, begins as a caterpillar and then—because he has been able to appropriate that surplus labor—turns into a butterfly.

All this is put into a simple, but brilliant form, when Marx offers three equations which define different periods of history and social structure. Commodities, which we will call C, can be bartered against one another:

$$C-C$$

Then, in a more complex society, money (M) can intervene to facilitate a much greater number of transactions. The proper formula is now:

$$C-M-C$$

In this second case, money is a medium of exchange. Now there is the capitalist equation.

$$M-C-M$$

Here the capitalist begins, not with a product to sell, but with money and a desire for a profit. He invests it in the production of a commodity, choosing that output that he thinks will give the highest yield and not thinking of social consequence. And if he is successful, he will end up with an increment: M, the caterpillar, has turned into M, the butterfly, the profit. Capital, to use our alienated, animistic speech, is money that "makes" money. (It is, in Marx's terminology, which is still to be explained on this count, value that generates additional value.)

Thus capital is a process from the point of view of the individual capitalist. But it is also a process from a national (or even international) perspective. It is in this area of his analysis that even Paul Samuelson credits Marx with a "stellar contribution" to economic theory. The businessman does not bother himself with the role of his product in the general scheme of things. But as a social system, capitalism is not simply engaged in production; it must reproduce itself on an expanded scale. Therefore, from this vantage it makes a good deal of difference as to what form capital takes. The output of the consumer-goods industry must equal the consumption demands of workers in that industry and in the capital-goods and luxury sectors. The physical output of capital goods must equal the need for them in all three sectors. If the metamorphoses of the individual capitalist do not take place—say he is unable to sell his commodities at a profit and drops out of the system as a bankrupt—that is only a private tragedy for him. But if there is an overproduction of the sum total of capital or consumer goods, an entire sector malfunctions and the whole system is imperiled.

It is in his analysis of this social aspect of capital that Marx's "procapitalism" becomes apparent. The point is important, for it differentiates Marxism from other, more emotional and sentimental attacks on the system. Taken individually, the capitalist may appear simply as a thief of surplus labor. But seen in his social function—as the agent of expanded reproduction during an entire historic epoch—he is much more than that. Marx writes of him:

> As a fanatic for the realization of value, he recklessly pushes mankind to production for production's sake, and thereby to the development of the social productive powers and to the creation of the material conditions of production which alone can provide the basis of a high social form whose basic principle is the full and free development of each individual.

Not that Marx idealized the capitalist. In his early historical incarnation, the entrepreneur was abstemious and puritanical. It was, therefore, "extremely important for bourgeois economics to celebrate accumulation as the first duty of the citizen and to preach without surcease that one cannot accumulate if he consumes his entire revenue. . . ." But then, as capitalism becomes more successful, the extraordinary productive powers of modern industry allow for pampering and waste. There is a growth in maids and personal servants (as well as in the "ideological" estates like law, the church, the military). Indeed, it is this trend that causes Marx to note that a new middle class was coming into existence and becoming "larger and larger . . . fed from revenues that weigh as a burden on the working people beneath them and increase the social security and might of the upper ten thousand." Marx, in short, assigned a historic place to both Max Weber's man of the Protestant ethic and Thorstein Veblen's creature of conspicuous consumption.

However, Marx's capitalist is never a mere wastrel. He accomplishes, in his own exploitative way, the absolutely necessary function of preparing the way for a new social order. The corollary to that proposition—one that very few Marxists have grasped—is that the essential objection to the capitalist is not that he steals surplus labor from the worker, and the crucial demand is not to share his luxuries with the populace on a democratic basis. That is the kind of populism that is directed against plutocrats drinking champagne from their mistresses' dancing slippers, and it has little to do with Marxism. What concerns Marx is that this process of accumulation is carried out in an antisocial fashion that causes depressions, wars and countless other miseries. The point, then, is not simply to make the distribution of wealth fairer, but to change the mode of production of wealth so that it is no longer accomplished by means of periodic crises and the brutalization of the producers. In this case, as throughout his analysis, Marx sees production, not distribution as crucial.[6]

VI

Capital, then, is for Marx a way of utilizing the instruments of production, raw materials and workers so that the owner of the means of production is able to extract a surplus from the labor power he buys. For over a hundred years, academic economics regarded this as the sheerest nonsense, above all because it asserted that there was an exploitative relationship inherent in the capitalist system.

The most famous formulation of this anti-Marxist theory was made by John Bates Clark in the 1890s. According to Clark, as long as the system functioned according to its own laws, "labor tends to get, as its share, what it separately produces; and capital does the same." Nothing could be fairer, or so it would seem; each factor of production is rewarded in proportion to its contribution to the creation of wealth. Indeed, there is such an air of justice and harmony about this thesis that it has survived to this very day. Paul Samuelson, for instance, quotes it with approval in his influential textbook.

Marx called the precursors of Clark's idyll the "trinitarian formula." In this analysis there are three unrelated sources of wealth: capital, land and labor. They are brought together and their prices —profit (or interest) for capital, wages for labor, and rent for land —measure what they bring to the final product. The latter's price is then simply the sum of these constituent elements. Marx first of all attacks the very notion of *capital,* which is so central to this conception.

Capital, he argues, is not a means of production, which is no more capital than gold or silver is inherently money; it is means of production monopolized by one class and counterposed to another class, which, because of its position in society, must sell its living labor to those monopolizers of dead labor. Typically, bourgeois economics equates two completely different kinds of categories: social relationships and physical things. Production instruments, the soil and workers are defined respectively as capital, landed property and wage labor. The first three terms identify the material preconditions of production in all social orders; the last three describe the peculiar forms that these preconditions take in capitalist society. In primitive societies, under slave systems and feudalism, the means of production are not capital, and work is not wage labor. (I leave out rent, because its peculiar complexities do not bear on the main point.)

However, the confusion of bourgeois economics in this area is quite functional. By equating the eternal preconditions of social life with the forms they take in a given epoch, one raises the latter to the status of facts of nature. Profit then arises ineluctably out of the very structure of reality itself. The result is a masquerade. The "thingification of societal relationships" produces an "enchanted, bizarre, topsy-turvy world in which Monsieur Le Capital and Madame La Terre lead a ghostly existence and are simultaneously social characters and mere things." The classical political economy, Marx acknowledges, saw through some of these inversions but, given its bourgeois limitations, it could never formulate the profundity of its own insights. Then, as the socialist threat grew, the academy stopped probing the identities of Monsieur Le Capital and Madame La Terre. It was more discreet and genteel to talk about relative prices.

A second aspect of the trinitarian formula has to do with a remarkable omission. If the gross product and gross income of the society are equal—as they must be, in the trinitarian formula, since the inputs are defined as revenues from the sale of the output—how are machines replaced? Wear and tear are not covered under profits or rent or wages, and yet they occur. Indeed, one of the ways that contemporary corporations lower or conceal profits—which is usually politically expedient in a welfare state—is by keeping their "capital consumption allowances" (the funds for depreciation) as high as possible. In doing so they violate the trinitarian formula; but, then, business is business. There is a method in this remarkable oversight; it supplied the basis for a theory of capitalist harmony, a theory that lasted from at least the time of Jean Baptiste Say (d.1832) to the triumph of John Maynard Keynes in the 1930s. For if gross product and gross income are equal, if one imagines that society consumes its entire product every year, then there can be no depressions. People will automatically have an income just large enough to buy everything that has been produced. As a result, all the complexities of the relationship between the capital-goods and consumer-goods sectors are abolished at a stroke. This idyll had a major and disastrous influence on economic policy for about a century, and it is a product of the trinitarian formula.

Finally, Marx points to yet another anomaly of the trinitarian formula, one that has figured prominently in recent discussions. In this analysis, profits, rent and wages divvy up what remains after the depreciation of capital has taken place. So this trinity shares in the new wealth that has been created. (If they are parceling out deductions from the existing stock of wealth, they are committing the most heinous of bourgeois sins, living off capital, and the system will break down if they persist.) The wages share, Marx argues, must provide a certain minimum to perpetuate the very existence of the working class. But he then immediately adds that wages normally deviate from that minimum (above it) and emphasizes that he is speaking "not only of a physical minimum but of historically developed societal needs." What is left after wages are paid is then available for distribution as profits and rent. In Marx's theory, those profits are a share of surplus labor time. But what are they a percentage of in the trinitarian formula (which is to say in most academic economics)? There is no satisfying response to this utterly basic question in established truth. And this, as will be seen, was one source of the crisis in economic theory in recent years.

Capital, then, is not in Marx's analysis simply a machine, although it sometimes takes that form. A machine can transfer value —through the wear and tear of the lathe, a piece of metal is shaped— but it cannot create it. That is why Marx calls the machine "constant" capital. It adds nothing new to the production process, and the increment of worth in the milled metal is equal to the depreciation of the lathe. More poetically, Marx regularly speaks of machines as "dead labor," in order to emphasize that whatever capacity they have to transfer value was created by a past expenditure of "living labor." (Piero Sraffa, one of the central figures in the War of the Two Cambridges, uses a similar concept, in which the means of production are reduced to "dated labor.") In other words, Marx did not deny the productivity of machines. Rather, he analyzed that productivity as the result of the human labor (mental as well as physical) which made the machines, rather than as the contribution of their legal owner. The latter, like Ricardo's landlord, could grow rich in his sleep.

Secondly, for Marx, capital is not finance, although it can take this form during its metamorphosis. It should be painfully obvious —though the fact has been ignored by a good many academic economists for about a century—that dollar bills and stock certificates play no role in the productive process. If their owner performs a managerial function his labor may well create new value (though Marx thought that the "wages of superintendence" were, more often than not, a false cost of production, a charge for keeping the workers in line). These pieces of paper are very real titles to the proceeds of production, but not to the process of production, and their owners can collect their reward without lifting a finger.

So Marx was profoundly critical of the "trinitarian formula" and, by clear implication, of the modern tradition first formulated by John Bates Clark. Moreover, he understood the apologetic function of such theories, and his comments on this point are relevant to this very day.

In them, he wrote,

> earth-rent, capitalist-interest and labor-wage present the various forms of surplus value and the structure of capitalist production, in an unalienated way, as foreign and indifferent to one another, *without any conflict* between each other. The various revenues are derived from quite different sources. . . . So, they do not exist as hostile to one another, because they are not at all interdependent. If they act together in production, it is a harmonious action, the expression of a harmony just as the peasant, the ox, the plow and the earth, in spite of their differences, work together *harmoniously* in agriculture. . . . To the degree that any antagonism occurs among them, it merely arises out of competition as to which factor shall appropriate more of the product, of the value, which they created together. If this occasionally leads to a fight, the end result of this competition between earth, capital and labor is that, in so far as they struggled with one another over distribution, their rivalry leads them to increase the product so that each gets a larger piece. The competition which spurs them on thus appears as only an expression of their harmony.

Given this idyll, the idea of a class struggle is sheer foolishness; and in so far as the workers pursue one, they are doing themselves harm. So, the three quarters of a century of bitter and often bloody disputes between capital and labor since Clark defined their harmonious position in society have been a mistake. One of the tests of a theory is how well it accounts for social reality. On this basis, Marx's definitions, which roughly predicted what has happened, are infinitely superior to Clark's, which lead to the conclusion that much of modern social history should never have taken place.[7]

VII

In the War of the Two Cambridges, the intellectual battle that pitted the theorists of Cambridge, Massachusetts (Harvard and the Massachusetts Institute of Technology), against those of Cambridge University in England (along with a number of notable Italian thinkers), Marx's questions and concerns proved themselves to be relevant to late-twentieth-century analysis.

It is a remarkable—I would say "fitting"—irony that academic economics, which so long hectored Marx for being metaphysical and unquantitative, recently found itself in a profound crisis because it had not thought through the concepts underlying its own quantities. Indeed, it turns out that the Marxian preoccupations—in particular the focus upon the impact of income distribution on the economic system and the related notion of the domination of the relations of production over the relations of distribution—were more useful than various theories of marginal utility. All of this is especially embarrassing to the mainstream of the profession, since it now turns out that it has been making increasingly complex and elegant mathematical models in which, however, a key term is not, and cannot be, defined.

As Joan Robinson put the problem, "there is no meaning to be given to a 'quantity of capital' apart from the rate of profit, so that the contention that the 'marginal productivity of capital' determines the rate of profit is meaningless."

Mrs. Robinson thereby made a devastating attack on her discipline. A brilliant young economist with egalitarian values, but a respect for the neoclassical tradition, Lester Thurow, put it this way:

Despite the problems associated with this idea of marginal productivity, economists are extremely reluctant to abandon it, since they do not know how to replace it and since it is central to much of the theoretical apparatus of economics. If it ever had to be abandoned, much of economics would have to be abandoned with it.

But what Joan Robinson is saying is that the moment feared by Thurow is at hand, and the marginal-productivity theory must be jettisoned. Thus, it would seem that the Marxist "critique" of bourgeois economics—the assertion that the entire science has faulty theoretical foundations—may be in the process of vindication.

Space and my own limitations will not permit anything but the briefest of surveys of some of the leading ideas of the War of the Two Cambridges. But even though this will take us into the area of abstruse simplicities, it is very important to the understanding of both the new and the future Karl Marx.

First, let us begin with a brief summary of the received faith. (It has countless variations, of course, but there is a continuity of over a century in these ideas.) The neoclassical synthesis argues that the prices of the factors of production—capital, land and labor —as registered on an impersonal market determine the prices of commodities and the distribution of income. The market mechanism is thus seen as having such universal import that its allocations can be analyzed without reference to any sociological data. Only a few assumptions are said to be needed to come to this conclusion. (I will merely note that these assumptions actually hold only in the bourgeois era; exploring this point, which would be quite important in other contexts, is not relevant to the immediate argument.)

One assumes that people are economizers. So neither capitalists nor consumers will buy a new unit of anything unless they are convinced that the utility they will derive from the purchase will be greater than the cost of it. This holds in the market, where the factors of production are bought and sold. One more unit of capital will be invested only if the profit it will help to produce is going to be greater than its cost. One more acre of land will be cultivated

144 THE TWILIGHT OF CAPITALISM

only if its yield is going to be more than its rent. And new laborers will be hired only if the value of their output will exceed their wages. The same rule holds for consumption. Consumer demand will be based on the utility (satisfaction, preference) that one more unit of a good will provide. The factor market where capital, land and labor are traded will thus accurately fix the costs that have to be paid to meet the patterns of demand set by the consumer market. (As noted earlier, this part of the argument ignores the crucial factor stressed by Marx: that demand depends on how much money a person has, which in turn is a function of the person's position in the production process and the outcome of the class struggle.) So the consumer market, where demand is set, and the factors of production market, where the cost of supply is fixed in relationship to that demand, mesh together.

In the process, the distribution of income is determined by these various market operations. For interest (or profit) represents the reward paid to the marginal efficiency of capital, wages the marginal efficiency of labor and rent the marginal efficiency of land. The political beauty in all of this is that it allowed the rich to picture themselves as humble servants of the market just like everyone else. If radicals wanted to cut down on profits, it could be pointed out that this was an unwarranted and artificial interference with an automatic mechanism. The well-meaning but incompetent left would thereby misrepresent the actual cost to society of new investment; indeed, it would thwart the real desires of working-class consumers by depriving business of the means to satisfy their preferences. Such a doctrine, as Gunnar Myrdal has pointed out,

> is not intended to be merely a scientific explanation of what course economic relations would take under certain specified assumptions. It simultaneously constitutes a kind of proof that the hypothetical conditions would result in maximum "total income" or the greatest possible "satisfaction of needs" in society as a whole.

The marginal-productivity analysis is, of course, a variant of the trinitarian formula analyzed by Marx in Volume III of *Das Kapital*. The attack on it, led by economists from Cambridge University in England—most notably John Robinson and Piero Sraffa—makes in its own way Marx's central point: that capital is not a thing. It does not, however, adopt all of Marx's solution to the problem, even though it moves in that direction. What follows is an exposition of a few of the major points in a critique that may well have subverted the foundations of economics as it has been known for the past hundred or so years.

First, the marginal theory assumes that capital is a homogeneous substance. In fact, it is not. It is assumed that there is something called "capital" that can be varied, upward and downward, while the other factors are held constant. Joan Robinson dubbed this mysterious substance "leets" (which is "steel" spelled backward, a joking reference to the fact that serious theorists on the other side have described capital as butter, or as a child's erector set with parts that can be switched around). With it "a change of production can be made simply by squeezing up or spreading out leets, instantaneously and without cost."

But then there is something in the real world that has some of the qualities of leets: money (or capital defined as finance). It seems to have the faculty of ubiquity, the ability to "flow" from one industry to another and to take many different forms and shapes. But there must be real capital goods that give the dance of money its meaning, and they are quite heterogeneous. Marx made the essential point in dealing with industrial capital. It "does not exist twice," he said, "once as the capital value of the property title, the stock, and the other time as the capital actually laid out in the undertaking. It exists only in the latter form, and the stock is nothing but a property title, pro rata for the surplus value to be realized through it."

Thorstein Veblen, the founding genius of institutional economics, elaborated this thought years ago in a classic critique of John Bates Clark. He wrote: "The continuum in which the 'abiding entity' of capital resides is a continuity of ownership, not a physical fact." On this count, Veblen is saying just about what Marx would say; and institutional economics, with its insistence on specifying the social and cultural context of an economic system, is clearly at least a cousin of Marxism. But Veblen also thought it possible to differentiate the technological basis of capitalism from its political and social integument and looked to engineers, who could be objective about society and production, and not the workers, as the natural leaders of a decent future. In this he is the precursor of the technocrats and the theorists of "industrial society" rather than a descendant of Marx.

Secondly, profits are supposed to measure the marginal efficiency of capital. But in the real world, the value of a machine will depend on the profit rate. When accountants determine how it is going to be depreciated, they must figure in that rate in order to determine its worth at any given point. Indeed, Marx demonstrates at length how one of the functions of a depression is to "devalue" some of the existing technology by creating conditions under which it is no longer profitable to continue using it. (And new inventions also have the same effect.)

Thirdly, Keynes pointed out that " 'the marginal efficiency of capital' . . . [is] merely the estimated future rate of return on the finance that a business commits to enlarging its productive capacity." Moreover, he noted that the system does not necessarily stabilize at a full employment of all the factors of production, as the neoclassicals had assumed. The Great Depression was a devastating case in point, and it helped Keynes to triumph as a theorist.

And fourthly, there must be at least some reference to Sraffa's enormous contribution to this debate. I say "some reference" since his slim volume of theory—the text is 95 pages long—is so densely packed with ideas that only the flavor of it can be suggested here.

Sraffa conceives of his book as providing the basis for a critique of the marginal theory of value and distribution. The marginalists, he points out, see the system of production as a "one-way avenue that leads from 'factors of production' to 'consumption goods.' " This, of course, is the modern version of the trinitarian formula— of the thesis that capital, land and labor are independent sources of productivity and that price is the aggregate of their cost. Sraffa rejects it on a number of grounds.

For one thing, he, like Marx, sees the economic process as circular and interdependent. So it is that the first section of Sraffa's book is devoted to an exploration of the interdependencies of a system of production, much in the spirit of Volume II of *Das Kapi-*

tal (or of the *Tableau Economique* of Quesnay, the precursor of the entire classical tradition in this area). It is because of this "mutual dependence" of the price of means of production, labor and profits in the production of basic products that Sraffa denies that there is an entity, "capital," which can be measured independently of, and prior to, the determination of the price of the products. If Sraffa is right on this count, then the "production functions" that are so important to contemporary theory are no longer viable. For one of the crucial terms in them, capital, turns out to be a confusion, not a definition.

Given this analysis of interconnections, Sraffa stresses that profits and wages are related and, therefore, potentially antagonistic. So, the harmonies of John Bates Clark and his numerous intellectual progeny are subverted. Then he turns to the "transformation problem" that has bedeviled Marxist theory for years: How can you translate labor "values"—that is, inputs and outputs defined in terms of hours of standard labor—into prices? In particular, why is it that industries which are labor intensive are not more profitable than those which are capital intensive? Given the labor standard, isn't it clear that they would yield much more value?

Sraffa's solution to this problem is extremely complicated, and I will not even attempt to summarize it here. But what is relevant is that he shows that an entire economic system can be reduced, rigorously and realistically, to quantities of "dated labor." In the process, he not only demonstrates that the Marxian analysis is consistent, but he also provides yet another ground for the criticism of the neoclassical synthesis. There is no such thing, he points out, as a "period of production" that can serve as a unit for the analysis of something called capital. For a machine contains not only the labor of the generation that made it, but also the labor of the generation that made the tools to make it, and that of the generation that made the tools that made the tools that made the machine, and so on. In this part of his analysis, he provides a brilliant application of the Marxist notion of the machine as "dead labor," as contrasted with the "living" labor of the workers.

All of this is not to suggest that Sraffa is a Marxist. He isn't. On the crucial question that separates Marx from Ricardo—whether labor is seen as the very substance of value, or whether it is merely a measure of value—Sraffa has more in common with Ricardo than with Marx. (And he has been criticized by Marxists on this and other counts.) What is, however, of tremendous importance is that he has placed the Marxian questions back on the agenda, even if he does not always give the Marxian answers to them.

But why, then did the War of the Two Cambridges take place in the 1960s? A good part of the reason is political. In the period of early capitalism, when the new system was struggling against the parasites of the old order, it fearlessly investigated "the laws which regulate the distribution of the produce of the earth between the classes of the community," for the truth in this case was bourgeois. But once capitalism was established, that same enterprise became subversive and socialist, and it was one of the functions of academic theory—in all sincerity and with considerable brilliance —to get the embarrassing issues off the intellectual agenda. But in the late twentieth century, life does not allow that evasion any more. The incredible turmoil of the immediate past—of world wars, anti-capitalist revolutions, fascism, the decolonization of the Third World, the emergence of state-planned capitalism—has forcibly pushed theory into a new contact with a tumultuous reality. And that is why Marx not only is relevant, but even in the academy once more is *seen* to be relevant.[8]

CHAPTER 6

THE SPIRITUAL MATERIALIST

FOR a long time one of the most popular libels against Karl Marx was that he was a materialist in the vulgar sense of the word, that he reduced all things to their lowest and most sordid common denominator. In this caricature—which some Marxists accepted as accurate—thought is to the mind as urine is to the kidney, the world of spirit is a mere reflex of matter. Then in recent years, particularly in the fifties and sixties, another, almost exactly opposite image of Marx emerged. It was for the most part the work of people sympathetic to the authentic Marxist tradition, and it emphasized its spirituality. As Erich Fromm put this new interpretation, "Marx's philosophy was, in secular, nontheistic language, a new and radical step forward in the tradition of prophetic Messianism; it was aimed at the full realization of individualism, the very aim that has guided Western thinking from the Renaissance and the Reformation far into the nineteenth century."

Both these readings of Marx are wrong, though not equally so. The first, the "materialist," is an outright travesty without the least basis in Marx's writings. The second, the "spiritualist," is an understandable reaction to the scientist interpretation of Marxism. Moreover, I am in general political sympathy with those who make out this case. It is just that they push their rehabilitation of Marx's philosophic and ethical concerns too far. Marx was, for instance, a basic and principled critic of Western individualism as it developed from the Renaissance and the Reformation into the nineteenth century, for he argued that it was inextricably linked with the rise of capitalism. He was not, as Fromm thinks, its apogee.

The truth about Marx in this area, as in every other, is dialectical: he was a spiritual materialist, the audacious synthesizer of philosophic traditions which had been at one another's throat for hundreds of years. That untranslatable Hegelian word, *aufheben,* really describes Marx's transformation of the spirit-matter, freedom-necessity antinomies. *Aufheben* means "to destroy, but preserve what is destroyed as part of a new and higher synthesis."

One can now almost hear the groans of those who opened this book in the hope of finding a "new"—that is to say, a usable—Marx. What can that project possibly have to do with a return to the murky debates of nineteenth-century German philosophy? Or with one more discussion of alienation, that most bedraggled cliché of contemporary culture? Didn't the mature Marx of *Das Kapital,* the scientist who rigorously probed the social order before his eyes, turn his own back on the metaphysical vapors of his youth? Friedrich Engels himself has told us that he and Marx had left the manuscript of the *German Ideology,* one of the philosophic works of that period, "to the gnawing criticism of the mice, and we did so willingly, since we had achieved our own purpose—self-understanding." So, some argue, it may be of scholarly or bibliographic interest to determine exactly what the young Marx felt about a "human nature" that he did not discuss in his mature masterpiece. That, it could be said, is hardly pertinent to a book that seeks a Marx who speaks to the twenty-first century.

I disagree. First, *Das Kapital,* which is to say the ultimate Marx, cannot be understood if one does not perceive its continuity with the youthful writings on philosophy. Marx changed in the course of his lifetime, deepened his analysis, rejected earlier opinions. For example, in somewhat less than two years, from the spring of 1848 to the fall of 1850, he advocated no less than three basic and contradictory strategies for the revolutionary movement. And yet his vision, his fundamental values, persisted throughout his life. They are not extraneous to the hard-minded presentation of the organic whole in *Das Kapital,* the stuff of Marxist sermons on Sunday which must not be allowed to interfere with the serious economic, sociological and political work of the rest of the week. Those values are so inherent in his tough-minded dissections of social reality that the latter cannot be read apart from them.

It is not accidentally that the humanism of the young Marx was declared a boyish aberration by the totalitarians who speak in the name of Marxism. They quite rightly understood that these speculative philosophic matters could incite subversion and even armed resistance. In addition, the Marxian concept of man has a profound methodological significance. Perhaps the most influential misreading of Marxism, as Chapter II showed, is the mechanistic theory that there is an economic base that immediately determines the content of cultural and political superstructure. That is, among other things, a theory about the nature of man; a way, for instance, of defining his freedom—and a bad way. It is not simply a matter of wrong values, but of wrong values that will lead to spectacularly erroneous analytic conclusions. A theory of human nature sets up expectations about human behavior, and that is why it is relevant to (and implicit in) sociology and economics as well as philosophy. Indeed, even the most practical of politicians are involved, willy-nilly, in these seemingly abstract issues.

Cuba under Castro is a case in point. As will be seen later on in detail, overly generous assumptions about human nature in a society of relative scarcity led Castro (and Che Guevara, the real source of this impulse) to play down "material incentives" in the middle sixties. This policy and the philosophic interpretation upon which it was based were then partly responsible for determining the level of sugar production. There is, of course, another interpretation of such events. It might be said that they did not result from a faulty reading of Marx, but from adapting to Marx's own, quite obsolete ideas. Could it be, as Herbert Marcuse has suggested, that Marx's basic values have been rendered utopian by the actual course of twentieth-century history?

These themes will weave in and out of this chapter. It will first turn to the famous debate over the young Marx versus the old as personified by Daniel Bell and Louis Althusser on the one side and Erich Fromm on the other. Then there will be a discussion of the very practical consequences that follow from Marx's spiritual materialism. And finally, there will be a consideration of the grim possibility that his intricate, dialectical and passionate vision of mankind, and particularly of mankind's potential for freedom, is one more casualty of this destructive century. I don't think so. Certainly not yet.[1]

<h1 style="text-align:center">I</h1>

Marxism, Louis Althusser holds, is not a humanism. That is to say, it is not based on a conception of the nature, or the essence, of man. Indeed, there is a "rupture" (*coupure*) in Marx's thought of the 1840s. On the one side of this intellectual chasm there is the young Marx who inveighed against capitalism in the name of human nature. On the other side there is the maturing and, finally, mature Marx who rid himself of the concept of "man" and interpreted history in terms of productive powers, the relations of production, determination in the final instance by the economic, and so on.

Althusser is, I think, quite wrong in his basic position. And yet, even though his torrent of definitions and lapidary formulas sometimes seems to be a Marxist scholasticism, he has the merit of a certain iconoclasm, a strange quality for a disciplined Communist. He refuses to take some of the most cherished of Marxist quotations for granted and asks embarrassing questions about them instead. Marx's famous assertion of 1844 that "the root is man" sounds sonorous on the tongue of a socialist orator. But precisely what, Althusser would ask, does it mean in the context of the Marxist analysis? So I propose to summarize a few of his main arguments, interrupting with critical comment only when that is absolutely necessary. The later sections of this chapter will constitute a reply to Althusser; for now I am concerned primarily with showing, in the briefest of outlines, his case against the very existence of a Marxist humanism.

To begin with, Althusser does permit himself to speak of "humanism" on occasion even though he considers it to be an "ideological" notion—that is, it does not help us to know the reality to which it refers. There is, he says in *Pour Marx,* a "class humanism." That is characterized by the dictatorship of the proletariat, as in China; and the Social Democrats who protest against it in the name of liberty do so on the basis of "bourgeois humanism." There is also a "humanism of the person (socialist)," which is incarnated in the Soviet Union and represents the culmination of class humanism.

These matters are presented by Althusser, like everything else in his books, in a style of Cartesian clarity and a spirit of scientific commitment. Only, it should be apparent to all but the most innocent of readers that there is a contemporary political dimension to his reading of Marx. For one of the things which Althusser is able to "prove" by attributing concepts like "class humanism" to Marx is that Marx himself would have approved of the dictatorship over the proletariat which is practiced both in the Soviet Union and in China. And one of the reasons—perhaps conscious, perhaps not— for making such an unsentimental and scientistic interpretation of Marxism is the one that motivated Stalin in his similar, if infinitely less sophisticated and more vulgar, enterprise: to make democracy, with its notion of the "rights of man," a mere bourgeois ideology, useful in its time and place, but irrelevant to the transition to a classless society.

So, even though he sometimes makes rhetorical concessions to those whom he considers to be tender-minded leftists, Althusser is basically antihumanist and a main thrust of his work is an attack on Marxist humanism. That humanist point of view, Althusser rightly notes, first arose after World War I. It was a response to the failure of the prewar Social-Democratic theories, which assigned a Darwinian inevitability to socialism, and to the success of the audacious voluntarism of the Bolsheviks in the October Revolution.

It was, then, a theory held by people who believed (even if erro-

neously, romantically) that the masses were by their own motion
about to create a society of genuine brotherhood. But what does
Althusser's interpretation of Marx represent? The period after that
wave of revolutionary hope and optimism—that is, the period of
Stalin's victory. Althusser, to be sure, is no simple Stalinist, and he
is opposed to what is euphemistically called "the cult of the personality"—which is to say, Stalin's totalitarian terror. But clearly
his antihumanism and his reading of texts from the 1840s is related to his critical support for a variety of Communist dictator-
ships in the 1960s and 1970s.

The Soviet leaders recognized the danger of Marx's humanism
very early on. An incomplete edition of the *Economic Philosophic
Manuscripts* appeared in Russian in 1927; the complete text in
German, Russian and French came out in 1932. Those were the
years of antifascism followed by World War II, and there was little
time in them for philosophy. But in the fifties the writings of the
young Marx came into their own. They became central to the revisionist—and anti-Stalinist—thinkers of Eastern Europe and to the
neo-Marxists of Western Europe. As one Soviet spokesman delicately put his attacks against these new interpretations of Marx,
they show convincingly "that revisionists are the agents of imperialism in the worker's movement." Althusser would never engage in such Stalinist bombast, but his intellectual conclusions,
subtle as they are, make the same point.

With this forewarning about the political dimensions of what
might seem to be only a scholarly undertaking, it is possible to
turn to a key term of Althusser's: the *problematic*. Aspects of this
idea were discussed in the text and appendix of Chapter I. Here, I
think is a valuable concept, even though Althusser ascribes much
too much precision to it. The answers in any theory, he notes, will
be profoundly affected by, and sometimes even settled by, the
questions that it poses. So, one must ask questions of these questions. How have the problems that it set for itself affected the solutions which it offers? And why, in terms of the issues which reality
thrust upon people at that particular moment, did a thinker choose
to ask this specific question? If one discovers that a philosopher

asked and answered irrelevant questions that is a clue to what is "ideological" in his thought.

A "problematic" arises when a new question is put that undermines the old assumptions. It happened when Lavoisier saw that Priestley's new gas was not "dephlogisticated air" but oxygen; or when Marx described profit, rent and interest as mere forms of surplus value. It develops "in the act of posing as a problem what had previously been given as a solution." This way of analyzing theoretical changes is quite useful in the case of Marx, particularly since he "borrowed" ideas from so many of his contemporaries.

Who was it, for example, who said the following?

> A mass of the population is condemned to the stupefying, unhealthy and insecure labor of factories, manufactories, mines and so on. Whole branches of industry which supported a large bulk of the population suddenly fold up because the mode changes or because the values of their products fall on account of new inventions in other countries, or for other reasons. Whole masses are thus abandoned to helpless poverty. The conflict between vast wealth and vast poverty steps forth, a poverty unable to improve its condition. . . . This inequality of wealth and poverty, this need and necessity turn into the utmost dismemberment of will, inner rebellion and hatred.

It was Hegel. Or who saw history as the process of a conflict between "master-slave, patrician-plebeian, lord-serf, the leisured-the worker"? It was Saint-Simon.

Are we, then, to say that the opening lines of the Communist Manifesto are Saint-Simonian, or that the Marxist theory of industrial crisis and class struggle is really Hegelian? Althusser provides a way out of such eclectic bookkeeping. If Marx used Hegel's thought—or, for that matter, his very words—but in a different problematic, if he asked un-Hegelian questions in using some insight of Hegel's, then he is no Hegelian. But if an essay, a book, or a period of his life was dominated, not simply by this or that perception of Hegel's, but by Hegel's questions, then he is still under the spell of the latter's problematic. So one does not say of a work that it is 20 percent Hegelian, 20 percent Saint-Simonian, 20 percent Feuerbachian and 40 percent Marxist. That is a mechanistic way of counting up "influences," as if they were so many sacks of potatoes. One asks, Are the book's basic questions Hegelian, Saint-Simonian, Feuerbachian or Marxist? For instance, where Saint-Simon had counterposed the "leisured" (*oisif*) to the worker, Marx wrote "capitalist." That is not the change of a word; it is the evidence of a new problematic.

Althusser argues that Marx's writings of 1843 were Feuerbachian. That is to say, their central concern is to contrast real, living men with the abstract humanism of the classical German philosophy. Then in the *Economic Philosophic Manuscripts,* Marx is seen as adopting the Hegelian problematic for the first time, focusing on how human nature is alienated from its true potential in capitalist society. This point is basically correct, yet Althusser makes it with excessive precision. He claims to be able to specify exactly when Marx takes leave of one question and asks another in its stead. But in 1843, in a "Feuerbachian" critique of Hegel, Marx employed a very Marxist class analysis in some critical passages. Such sloppiness is anathema to Althusser. He writes of Marx's *Theses on Feuerbach* that they are "the extreme anterior bank of his rupture [with Feuerbach and Hegel], the place where, within the previous consciousness and language . . . the new theoretical consciousness already thrusts through." This is to make the flow of a man's thought mechanistic, to run a film of his mind at such a slow speed that every frame is visible. That is neither possible nor desirable.

But the problem is not just the pseudo precision of Althusser's method. The basic objection has to do with his content. At the beginning, Althusser argues, Marx was a rationalist liberal in the tradition of Kant and Fichte. The essence of man was reason and liberty, and the Prussian state did not conform to it and was therefore to be criticized. "Philosophy," Marx wrote in this mood, "asks that the state be the state of human nature." In the second stage, as Althusser describes it, Marx becomes a humanist in Feuerbach's mode. Now the state is seen as the enemy of reason and man is a creature of reason and liberty only in his "community being," in his relationships with other men and with nature.

Then came the rupture. Althusser writes:

> From 1845 on, Marx radically broke with all theories which based history and politics on an essence of man. This unique rupture had three inseparable theoretical aspects: 1. Formation of a theory of history and politics founded upon radical new concepts: concepts of social formation, productive powers, relations of production, super-structure, ideologies, determination in the final instance by the economy, specific determination of levels, etc. 2. Radical critique of the theoretical pretensions of every philosophic humanism. 3. Definition of humanism as an *ideology*.

Some of the terms in Althusser's statement may be unclear, since they refer to aspects of his interpretation that have not been treated here. But the main thrust is plain. After 1845 Marx stopped talking about man and human nature, because he regarded those terms as ideological, as the products of a false consciousness. From that point on he is concerned not with individuals, but with social classes and relations of production. The actors in history "are not, contrary to all appearances . . . 'concrete individuals,' 'real men' . . ." Rather, "the true 'subjects' [of history] are . . . the relations of production" and the social, political and ideological relations. Men simply occupy the places assigned to them by the relations of production; for Althusser's Marx they are not concrete individuals but the "bearers," the occupants, the functionaries of relationships which lie outside of themselves.

As Althusser puts it in another context,

> The untenable thesis upheld by Marx in the 1844 *Manuscripts* was that History is the History of the process of alienation of a Subject, the Generic Essence of Man alienated in "alienated labor." But it was precisely this thesis that *exploded*. The result of this explosion was the evaporation of the notion of subject, human essence and alienation, which disappears, completely atomized, and the liberation of the *concept of process* . . . *without a subject,* which is the basis of all the analyses in *Das Kapital*.

The full meaning of this passage is complex and perhaps murky. Its central point, however, is clear enough. "Man" is not the pre-existing subject who undergoes and shapes history. Man is part of a historical process, its result rather than its creator, and he occupies the place that is assigned him by the relations of production. So what is central is not man but that process. (See Appendix E, § 1, p. 384.)

My own critique of Althusser's thesis will come later on in this chapter. For now, there are just a few, preliminary comments about the embarrassment that he suffers because of Marx's *Grundrisse,* the "raw outline" of *Das Kapital* from the late 1850s. The *Grundrisse* is, Althusser himself is forced to recognize, filled with "Hegelian"—that is to say, *philosophic*—references. Althusser notes bitterly, "It can be predicted with some certainty that, along with *The German Ideology,* the *Grundrisse* will provide all the dubious quotations needed by idealist interpreters of Marxist theory." So Althusser has a rather mature Marx committing a Hegelian deviation, which is more than a thousand pages in length. It is a dangerous procedure in any case to declare that a world-historical genius has misunderstood himself, not in a few pages or in an essay or two, but in a major work. And it is particularly questionable for an author who has insisted that a particular genius went through a series of clearly defined intellectual stages to adopt this procedure. How, then, account for a juvenile regression to the concept of alienation on the part of a Marx who was on the eve of writing *Das Kapital?*

An accident of publishing history makes all this even more bothersome for Althusser. The 1857 Introduction to the *Critique of Political Economy* was a part of the manuscripts which make up the *Grundrisse.* It was, however, published separately by Karl Kautsky in 1903, and it was widely translated and quoted. The *Grundrisse* itself first appeared in Moscow in 1939, and a new edition was brought out by the East Germans in 1953. Althusser regularly—and rightly—cited the 1857 Introduction as a classic and sophisticated statement of the Marxian method. Then he had to confront the *Grundrisse* itself. But how can one downgrade a volume that contains an Introduction which you have hailed as brilliant? If Marx abandoned all thought of alienated human nature in 1845, then he was hopelessly confused in 1857, backsliding to youthful concerns and writing a manuscript that is simultaneously the quintessence of maturity and an act of theoretical infantilism.

The truth, as Leszek Kolakowski pointed out in a stinging critique of Althusser, is not so hopelessly convoluted. All of these contradictions vanish as soon as it is recognized that the *Grundrisse* and *Das Kapital* are infused with the values and humanist concerns of the young Marx. In the *Grundrisse* those themes are explicitly generalized; in *Das Kapital* they are implicit in everything that is said. For the plain fact of the matter is that Althusser's analytic chronicle of Marx's thought cannot account for its actual development. This would have come out in the end in any case, for it can be demonstrated without a single reference to the *Grundrisse*. The fact that Althusser stumbled over the peculiar publishing history of that volume only makes it a little easier to show how flawed his fundamental theory is.

Althusser's political bias, his Communist penchant for a scientistic Marx, has already been noted. But how, then, explain that Daniel Bell, a Western scholar and an anti-Communist, shares Althusser's reading? The answer is that there is a symmetrical prejudice. Althusser is fearful of a Marxist critique of Communism based on Marx's humanism; Bell rejects a Marxist critique of capitalism based on Marx's economic work. Althusser's tough-minded, unsentimental and ahumanist Marx helps rationalize totalitarianism as necessary for progress. Bell agrees that the real Marx is described by Althusser and rejects him because his tough-mindedness is narrow and his ahumanism inhumane.*

So it is that Althusser and Bell misunderstand the same Marxist concept in similar fashion. Bell quotes Marx from his 1867 Introduction to Volume I of *Das Kapital* (as does Althusser):

* As far as I know, Bell has not published anything about Althusser. When I talk of their agreement it is only to indicate that they have come to the same conclusion as to what is authentic and essential in Marx, but not that they have done so jointly or that they have necessarily even influenced one another.

Here individuals are dealt with only insofar as they are the personifications of economic categories, embodiments of particular class relations and class interests. My standpoint, from which the evolution of the economic formation of society is viewed as a process of natural history, can, less than any other, make the individual responsible for relations whose creature he socially remains, however he may subjectively raise himself above them.

Bell then comments (and Althusser would almost certainly agree): "Thus individual responsibility is turned into class morality, and the variability of individual action subsumed under impersonal mechanisms." Bell adds, "And the ground is laid for the loss of freedom in a new tyranny that finds its justification in the narrow view of exploitation which Marx had fashioned." Althusser would, of course, reject that last sentence, but he would certainly agree that his and Bell's reading of Marx provides a justification for Soviet society. The difficulty with the Bell-Althusser version of this passage is that it distorts Marx's thought in the most extraordinary way.

To begin with, Bell omits the first two sentences of Marx's paragraph and then quotes the rest. In the original, one finds this preface to the passage cited: "One word in order to avoid a possible misunderstanding. The depiction of the capitalist and landlord is in no way done in a rosy light." Then follows: "But here [in this volume] it is not a question of persons . . ." That is, Marx is forestalling the objection that he has described capitalists as men of unrelieved evil by noting that *in this book* he only considers them under one functional aspect. This does not in the least mean that Marx thinks that capitalists and landlords are "only personifications of economic categories"; only that they will be treated exclusively in that light in what follows. If anything, Marx is saying the opposite of what Bell and Althusser attribute to him, declaring that he knows that people, including capitalists, are not simply personifications, but that he will treat them in this way for a specified analytic purpose.

This relates to the important distinction made in the previous chapter between a mode of production and an economic-social formation. The latter, it will be remembered, describes the complex richness of an actual society in which, as in contemporary England, a capitalist economy and the feudal institution of the monarchy complement each other. The mode of production, on the other hand, is an abstraction that treats all this complexity from the primary vantage point of only one of its relationships, the economic. *Das Kapital* employs this second kind of analysis. In it, therefore, the capitalist, by definition, can appear only as the personification of an economic category.

Secondly, and even more substantially, it is true that Marx believed that capitalism tended to reduce people to personifications. This is a point that he makes explicit both in the 1844 *Manuscripts* and in *Das Kapital*. And it hardly can counterpose the young Marx to the old, since they shared it. But if there is a limited truth to the notion that "the variability of individual action [is] subsumed under impersonal mechanisms" under capitalism, it is a truth that Marx abominated and proposed to destroy. So Bell and Althusser are wrong on two crucial counts: They first artificially reduce Marx's image of man to a class-determined, impersonal concept; and then they act as if Marx positively accepted the concept—when, in fact, he fought all his life to shatter whatever unfortunate truth it contained.

Bell, again like Althusser, also trips over the *Grundrisse* (and *Das Kapital,* for that matter, but that is not quite so obvious). After 1846, he writes, Marx never returned to the philosophical preoccupations of his youth "except for some gnomic references in the *Critique of the Gotha Programme* in 1875 . . ." One of the many problems with this statement is that we know that Marx received some volumes of Hegel from his friend Freiligrath in the fall of 1857. In January 1858, Marx reported to Engels on the impact of that gift: ". . . I have thrown out the entire theory of profit as it was. In the *method* of working this out, a great service was done for me by mere accident—Freiligrath found some volumes of Hegel which originally belonged to Bakunin and sent them to me, and I paged through Hegel's *Logic* again." This was the period in which Marx was writing the *Grundrisse,* and even if we did not have letters showing that he had a second, rather important encounter with Hegel in that period, we could deduce it from the text itself. We have at least a one-thousand-page exception to Bell's assertions that Marx's philosophical references after 1845–46 were only "gnomic." The *Grundrisse* has been, in short, like a reproach from Marx's grave addressed to the carelessness of his friends and enemies.

There is, then, one version of Marx's humanism: that he got over it, quickly and decisively, when he was twenty-seven (Althusser) or twenty-eight (Bell) years old. In this reading, the mature Marx is not a spiritual materialist, or spiritual in any sense of the word. He is a prophet of impersonal economic and social structures that tower over puny men and assign to them the personifications they must assume. There is a part truth in this, for Marx did depict such an alienated world—but, then it must be quickly added, it horrified him precisely because he maintained the humanist values of his youth. And even if one abstracts from Marx's ethical judgments and simply focuses on his analysis of social reality, he never made man insignificant.[2]

II

Given this rejection of Bell and Althusser, there is hardly any need to explain my sympathy for Erich Fromm's defense of the spiritual element in Marx's materialism. Indeed, Fromm has his own description of the Marxian underground which is a central idea of this book. Moreover he makes some extremely shrewd comments on Bell, picking up one misquotation of the *Theses on Feuerbach* that fits in with the misinterpretation of the Foreword to *Das Kapital*. Therefore it is with some reluctance and in a fraternal spirit that I make this critique of Fromm. It is dangerous to sentimentalize or overspiritualize Marx—though not as dangerous as turning him into a philosopher of totalitarianism. I deal, then, with an understandable, fruitful error.

Fromm, as I noted earlier, sees Marx as aiming at the "full realization of individualism, the very aim which had guided Western thinking from the Renaissance and the Reformation far into the nineteenth century." And he insists, quoting Marx, that the latter

interpreted history "based on the fact that men are 'the authors
and actors of their history.' " Socialism, he writes,

> must satisfy man's need for a system of orientation and devotion;
> . . . it must deal with the questions of who man is and what the
> meaning and aim of his life are. It must be the foundation for
> ethical norms and spiritual development beyond the empty phrases
> stating that "good is that which serves the revolution" (the work-
> er's state, historical evolution, etc.)

Let me turn to this last comment first, for it has to do with the
spirit in which one approaches Marx's philosophy. In the classic
period of the Second International, Marxism in Central Europe
unquestionably functioned as a kind of substitute religion, and it
has performed that function for some intellectuals, but not for a
coherent mass movement, since then. Marx himself, I suspect,
would have been quite suspicious of that trend and, however one
reads the thoughts of a dead man on this issue, living Marxists
certainly should be. There is a philosophy, a vision of man, that is
at the center of Marxism, and it informs its analysis as well as its
morality. But it is not and cannot be the basis of a "system of ori-
entation and devotion." For every time someone has tried to turn
Marxism into a faith, a *weltanschauung,* the results, from Friedrich
Engels on, have been unhappy at the very best.

Marx did not even address himself to questions that are at the
very heart of religion. He was an atheist who accepted the world
stoically, and understood that even communist revolution would
not totally transform the human condition. Death, which is at the
center of so much religious meditation, would remain. Indeed,
Marx had no response to all those who had died or would die mis-
erably in that charnel house of history which precedes the socialist
possibility. The short and brutish existence to which most people
had been condemned would not somehow be justified by being seen
retrospectively as a moment in "mankind's" progress. Indeed,
Marx thought it the religion of servility to counterpose "mankind"
to the self. He left many questions unanswered because he thought
them unanswerable; Promethean that he was, he always understood

that there were unalterable limits to human life. It is precisely on the outer edge of those limits that religion stands with its transcendental reply to death and evil. Marx thought such an enterprise hopeless and superstitious even though in the premodern age it had been the most profound expression of the human spirit.

Now, it is clear that Fromm is not trying to set up a new atheistic religion. He is emphasizing a certain community of impulse that links Marx to the Messianic tradition and that properly helps dispel the myth of his crass, sordid materialism. But Fromm blurs Marx's dialectical relationship to that tradition: that he breaks with and turns on it, even as he continues it in a new and secular form. In so far as Fromm overemphasizes that continuity between Marx and the great moralists, he understates what is distinctive in him and—inadvertently—lays the basis for a Messianic interpretation of an anti-Messianic thinker.

An undialectical one-sidedness is visible in the other quotations from Fromm. Marx indeed believed that men are "the authors and actors of their history," but from first to last he always immediately added that they were also creatures of that history. The world of the previous generations, with its economic, social and political structures, is the necessity within which men assert their freedom. It is significant that Fromm, who obviously is perfectly well aware of this Marxian truism, does not mention it at crucial moments in his analysis. The brilliant psychoanalyst, one suspects, makes a political Freudian slip.

The same trend is visible in Fromm's assertion of Marx as the culmination of the individualist tradition. For Marx—and Fromm himself was one of the first scholars to develop this theme—there is a relationship between personality and social structure. In precapitalist societies, the young Marx stressed, the individual is integrated into a community. His station in life is inherent in the work he does, his economic position and his political status are identical. In the bourgeois order, on the contrary, politics are institutionally divorced from social class. Rich men and poor men are "equal" before the law and unequal in fact. The private man, who is really crucial, is divorced from the public man. Individualism, as Marx defines it, is the ideology that takes this historically specific personality of the capitalist era and considers it to be the norm of "human nature."

The mature Marx reiterates this insight in the profound philosophic meditation of the 1857 Introduction to the *Critique of Political Economy*. The individual is taken by the great bourgeois thinkers of the eighteenth century to be a fact of nature. Actually, he is the product of a long and complex historic development.

> The deeper we go back in history [Marx writes], the more the individual, and therefore also the producing individual, appears as dependent, the member of a great whole, first of all quite naturally in the family and then in the expanded family of the tribe, later on in the communes that arise out of the opposition and fusing of the tribes. It is only in the eighteenth century, in the "civil society," that the various forms of social interrelationship are counterposed to the individual as mere means for his private ends, as an external necessity. However, the epoch which brings forth this standpoint, that of the isolated individual, is precisely the one in which there are the most developed social . . . relationships.

Individualism, then, was a distorted way of viewing the development of society's social powers as if they were the work of private men. As such it was bourgeois through and through, duplicating in its conception of man that very private-social schizophrenia that is the foundation of the capitalist economy. This is the way in which human beings appear in a society in which there is the universal and reciprocal dependence of people who are indifferent to one another. And here, as throughout bourgeois thought, the great error was to take human nature as it was defined under capitalism and equate it with human nature as such. So, for example, an Adam Smith would argue that it is of man's essence to truck and barter. But that, Marx would say, is not his "essence"; only his characteristic behavior in one transitory era.

Marx, of course, prized the accomplishments of individualism as much as he did those of capitalism. He acknowledged his profound debt to the great thinkers who articulated this philosophy, and he saw them as participants in the great advance of the bourgeois revolution. But, when all is said and done, he was also their firm and principled opponent, insisting that the increasingly social reality of the bourgeois economy and society could no longer be contained within capitalist, individualistic structures. He was, after all, the prophet of consciously socialized man. Fromm, with an understandable and even commendable desire to rescue Marx from the calumny that he advocated anthill regimentation, overreacts and turns the inspired critic of individualism into the culmination of the system he was trying to destroy. So, man for Marx is not the mere plaything of social structures, as Althusser and Bell think; but, then, neither is he primarily spirit, will, activity, as Fromm intimates. At a given historic moment he is both, and the intermix of freedom and necessity will vary in a complex way in different societies.[3]

III

But does all this mean that there is a seamless philosophy to be found in Marx, a spiritual materialism that inspired both his youth and his maturity? It would be absurd to argue that there was no change, no growth, in Marx. When he wrote the *Economic Philosophic Manuscripts* in 1844, he had just begun to read economics. (He later said that he found himself for the first time in the "embarrassing position" of having to speak on "the so-called material interest" in 1842–1843.) Clearly he led a rich intellectual life and deepened his ideas enormously and changed some of them. Moreover, the political situation, as Lucien Goldmann has pointed out, oriented his attitude on philosophic issues in different ways at different times. The young Marx first thought the proletariat would be the "heir" of classical German philosophy; he then seemed to turn on philosophy as such, out of a disgust with the vagaries of the Hegelian left; and later on he became angry that Hegel was being treated as a "dead dog" and emphasized his debt to him.

Still, there are remarkably persistent underlying values that can be found in *Das Kapital* as well as in the *Manuscripts* of 1844, and they are united by a common conception of man. That conception is not, with one possible exception, terribly complicated, and it is clearly profoundly influenced by a Western tradition that goes back to Aristotle. Yet, even though these basic Marxist themes may sound simple and even obvious in this brief restatement of them, scholars who have ignored them have been led into major errors of interpretation by that fact. Last, but most certainly not least, I believe that the Marxian vision of man is accurate and provides the firmest foundations for a twenty-first-century humanism.

Man, the young Marx writes, is a "species being," a concept which, in part, he borrowed from Kant. This means a number of extremely important things.

First, "in the mode of life activity lies the entire character of a species, its species character, and free, conscious activity is the species character of man."

> The animal is immediately one with its life activity. It does not differentiate itself from it. It is *it*. Men make their life activity itself an objective of their will and consciousness. . . . Conscious life activity differentiates men immediately from animal life activity. Only through it is man a species being [*Gattungswesen*]. Only in this is his activity free activity.

So, man's "species being" is that which, first of all, distinguishes the human species from all the rest of nature.

Marx continues:

> In the practical creation of an *objective world,* in *working-up* [*Bearbeitung*] inorganic nature, man proves himself to be a conscious species being. . . . To be sure, the animals also produce. They build nests, dwellings, like the bees, beavers, ants, etc. But they only produce what they, or their young, need immediately. They produce one-sidedly, while men produce universally; they produce only under the domination of immediate physical needs, while man produces even when he is free from physical needs and first truly produces in freedom from them. . . .

In saying these things, Marx is defining both a reality and a potential. It is free conscious activity that differentiates the human species from the animals; and it is through labor, through a transformation of nature that also transforms its author that this species activity manifests itself. Yet, labor is alienated labor, and in it the worker "does not affirm himself but denies himself, feels not happy but unhappy, does not develop his free physical and spiritual energy but mortifies his body and ruins his mind." So, man the worker comes to feel more at home in his animal functions of eating, drinking and procreating, and perceives himself as animal when he engages in the specifically human process of shaping his environment. He is alienated, both in the act of production, where capitalism degrades him as an adjunct of the machine, and in the distribution of the products he has made, where his socialized powers create the means for others to exploit him better.

Man, then, is a "species being," in a double sense: subjectively in that he, and he alone in nature, is conscious of himself as part of a species; objectively, in that he transforms the world and increasingly lives in a second nature of his own making. Indeed, in the process man creates his own senses. Marx writes, in an extremely important passage, "The formation of the five senses is a work of all previous history." Senses that exist under raw, practical needs are not truly human; the starving man wants to stuff himself and has no concern for truly human food; the miserable man has no taste for theater, and so on. Thus "the objectification of the human essence, in both its theoretical and its practical aspects, is necessary to make men's senses *human* . . ."

Now this, as Leszek Kolakowski has pointed out in a brilliant essay, is a most radical proposition, one that undermines much of what has passed for Marxist epistemology for years. The senses do not, in the Marxist view, "reflect" an external reality that is independent of the subject. That has been an article of faith for realistic philosophers from Aristotle through Locke to some contemporaries, and since both Lenin and Stalin held a version of the thesis, it has been a dogma of the world Communist movement for over half a century. Only Marx, with his rigorous and revolutionary insistence on the self-creation of humanity, did not hold this position. For him, the data of man's senses were not simply given by a world out there; rather they were progressively human products, human needs, human responses. The way we see and touch and hear is the work of our previous history, not of blind, inanimate, deaf nature.

There is, Kolakowski says in summarizing the Marxian vision, "a continuing dialogue between human needs and their objects.

This dialogue, called work, is created by both the human species and the external world, which thus becomes accessible to man only in its humanized form. In this sense we can say that in all the universe man cannot find a well so deep that, leaning over it, he does not discover at the bottom his own face."

All this, one might object, sounds attractive and poetic, particularly in Kolakowski's breathtaking image. But is it Marx? I would argue that this view of man in the world runs through every serious work that Karl Marx wrote and that a central theme of his whole life—that people were turned into things and things into persons—cannot be understood without it. This seemingly simple distinction between man and the animals is, as Bertell Ollman rightly remarks, "the generally unrecognized foundation on which Marx erects his entire conception of human nature." (See Appendix E, § 3, p. 387.)

For example, compare this passage from Volume I of *Das Kapital* with the quotations from the 1844 *Manuscripts:*

> Labor is first a process between man and nature in which man mediates, regulates and controls his interchange with nature through his own act. He is counterposed to the stuff of nature as a natural power. He sets in motion the natural forces that belong to his own body, arm and leg, head and hand, in order to appropriate the stuff of nature in a form that is useful for his own life. As he thus works upon and changes nature outside of him, at the same time he changes his own nature. He develops the powers slumbering within him and subjugates the play of their powers to his own domination. We are not here concerned with the first, instinctive, animallike form of labor. . . . We understand here labor in a form in which it belongs exclusively to men. A spider performs operations which resemble those of the weaver, and in the construction of its hive a bee shames the human architect. And yet, what distinguishes the very worst of architects from the very best of bees from the outset is that the architect builds the structure in his imagination before he erects it in reality. At the end of the labor process there is a result which at the beginning only existed in the imagination of the worker, and thus in an ideal form. Not only does he accomplish a transformation of the form of nature; he also effectuates in nature his own purpose, which he is con-

scious of, and which determines the mode and manner of his action as a law to which his will must subordinate itself.

This passage is obviously infused with the same vision as the 1844 *Manuscripts:* it is free activity and purposiveness that differentiate man from animals; it is through labor that man creates his own essence; and so on. If Althusser and Bell had understood this relatively simple proposition, they would never have made the error of assuming that, when Marx described the subordination of the human personality to social-class mechanisms, he was depicting a fact that was both permanent and good. For the values contained in the writings of 1844 and in *Das Kapital* lead straight to a central point that was crucial for Marx throughout his life: that the transcendence of this alienation, in revolutionary practice as well as in analytic thought, is the basic task of socialism.

This idea can be found in a document that Marx wrote in 1843—that is, long before the supposed rupture between his youth and his maturity—and find these words: "As religion does not create men, but men create religion, so the political order [*Verfassung*] does not make the people, but the people the political order." This concept, which is so central to Marx, is not original with him. It was, among other things, basic to Feuerbach and his critique of Hegel. Hegel, Feuerbach said, and Marx repeated on numerous occasions, had inverted subject and object—that is, he had made the idea the principle of reality rather than the other way around. "The new philosophy," Feuerbach said in counterposing it to Hegel, "does not have the *subject,* the *I, the absolute,* as its principle of knowledge, not *reason in the abstract,* but the actual and entire being [*Wesen*] of man."

Marx and Feuerbach agreed that Hegel turned things into ideas and ideas into things. But then they disagreed on a crucial point. Feuerbach thought that Hegel could be turned upside down rather easily. He argued that if only people became aware of his inversion, then man would appear as he actually was, a free and universal being. Marx saw that potentiality in humans, but he knew that it was not yet a fact, because of the limitations of presocialist history. For capitalism (and class society in general) had its own version of

Hegel's proposition; only, it carried it out in reality rather than speculated about it in thought. In this society, spirit was "thingified," and things came to seem to be persons; workers became the instruments of their machines; money took on a mystic, self-generating quality. In short, Marx took Feuerbach's analysis of Hegel and socialized and historicized it. That marks a critical difference between a brilliant philosopher and a genius of epochal rank.

The insight that Marx thus developed as a philosopher will be found at a climactic moment of his intellectual life, in Section 4 of Chapter I of *Das Kapital,* "The Fetish Character of the Commodity and Its Secret." The image of the fetish—of a thing endowed with spiritual qualities by a superstitious people—had been with Marx all his life, and it was obviously ideally suited as a metaphor for the inversion of things and persons. The very first time he spoke on the "material interests," in 1842, Marx had commented that the Cuban natives thought that gold was the fetish of the Spaniards. But, he added, ironically, at least the natives used their fetishes to protect men. The Spaniards and the Germans did not.

The "fetish character" of the commodity arose because the source of its value, the social labor of man working in interdependence, was transmuted in capitalism into an objective character of the product, into a price. That interdependence was isolated and indifferent; it could not straightforwardly assign value to the satisfaction of needs, but only to sales on the market, the only place where private labors became social. Thus, as Chapter 5 showed, the productivity of socialized man was seen as the productivity of "capital," of machines or money, and human relationships were turned into commodities. Given the central position that this concept of fetish, of the inversion of persons and things, occupies in both the early writings (as far back as 1842) and *Das Kapital,* it is small wonder that Louis Althusser suggests that the first chapter of Marx's masterpiece be rewritten to rid it of what he regards as a Hegelian focus. The only problem is that this "Hegelianism" involves the basic values and perspectives of *Das Kapital* and all of Marxism.

It would not do, however, to respond to Althusser's absurdity about Chapter 1 with a counterabsurdity: that in 1842, when he first concerned himself with the social question, or in 1844 when he wrote the *Manuscripts,* Marx's use of the word *fetish* means that he had already developed the basic theory of *Das Kapital.* That is obvious nonsense. Indeed had Marx died in 1844 he would have gone down in socialist intellectual history as a brilliant and perceptive man, but he would not have inspired a movement or made a permanent, major contribution to modern culture. Most of the insights and perceptions of those early writings are to be found in other authors—in Kant, Saint Simon, Hegel and Feuerbach, in particular—and in the art of the era, especially romanticism. Early on, Marx began to give them his own characteristic interpretation, but that hardly constituted a significant breakthrough.

What happened between 1842, when Marx used the concept of fetishism to explicate a debate in the Rhineland legislature, and 1867, when the first volume of *Das Kapital* was published, was that he made a rigorous analysis of exactly how fetishism was built into the capitalist system. What had been an accurate perception now informed one of the most remarkable syntheses in the history of thought. Marx's basic values—his "philosophy," in the popular sense of the word—did not change with regard to the essentials, but it became part of an analytic achievement that he could not even have imagined as a young man. And yet, if one ignores those deceptively simple generalizations about the human species from the early years, then it becomes impossible to understand the intricate intellectual structure of Marx's maturity.[4]

IV

As a tool of social and economic analysis, the concept of man as a spiritual materialist is almost empty of meaning. That is, it provides some very broad and basic guidelines—in any society at some time there will be an interaction of freedom and necessity, of men as simultaneously creatures and creators of their environment—but that will tell almost nothing about a specific situation. The algebraic formulas have to be filled in with the numbers of real life and the personal skill and insightfulness of a Marxist will have a great deal to do with how well he uses Marx's categories. It is a dream of the small Marxist sects (usually based on a simplistic interpretation of the career of V. I. Lenin) that Marxism provides them with a philosopher's key, that they somehow can anticipate the future and therefore be so much better prepared to meet it than any one else. Only, this is never the case.

Still, when one looks at Marxist failures, or at pseudo Marxisms, it is often possible to see the basic flaw in a one-sided reading of the fundamental Marxist perspective. It then turns out in retrospect that the methodology that such thinkers employed was—as every methodology in the study of society is—an implicit assertion about the nature in man. Two brief examples, one from American Populism, the other from Cuban Communism, can serve as illustrations of how values and moral vision can affect and distort political analysis.

American Populism, it has been understood for some time, presents itself as a curious amalgam of the right and the left, of xenophobia and anti-Semitism on the one hand, and militant hostility to Wall Street on the other. One reason for this strange mixture was brilliantly dissected by Christopher Lasch in his *Agony of the American Left*. It is particularly relevant here, because the assumptions about human nature which led the Populists astray are often confused with Marxism—sometimes by Marxists.

Lasch writes:

The Marxian tradition of social thought has always attached great importance to the way in which class interest takes on the quality of objective reality, so that the class basis of ideas is concealed both from those whose class interests they support and from those whom they aid in exploiting. Lacking an awareness of the human capacity for collective self-deception, the Populists tended to postulate conspiratorial explanations of history. These were by no means the crude fantasies that some historians have seen as the Populist's only contribution to political discourse. They could take the form of a sophisticated economic determinism—as in Charles A. Beard's economic interpretation of the Constitution—according to which men consciously manipulate events to serve their immediate personal interests. Many American Marxists have themselves embraced an economic determinism that owes more to the Populist tradition than to Marxism, so that it is not surprising if Marxism is so often confused, by Marxists and non-Marxists alike, with the economic interpretation of history.

Marxism, Lasch rightly concludes, "implies a radical break with the psychology of interests, according to which men rationally perceive and act upon their self-interest." But the Populist thesis is, of course, also an assertion about human nature. In it, men and women are crass materialists in the most sordid sense of the term. Only, the Populists themselves—because they are honest toilers and, in America at least, usually country folk—are exempted from this charge of universal venality. Politically, this belief creates a mood of paranoia and suspicion in which the hated banker is easily transformed into a Jewish banker and a social problem becomes the result of an international Zionist plot. Intellectually, it leads people to look for conspiracies and to assume a nonexistent and immediate identity of objective economic interest and subjective motivation. That robber barons will try to make as much money as possible is a truth which hardly required a Marx to illuminate; that they will thereby promote the rise of the corporation, and their own extinctions, is a complex historical process that needs a Marx to explain it.

Such a pseudo Marxism (or genuine Populism) takes one side of the spiritual-materialist notion and forgets the other, abstracting from the complexities of human consciousness and freedom. It cannot, Antonio Gramsci brilliantly understood, account for errors in history, since every political act is seen as "determined, immediately, by the structure . . ." There is a symmetrical opposite of this mistake. Che Guevara provides a good example of it.

Before turning to the case of Guevara, it is necessary to state in slightly greater detail some assumptions of my own, which were alluded to in Chapter 2. (They are detailed and documented in Chapters 7, 8 and 10 of *Socialism.*) Communist society is not socialist, but bureaucratic-collectivist. It arose in the most backward of the Western nations because there was no bourgeoisie capable of carrying out the capitalist revolution. The material and human preconditions for socialism—a technology of abundance; an educated, urban working class capable of mastering it—were lacking. So a movement calling itself socialist socialized poverty, not wealth, and since there was not enough to go around, classes developed despite all pretensions to classlessness. Modernization occurred under the control of a totalitarian bureaucracy whose monopoly of political power was the means of imposing economic and social control on the workers and peasants. Thus, the dictatorial political structures have the economic function of extorting a surplus from the direct producers and investing it in a way that conforms to the interests of the bureaucracy rather than those of the masses of the people. In such a setting, "socialism" is an ideology—a mask for class rule.

What has just been said applies most closely to Russia, the first bureaucratic-collectivist state. The other countries with this social system reached it in their own distinctive fashions: in Eastern Europe, except Yugoslavia, by an alliance of the national Communists with the Soviet bureaucracy (and its Red Army) immediately after World War II; in Yugoslavia by a revolution carried out within the struggle against fascism; in China and in Cuba by different kinds of revolutions in quite different types of Third World countries. But, for all the distinctions dividing the powers calling themselves Communist—in the Sino-Soviet dispute they are so murderous that they still could end up in war—they have similar modes of production, similar problems and similar limitations. It is from this general perspective that I analyze events in Cuba.

Che Guevara was an idealistic totalitarian who railed against, and sought to transcend, the limitations that history had placed upon him. In the process he put an exorbitant stress upon the spiritual element in Marxism, ignoring its materialist dimension. In a sense, that is very much to his credit, since it meant that he chafed under the rationalizations of Communism. Yet these were and are deeply rooted in a reality that eventually overwhelmed Guevara. Without trying to psychoanalyze a dead man, one cannot but wonder whether he did not seek his own martyrdom because the world (or the Cuba) in which he lived would not permit him to act on his own idealism. That question, however, is not the focus of these brief reflections on Guevara's life and thought. What is apropos here is how a one-sided reading of the Marxist conception of man had the most momentous political consequences.

Guevara himself defined his situation in terms of the young Marx and the old Marx. In a discussion of how enterprises should finance themselves under socialism—whether they should rely on moral incentives, as Che wanted, or upon material incentives as in most Communist countries—he begins with a quotation from the *Economic Philosophic Manuscripts*. It speaks of communism as "fully developed humanism" and "fully developed naturalism." Guevara introduces the text almost apologetically:

> Even in his language, at this time, the influence of the philosophic ideas that contributed to his development was very evident, and his ideas on economics were less precise. Nevertheless, Marx was in the prime of his life and had already embraced the cause of the poor and explained it philosophically, although without the rigorous scientific method of *Das Kapital*. He thought like a philosopher; therefore, he referred more specifically to man as a human individual and to the problems of his liberation as a social being. He did not yet undertake an analysis of the inevitability of the cracking of the social structures of his age and the subsequent period of transition, the dictatorship of the proletariat. In *Das Kapital* Marx emerges as the scientific economist . . . he does not permit philosophical disquisitions to enter into the discussion.

Without becoming mechanistic and describing ideas as a mere reflex of material life, it is possible to see Guevara's position on the scholarly question of the young Marx and the old, in terms of the ambiguities of his own political plight and that of the Cuban revolution. On the one hand he is clearly and strongly drawn to the humanism of the young Marx. On the other hand, he accepts the myth that the mature Marx "did not permit philosophical disquisitions to enter into the discussion." And in parallel fashion, he was both a supporter of Communist totalitarianism, which he pictures as the vision of Marx when he is most intellectually profound, and a partisan of the humanism of the early Marx. The conditions of life in Cuba, formerly a colonial island menaced by an imperial neighbor, did not allow the genuine Marxian synthesis to be put into practice. There was not the secure abundance that could make a society of freedom and classlessness possible; neither was there a vast socialist and democratic movement that, through long struggle, had learned how to assert its own goals in its own way.

In this setting, Guevara interpreted Marx schizophrenically. He accepted the legend of the mature Marx as the scientist of the inevitable triumph of socialism who was an advocate of dictatorship, for that mythic figure justified what was actually being done in Cuba. But, to his credit, Che could not forget that humanist vision that he thought was found only in the young Marx.

The practical issue on which Guevara focused was *incentives*. "We do not deny the objective need for material incentives," he writes, "but we certainly are unwilling to use them as a fundamental driving force. We believe that, in economics, this kind of force quickly becomes an end in itself and then exercises its power over the relationships among men." He asked, Is it possible that a concern with conscience can retard production?* And he answered: "We maintain that in a relatively short time the development of conscience does more for the development of production than material incentives do." But this is precisely his error. He assumes that the Marxian vision of what man can become under conditions of democratically planned and socialized abundance can be operative in a society of scarcity. Where the Populists tend to see a good many people as more maliciously evil than they actually are, Guevara perceived the workers and peasants of his adopted island as more idealistic than the conditions of their life would permit them to be. He was, if you will, an armed Feuerbachian.

So long as the Cuban revolution acted, even if only in a very restricted way, on the premises of a developed Marxian humanism in a situation where they did not apply, it was involved in practical, as well as philosophic, contradictions. Eventually Guevara departed for what still seems to me to have been a Quixotic rendez-

---

* In Spanish, as in French, one word means both conscience and consciousness. *Conciencia,* which is surely the word being translated in these passages, thus has a fecund ambiguity, and the reader could replace "conscience" in the quotation with "consciousness" to get another layer of meaning.

vous with death; Fidel became an orthodox Moscow Communist, even approving the imperialist Russian invasion of Czechoslovakia in 1968. In part, these events were profoundly influenced by conceptions of human nature.

For the fact is that where there is still a pervasive scarcity, most ordinary people cannot afford to be nice to one another. Every one eats his or her daily bread at the peril that someone else will covet and seize it; most effort is, perforce, directed to maximizing a private interest. For people to be able to love one another—for human nature as it has been to be radically transformed into what it could be—it is not enough to have a will. There must also be a way, a material, economic, bread-and-butter way. In Cuba moral incentives were employed in a setting where they could not work. But then the society had to find a substitute for them, and it was embarrassed to go back openly to the material incentives. In Cuba, then, force took over from both moral and material incentives.

I have documented this assertion elsewhere, relying solely on observations of long-time friends of Fidel's regime. I would only add here a more recent statement by a former partisan of the regime. Irving Louis Horowitz wrote in 1972 that in Cuba

> the concepts of heroism, or the heroic economy, or the new socialist man, or working for moral goals are insured ultimately by coercion rather than by a new level of consciousness. The rise of widespread apathy among the Cuban working class, both of the factory proletariat and the peasantry, who are not responding with the anticipated enthusiasm to government calls to hard work, has not been met simply by criticism, but by implied forms of terror.

Clearly, I would prefer not to have to insist on the limitations upon social heroism. It would be a much more humane world if Guevara, instead of Marx, were right. But Marx is right, and facing up to that dialectical relationship of freedom and necessity is the only way to act so as to eventually transcend it. Moreover, the case of Guevara is one more example of how the Populist theory according to which men necessarily act upon the immediate economic self-interest is wrong. In a famous formulation, which might apply to Guevara, Engels understood brilliantly how much more complex is the relationship between consciousness and politics.

He was describing the German peasant revolution of the sixteenth century and dealing with the fate of its radical, communistic left wing led by Thomas Munzer—

> It is the worst thing that can happen to the leader of an extreme party when he is forced to seize power in an epoch which is not yet ripe for the rule of the class which he represents, and for the carrying-out of the measures which this class demands. What he *can* do does not depend upon his will, but upon the level of the conflict between classes and of the development of the material conditions of existence. . . . What he *can* do contradicts all his previous positions, his principles and the immediate interest of his party; and what he *should* do cannot be done. He is, in a word, forced to represent, not his party, not his class, but that class for whose rule the time is ripe.

This is a crucial passage, and it deserves to be seen in all of its complexity, as it applies both to Fidel and Che and to the analysis of society in general. Marx, his critic Karl Popper freely admitted (crediting Karl Polanyi with the original insight), "first conceived of all social theory as the study of the *unwanted repercussions of nearly all our actions . . .*" That is, so to speak, the impact of historical necessity upon human freedom; we do not choose the circumstances under which we act, we are in part the creature of the moment. But then this necessity asserts itself in the consciousness of individuals honestly and sincerely. Che Guevara's bona fides is not an issue, and it is only in the Populist perversion of Marxism that his betrayal of principle—or his tortured betrayal and affirmation of it—is seen as the outcome of a plot. And finally, it is precisely the function of socialism to reduce the realm of the unintended consequence by expanding the realm of free consciousness.

Apply Engels' brilliant formulations to Fidel and Che. They both began with the premises of a humanist socialism; they both were forced to confront the fact that the preconditions did not exist that would permit those ideas to become reality. The one went to Bolivia and death; the other became a supporter of orthodox Communism, representing, not the working class in whose name he speaks, but a new bureaucracy carrying out the modernization of his nation. In all of this, one sees in dramatic, but "real-life," form the possibilities and limitations of a spiritual humanism at a given moment of historic time. In the case of Cuba, both the conception and the reality of human nature at that particular epoch had the most critical practical consequences.

Finally, most important distinctions must be made: between Marx's conception of man as the basis of an ethic, as a human-behavior hypothesis which is important to analysis, and as a prophetic anticipation of what mankind can become. On the first two counts, Marx is on demonstrably solid ground. On the third, he may be right and he may be wrong, which is one more way of saying that his thought is not a closed system. It cannot, like bourgeois thought, refuse to contemplate its own death. It insists upon its own humble, and possibly transitory, origins in historic time.

First of all, there is the Marxian "should." It is, of course, well known that Marx fought against all those who would locate the ethical imperative in the imagination or the spirit. He insisted that it was a matter of social and historic reality, that what should be done was always limited by what was possible. As he wrote in 1875, "rights can never be higher than the economic forms of society and the cultural development which they condition [*da durch bedingte Kulturentwicklung*]." When, as in Engels' analysis of the Peasant War in Germany, a leader (or a follower) tries to act upon an ethic that is not historically ripe, then there will either be failure or self-betrayal.

All this is well known and carefully emphasized by those who prefer their Marxism without a horizon, who make it into a justification of the brutalities of the present (much like that famous Hegelian phrase that whatever is real is rational). Only, Marx himself would not accept such a pragmatic simplification of his thought. Even though he thought that British imperialism in India was awakening a nation from its torpor and doing the work of progress, he condemned the acts of the army that effected this process as criminal and immoral. That was because, in addition to his insistence on the social relativity of morality, Karl Marx held to a theory of human nature that provided him with a quasi-absolute standard of that morality at any given moment.

Marx's absolute is not, of course, absolute in a philosophic sense; it is relative to the human era. Man as a species being characterized uniquely by free conscious activity emerged at a point of time, beginning the creation of himself. His nature is clearly finite. But once man did appear, he activated the potential of his exclusive powers; and those powers themselves, even though they change and develop constantly, have a nature of their own. As Marx put it in that passage from *Das Kapital,* man "develops the powers [*Potenzen*] slumbering within him . . ." There is, in short, a potential in human nature that can be perceived even before it is actualized—which, of course, is precisely what the socialist vision does. When the British raj shattered the somnolence of Indian society, it made progress possible and at the same time violated the standards of human conduct based upon the nature of the species.

I find this first aspect of the Marxian conception of man persuasive. Morality must be relative, in that it recognizes the historic and social transformations of its values, and yet also absolute, at least in what concerns specifically human history, for there is a persistent humanity asserting itself in the midst of all the flux. And it provides a norm of right and wrong which is not totally dependent on time and place.

Secondly, the Marxian conception of man is a scientific hypothesis about man's behavior. It holds that man in history and society is best understood by means of a dialectic that sees him as the simultaneous creature and creator of his circumstances. That, it seems to me, is quite true; but its worth as a tool of analysis depends in considerable measure upon the skill and insightfulness of the person who employs it. Marxism is not a system of thought guaranteed to turn every individual into an inspired social scientist.

Thirdly, Marxism is a vision of the possible future. It does not, like Feuerbach, idealize existing men, seeing them as free and universal in their present state. It insists, rather, that class society deforms and stifles that universality and freedom which "slumbers" in man, that they are not "given," but must be won through the most bitter struggle. But it does see, even in the midst of class society, that extraordinary potential of man's species being. There are, however, some who were raised in the Marxist tradition who have come to think that vision utopian. Herbert Marcuse is one of them.

Marcuse writes:

> Not only the political but also (and primarily) the technical apparatus and production itself have become systems of domination into which the laboring classes are incorporated and incorporate themselves. The "inner logic of their condition," according to which they were the historical agents of socialist humanism, is no longer *their own*. The objective identity of socialism and humanism is dissolved. . . . Marx underrated the extent of the conquest of nature and of man, of the technological management of freedom and self-realization. He did not foresee the great achievement of technological society: the assimilation of freedom and necessity, of satisfaction and repression, of the aspirations of politics, business and the individual.

What Marcuse and many others are saying is that repressive society has become so technologically accomplished that it can afford to bind its people with comfortable, golden chains. He therefore does not look to the workers, whom he deems integrated into the alienated order, but to the marginal people, the underclass, the minorities and the like. That alternative to Marxism is no more compelling than when Bakunin first gave it its classic articulation. The *Lumpenproletariat,* with all its problems of internal demoralization and disintegration, is not going to take over an advanced technological society and run it along humanist lines. It must help to destroy that society, but it simply does not have the cohesiveness, the discipline, the democratic tradition, required for the makers of a technologically humanist world.

I take Marcuse's case as being more radical than he himself is willing to admit. It really asserts that Marxism—that is, the dream of a mankind controlling its own destiny through its free and conscious activity—no longer correctly anticipates the future. That may be; it may not be. For in this last portion of the incredible twentieth century, the variables are in such whirling motion that only a fool can say that he or she knows their outcome. Therefore, it seems to me that Marxism must be more chastened, but not less militant, understanding that its humanism is not an inevitability, but simply the best possibility that mankind can struggle for.[5]

CHAPTER 7

THE MARXIST PARADIGM

THERE is a Marxist paradigm.

Even though it shares insights with, and has influenced, the various social sciences, it is distinctive and cohesive both as a method and in the results it facilitates. It is not, it should be obvious by now, a rule book or a set of equations that can be used with automatic brilliance by enthusiasts or impartial observers. It poses the right questions about the contemporary world; it suggests some profound ways of seeking out the answers; and it is therefore relevant to the theory and practice of the twenty-first century.

However, before I attempt a summary outline of that paradigm as it has emerged in the last six chapters, I want first to confront a serious objection to its very existence. This is not to make one more refutation of the refutations of that mechanistic and simpleminded "Marxism" that has worked so many indignities upon Marx's memory and meaning. It is to take up the sophisticated assertion that all that is worthwhile in Marx has been co-opted by the academy, while the embarrassing, Hegelian pretenses have been mercifully forgotten.

Two of the finest Marx scholars, T. B. Bottomore and Maximilien Rubel, put the case in this way:

A great deal of Marx's work is a permanent acquisition of sociological thought; the definition of the field of study, the analysis of economic structure and its relation with other parts of the social structure, the theory of social class and the theory of ideology. But the incorporation of Marx's ideas entails the disappearance of "Marxist" sociology. Modern sociology is not the sociology of Marx any more than it is the sociology of Durkheim or Weber or Hobhouse. It is a science which has advanced some way towards freeing itself from the various philosophic systems in which it originated, and with which its founders were still embroiled.

I think Bottomore and Rubel are wrong. Academic sociology obviously has incorporated many Marxist insights and preoccupations into its discipline. Even the functionalists, the conservatives who dominated American sociological theory in the fifties, could pick and choose from a Marx they basically opposed. In part, the functionalists, who first emerged within the discipline of anthropology, helped overcome that parochialism of the Western mind that Marx found so limiting in Adam Smith and David Ricardo. For instance, they saw a kinship pattern that seemed bizarre by European standards, not as an immature or perverse precursor of today's institutions, but as an adaptation to the requirements of a time and place. But functionalism also had a conservative bias and its source is quite revealing in terms of the Bottomore–Rubel thesis. It focused upon what held a social order together; it lacked a sense of creative malfunctioning within a system. It borrowed from the Marxian tradition—as W. G. Runciman has brilliantly noted, it, too, is descended from the concept of the organic whole—but it carefully omitted only the essential.

The problem is, as E. J. Hobsbawm has said, that the Marxian model is a synthesis of the functional and the dysfunctional, of stabilizing and disrupting forces. Indeed, all of Volume II of *Das Kapital* is a brilliant demonstration of how capitalism works to expand society's productive powers, and Marx himself noted that one set of his equations could be used to defend the status quo. The academicians tend to focus on the functional and stabilizing in the Marxist analysis, or else on the peripheral. The Marxian sects concentrate on the dysfunctional and disruptive and, in the classic fashion of millenarians, always see the apocalypse at hand. But the genuine Marxian paradigm unites both of these polarities.

Academic sociology, then, could, just as Bottomore and Rubel say, co-opt Marx's theory of social class and ideology and all the rest, but on one condition: that the various Marxist perceptions were wrenched out of their context—that is, out of a theory of society in which the sociological as such, as an independent factor, did not exist. A brief history might illuminate this important point. It shows how mainstream thinkers—with the best will in the world, I am sure—performed a prefrontal lobotomy on Karl Marx. It was only after his more subversive spirit had been surgically neutralized by the economists that he could be sent over to the sociologists for kind treatment. The whole Marx was not, and could not be, taken over by the professoriate, which is one of the many reasons why this book seeks to put him back together again.

Bottomore and Rubel provide an excellent historical summary of Marx's fate among the sociologists. At the first Congress of the Institut International de Sociologie in 1894, Marx was discussed by Enrico Ferri, Ferdinand Tonnies, P. de Lilienfeld and others. (Ferri, who was to make a scientistic reading of Marxism, typically cited the preface to the *Critique of Political Economy*.) In this period Sorel treated Marx as a continuation of Vico, the great Italian historian, and the *Année Sociologique,* under the editorship of Durkheim, paid much attention to Marx in its early years. Max Weber, of course, treated Marx's ideas with great seriousness and they also influenced American scholars, most notably G. H. Mead and Thorstein Veblen.

In saying this, I do not want for a moment to suggest that the sociologists rallied to the Marxist cause. It has been argued that Weber carried on an "epic campaign against the influence of Marx." That is an overstatement, but the overstatement of a truth; and it is certainly important to remember that Weber was to become, in the fifties, patron saint of American academic sociology, which contrasted his insistence on being "value-free" (which was often oversimplified) with Marx's allegedly unscientific political commitments.

Alvin W. Gouldner, the author of an influential critique of academic sociology, even speaks of a "binary fission" in this discipline. On the one side there is

> a protean tradition whose persistent theme has been a criticism of modern society in the name of man's human potentialities and their fulfillment. (It derives from Marx.) The other side of this fission at first crystallized as Positivistic Sociology, which provided the roots of conventional Academic Sociology, as it passed from Comte through Emile Durkheim and English anthropology, to become one of the central sources that Talcott Parsons was to draw upon for his own theoretical synthesis.

Gouldner even reports that in the thirties, Parsons, who was to become the dominant figure in American sociology in the post-World War II period, was a member of a Harvard seminar that studied Vilfredo Pareto in order to mount a counteroffensive against the popular Marxism of the Great Depression.

It was not, then, that the sociologists all became Marxists. But this discipline, from its very inception, did take Marx seriously and regarded him as a relevant man of science. The anti-Marxist concerns of thinkers like Weber and Parsons testify to the existence of a living Marxist current in their field. Gareth Stedman Jones described Marx's influence in much this fashion, speaking of

> Pareto, Durkheim, Croce, Sorel, Michaels, Sombart, Troteltsch and Schumpeter, all examining, developing or attacking Marxism as a system and nearly all published in the years between 1895 and 1910. It might be further suggested that (with the possible exception of Durkheim) the most fruitful work of each of these writers was developed as a reaction to Marxism and can be interpreted as a tortured counterpoint to Marxist propositions.

In economics the situation was quite different. The influential Austrian school of the late nineteenth century was consciously and specifically anti-Marxist. Boehm-Bawerk—Schumpeter called him "the bourgeois Marx"—wrote his famous critique which purported to show all of *Das Kapital* rested upon a gigantic contradiction between Volume I and Volume III. Thus, for over half a century, Marx was treated by most economists as an intellectual pariah. A giant like Schumpeter was an exception to this rule; so was and is

Wassily Leontief. But by and large the profession shared Paul Samuelson's contemptuous opinion: "A minor post-Ricardian, Marx was an autodidact cut off in his lifetime from competent criticism and stimulus." Samuelson, as Chapter 5 noted, has since modified his view somewhat. And yet there was good reason to believe in 1973 that Samuel Bowles and a number of other young Marxist economists were denied tenure at Harvard University because of their intellectual identification with a great heretic who had never run his data through a single computer. (Paul Sweezy had met much the same fate at Harvard one generation earlier.)

How does one explain the very different reception that Marx received from economists and sociologists? Part of the answer has already been suggested in Chapter 5. In the second half of the nineteenth century, economics changed its basic questions (its problematic, or paradigm). It no longer inquired about the distribution of wealth as between the classes of society. It now concerned itself with the determination of relative prices. This shift, as we have seen, coincided with the rise of a working-class socialist movement which made it embarrassing, from the point of view of the bourgeoisie, to discuss the old questions about the distribution of wealth in public. This is not to imply that there was a conspiracy and that venal scholars were paid off by the ruling class to change their basic concerns. There were many other factors at work, including the application of calculus to economic analysis, a method that fit the new marginal theories like a tailor-made glove.

And yet the economists were aware of what was going on outside the wall of their studies, and they responded in sincere, ingenious and conservative fashion. They explained patiently for almost a century that economic crises could not happen if the system were allowed to function properly, and each depression that did take place was shown to be the result of unwarranted interference with a basically sound, laissez-faire, mechanism. It took the catastrophe of the 1930s, when the capitalist roof caved in around the world, to win acceptance for a moderate like Keynes. In America, Keynes is sometimes pictured as a radical, or even as a quasi-Marxist. However, he proudly proclaimed "the class war will find me on the side of the educated bourgeoisie" and described Marxism as "a creed which, preferring the mud to the fist, exalts the boorish proletariat above the bourgeoisie and the intelligentsia." The author of the Keynesian "revolution" was thus a principled antirevolutionary.

But why this remarkable contrast between the respectful reception of Marx among the sociologists and the derision heaped upon him by the economists? Unlike economics, sociology does not deal directly with the distribution of wealth and government policy affecting it. As long as it deals with class status and power, but not with the economic factors working within these categories, it is a relatively "safe" social science. Brilliant, probing descriptions of the alienation of the workers or the anomie of the masses do not lend themselves to translation into contract demands on the part of a union or arguments for a tax on wealth.* Therefore, sociology, so long as it kept its distance from economics, could be allowed a much greater degree of radicalism and could even comment appreciatively on Marx, particularly when he was turned into a theorist of functionalism.

In the case of the volume which introduced Marxism to the American academy—and deeply influenced the young Charles Beard—one does not have to speculate about these matters. E. R. A. Seligman's *Economic Interpretation of History* was first published in 1902. Ironically, since it was based on a knowledge of the original materials, and particularly on the aging Engels' repentant efforts to correct the mechanistic reading of his friend's theory, it is more sophisticated and subtle than almost all of the scholarly books on the subject since then. But what is interesting in the present context is that it explicitly argues for separating Marx's socialist politics and his analyses of the economic crises of capitalism from his method for dealing with history.

* There is some evidence, both in America and in Europe, that this situation may be changing in the seventies and that concern for, and agitation about, life on the assembly line may be spreading among the workers. If this is the case, at least one of the reasons for this development is the *relative* material well-being of those workers as compared with the generations of their fathers and grandfathers. It was, in short, only when a large number of workers felt themselves securely raised above the subsistence level, or at least protected by the welfare state from the more drastic consequences of economic crisis, that they could permit themselves the luxury of worrying about the quality of their daily lives.

This relates to the Bottomore-Rubel thesis about the co-optation of Marx in two ways. First, it suggests that this co-optation could take place only if Marx were split in two, with his dangerous side being laughed out of intellectual court by economists, while his less threatening side was granted a certain legitimacy by sociologists. Secondly, and more important from the point of view of a chapter that will try to summarize the Marxian paradigm, it emphasizes a critical aspect of that paradigm itself: its analysis of the mutual interaction of the factors that are treated by academic social science within separate, and often hermetically sealed, disciplines. For it is this aspect of the Marxian theory that treats of social class, not simply as an effect of the mode of production, which is studied in and of itself, but as a cause and effect in a coherent economic-social formation that turns people into things or into mere members of social classes, which is one variant of the reifying process.

So, Bottomore and Rubel write quite accurately if one takes Marxist sociology to be defined in the same way as academic sociology, as a discrete specialty. (Or, should one write, a discreet specialty?) Only, Marxist sociology cannot be defined in that fashion and remain Marxist. And therefore, even though I have enormous respect for these two scholars, I think they mistake exactly what it is that has been co-opted. It is not Marxism, but some ideas taken from Marx in defused form. There is, however, another objection to the notion of a Marxist paradigm, and it is found in Marx's own writing.

For Marx, form and content are integrally related to each other. The method adopted for the study of capitalist society is, in considerable measure, determined by the very character of that society itself. Thus, when one has decided how to approach an issue, one must have already done most of the work in settling the issue itself. In such a Marxist perspective, it is impermissible to present a list of methodological propositions that are abstracted from the problems they are supposed to illuminate. So there is no such thing as *a* Marxist paradigm, unless one stays on a level so general that it is not particularly profound. Rather there are a series of actual and potential Marxist paradigms. The one outlined in this chapter is derived from Marx's own dissection of capitalism. It is then somewhat modified in Part II of this book as it is used to analyze, not a completely different social-economic formation, but a new stage of that organic capitalist whole that Marx himself so brilliantly described. In a very real sense, one must reinvent the Marxist method each time it is turned toward an emergent historic reality.

Henri Lefebvre well understood how Marxism is inherently restless, dissatisfied with all fixed and certain theories, including the Marxist ones; how it is congenitally "revisionist."

> The research which extends Marxist thought [Lefebvre wrote] doesn't try to discover or construct a coherence: an "urban system" of structures and urban functions in the interior of the capitalist mode of production. A really Marxist approach subordinates coherences to contradictions. If it is necessary to state and accept the inverse, to understand the subordination of conflicts to the forces of cohesion, then Marx is wrong, his thought is obsolete, the bourgeoisie has won.

One final stricture is in order before proceeding to a brief summary of the Marxist paradigm. The recent vogue of this concept is the result, we know, of Thomas Kuhn's brilliant use of it in his *Structure of Scientific Revolutions.* Kuhn uses it to explain the development of the physical sciences. That, however, does not in the least mean that the notion can simply be transferred from chemistry to sociology or economics, particularly if one is a Marxist. The social sciences deal with an area of political policy importance, which is to say, of class struggle. Their very data are, more often than not, works of art, arguments in the guise of facts, rationales that pretend to be mere definitions. As a result, there are immediate and direct motives (usually unconscious and sincere) on the part of the powers that be, both material and intellectual, to avoid even the discussion of unpleasant truths.

The subject matter of the physical sciences is not alive, and the data do not talk back deceptively. Moreover, it is obviously easier to test hypotheses in this area. Even if it is no simple matter to "empirically verify" a proposition in physics or biology, and one has to content oneself with a modest demonstration that a thesis can be, but has not been, falsified, the nature of the facts and experiments make it possible to get much more of a consensus than in the social sciences. The latter are, in many cases, still arguing about first principles and basic method; as we have seen, economists can suddenly realize that they have forgotten to define their central term.

So, when I speak of the Marxist "paradigm" in this chapter, I do not want to suggest that there is an agreed-upon Marxist model of society which its proponents and opponents are busy testing, like a theory in molecular biology. The word is used much more modestly here: to suggest that there are some distinctively Marxist questions, and ways of answering them, and that both are pertinent to the understanding and shaping of the future present in which we live. What follows, then, is a modest, even chastened, attempt to summarize some important Marxist methodological themes. The proof of whether I have usefully integrated them into my own thinking waits upon Part II, in which they are used rather than described.[1]

First. The Marxist paradigm is critical about its own definitions and data. Like other theories in the social sciences, it realizes that the facts are not given, that they must be selected on the basis of criteria of relevance and importance. Unlike the rest of the social sciences, it looks for the class bias in the most obvious definitions of "fact." It asserts that the common sense of any given society is a rationalization for that society, that vocabularies normally conceal as well as communicate, particularly when they speak of anything that has to do with power. Marxism, then, is a "critical" theory in the Kantian sense of the term—it probes its own concepts and terms as well as those of its opponents; it seeks to articulate the unstated assumptions of an era and regards their unstatedness as eloquent clues to what a society really means.

Second. Marxism makes no pretense at being "value-free"; yet it seeks to be rigorously scientific. The great vogue of an impersonal and value-free sociology occurred in the intellectually conservative period of the 1950s. As Alvin Gouldner described the situation in a famous essay in 1962,

Today, all the powers of sociology, from Parsons to Lundberg, have entered into a tactical agreement to bind us to the dogma that "Thou shall not commit a value judgment," especially the sociologists. Where is the introductory textbook, where the lecture course on principles, that does not affirm or imply this rule?

In recent years, there has been a retreat from that position among sociologists. Yet, it is still a favorite pose of economists, who present themselves as the humble servants of the equations they write. And even those who now admit the relevance of values in sociology do not do so in anything like a Marxist fashion. So, it is important to linger for a moment over this distinctive aspect of Marx's thought.

Marx's commitment to socialist values is not a political act external to his intellectual work. That is the meaning of the anti-Marxist and Communist doctrine of *partinost,* which requires that the scholar follow the party line on the most abstruse questions of theory. So it was that when Joseph Stalin published an article attacking the linguistic analysis of N. J. Marr, every Soviet member of that discipline promptly executed a 180-degree turn with regard to the basic questions of their subject matter. After all, as Leszek Kolakowski so well put it, "the Greatest Philologist in the World" had spoken. That was, and is, obscene. Unfortunately, there are serious scholars who confuse this vicious anti-intellectualism with Marx's own attitude. Marvin Harris, an anthropologist much more sympathetic to Marx than most, writes that "the Marxist sociologist would seem to enjoy a mandate to change data in order to make it more useful in changing the world. . . ." This does not simply do grave injustice to Marx's actual position, which was scrupulously scientific; it is also internally contradictory. How can falsified facts make it easier to change the world?

Indeed, it is precisely the assertion that the most rigorous objectivity is in the subjective interest of the socialist struggle that is at the center of Marx's attitude. As we have seen, Marx believed—and I think history has proven him right—that economics was intellectually fearless when it was allied with the bourgeoisie in the struggle against feudalism, but that it became timid and even deluded once its patrons had conquered power. The socialist, he held, could afford to be utterly truthful about society because of his or her class position. More generally, the Marxist paradigm suggests that one's analytic view of society will vary according to one's social perspective. From the standpoint of the ruling class, stability is an obvious and overwhelming value; from the standpoint of the workers, or the minorities, this is not necessarily the case.

Normally, however, almost everyone in a society thinks in the terms defined by the dominant class—"The ideas of the ruling class in each epoch are the ruling ideas, i.e., the class which has material power in society is also the possessor of *spiritual* [*geistige*] power." Therefore the workers under capitalism do not ordinarily see through their exploitation; they "feel at home" in their alienated existence. But some workers and some intellectuals who identify with the working class can penetrate the deceptions of society. They do not do so by adopting the actual, existing consciousness of the oppressed, but rather by developing ideas that objectively express their needs. The proof of whether or not this has been rightly done occurs when a crisis takes place and the great mass of people are suddenly awakened from the hypnotic spell that stable, ongoing power has cast upon them. If their perceptions then coincide with the minority who spoke in their name, the latter articulated a genuine class interest.

In this analysis, a great deal of intellectual work concerned with the study of society is ideological. To Marx this means that even serious thinkers doing useful work are bound to, and limited by, the unconscious assumptions that are part of the stabilizing apparatus of the society. So it was that Smith and Ricardo performed tremendous feats in economic theory and yet committed the basic and typically bourgeois error of ascribing capitalist behavior to "human nature."

In effect, then, the Marxist paradigm argues that all theorists who do not make their social-class perspective explicit to themselves and to their audience are operating on the basis of the unstated premises of their time and place. However, a simple declaration to the contrary, an act of fidelity to the cause of the exploited, hardly assures a thinker that he or she will incisively develop the insights which are potentially available from this vantage point.

There are stupid and inept Marxists. But the very content of Marx's critique of capitalist society is inseparably linked to his declared solidarity with the working class. In his perspective, that is a way of intellectual enrichment as well as of political identification.

Third. Men and women are both creatures and creators of their society. In part, their actions are to be explained in terms of their avowed purposes and conscious intentions. But in part, they do only that which can be done at a given moment in historic time. There is, therefore, a dialectic of necessity and freedom, and it constantly leads to consequences influenced by the given circumstances at least as much as by the individual actors.

Fourth. Again it is helpful to recall the Marxist paradigm of the essential determinacy of the economic element in the structure of society, with the reciprocal interaction, at the same time, of the political, social and cultural. One part of the analysis in Chapter 5, above, deserves to be stressed here: The mature Marx did not see his theory of the mode of production as a key to the historical progress from the family and the tribe at the dawn of history to the communist relationships at its close. He insisted, as has been seen, that capitalism was unique in that it was the only mode of production in which domination did not involve personal relationships of dependence. Almost one hundred years after Marx's death, then, we are still on the threshold of Marxism.

Moreover, it is clear, as the concluding chapters of this book will document, that the successor to capitalism will be based on conscious economic planning. It could take the socialist form that Marx looked for—that is, democratic planning by and for the majority of the society—and it could take a form that he did not anticipate—that is, a bureaucratic and exploitative collectivism. In either case, there will have to be a basic modification of the Marxian analysis and its methodology derived from the capitalist separation of the political and economic spheres. Therefore, even as one sketches the Marxian paradigm, it must be understood that events will require us to change it. That change, however, can be accomplished in a Marxist spirit—that is, by focusing upon the new relationship between the direct producers and the surplus that they create. That relationship remains crucial to the Marxist paradigm, even under the unprecedented circumstances of the twenty-first century.

This last point raises an important question of emphasis. Because vulgar Marxism, with its simplistic derivation of political and cultural superstructure from the economic "base," has been the most popular misunderstanding of Marx, it has been ruthlessly criticized throughout this book. But that hardly means that the economic is just another factor, on a par with the social and the cultural. If all of these aspects of the organic whole are seen as interpenetrating one another, the economic still remains primary, both as the *sine qua non* of life itself and as the source of the pervasive light that bathes the entire society. It is, of course, impossible to define this concept with any precision in generalities. One extremely important contemporary case in point should illuminate it in Part II. For now, there is this inadequate summary that is, however, necessary to any broad statement of the Marxist paradigm.

Fifth. The Marxian paradigm looks for contradictions as a key element in the social dynamic. This does not mean, as Engels suggested at length in *Dialectics of Nature,* that there is some universal, Hegelian principle of contradiction in nature and society. It does not even mean that contradictions must play a decisive role in every society. In Marx's analysis of India, for example, there are centuries when they do not. It does suggest, however, that capitalist society is structurally contradictory and that the conflict between its increasingly social way of working together and its still private mode of decision making and allocation of resources is a basic fact of life of the system, the origin of its "law of motion." This has been abundantly confirmed during the last century.

More broadly, the Marxist paradigm contains a theory of social evolution which, if it is used with the scrupulous care that Marx himself observed, can be an enormous aid. It is not the universal key to history, of which the youthful Marx and Engels dreamed, because there are entire historic epochs—the centuries-long stagnation of Indian society—which do not conform to it. But where there is systemic change, this pattern is of extreme importance. Historical evolution and revolution, Marx argued, are powered by a contradiction between the powers of production (which, it will be remembered, include science and the social mode of working together as well as technology) and the relations of production. So it is that the reality of domination and scarcity, along with their ideological rationalizations, which were functional necessities at the outset of a given society, come into conflict with the increased productivity that opens up new possibilities. This process is visible primarily in the economic sphere only in capitalism; in other forms of society it is mediated by politics, religion and even kinship. In the current period, with its exponential explosion of productivity within a creaking institutional framework, it is both the ultimately determinant and immediately dominant fact of human life.

Sixth. The economic takes social form in the shape of the classes which, under capitalism, are determined in the production process. This is not to say, as Ralf Dahrendorf and other critics of Marx think, that the Marxist definition of social class can be reduced to some simple formula—that is, capitalists are owners of the means of production, workers nonowners who toil with those means. In fact, Marx had a complex, developing attitude toward social class and died before he could generalize his own findings and revisions. To the young Marx of the Manifesto, the "distinctive feature" of the modern epoch was that "it has simplified class contradictions. The entire society more and more divides itself into two great, hostile camps, into two classes directly counterposed to one another: the bourgeoisie and the proletariat."

But as Marx matured, he realized that this stark statement had to be modified. As capitalism developed, it economized on labor through an increasing investment in machines and therefore liberated people for all kinds of nonproductive employments (or nonemployments). This economic trend was, as we have seen, the basis of the shift from capitalist asceticism to self-indulgence, from Weber's Puritan ethic to Veblen's conspicuous consumption. "What a fine arrangement," Marx wrote, "that permits a factory girl to sweat for twelve hours so that the employer can use a portion of her unpaid labor to hire her sister as a maid, her brother as a groom and her cousin as a soldier or a policeman." This also made it possible to support a new middle stratum, which stood between the capitalists and workers. And at the same time, the nonowning managers were on the rise within the structure of the corporation: the famous separation of ownership and control, discovered for American social science by Berle and Means in the 1920s, was clearly recognized by Marx in Volume III of *Das Kapital* more than fifty years earlier.

Marx's own theory of class, then, must be inferred from what Althusser calls a "symptomatic reading" of his writing—that is, one generalizes the theory implicit in his actual analyses, but never developed by him. The most important work in this area has been done by Nicos Poulantzas. In Part II I will use Poulantzas' categories to help in the understanding of the American welfare state. For now, a brief statement of two of his most important interpretations should suggest the complexities with which we must deal.

Capitalism, it is well known, is the society produced by the bourgeois revolution. Therefore, it would seem, Marx argued that the bourgeois (or capitalist) class was in charge of that revolution. In fact, as Poulantzas notes, his historical and political writings make almost the opposite point. In England, the bourgeois revolution is, until 1832 at least, largely the work of aristocratic landowners with roots in feudalism. In France, the bureaucracy of Napoleon III (or the rule of Napoleon I) plays a crucial role; in Germany, Junkers, feudal landowners, take the lead under Bismarck. In Japan, the Meiji Restoration is also an aristocratic capitalist revolution from above. Indeed, the evidence is so compelling in this case that one does not even have to make a "symptomatic reading." Engels has already done it for us.

"It seems a law of historical development," Engels wrote in 1892, "that the bourgeoisie was unable to conquer political power in any European land—at least not for a long period of time—in the way that the feudal aristocracy did during the Middle Ages." But, then, this insight is hardly original with Marx or Engels. It can, for instance, be found in the writings of Walter Bagehot, the conservative who edited the *Economist* during part of Marx's lifetime. Moreover, it has been almost universally understood by sophisticated Marxists—which is to say, by a tiny minority—for more than a century. Here, for instance, is one of Max Shachtman's statements of it:

The bourgeoisie was revolutionary primarily and basically only in the sense that it was at once the agent, the organizer and the beneficiary of capital. . . . But never—more accurately, perhaps, only in the rarest of cases—was the bourgeoisie revolutionary in the sense of organizing and leading the political onslaught on feudal or aristocratic society. That would have required either a radical break with the feudalists, for which it was not prepared, or the unleashing of "plebeian mobs and passions," which it feared—or both."

But, then, if one takes this Marxist point seriously, as Marx, Engels and every Marxist of any consequence did, there is an important consequence, one which Poulantzas stresses. Marx did not, and could not, have a purely "economic" definition of social classes, since, in the cases cited, it was possible for the class with the progressive economic "base" to be passive, while a class with a reactionary "base" shouldered the political work of the revolution. These complexities will take on a contemporary importance when we examine the relationship of the business leaders to the welfare state. They will help explain, for instance, why the bourgeoisie which Franklin D. Roosevelt rescued by the New Deal kept throwing the life preserver back at their savior. For now, it will be simply noted that the question of class is crucial to the Marxist paradigm— and not in the least simple.

Seventh. In the Marxian paradigm technology is an extremely important variable. It is not, however, determining for a social system as a whole. For one of the two or three central points of *Das Kapital* is the demonstration that it is not the physical capital itself that is decisive, but the way in which a given economic-social formation uses it. In this analysis—which contradicts the most basic assumption of the current theorists of "industrial" and "postindustrial" society—a factory in the Soviet Union that is identical to one in the United States represents a qualitatively different kind of social fact. It is, of course, still important to analyze the way in which technological change interacts with the structures which give it its basic direction, but it is the structure which is central.

Eighth. Clear distinctions must be kept in mind, as Schumpeter insisted, between Marxian possibilities, symptoms and causes. The possibility of crisis is inherent in the very structure of capitalism, in Marx's analysis. It arises, for instance, out of the fact that the capitalist must lay out his money and produce his commodity without really knowing what the market is. As a result, it is always possible that he will overproduce, and he can even be forced to sell at a loss. But that possibility is not actualized at every moment of the capitalist system. Rather, Marx discerns (and he was the first to do so) cycles of recovery, boom, bust and recovery which take place over a number of years. It is necessary to explain why at a certain point, and not at another, the possibility of crisis becomes real.

But then, in analyzing the actual events which lead to a crisis, another distinction becomes important: between causes and symptoms. The basic cause, Marx argues, will be found in the process of accumulation. In the pursuit of surplus value, capitalism constantly expands its productive capacity and eventually outraces the market itself. So it is that the crash is a crash—that is, a sudden and sickening dive from the top of a boom in which the accumulation of capital had generated prosperity, high wages and the like. One result of this pattern—a symptom of it—is that credit expands on the ascending side of the cycle and contracts on the descending side. "The superficiality of political economy," Marx comments, "shows itself when it makes the expansion and contraction of credit, a mere symptom of the successive periods of the industrial cycle, into the cause of the cycle."

These careful distinctions between the possibility, causes and symptoms of capitalist crisis are regularly ignored by almost all Marx's enemies and a good number of his self-styled friends. The ultraleft Marxists, in particular, like to picture the system as on the verge of collapse at each and every moment because it does indeed contain a built-in tendency toward crisis. But they do not bother with the complex ways in which this general tendency becomes an actuality; they overlook the fact that Marx is a theorist who insists upon periodic capitalist prosperity as well as periodic capitalist crisis. Understanding that requires scrupulous attention to the actual workings of the system at a given moment, not generalities about its structural (and undoubted) iniquity.

These, then, are eight aspects of the Marxist paradigm. They are distinctive in that they provide a framework which is unlike that of the mainstream academic disciplines. Moreover, as we have seen, they integrate subject matters which are normally treated as separate branches of knowledge about society, and that is, in a sense, a ninth, and crucial, aspect of the paradigm. One can say, as against Bottomore and Rubel, that Marx has not been co-opted, that there is a coherent and unique Marxist approach to the analysis of the social world.

But, finally and once again, this paradigm is worthless—or rather, it is obsolete, after having been brilliantly employed once upon a time in the nineteenth century—unless it informs a careful, original and empirical study of new and unprecedented realities. So the proof of the existence of the future Karl Marx must now move from theory to practice, from generality about analytic method to the application of that method to the understanding of the contemporary welfare state in America.[2]

PART II

The Future Karl Marx

or

The Secret History of the Contemporary Crisis

CHAPTER 8

INTRODUCTION TO A SECRET HISTORY

IN the middle seventies, every capitalist nation in the Western world found itself in a crisis more serious than any that had occurred since the Great Depression of the 1930s. In Britain, which had pioneered and named the welfare state, there was talk of the collapse of the system. Even in the United States, still the strongest power in the world, the serious, established men of power began to speculate publicly on whether a simultaneous depression-inflation might not rend the very fabric of democracy itself.

And yet, most people in the West did not think that these events had anything to do with the capitalist economy as such. They seemed, rather, to be the product of external and fortuitous circumstances—of the cartel of the Organization of Petroleum Exporting Countries (OPEC), which had quadrupled the price of oil between 1973 and 1974, of the increasing demand for food on the world market, and so on. These accidents, including the vagaries of the weather which affected the harvests and thereby the market, were indeed important, and one could hardly blame capitalism for them. But if capitalism could not be held responsible for circumstances beyond its control, it was responsible for what it made of them.

It is the argument of Part II of this book that it was and is the structure of capitalist society that turned the historical accidents of the 1970s into calamitous necessities. The West carefully helped to fabricate its own bad luck. Moreover, this extraordinary process can be understood only in the light of the themes developed by Karl Marx in *Das Kapital* and, above all, in its first chapter.

That last proposition must seem absurd on its very face. *Das Kapital* was written about a mid-nineteenth-century economy, which is as distant from the 1970s as the nuclear reactor is from the steam engine. And Chapter I of that book, we know, is a conscious and extreme simplification of that relatively simple system. What could Marx's Hegelian definitions of use value and exchange value, his theory of the fetishism of commodities, have to do with our world? This anti-Marxist point should be particularly persuasive, since capitalism has been profoundly modified by the welfare state. Isn't it obvious that the system no longer operates according to the "law of value"? It is now planned by governmental bureaucrats; it ceased to rely on the invisible hand of the market years ago, even though it pretends that this is not the case.

The extraordinary fact of the matter, as the next five chapters will demonstrate, is that this welfare state, which has indeed effected profound modifications of the capitalist structure and is even potentially anticapitalist, still follows the basic logic described in *Das Kapital*. Specifically, since the dominant economic institutions of the welfare state are private corporations producing for profit, that state observes capitalist priorities even when they are carried out in what seems to be an anticapitalist manner. In Chapter I of Volume I of *Das Kapital,* Marx made the claim that the fundamental character of the system derived from the few variables with which he constructed his first highly abstract model of it. He did not for a moment suggest that this model exhausted the subject. He only argued that it was the fundamental key to understanding its further development. That still holds in the case of welfare capitalism.

This is not to say that the welfare state is a simple phenomenon. On the contrary, it will be seen that although it is the salvation of capitalism, it is also anticapitalist. It is planned, yet the most important consequences of its foresight are often unintended. It is a triumph of the rich and of the workers and the poor; it is the road toward socialist classlessness and toward an antisocialist new class. It must be defended against its reactionary enemies and attacked because of its reactionary friends. And yet, at the very bottom of these dialectic paradoxes, the welfare state is most decisively capitalist.

The data for demonstrating this last proposition will be taken primarily from the American experience—which is to say, from the most laggard and pinch-penny of the advanced welfare states. But the national differences will be carefully noted and, in any case, the basic mechanisms which operate in the United States are also at work in the capitalist democracies of Western Europe, Canada, Australia and Japan.

The next chapter will begin to describe how the welfare state remains capitalist despite all the modifications of that system. Then Chapter 10 will focus more precisely on the connection between capitalist economic power and welfare-state politics by examining a single, but huge, case in point, the joint corporate-governmental contribution to the energy crisis. Chapter 11 will analyze a group of brilliant, neoconservative theorists whose failure to understand the welfare state derives precisely from their ignoring or denying its capitalist character. In Chapter 12, this theory will become more complex as it takes into account the ways in which the welfare state is not simply capitalist. And the final chapter will attempt a summary statement that, I hope, will show that the Marxist method has permitted us to make a unique dissection of a phenomenon that was not even dreamed of in the writings of Karl Marx. In short, the new Karl Marx of Part I will be seen in Part II as a thinker with a future.

CHAPTER 9

BOURGEOIS "SOCIALISM"

IN the Communist Manifesto, Marx and Engels described "conservative, or bourgeois, socialism."

> A part of the bourgeoisie [they wrote] wants to remedy *social grievances* in order to ensure the stability of bourgeois society. . . . They want to have the existing society, but without the revolutionary, transforming elements.

The function of this "socialism," they went on to say, was not

> the abolition of bourgeois relations of production, which is possible only in a revolutionary way, but administrative improvements, which can go forward on the basis of this mode of production, which thus alter nothing in the relationship of capital and labor, but in the best case lessen the cost of bourgeois domination and reduce its public budget.

It would be nonsense to suggest that this passing *aperçu* of Marx and Engels (which appears in a rich, but often unread, section of the Manifesto) anticipated all the developments of the welfare state. It would be equally silly to ignore the fact that it provides a remarkable organizing insight for the analysis of some of the events of the past century. Indeed, there is a contemporary example of the theory of "bourgeois socialism," one which has been encountered earlier in this book and which is one of the most influential sociological and political ideas of the times. It is the notion of industrial (or postindustrial) society associated with thinkers like Raymond Aron and Daniel Bell.

This concept will be examined in greater detail later on in this chapter and in Chapter 10. For now, one aspect of the theme of industrial society is pertinent. This holds that capitalism, both as a reality and a term for analysis, has been transcended in the advanced Western nations. Where once feudalism, capitalism and socialism were a relevant progression, defining social structures on the basis of their property relations, there is now a new phase of Western society which does not fit into the old categories. Its determining facts are theoretical knowledge and economic growth and it is best described as the "postindustrial" society, which follows upon preindustrial and industrial society.*

In the early version of this theory—say in Bell's *The End of Ideology*—it conformed quite closely to Marx's "bourgeois socialism." In the West, one was told, "there is today a rough consensus among intellectuals on political issues: the acceptance of a Welfare State; the desirability of decentralized power; a system of mixed economy and of political pluralism." And "the workers, whose grievances were once the driving energy for social change, are more satisfied with society than the intellectuals." The conservative utopia derided by Marx was said to have been achieved: a "mixed economy" —that is, a capitalist society with government intervention and a Welfare State—which commanded the loyalty of workers even more than that of intellectuals. Then the 1960s were a period of extraordinary intellectual discontent and, in Western Europe, of working-class militancy. The thesis had to be revised.

---

* There is a certain semantic confusion because Aron and Bell mean roughly the same thing by "industrial" (Aron) and "postindustrial" (Bell) society. Since Bell's book is the more recent and systematic statement of the theme, I will use his vocabulary.

In the more recent statement of it, Bell makes room for political conflict, and yet he still holds that there has been a bloodless, practically invisible revolution since World War II and that it has brought a new class to power. So, once again, capitalism is seen as having been fundamentally transformed, although the 1970s' version of how this was done differs somewhat—and not accidentally—from the 1950s' version.

It is the contention of this analysis of the welfare state that Bell and Aron are wrong and that their revolution did not take place. The most important thing about contemporary society is that it is capitalist, even though that fact has to be understood in a way that revises Marx's first statement of it. In developing this theme, I propose to go back in history, showing that state intervention, accompanied by theories that capitalism was being fundamentally changed, is at least one hundred years old. In noting these precursors of the idea of "postindustrial" society, one does not simply establish its political and intellectual genealogy; one also begins to grasp how basic capitalist structures persist through the most extraordinary permutations. And that is germane to the thesis that they dominate the contemporary welfare state, shaping the disastrous necessities of its response to the accidents of recent years.[1]

I

State management of the economy on behalf of the capitalists dates back at least to Bismarck's Germany.

To be sure, one could locate the origins of the welfare state at an even earlier point in history. There were, as Joseph Schumpeter pointed out, writers who dealt with *"Wohlfahrtsstaat"* themes in the Germany of the eighteenth century; and there were precursors in mid-nineteenth-century France both in theory (Charles Dupont-White) and in practice (Napoleon III). For my purposes, however, the truly decisive moment occurred under Bismarck in the 1870s and 1880s, for it was then that the reform of capitalism was seen as the transformation of capitalism. Engels and his fellow Marxists called the proponents of that notion "state socialists" and considered them to be the heirs of Rodbertus, who had proposed a social monarchy as early as the 1850s.*

In a shrewd comment, which clearly had its ideological origins in Marx and Engels' notion of "bourgeois socialism," Karl Kautsky, the dean of German Marxists, wrote in 1891 that "state socialism" was governmental intervention into a capitalist economy and that it seeks "to put an end to the class struggle between proletarian and bourgeois and to introduce 'social peace' by 'abolishing social classes' and proposes a strong monarchistic state which stands above and independent of the classes." The right wing of Kautsky's own party had mistaken this development with the triumph of socialism itself. In France there was an analogous development as the number of school teachers and civil servants doubled between 1870 and 1913, convincing many of the employees in the expanded public sector that they were building socialism. In Britain, the reform movement of the first decade of the twentieth century often looked to Bismarck. As Winston Churchill, then a Liberal, put it, "Thrust a big slice of Bismarckianism over the whole underside of our industrial system."

Even in the United States, always the most backward of the Western nations in these matters, there were a few shrewd corporation men who saw the possibilities of friendly state intervention. As William Appleman Williams described Mark Hanna's response to the demand for the nationalization of the railroads: "Acknowledging its economic relevance in stabilizing a crucial element of the private-property market place, he merely commented that it was perhaps a good idea—provided it was not done until the corporations had extracted the first-run profits from building and establishing them." And one analyst of American history, Gabriel Kolko, sees the entire Progressive Era at the turn of the century as the triumph of a "political capitalism" in which government and business joined together.

* The phrase "state socialism," is misleading, and it is unfortunate that Engels borrowed it from his opponents even as he was criticizing it. The whole point of that criticism was that "state socialism" was, in fact, state capitalism and it is the latter term which has been used by most twentieth-century Marxists.

Strangely enough, the most perceptive description of the new, statist phase of capitalism at the turn of the century occurred while it was still beginning. Rudolf Hilferding's *Finanzkapital* was a brilliant analysis of how capitalism was centralizing, cartelizing and intertwining with the government. It was, he understood, still very much capitalism, although he opened up the theoretical possibility that total political control of the economy could lead to a new form of society. Later Hilferding was to argue that the possibility of a planned, anticapitalist and antisocialist economy had actually come to pass in the Soviet Union. What is significant, though, is that a major Marxist theorist had exhaustively and critically dealt with a planned capitalism as early as 1909.

Bismarckian "socialism" was one impetus to the illusion that a directed capitalism was not capitalist. The economic policies of the belligerent states in World War I was another stimulus to the same idea.

In every one of the warring countries, the government mobilized the economy, often taking control of critical industries. N. Bukharin, the Bolshevik theorist, commented on these developments in 1915: "The exigencies of the war and imperialist preparations for war, force the bourgeoisie to adopt a new form of capitalism, to place production and distribution under state power, to destroy completely the old bourgeois individualism." Bukharin noted that the "state socialists" (in Engels' sense of the term) were heartened by this trend. He quoted Max Krahman on how the war is bringing a "nationally consolidated Socialism." "Such a Socialism," Krahman said, "we now approach. This is not democratic Communism, less so aristocratic class domination. But it is a nationalism that reconciles the classes."

Bukharin was not taken in by this "socialism." It was, he argued, only capitalism in a new guise. There was no principled difference between a private monopoly and a state monopoly, particularly when the latter had to compete on the world market. Indeed, Bukharin felt that the internal contradictions of capitalism were being collectivized within the various nations, but then were being transposed into the anarchy of international production. In the 1920s Bukharin was a leader of the new Soviet state—until Stalin turned on him at the end of the decade—and he extended his World War I analysis to see in the "trustification of state power" the basis of the stability of world capitalism in the 1920s.

But in his earlier studies of military "socialism," Bukharin had glimpsed the possibility that Hilferding had identified: that these developments might conceivably become the basis for a completely new form of society.

> Were the commodity character of production to disappear [he wrote] (for instance, through the organization of all the world economy as one gigantic state trust, the impossibility of which we tried to prove in our chapter on ultra-imperialism) we would have an entirely new economic form. This would be capitalism no more, for the production of *commodities* would have disappeared; still less would it be *socialism*, for the power of one class over another would have remained (and even grown stronger). Such an economic structure would, most of all, resemble a slave-owning economy where the slave market is absent.

This notion of an anticapitalist and antisocialist successor to capitalism has an obvious relevance to Communist societies. For now, however, the point to emphasize is that Bukharin saw military "socialism" as planned capitalism.

After World War I, a small but significant number of serious thinkers understood that capitalism was now state capitalism. The German Marxist, Rudolf Goldschied, said that the choice was now between "state capitalism or state socialism." He wrote that "the basic problem of the state becomes whether it is more and more in the hands of the private economy, or it has the private economy in its hands." In England, the Liberal John Maynard Keynes announced "the end of laissez faire," and the young conservative and future Prime Minister, Harold Macmillan, agreed. In the United States, Thorstein Veblen perceived the possibility of a new elite of engineers and technicians; in Germany, Walter Rathenau described corporations that were becoming a self-perpetuating law unto themselves, independent of their stockholders.

The recognition of a statified, rationalized capitalism was, then, obviously not a uniquely Marxist insight. But what was Marxist—

and here Goldschied and Bukharin, the Social Democrat and the Bolshevik, were in accord—was the insistence that this whole process was a moment in the history of capitalism, a mechanism for the perpetuation of class domination rather than its transformation. That judgment was catastrophically corroborated when capitalism, for all its modifications, proceeded to break down in an absolutely classic fashion in the Great Depression. And yet, a powerful and dangerous notion had been set loose in these theories of a "socialist" capitalism. In a fatefully influential book of 1920, *Prussiandom and Socialism,* Oswald Spengler saw the future as belonging to just such a "socialism": to an order of discipline, hierarchy and obedience, in which the "human vermin"—the workers—would toil twelve hours a day.

In 1933, Adolf Hitler took advantage of the collapse of world capitalism and turned Spengler's dream into a monstrous reality. There were many who thought that this German fascism represented a new, non- or anti-capitalist, form of society. Some, like James Burnham, were superficial, but reached a wide audience; others, most particularly some members of the Frankfurt school of social criticism, were profound even if their profundity was recognized only by a relatively small group of scholars.* Dissecting the organized horrors of Nazism, they produced what might now be termed an early, pessimistic and sometimes even despairing version of the theory of post-industrial society.

The Nazis themselves seemed to give credence to the notion that they were creating a new system. Their party's full name was the National Socialist German Workers Party. In their struggle for power, particularly during the twenties, the Nazis did not hesitate to stress the "socialist" appeal of their program. "We call ourselves

---

* The Frankfurt school originally thought of itself as Marxist, but did not use the word officially, for political-diplomatic reasons. Later on it developed some criticisms of Marx, which are summarized in Albrecht Wellmer's *Critical Theory of Society.* In my opinion, however, the School remained within the Marxist framework, albeit in a revisionist mood. Indeed, Jurgen Habermas, its best-known contemporary exponent, is one of the most brilliant Marxists at work today. An interesting summary of the Frankfurt theories of fascism can be found in Chapter V of *The Dialectical Imagination* by Martin Jay.

a workers' party," said that evil genius Josef Goebbels, "because we will make labor free, because for us labor is the progressive element in history, because labor means more to us than ownership, education, status and bourgeois rule." And he concluded, "How can we take upon ourselves the ethical right to fight against the doctrine of the proletarian class struggle, if we do not first smash and destroy the basis of the bourgeois class state and replace it with a new socialist organization of the German community."

There were many, including a significant number of Nazis, who believed in this "socialist" rhetoric; so did some of the industrialists who helped Hitler to power, like Fritz Thyssen. And even after Hitler came to power, there was talk of a "second revolution" that would break completely with the old capitalists and politicians. Hitler dealt with that threat by means of a bloody purge in June 1934, yet the grandiose verbiage continued to fool some people. One of them was James Burnham, whose book *The Managerial Revolution* had a considerable intellectual vogue in the forties and fifties. "In capitalist society," Burnham simply asserted, "the role of government in the economy is always secondary," a judgment that ignored the brilliant theories of Hilferding and Bukharin, as well as more than fifty years of capitalist history. From that oversimplification, it was a short step to the proposition that "the basis of the economic structure of managerial society is governmental (state) ownership and control of the major instruments of production." And this, in turn, led to the remarkable conclusion that the New Deal in America was moving in "the same direction as Stalinism and Nazism."

Burnham's thesis is a warning to all those who think statification and capitalism are antithetical; the "thousand-year Reich," which was supposed to be a major component of the managerial wave of the future, collapsed four years after his book appeared, and it was replaced, in West Germany, by Adenauer's conventional version of capitalism. And yet, impressionistic and sloppy as his insight was, Burnham was talking about an important trend in the world economy. (See Appendix F, § 1, p. 390.) The Frankfurt school responded to that same trend, with the difference that its work has lasting value.[2]

II

Actually, there were two tendencies in the Frankfurt analysis. One was represented by Theodore Adorno, Max Horkheimer, Herbert Marcuse and Frederick Pollock; the other, by Franz Neumann. Adorno and Horkheimer wrote their *Dialectic of the Enlightenment* in 1944. What happened in Germany, they suggested, was the unintended consequence of the Enlightenment itself. It was during the Enlightenment that man's intelligence was redefined in an instrumental, positivist fashion, so that one knew the world only in so far as one could manipulate it. This "scientific" ideal prefigured the dictator's relationship to the people. In Nazism, this trend reached an insane culmination. The system—unlike capitalism, which was forced to observe Marx's law of value—recognized no rules; it administered reality, including human reality, and its leaders thought of themselves as the engineers of world history. In the process, the individualistic psyche, which had emerged in the bourgeois age, was expropriated, and the very images in the minds of men and women were put there from on high.

There is an unforgettable literary image of Adorno and Horkheimer's theme. Thomas Mann, who became friendly with them when all three were exiled in the United States, described the composer Adrian Leverkuhn in Dr. Faustus. Driven mad by venereal disease at the same time that German society itself had become insane under the Nazis, Leverkuhn wants to "take back" Beethoven's Ninth Symphony, to repudiate a culture which could have told such rationalist and optimistic lies about the human condition as that magnificent piece of music. For Mann, as for the Frankfurt scholars, the entire humanist tradition was challenged by a Nazism which it did not prevent, which it may even have unwittingly helped to promote.

But if this were the case, then it was not the capitalist use of science and technology, but science and technology themselves, which were the cause of this terrible turn in human affairs. Herbert Marcuse, a onetime colleague of Adorno and Horkheimer, eventually carried the logic of their position to its extreme. In *Reason and*

Revolution, the book that he published in 1941 to defend Hegel against the charge of being responsible for Nazism, Marcuse still used fairly orthodox Marxist categories. Like his friend Franz Neumann, he believed that under fascism "the most powerful industrial groups tended to assume direct political power in order to organize monopolistic production, to destroy the socialist opposition, and to resume imperialist expansionism." In that perspective, Hitler's new order was a totalitarian form of capitalism, but still capitalism.

But by the sixties, Marcuse had reached a position quite similar to that of Adorno and Horkheimer in the *Dialectic of the Enlightenment*—only now he applied it to democratic capitalism, and not just to Nazism. "Domination," he wrote in 1964, "is transfigured into administration. The capitalist bosses and owners are losing their identity as responsible agents; they are assuming the function of bureaucrats in a corporate machine. Within the vast hierarchy of executive and managerial boards extending far beyond the individual establishment into the scientific laboratory and research institute, the national government and national purpose, the tangible source of exploitation disappears behind the façade of objective rationality." (See Appendix F, § 2, p. 391.) This is the left-wing version of the theory of postindustrial society; it describes an essentially postcapitalist, managed system.

But what, then, was the precise character of the new economy? All of the thinkers who interpreted fascism (or postindustrial society) as post-capitalist were fairly specific about the sociology, culture and philosophy of the unprecedented system they described; but they were somewhat vague about its economics. Another colleague of Adorno and Horkheimer's, Frederick Pollock, tried to work his way through that problem. The growth of state intervention throughout the Western world, in both its totalitarian and its democratic variants, was, Pollock argued, a phase of "state capitalism." He used that term because the alternative formulations—that this new order was bureaucratic collectivism or managerial society or state socialism—ignored the fact that "profit interest still plays a significant role and that it [the managed economy] is not socialism."

On the last two counts Pollock was quite right. But then, in the spirit of Adorno and Horkheimer, he added a comment that contradicted his own definition: "With the autonomous market, the so-called economic laws disappear." But if economic laws had disappeared, in what sense could a society be called capitalist? Pollock himself later all but admitted the substance of that point, even while insisting on the term *state capitalism.* "The replacement of the economic means by the political means as the last guarantee for the reproduction of economic life," he wrote, "changes the character of the whole historical period. It signifies the transition from a predominantly economic to an essentially political era."

Pollock was, I think, wrong. Franz Neumann, something of an outsider in the Frankfurt School, was right. In his analysis of Nazism, *Behemouth,* Neumann argued that Hitler Germany itself was run by capitalists, for capitalists and according to capitalist priorities. The consequence of accepting the idea that politics has taken complete command of the economy, Neumann said, was that the "system of mass domination is so flexible that it seems potentially invulnerable from within." In fact, even the Nazis themselves in a candid mood admitted the persistence of capitalist relations. As one fascist editorial put it, the regime recognized "the fundamental importance of the decisive participation of the German big enterprises in the oil and coal industry."

And in another extremely important insight, Neumann showed how the demands for democratic reform had come into conflict with capitalist social structure in the pre-Hitler period. He argued that

> Democratic planning failed because democratic planning must satisfy the needs of the large masses. . . . To satisfy the demands of the large masses, however, means to expand or at least maintain the consumer's good industry; this necessarily restricts the profits of heavy industry. Moreover, in the dynamics of the democracy, one achievement of the masses will lead to further demands.

A capitalist like Krupp, Neumann comments, would not make any concessions to the democratic movement because he feels that to do so would be to concede his class privileges; but under Nazism, where he is no longer menaced from below, he can be "reasonable." Michael Kalecki developed the same thought: "One of the impor-

tant functions of fascism, as typified by the Nazi system, was to remove the capitalist objections to full employment."

On the whole, Neumann had the best of the argument within
the Frankfurt School. Adorno, Pollock, Horkheimer and Marcuse
were right that unheard-of modifications were being made in the
capitalist system; they would even have been right if they had said
that these modifications are the portents of a new order. But in so
far as they suggested that the new order had already arrived, they
were wrong. How else explain the extraordinary vitality of the
capitalist infrastructure in West Germany, which, a generation
after the collapse of Hitler, had built on the ruins of the Third
Reich the most successful economy in Europe? Where Adorno and
the rest went wrong, I think, was in not being sufficiently dialectical
about Nazism, in not seeing that its seemingly, and perhaps potentially, anticapitalist departures were contained within a system
that remained capitalist.

There were, to be sure, revisions required in some of Neumann's
theses in the light of new evidence unearthed after World War II.
Businessmen, it was realized, made much less of a financial contribution to the Nazis' rise to power than had been assumed; and
there was more political control of economic power than Neumann
had been willing to admit. And yet the academic scholarship of
recent years, as Stuart Hughes has pointed out, confirms Neumann's basic propositions. On the Marxist side, Nicos Poulantzas
has demonstrated how, once the Nazis had taken power, many of
the true believers were pushed aside and the bourgeois elements
became dominant.

Max Horkheimer once said, "Whoever is unwilling to speak of
capitalism should keep silent about fascism." He was right.

This does not prove that the theory of postindustrial society is
wrong about the 1970s in the industrial West. Just because capitalism persisted in its Bismarckian, military and fascist permutations is no demonstration that it is dominant in the welfare state
today. I think that is the case, but it has not yet been documented.
What has been shown—and it bears importantly on what will be
argued—is that capitalism has an extraordinary adaptability, that
it is compatible with widespread, and even totalitarian, planning.

Ironically, it takes a Marxist to be properly respectful of the vitality of this system in its obsolescence.[3]

III

Before turning to the data which show that the contemporary American welfare state, for all of its governmental intervention into the economy, is still capitalist, it is only fair to outline some of the contrary propositions of the theory of postindustrial society in a little more detail. Daniel Bell is again the case in point.*

For Bell, three events led to the emergence of the postindustrial society. First, there was the Great Depression, which forced the recognition that the direction of the economy is "a central governmental task." Second, there was state subsidy of the new science-based technology, which became a decisive factor in the 1950s. And thirdly, there was the response to the social demands of the sixties which, though "pell-mell and piecemeal," led the government to make a commitment "not only to the creation of a substantial welfare state *but to redress the impact of all economic and social inequalities as well."* This thesis, it will be noted, is essentially a generalization of the Keynesian experience. The other antecedents of planned capitalism, which were outlined in the previous section, are either briefly mentioned or ignored.

Bell introduced his analysis of this evolution in *The Coming of Post-Industrial Society* with a modest disclaimer. He wrote that he had resisted the impulse to make too large a generalization.

> Instead [he went on], I am dealing here with *tendencies,* and have sought to explore the meaning and consequences of those tendencies if the changes in social structure that I describe were to work themselves to their logical limits. But there is no guarantee that they will. . . . Thus I am writing what Hans Vahinger called an "as if," a fiction, a logical construction of what *could* be, against

---

* I treated Bell's argument in *Socialism,* and there will be some unavoidable repetition of ideas from that book in this section. I have tried, however, to confine myself to brief summaries of statistics and arguments from that earlier work, and I have added new information—and, I hope, new insights—which have arisen since its publication.

which the future social reality can be compared in order to see
what intervened to change society in the direction it did take.

The only problem with this humble agnosticism is that Bell does not
act upon it. He continually makes assertions about facts, not tendencies, i.e. that the welfare state seeks *"to redress the impact of all
economic and social inequalities."* That claim, as will be seen, is
simply not true; but what is important at this moment is that the
very fact that it is made indicates that Bell's "as if" image of his
thesis is an escape clause, not a description of his work.

There are, Bell says, five "dimensions, or components" of the
term, "postindustrial society." In the economic sector there is a
shift from goods producing to a service economy; occupationally,
there is the "pre-eminence" of the professional and technical class;
the axial principle of the society is "the centrality of theoretical
knowledge as the source of innovation and of policy formulation
for the society"; there is technological forecasting; and decision-
making takes place by means of a new " 'intellectual technology.' "
All of this is clearly related to the growth of the welfare state, particularly in its role as manager of the economy. Bell writes, "A post
industrial society . . . is increasingly a communal society wherein
public mechanisms rather than the market become the allocators
of goods, and public choice, rather than individual demand, becomes the arbiter of services." So, ". . . if the major historic turn
in the last quarter of a century has been the subordination of economic function to societal goals, the political order necessarily becomes the control system of the society." Therefore, "what the
traditional classes fought out in the economic realm . . . is now
transferred to the political realm."

Although Bell does not make the point explicitly (he waffles on
this count), these assertions add up to the theory that the postindustrial society is also postcapitalist. Indeed, if economic function
has been subordinated to "societal" goals, that might even imply
that it is socialist. But then, Bell would argue that the very terms
"capitalist" and "socialist" have become, if not meaningless, not
very useful and that he, and his colleagues, are inventing a new
vocabulary to deal with a new reality. That is his and their right. If,

however, the factual assertions that underpin the new definition—
say, that economic function has been subordinated to "societal
goals"—are inaccurate, then Bell's linguistic innovation is invalid
too.

A critical point that allows one to check the worth of the post-
industrial categories of analysis concerns the ruling class in contemporary society. "If the dominant figures of the past hundred
years have been the entrepreneur, the businessman and the industrial executive," Bell argues,

> the "new men" are the scientists, the mathematicians, the econo-
> mists and the engineers of the new intellectual technology. . . .
> The basic values of society [prior to the postindustrial shift] have
> been focused on business institutions, the largest rewards have been
> found in business, and the strongest power has been held by the
> business community, although today that power is to some extent
> shared within the factory by the trade-union, and regulated within
> the society by the political order. . . . In the post-industrial soci-
> ety, production and business decisions will be subordinated to, or
> will derive from, other forces in society; the crucial decisions re-
> garding the growth of the economy and its balance will come from
> government, but they will be based on the government's sponsor-
> ship of research and development.

This means, Bell holds, that "the long-run historical trend in
Western society" is "the move away from governance by political
economy to governance by political philosophy . . . a turn to noncapitalist modes of thought." But, if the experts are thus in the
process of replacing the capitalists as decision-makers, surely the
outcome of those decisions, made by new men on a new calculus,
must be observably different from those of the old order. In fact,
this is not the case. There are indeed changed structures; only, they
have an old, and quite capitalist, content.

In the course of empirically challenging Bell's theory by showing
that the results it predicts do not take place, not even incipiently,
a basic proposition of the entire second half of this book will begin
to emerge. When the government intervenes into an economy dominated by private corporations to promote the common good, those

corporations will normally be the prime beneficiaries of that intervention. The planners may be liberals, or even socialists, but they will not be able to carry out policies that run counter to the crucial institutions of the society unless they have the support of a determined mass movement willing to fight for structural change. Since this condition usually is fulfilled only in exceptional crisis circumstances, the normal tendency of the welfare state, even with the "new men" admittedly much more in evidence and conscious planning taking on a greater importance, is to follow the old capitalist priorities in a new, sophisticated way.

Marx and Engels glimpsed the essential mechanism of this phenomenon long ago (which is hardly to argue that they said the last word on it). Proudhon had proposed that the government provide cheap credit for cooperatives and small business. If that were done, Engels wrote to Marx, the workers' societies and small producers would not be able to qualify for credit at the state bank, but big business would. It would have the collateral to prove that it was a good risk and the expertise to take advantage of the cheap money. John Maynard Keynes understood this point in his own way. Businessmen, he said, must be treated more gently than politicians. "If you work them into the surly, obstinate, terrified mood, of which domestic animals, wrongly handled, are so capable, the nation's burden will not get carried to market; and in the end public opinion will veer their way."

John Kennedy was forced to learn this depressing fact during his brief Presidency. He confronted this reality when he tried to deal with the balance-of-payments issue. "It's a ridiculous situation," he said, "for us to be squeezing down essential public activities in order not to touch private investment and tourist spending —but apparently that's life." That was not "life," but *life under capitalist conditions,* and as the next chapter will show, the argument that Kennedy faced—that government must sacrifice its priorities to profit in order to provide for investment—is still very much with us in the seventies.

The macroeconomic planning of the welfare state, then, follows, and must follow, capitalist priorities. The government and the "societal goals" which it articulates is subordinated to private purpose

—not the other way around, as Bell thinks. This will be documented at length in the next chapter, which will show how Washington made the aims of the oil companies the public policy of the United States with disastrous social consequences. In this particular case, one sees vividly how the capitalist structure of the welfare state was the decisive reason for the great Inflation-Recession of the seventies.

It might, however, be argued that oil is an exceptional case. Its giant American enterprises are vertically integrated and part of an international corporate conspiracy that has existed since the 1920s. Moreover, oil is the only instance in which there has been a dramatic increase in American overseas investment in the Third World; the more typical multinationals are involved in Europe and Canada. So, it would be well to outline how the patterns that will be treated in some detail in the next chapter apply to all of big business in the United States.

First of all, there is the case of federal housing policy during the past forty years. It too has followed corporate priorities. The migration of the middle class and the rich to the suburbs, as I documented in *Socialism,* has been subsidized by Washington. Over a period of three decades, the government helped to build ten million units for the better-off and 650,000 units of low-cost housing for the poor. In 1969, the *Wall Street Journal* reported that there were $2.5 billion in subsidies for the urban freeways, which facilitated the commuting of the privileged, and only $175 million for mass transit. All of this made good commercial sense even though it helped to perpetrate the social disaster of the disintegration of the central cities, the consequent isolation of the racial and ethnic minorities, the subversion of the passenger rail system, and so forth.

As the Council of Economic Advisors put it in its 1969 report, "Investing in new housing for low-income families—particularly in big cities—is usually a losing proposition. Indeed the *most profitable investment* is often one that demolishes homes of low-income families to make room for business and high-income families." What did this government agency mean by "profitable" in this statement? It could not possibly have been referring to a social conception of increased benefits, since the process that it was describing had exacted a high public cost in crime, welfare expenses and, above all, wrecked human lives.

The Council was, of course, talking about the private-profit criterion. And that was, not simply in theory but in fact, the one that the government had followed. Those billions of dollars had been assigned to the housing of the affluent on the grounds that their discarded dwellings would eventually "trickle down" to the poor. That did not happen; the central cities were turned into devastated regions instead.

In 1973, when the postindustrial theorists were talking of how the economic process had been subordinated to societal goals, I described the dying of New York City in *Fragments of the Century*. "Federal policies," I wrote, "helped transform the class and racial composition of the great cities in a way that made them helpless to deal with a crisis subsidized by Washington. In New York City that meant a vast increase in the number of those whom the society had made more desperate as well as an equally vast exodus of more stable families. . . . Most of the government programs, from agriculture through housing to highways had the consequence (sometimes unintended) of constantly socializing on behalf of the rich rather than the poor, or worsening (sometimes even creating) crises that the government then deplored. We did indeed act massively and audaciously—but thoughtlessly and in the wrong direction."

In 1975, those forces resulted in the effective bankruptcy of New York City—and they will eventually bring all the great cities of America to their knees. This development cannot be understood if one assumes that there are scientifically trained new men making decisions according to a new calculus (unless one stipulates that those new men are perversely anti-urban). It can be grasped if it is realized that a hidden agenda unites all of those various Federal policies: the agenda of making government choices conform to, and promote, corporate, which is to say capitalist, priorities.

A second case in point is food.

When one thinks of American agriculture, one usually envisions a mythic image of the yeoman farmer. In reality, it is a sector dominated by gigantic agribusinesses. Between 1960 and 1974, the number of farms in America decreased by 25 percent, but the larger units (with more than $20,000 a year in sales) went up by 80 percent. In 1971, 21 percent of the largest farms received approximately 80 percent of the cash receipts from farming. Among the "farmers" in America, one finds I.T.T., the John Hancock Mutual Life Insurance Company, Tenneco (which used to be the Tennessee Gas and Transmission Company), Gulf and Western, Boeing Aircraft, and other giant corporations. And the average investment in reproducible farm capital (machinery, livestock, etc.) in the United States was $18,000 in 1964. (In Latin America it is less than $500.)

These big businesses on the land have been the prime recipients of tens of billions of dollars in federal subsidy. In the thirties, when the Depression wreaked havoc on the farm, Washington embarked upon a program of planned, socialized scarcity, even though people were (and still are) hungry. It was an almost classic acting-out of the scenario described by Marx in Volume I of *Das Kapital*. Agricultural productivity had grown enormously and was "overproductive" for a society of restricted, maldistributed income. Therefore, the accomplishments of agricultural technology became, quite literally, a fetter upon the system. Farm animals were killed, farmers were paid for not growing crops. This latter policy benefited mainly the largest landowners and producers; it provided nothing for subsistence farmers and a pittance for small units. Thus, the trend toward agricultural concentration—the destruction of that sturdy, independent yeoman of the Jeffersonian myth and his replacement by a corporation—was expedited at enormous federal expense. It was, after all, "sensible"—within a capitalist definition of the term—to orient policy toward the most successful, and politically powerful, producers.

In 1974, a study carried out by the National Farmers Union documented the consequence of the government's pursuit of corporate priorities in the fields of America. Between 1968 and 1973 —that is, in the five years immediately prior to an incredible inflation of food costs of America and the emergence of starvation as a reality in the poor countries—Washington paid $15.5 billion to farmers in return for their idling 233 million acres of land that would have produced an estimated grain crop of 23 million metric tons. "Assuming yields of only two thirds of the national average for the grain best suited to the various lands held out of production," the study said, "the five-year total would have reached the equivalent of 8,609 million bushels of wheat. This is nearly a billion bushels more than the actual total harvest of 7,669 million bushels of wheat in the U.S. during those five years."

It cost billions of dollars not to produce those bushels of wheat in a hungry, partly starving, world. As the Joint Congressional Committee staff computed the price for nonproduction in 1970, there were $5.2 billion in direct federal outlays to the farmers, and food cost the consumer an extra $4.5 billion in higher prices due to the scarcity he had already subsidized in his role as a taxpayer. So, the total cost in 1970 to the people of the United States was $10 billion to keep crops from being planted. This is perhaps the most obvious single case of how the business pursuit of profit is institutionalized in welfare-state policy and takes precedence over the most basic of all economic processes, the production of food. Moreover, as will be seen, these tens of billions of taxpayers' dollars made an important contribution to the inflation of the 1970s and helped limit America's ability to respond to the crime of global malnutrition.

The tax system in the United States is one of the most important instrumentalities of corporate values. It is utterly dominated by "political economy" (corporations) and not by "political philosophy" (liberal technocrats).

First of all, there has been no trend toward equality in the United States during the past generation (i.e., since 1945) and it is questionable whether there was any equality trend at all during the twentieth century. The relative shares of wealth are at least as maldistributed today as they were at the end of the Great Depression. The figures are difficult to pin down—this is after all the "dirty little secret" of American democracy—and some of the most reliable are more than ten years old. However, the basic and intolerable fact is not really in dispute; it was, for instance, admitted

by Richard Nixon's Council of Economic Advisors in 1974. As
the economist Lester Thurow assembled the data:

U.S. DISTRIBUTION OF FAMILY WEALTH 1962

% of Total Families by Wealth		% of Total Family Wealth
Lowest	25.4	0.0
Next	31.5	6.6
Next	24.4	17.2
Top	18.7	76.2
(Top	7.5)	(59.1)
(Top	2.4)	(44.4)
(Top	.5)	(25.8)

So, the wealthiest Americans—0.5 percent of the families own
more (25.8 percent of the total) than the bottom 81.3 percent
(who own 23.8 percent of the country).

In theory—and in the imagination of most Americans as well as
in the propaganda of big business—the tax system is progressive.
If this were indeed the case, one would expect that the trend toward
the concentration of wealth would be offset by the various federal,
state and local levies. In fact, the way in which taxes are collected
is only most mildly progressive (if it is progressive at all); and the
way in which tax expenditures are allocated favors the rich with
billions and even tens of billions in subsidies a year. More to the
point of this chapter, the rationale whereby the government redis-
tributes burdens from the wealthy to the working people is that it
is necessary to make the capitalist system work.

Joseph Pechman and Benjamin Okner did a careful study of the
tax burden in the United States. Before noting their conclusion,
an important, but unfortunately abstruse, methodological point has
to be made. Most government statistics omit capital gains as an element in family income; thus, the growth in the value of the equity
held by the rich in boom years is not counted. (This is the *only*
form of income which is not taxed when it is made, and this fact,
along with the weakness of the inheritance laws, allows the rich to
evade billions in taxes.) However, if capital gains are included,
then the income inequality in the United States increases dramati-

cally. Using the government's figures, the top 1 percent of the people get "only" 4.8 percent of the annual income; using the adjusted figures, their take goes up to 10.5 percent.*

Pechman and Okner's point is recognized even by the conservatives in government, although they prefer, for obviously political reasons, to publish statistics that play down the maldistribution of income. If the adjusted figures are used, and if the reasonable assumption is made that corporation taxes are shifted, in whole or in part, to consumers, then the effective rate of taxation on the very rich is only 5 percent more than that paid by most families. The federal tax system is thus not progressive, but proportional "and therefore has little effect on the distribution of income."

It is a scandal that the tax system is not, as is so often claimed, progressive. One might infer that this is the case because of the political power of wealth in America. However, when one turns from the way in which taxes are collected to the manner in which tax expenditures are made, there is no need for inference. The government proudly and openly states that these are motivated by capitalist considerations.

A tax expenditure occurs when Washington decides that some particular class of taxpayers need pay no tax, or will be forgiven a portion of their tax. It has the same effect as a direct expenditure of government money since lowering one group's rate effectively increases the rates of everyone else. For instance, realized capital gains are taxed at lower rates than any other form of income.† People with incomes of $20,000 to $25,000 a year, a Congressional Committee reported in 1972, receive $100 in benefits from this provision; while those with incomes of $1 million get $640,000 a

---

* Income, it will be noted, is less maldistributed than wealth; the top 1 percent have 10.5 percent of the income, but the top 0.5 percent have 25.8 percent of the wealth. This simply shows that the rich have most of their holdings in long-term assets, which are not subject to income tax, and that they have a positive incentive to minimize their income. Either figure is outrageous; both are only the different sides of the same golden coin.

† When capital gains are realized—when stock is sold and a profit is taken—they are income. The capital gains that Pechman and Okner computed are "accrued"—that is, they include both those gains which were turned into cash and those which were held as part of a continuing investment.

year from it. More generally, the deductions—or tax expenditures —in the Internal Revenue Code provide 10 percent of the benefits for the 50 percent of the people at the bottom of the society and 15 percent of them for the 3 percent at the top.

In 1975, the projected federal budget for 1976 contained no less than $91.8 billion in tax expenditures. These figures, it should be noted, were computed on the basis of very conservative assumptions—the fact that imputed rental value of an owner-occupied house was not considered to be a tax expenditure and neither was the failure to count in the accrued value of capital gains during a tax year. But even with these definitions, which made the Internal Revenue code look fairer than it is, there were shocking notations. For instance, the deductibility of mortgage interest and property taxes yielded homeowners a tax subsidy of almost $13 billion— almost ten times as much as was spent on public housing assistance in 1975!

In 1975, the Treasury prepared, at the request of Senator Walter Mondale, an analysis of tax expenditures as they showed up in 1974 spending. In that year, the two tenths of one percent of the taxpayers who had incomes of more than $100,000 a year received 12.6 percent of the subsidies in a number of major categories; the 46.9 percent of the taxpayers whose incomes ranged up to $10,000 that year, got a mere 16.6 percent. And the top 1.2 percent got a third more than the bottom 46.9 percent. In theory, such policies are supposed to stimulate business and individuals to act in a way that will promote the common good. In fact, as Senator William Proxmire pointed out when releasing a Joint Economic Committee Analysis, "our studies have shown that many subsidy programs do not work well economically, they are often directed at outmoded or nonexistent objectives, they redistribute income to the affluent, and in many cases their costs far exceeded their benefits to the society as a whole."

So, in many cases the argument for a given deduction was clearly fallacious. The privileged treatment of the capital gains of the rich was worth $14 billion in 1971. The theory was that the government thereby encouraged people to save, which in turn provided investment funds for new jobs, and so on. In fact, as Benjamin Okner pointed out to the Joint Economic Committee, only a small and declining portion of corporate investment in 1971 came from external financing. So, most of the $14 billion was a handsome, if unconscious, gift to the wealthy from the less-well-off.

But, then, this systematic bias does not operate simply in this or that case. It informs all of macroeconomic governmental policy in the United States.

In this post-Keynesian era, the tax system is not conceived of as a mechanism for collecting and disbursing public revenues. Its prime function is to facilitate countercyclical policy, to expand demand when there is excess capacity and unemployment, to restrain it when the opposite is the case. (However, as Chapter 12 will show, this neat thesis does not work out in practice.) Since corporations are the primary economic units in the society, such countercyclical tax policy must, as Keynes so well understood, be kind to executives. Over thirty years ago, Michael Kalecki shrewdly anticipated the problems that would arise in such an undertaking. Business, he said, is opposed to government spending for three reasons: a dislike of government intervention in the economy, as such; opposition to the direction of government spending (public investment and subsidizing competition); and fear of the undisciplined work force that would result from a full-employment economy.

One of the ways to deal with this corporate hostility to government intervention, Kalecki argued, was to have the state stimulate and subsidize *private* investment. That would make businessmen less grumpy about bureaucratic interference, since they would make money from it; and it would not put public money into public investments, nor would it underwrite the consumption of the masses. Kalecki's reading of the political dimensions of Keynesian policy in a capitalist economy proved prophetic, above all, in the United States.

Indeed, this point helps to explain the function of the warfare state within the welfare state. Military spending has the marvelous quality of conferring subsidized profits on inefficient corporations which produce goods that do not, like the power generated by the Tennessee Valley Authority, compete with the output of other firms in the consumer market. It thus neatly synthesizes the worst potential of both capitalism and socialism. This does not, however, mean that a massive arms sector is a necessity for capitalism, a precondition for its continuing existence. As Seymour Melman has pointed out, Germany and Japan did quite well after World War II, even though defeat deprived them of the right and duty of wasting a good portion of their substance on the means of destruction. For that matter, the Pentagon's share of the Gross National Product has declined somewhat in recent years. Moreover, it is a mechanistic and silly economic determinism to try to reduce all of the complicated international politics of the postwar decades to a reflex of a militaristic economy. The tragic, unconscionable American intervention in Vietnam, to take but one case in point, was also senseless from a rationally calculated capitalist (or imperialist) point of view. The financiers and Wall Streeters who participated in considerable numbers in the antiwar campaigns of 1968 understood this even if some self-proclaimed Marxists did not.

And yet, if capitalism is not inevitably and intrinsically militarist, the great fact remains that arms spending is peculiarly congenial to it. The businessmen who refused to let Roosevelt engage in social spending at a rate that would have ended the Great Depression became patriotic "dollar a year" men as soon as war broke out. In part their reaction was sincere; in part, it expressed the knowledge (or, at the time, the *intuition*) that military "socialism" is profoundly antisocialist. But, then, even when the system adopts pacific measures of government intervention—and does so under liberal auspices—it has the same point of maintaining, and extending, the status quo. Military spending is only one instrument of capitalist survival, albeit an important and fearful one.

When, for instance, John Kennedy wanted to get the economy moving again in the early sixties, he could have done so, as Kenneth Galbraith and the AFL-CIO urged, by direct outlays for social investments. That, however, would have pitted him against the political power of business (and of reaction in general). Just as Kalecki predicted, he came out for a tax cut that would benefit the corporations more than anyone else. In a speech defending his policy before the Economic Club of New York, he waxed so conservative that Galbraith said that he had given "the most Republican speech since McKinley," and *Time* Magazine noted that he sounded like the National Association of Manufacturers.

This did not mean, as many on the left would probably assume, that Kennedy had "sold out." It is much more profound than that, and one can concede Kennedy's *bona fides* without harm to the essential point. The President of the United States was bowing to the power relationships of an economy dominated by private corporations. In such a setting, he could—particularly if he had been much more powerful in the Congress than he was at that time— have acted otherwise; but all of the institutional, structural pressures in American society urged him to act as he did.

As a result of this general tendency of the political economy of a capitalist society, all of the tax reductions between 1964 and 1973 favored the rich. Some 16.1 percent of the tax returns in that period came from people with incomes under $3,000; they received 7.9 percent of the tax cuts. They were only 4.7 percent of the returns in the $20,000-to-$50,000 category, but they received 10.3 percent of the benefits; and the 0.6 percent of the people with incomes over $50,000 got 0.9 percent of the cuts. At the same time, the corporations got bonanzas in the form of investment tax credits. The economy of the United States was thus stimulated by pampering the rich and slighting the poor.

So macroeconomic policy is procorporate in two basic ways. First, it stimulates private investment and thereby allows the executives to determine the actual form that the public expenditure will take. Instead of direct outlays for health, mass transportation, education, and the like, there are tax cuts that allow the private sector to build and sell whatever it pleases without any reference to social usefulness. And secondly, the benefits of the public expenditures are assigned in inverse proportion to need, with the corporations and the rich getting the most and the poor the least.

A carefully documented and even ingenious study by an academic moderate, Harold Wilensky's *The Welfare State and Equality* disputes the kind of argument I have made. The welfare state, Wilensky asserts, has an egalitarian effect, because the "payout is typically more progressive than the financing is regressive." That conclusion is wrong, but Wilensky honestly arrived at it on the basis of a flawed, but revealing, method. In computing the regressivity of the financing, he excludes capital gains and expense accounts. But capital gains, as we have seen, are the most inequitable and massively subsidized source of the privilege of the wealthy. By one stroke of a statistical definition, Wilensky thus biases his case. Secondly, he treats the welfare state narrowly, concentrating on social security programs, but ignoring the tens of billions paid out in the dole for the rich in the Internal Revenue Code as well as the gains made by the corporate class as a result of federal economic management. And finally, Wilensky is much too optimistic about the progressiveness of the welfare state "pay out." This is a point that deserves some attention in its own right.

Medicaid is the federal program designed to bring health care to the poor. It is financed both by Washington and by the individual states. Predictably, the richest states—New York, California, Massachusetts—take a maximum advantage of this law; the poorest states do the least. There are 46 percent of the poverty-stricken in the South, but only 17 percent of the Medicaid payments are made there, and the three affluent states disburse 50 percent of the funds. And even social security itself refracts the basic unfairness of America's class structure. It may well be that the poor do not get more benefits from it, because they die earlier and work longer than anyone else in the society. Moreover, we do know that whites use Medicaid more than blacks (because of the shortage of doctors in black areas) and that the elderly with a $15,000 income get twice as much from Medicare as those with less than $5,000 a year. Considerations like these led the Brookings Institution, a center of moderate, pragmatic liberalism, to conclude that there is no redistribution of wealth from federal programs for "transferring" income—theoretically, but only theoretically—from the rich to the poor.

All of these facts are at odds with Bell's theory of a postindustrial society. One of the quintessential domains of the "new men" was and is economic policy. This is an example of a new intellectual technology, of the rise of nonmarket forces and so on. And yet it turns out that, even under a liberal administration like Kennedy's, those new men are forced, willy-nilly, to follow corporate priorities when they elaborate the government's program. And this is so because the macroeconomics of the welfare state, for all the momentous changes that have taken place, are still filled with a capitalist content. That welfare state, then, is not a new form of society, any more than Bismarckian "socialism" was; it is, rather, a new way of protecting the old order. That, as Chapter 12 will show, is a problematic and ambiguous enterprise, for the welfare state also contains contradictory tendencies, the seeds, not of one new order, but of two. As of now, however, it is primarily and fundamentally capitalist, and this is the key to the secret history of the great economic and social crisis of the seventies.

One aspect of that crisis was the formation of an oil cartel in 1973, the Organization of Petroleum Exporting Countries (OPEC). It would seem preposterous to put the blame for this event on the internal system of the Western capitalisms. And indeed, there is no doubt that the quadrupling of oil prices had an independent and profound impact upon the Recession-Inflation of the middle seventies. But the way in which that "accident" impinged upon America and Europe was not accidental. It was precisely because the welfare state was operating on the basis of corporate priorities that the disaster was possible. So the next chapter, on American energy policy, will focus on a case in point of the general trend described in this chapter, one that bears greatly on the current crisis.[4]

CHAPTER 10

THE COMMON GOOD AS
PRIVATE PROPERTY

DURING the past generation, the people of the United States paid hundreds of billions of dollars in handouts to some of the richest corporations in the world. One consequence of this extraordinary act of charity was that it helped the nation become criminally profligate with energy and vulnerable to the cartel policies of the Organization of Petroleum Exporting Countries (OPEC) in the 1970s. One would be hard put to find a better example of how the welfare state follows capitalist priorities.

Indeed, the only problem is that this example is almost too good. As a Ford Foundation study rightly pointed out, the energy industry "possesses a unique combination of political advantages, which has enabled it to exert considerable influence on public policy." Oil companies are gigantic; four of them are among the ten largest industrial corporations in America, seven rank in the fifteen largest multinationals in the world. Moreover, in the United States this industry has the political leverage that comes from producing (coal, oil, natural gas, nuclear power, etc.) in a majority of the states.

So the claim is not made here that the oil case is typical. On the contrary, the reader is warned to be very careful in making analogies between this incredibly powerful industry and the other sectors of American capitalism. And yet, the fundamental policy assumptions and decisions which are writ so large in this instance are at work throughout the entire society. For what is crucial to the analysis of this chapter is not the proposition that these companies used their economic power in a conscious political way to enhance their self-interest. That is a self-evident—and sometimes deceptive —truth which can divert attention from a much more basic proposition. The bias of the welfare state toward oil corporations, or any other form of big business, is the consequence of its capitalist structure, not of conspiracies in the board room.

This point must be stressed at the outset, since a surprisingly broad political stratum agrees on the basic "facts" in this case, and it is the interpretation of them that is really at issue. In his 1975 State of the Union Message, for instance, President Ford spoke of the energy crisis and conceded that "we cannot put all blame on the oil exporting nations. We, the United States are not blameless. Our growing dependence on foreign sources has been adding to our vulnerability for years and years." And the *Wall Street Journal* went even further, commenting editorially that the quadrupled price of oil caused by the OPEC cartel threatens the advanced capitalist nations "only because of the prior and present economic mismanagement by the Western governments themselves."

Perhaps the most concise statement of this theme was made by David Haberman, an attorney who had worked on an antitrust case against some of the oil majors for fifteen years. Haberman told a Senate committee that

> the current international oil crisis did not just suddenly spring full blown when a few Middle East governments decided to impose their oil embargo upon the consuming nations of the world. Rather, I suggest that you will find that Middle East government actions and the world oil crisis which they precipitated, represented but a logical extension, indeed the inevitable culmination, of a long, well-defined historical process. . . . That process saw the evolution and exploitation of a most complex and extraordinarily symbiotic relationship between these seven major interna-

tional oil companies on the one hand [Standard Oil (New Jersey), Socony Vacuum, Standard of California, the Texas Company, Gulf Oil, British Petroleum, and Royal Dutch Shell] and the several governments of the United States, Western Europe, and the Middle East on the other.

Clearly, then, one need not be a Marxist to understand that there is some connection between America's domestic economic structure and its vulnerability to the energy crisis of the seventies. Where the analysis of this chapter differs sharply from President Ford, the *Wall Street Journal* and even Haberman—where it is Marxist—is in showing that these events happened as they did, in considerable measure, because the welfare state is capitalist. So oil is the subject of a detailed and specific chapter in the secret history of our present calamities.[1]

I

I will arbitrarily begin this narrative in the middle of World War II.

There is, of course, a rich prehistory of governmental involvement in the energy industry. During World War I, Washington played a major role in it as a part of the military mobilization, and there were even sober public figures, like Josephus Daniels, who wanted to nationalize the oil wells in order to protect the Navy's source of supply.

The United Mine Workers of America also demanded public ownership, but for left-wing reasons. Then, right after the war, there was a panic. Scientists told the nation that its oil reserves would be exhausted within ten years of average consumption. Part of the Federal response was to demand an "Open Door" in Iraq, where a British-Dutch-French monopoly was seen as threatening American interests.

But by the time American power had kicked the door open in the Middle East, the industry was worried about a glut rather than scarcity. During the most momentous grouse hunt in history, at Achnacarry Castle, in Scotland in 1928, Exxon (I use current corporate names throughout this chapter), British Petroleum and Shell agreed to divide up world production and distribution in an orderly manner. Back in the United States the market was similarly rigged. It began when the producers in Texas and Louisiana seemed about to pump entire fields dry as each tried to get the maximum out of the common pool to which a number of them had access. An executive of Humble Oil (now Exxon) remembered, "We had to let a president of Humble quit to become governor" in order to deal with the crisis. The solution was *dirigiste:* the states fixed production quotas, and the federal government helped enforce them with the passage of the Connally Hot Oil Act of 1935 which banned interstate shipment of oil produced in violation of those quotas.

Indeed, Washington's involvement in this area generated the greatest governmental scandal in American history prior to Watergate. In the Teapot Dome case, the Secretary of the Interior was convicted of taking a bribe to allow a major oil company to drill on a Naval petroleum reserve. That, however, was only one more example of a perennial corruption that has existed in American politics since the foundation of the Republic. The history of the Petroleum Reserve Corporation, in contrast, reveals the specific mechanisms of the welfare state's inherently capitalist prejudices. It introduces the classic rationale for legal and honest governmental favoritism toward corporations: that the national security of the United States—sometimes it is said, the security of the entire Free World—depends upon the profit-making multinationals of the oil industry.

In 1943, the American military's energy situation seemed precarious. Herbert Feis, a historian and a participant in these events as a government official, notes that the Germans had captured the Rumanian oil as well as two important Russian fields. "For a time," Feis wrote, "it seemed likely that they would capture the other Russian fields and close in upon the fields of Iraq and Iran." In June of 1943, William C. Bullitt, the Under Secretary of the Navy, put the problem in long-range perspective. The crude petroleum reserves of the United States will be "totally exhausted" in fourteen years, he wrote to President Roosevelt. "To acquire petroleum reserves outside our boundaries has become, therefore, a vital interest of the United States." Standard of California and the

Texas Company, Bullitt continued, were worried about British dominance in Saudi Arabia and wanted Washington to help them.

The companies asked the government to support them in their Saudi venture—that is, to move, not against the Nazi enemy but against the British ally. But though the United States would, in their scenario, supply the political power that would win them the Saudi concession, the oil companies would remain in control of the whole operation. Bullitt was prophetic on this point. He wrote to Roosevelt: "To accept such a proposal would be to relapse into the 'dollar diplomacy' of a dead era. The Government of the United States would be undertaking to back up with all its diplomatic and other resources private capitalists whose concessions will be relatively valueless without government support." This, as will be seen, is exactly what has in fact been happening during the past generation.

At first it seemed that the companies were not going to prevail. Roosevelt was impressed by Bullitt's arguments against "dollar diplomacy," and he also listened to his feisty and independent Secretary of the Interior, Harold L. Ickes. Among Ickes' duties at that time was supervision of the petroleum war effort. So he proposed that a government corporation be set up to assert the public interest in this area. In 1943 the Petroleum Reserves Corporation was established, with Ickes as president, and it was empowered "to buy or acquire reserves of crude oil outside the United States, including stock in companies, to transport, store, process and market, and otherwise dispose of such crude and its products, with power to operate refineries, pipelines and storage tanks outside the United States." The Petroleum Reserves Corporation's first act was to try to buy all, or part, of California Arabian, the joint venture of Standard of California and the Texas Company, which were seeking the Saudi concession.

The corporations were outraged. As Herbert Feis put it,

> they had gone fishing for a cod and caught a whale. They had first made their way to Washington in search of protection against enemies hard to name and desirous of help in developing their properties. Perhaps also with the inner thought that skillful persuasion might save them from the need to make further advances to local

rulers. Then, one day, they walked into the Interior Building and were met with a suggestion that they sell their property to the government and withdraw from their enterprise.

The companies managed to throw the whale—the United States government—back into the ocean as if it were an underweight fish. They flatly refused to sell the Petroleum Reserves Corporation their Saudi subsidiary or even to allow it to become the majority stockholder with the actual management left to Standard of California and Texaco. Meanwhile, the industry front group—the National Oil Policy Commission of the Petroleum Industry War Council—thundered that the whole scheme was "fascist." As a colonel at the State Department summed up the corporate attitude, the companies were saying, "We are under no obligation to our government, we don't trust you, but if you'll invest one hundred and fifty million dollars in facilities as a guarantee that you will protect us, we will agree not to trade with your enemies and will give you a discount on some future oil."

The companies were not alone in their opposition. There were liberals who were against the undertaking on anti-imperialist grounds, as well as isolationists who objected to any involvement beyond the nation's shores, and Zionists who were concerned about the implications of this move for their cause. But, as Feis says, the issue was not settled on its policy merits. The Petroleum Reserves Corporation

> was rejected mainly because of the opposition of groups who believed that it would have an adverse effect upon their business position or prospect. Virtually the whole of the American oil industry condemned the proposed measures as needless and unfair. It was, the industry argued, needless because all the oil the United States might need could be, and would be, supplied by the American oil industry—from American resources in the main, supplemented by foreign production.

From the vantage point of the seventies, we know that the industry's argument was fallacious. Indeed, the fact that Washington accepted it and acted upon it is one of the reasons why there is an energy crisis. Moreover, one sees here an early appearance of the fateful theory that the common good of the United States is served by maximizing the private interest of the oil corporations. In saying this, it should be noted that there were indeed problems in 1943: the short-term difficulties of assuring military petroleum supplies, particularly if the Germans were to expand into Iran and Iraq; the long-term energy needs of the United States. In response, it was decided after a brief struggle that the oil companies were the anointed instruments of the people of the United States in facing up to those problems. That makes excellent antisocial sense in an economy in which the dominant producing institutions are corporate. The way in which the industry forced Washington to accept this logic was political—that is, by effectively threatening a wartime strike of capital if its demands were not met. But the very structure of the economy was an argument in favor of the company's position, and Ickes could not long resist that fact.

In February of 1943, Franklin Roosevelt declared that "The defense of Saudi Arabia is vital to the defense of the United States," thereby committing the government to spend more money than the British in this area in order to ensure the Saudis' friendship with the American corporations. Then, as Harold Ickes told the Senate in 1945, once "Rommel had been chased out of North Africa they were secure in their concessions and more disposed to thumb their nose at us." So much for capitalist patriotism.[2]

II

With the Cold War the argument that the government and industry interests were one and the same took on even greater weight, with momentous consequences. Two cases in point are the special deal that allowed oil companies to avoid taxes (and provided them with an incentive to misallocate resources) and the cancellation of a federal antitrust suit against the biggest of these corporations.

George McGhee, who was Assistant Secretary of State for Near Eastern, South Asian and African Affairs between 1949 and 1951, told a Senate committee in 1974 of how a multibillion-dollar tax subsidy to the oil industry was justified in the name of anti-Communism. In 1949, McGhee testified, "the Middle East was perhaps the most critical area in the world in the contest between ourselves and the Soviets. The governments in the area were very unstable. We had no security pact covering the area. The Soviets had threatened Greece, Turkey and Iran." So, Washington decided that the Arab powers should get more money.

There was more than a little cynicism in the decision. A 1950 State Department Background Paper, prepared for a meeting with oil executives, was remarkably candid. It said:

> Communism's alleged support for the underdog, in an area of underdogs, and its promise of quick relief have opportunity for expansion in the Middle East, where masses of people live in circumstances of exceptional poverty and ignorance, where governments are often corrupt, inefficient and of, by and for the upper classes, and where increasing numbers of partially educated frustrated younger generations are becoming available for explosive action. Communist propaganda tries to exploit this internal situation and to place responsibility on the West.

This is excellent sociology but unconscionable politics. For there was no argument that the proper American policy would be to help the masses escape their exceptional poverty and ignorance. Instead, there was to be skillful deception. The memo, for instance, notes that "The U.S. Government should endeavor to minimize publicity of Anglo-American 'collusion' on oil in the Middle East while at the same time avoiding Anglo-American conflicts over oil . . ." That is to say that the government should simultaneously deny and sponsor the Anglo-American collusion. More substantially, Washington also figured out how to simultaneously subsidize conservative Arab rulers—those administrations which were "often corrupt, inefficient and of, by and for the upper classes"—and heap even more favors on the wealthy American oil enterprises.

Aramco, the American consortium operating in Saudi Arabia, was worried that the Saudis were going to follow the Venezuelans and demand a 50-50 split on the value of their oil. If the companies resisted, they might be nationalized. Washington, therefore, urged them to accept the higher payments, but then ingeniously allowed them to send the bill to the American taxpayer. It was decided that the royalties paid to the Arab powers would be treated as taxes. Thus they would not simply qualify as a business expense which was deducted before the payment of corporate taxes; they would be a hundred percent tax credit.*

In developing this technique of paying the oil industry's new costs with taxpayers' money, the government had the full cooperation of the companies, needless to say. A startling and important detail about this fact, however, is that the actual procorporate proposal came from the government side. One witness testified that "we wanted the best brains available . . . and a lot of those brains happened to be with oil companies. So, under George McGhee's leadership, we had regular meetings with the oil companies." Yet McGhee himself reported that the tax-giveaway idea had come from his side of the table. In other words, the oil companies were not using the government as an instrumentality, which is the conspiratorial interpretation of the events that are documented here. Rather, industry and government were honest and sincere participants in a process in which both articulated a policy that was logically based on the very structure of the American economy. Under such circumstances, the notion of giving away billions of federal dollars to private interests could and did come from the federal bureaucracy itself, with no hint of corruption involved. (There was an almost comic moment when these events were narrated before the Senate committee. The civil servant who had thought up this plan, Senator Percy said, "reminds me of my own comptroller, Harold Geneen. He was always coming up with ideas like this." Some years later, Geneen in his own name, as president of I.T.T.,

---

* The Ford Foundation study illustrates the difference between treating payments as royalties and treating them as taxes: ". . . assume a U.S. oil company earns $100 million abroad and pays a foreign tax of $60 million. If this tax were treated as a business expense, the U.S. tax would be levied on $100 million — $60 million = $40 million net income, which at the U.S. tax rate of 48 percent would be . . . $19 million. But if the host country take is assumed to be an income tax, the same company would not pay any U.S. tax at all, having already paid more ($60 million) income tax to the host country than the U.S. tax liability. . . . Instead, it ends up with a credit of $60 million — $48 million = $12 million." That credit may be used to offset tax liabilities incurred in the United States, or it may be "stockpiled" and applied five years later.

was to come up with another brilliant idea: persuading the American government to overthrow Allende in Chile.)

So the companies got to treat royalties like taxes, to their great advantage. But then they took care to see to it that the price of Middle Eastern oil was paid out primarily in taxes anyway. The "tax price" of a barrel of oil was pushed higher and higher, since it was, even under the normal rules, completely deductible from the American tax liability; the royalty stayed rather modest. So it was that the "income tax" on oil amounted to over 80 percent of its price. Had the royalty portion been higher, it could only be charged off as a "business expense." As Senator Charles Percy put it, there is a "credibility gap" when the corporations "have a billion in income and . . . are paying 80 percent in income taxes to the Arab nation and 1.2 percent to the U.S. Government."

There were a number of consequences which flowed from this "anti-Communist" tax policy. First, it was one of the factors that allowed the oil corporations to avoid billions in taxes. In 1971, for instance, American companies paid roughly a 40 percent tax on their income, the oil multinationals, 5 percent. Had the oil industry paid at the regular rate, the U.S. Treasury would have been richer by $2.5 billions in that one year. Secondly, this tax structure motivated the companies to spend money outside the United States and to shirk the more arduous tasks of developing American energy sources. This was and is a particularly important consideration, since the oil giants have major holdings in all forms of energy. Of the fourteen largest petroleum companies, seven (including the four biggest) have moved into every other branch of the industry, into gas, oil shale, coal, uranium and tar sands.

As Arnold Miller, president of the United Mine Workers of America, told a Senate committee in 1973, "The reason for the failure of coal to assume its rightful share [of the American energy output] must lie in the monopolistic position of the energy companies and their ability to control the use of various fuels, since they own a great part of the reserves of all fuels." To which it might be added that the tax policy initiated in 1950 gave a mighty incentive to the American-owned multinationals to let their nation's economy become dependent on Arab oil. The government in effect spent a generation paying them billions of dollars to do just that. Therefore, the results of the patriotic tax policies of the Cold War were not simply outrageous in that they lessened the burdens on giant oil corporations and thereby increased them on everyone else; they also made a major contribution to the misallocation of American and world energy resources.

During the hearings on these developments, Senator Church understood this last point, but George McGhee, making a retrospective defense of the policy he had helped to initiate, nimbly finessed it. "Although it may not have been apparent at the time," Church commented, "it must have become apparent to the State Department as time passed and as we are no longer an oil-export country, as our dependency on foreign sources began to increase and then grow very rapidly, that these policies, these decisions operated as a strong economic inducement to the companies to invest abroad rather than in the United States . . ."

McGhee answered that the real incentive to go abroad was that oil resources at home were running out. What he did not talk about —because it would have destroyed his thesis—was why the corporations failed to develop the other domestic sources of energy which they already owned. The answer, as Arnold Miller realized, is that their monopoly position plus the tremendous largesse of Washington made it more profitable to distort the American energy economy and to prepare its vulnerability for the OPEC cartel than to follow social priorities for the creation of a rational energy system.

And, once again, the rationale for this extraordinary use of the public power to subvert the common good was the identification of the national interest with the private, corporate interest. If one believed that the oil companies were, as Senator Percy put it, "the bargaining agents for the free world," then one treated them lavishly. At first there might be a temptation to dismiss Percy's rhetoric as a typical excess of the Cold War mentality. It is certainly that, but it is also the statement of a profound truth. In American capitalism, where government is supposed to have a subordinate and ancillary role but does not intervene in production, private corporations are indeed the representatives—unelected, to be sure—of the entire society. The point is not to deny the absurd statement that rapacious and profit-seeking institutions are the "bargaining agents of the free world"; the point is to analyze the social-economic formation in which that absurdity makes sense. (See Appendix G, § 2, p. 393.)

The second, extremely illuminating example of this crazy logic has to do with antitrust. Here too the public policy of the United States was consciously subordinated to the needs of the oil corporations on the grounds that they were the effective instruments of the national purpose.

In August 1952, the Federal Trade Commission published a 378-page report on "The International Petroleum Cartel" and submitted it to a Senate Committee on Monopoly. Late in 1952, the outgoing Truman administration initiated a grand jury investigation that could have led to criminal charges. Five American companies were to become involved in this legal process: Exxon, Mobil, Socal, Texaco and Gulf (again I use their present names). The defendants, and their allies in the State Department immediately raised the issue of national security. Indeed, as one government lawyer was later to recall,

> Special Assistant to the Attorney General Leonard Emmerglick [the head of the Justice Department staff on this case] was put in the anomalous position of having to persuade the court that he—and not defense counsel—was the duly authorized legal spokesman for the policy position of the U.S. government with respect to security and sensitivity.

The Justice Department argued that the corporation's monopolistic policies were actually endangering the security of the United States by maintaining their reserves at too low a level. The reason for seeking criminal indictments was that this method would allow for speedy action; a civil case was likely to drag on from four to eight years. On January 12, 1953, President Truman instructed the Attorney General to drop the criminal case because of the interests of "national security." Then, with the probusiness Eisenhower administration in office, the official line became even more precise. Because of America's need for Middle Eastern oil and friendly relations with the Arab powers, the companies were effec-

248 THE TWILIGHT OF CAPITALISM

tively exempted from the antitrust laws. The case dragged on for several years and was eventually settled by consent decrees which represented a decisive victory for the industry.

The public record was strewn with documentary evidence that the international oil cartel had rigged supply and prices, used quotas, and generally engaged in monopolistic practices. But because the American members of this conspiracy were seen as "bargaining agents of the free world" they were never brought to justice. In an even more bizarre event in the 1970s, they were given immunity from the law before their collusion began. That saved the court costs of prosecution and the embarrassment of openly subverting government policy.

This incident began with the overthrow of the Idris regime in Libya in 1969. That government, as a State Department official candidly confessed to a Senate committee, "was certainly one of the most corrupt in the area and probably one of the most corrupt in the world." It was, in short, the kind of a government that Washington and the companies like to deal with. It was succeeded by the military rule of Qaddafi. Under him, the Libyans proposed in 1970 that their share of the oil take be increased. The companies thought these demands were too high. Washington, the State Department official conceded, had no way of knowing what the facts really were, since it had to rely on the corporations for all of its data.

"Why is it," Senator Church asked, "that the U.S. Government is in this position with respect to the oil companies? Why can't we obtain information as a matter of right?" James Akins replied for the State Department. "I don't think we can go in and ask similar information from a copper company or a steel company or an automobile company or I.B.M. or what have you." The companies are considered as public agents, deserving of military, economic and political support and of exemptions from antitrust laws, on the one hand; but when the government wants to find out the facts with regard to an issue that bears on both economic and military security, the same companies suddenly turn into "free enterprises" with all the prerogatives of managerial secrecy.

If the companies wanted to keep the government uninformed,

they also wanted to meet together and to discuss how to handle the Libyan situation without fear of prosecution under the antitrust laws, which they were violating. The description given the Senate committee of how this was done would be hilarious if it only did not involve degrading the sovereignty of the American people to the benefit of the oil industry.

A major figure in these events was John J. McCloy. McCloy has been Assistant Secretary of War, President of the World Bank, United States Military Governor of Germany, Chairman of the Board of the Ford Foundation, Disarmament Advisor to President Kennedy, and a member of the Warren Commission that investigated the assassination of Kennedy. He is a lawyer, a partner in one of the most powerful of the New York firms, and a former chairman of the board of the Chase Manhattan Bank. In a statement of unwitting brilliance, Senator Percy captured McCloy's distinctive quality: "I would just like to say, as one member of this subcommittee, that we are very fortunate to have John McCloy here. He can walk in several pairs of shoes, he has been on both sides of the fence . . ." Somewhat more soberly, but just as accurately, Senator Clifford Case told McCloy, "You represented everybody, including the U.S. government without the U.S. government knowing what was being done until you told them about it." That is exact.

McCloy himself invoked the usual rationale for his wearing "several pairs of shoes." Since Woodrow Wilson, he told the Senators, the government had been supporting the oil industry in the name of national security, and that was good and proper.

> Through the energies and activities of the American oil companies and their associates—and I keep referring to the fact that I represent not only American companies but also some foreign companies in this Middle East area, which are companies of our allies, we have been able to accomplish much of what U.S. statesmen in the immediate postwar period set out to achieve, and our economy and our security have been advanced as a result of it.

It is, of course, the argument of this chapter that all this is nonsense, and that oil profiteering, as subsidized by the government, tended to ignore the priorities of the United States in every sense of the word.

This rationale, however, served when the companies, with Mc-Cloy's assistance, wanted to get their exemption from the antitrust laws. In the process, there was an incredible scene, described by James Akins of the State Department. The oil corporation executives met behind closed doors in McCloy's law office. Akins and an associate, the representatives of the American government, sat in an anteroom. The companies wanted a "business review letter" which would effectively allow them to formulate a common policy without fear of Washington's intervention. So, McCloy and his friends drafted policy statements. From time to time, McCloy or some other member of the policy meeting would show a draft to the State Department representatives. Their comments would be heard, and then McCloy and his friends would get on with the job of developing what was, in effect, the policy of the United States government. As a result, a "London policy group" was established by the oil companies which held in the neighborhood of fifty meetings, starting in January 1971. This conspiracy was blessed by the United States in a benediction prepared by its own lawyer. The people of America sat, hat in hand, in the anteroom; McCloy and the industry occupied the executive suite.

Even though this narrative demeaned the nation's very sovereignty, the Senators were deferential toward such a veteran Establishmentarian as McCloy. Yet, some pertinent questions were raised, even if they were not pursued. A staff member asked Akins if "the U.S. government ever considered what it was they were going to get in return from the companies." He pointed out that these corporations are major fertilizer producers, and that the nation faces a fertilizer shortage. "Was there," he wanted to know, "any concept of linkage whereby the companies in return for these various actions on the part of the United States would indeed commit themselves to meeting a variety of U.S. domestic needs?" The answer was no.

The committee also produced evidence that the companies had rigged supply so as to get higher profits—that is, had played the game of the OPEC cartel before the OPEC cartel became an effective instrument. There was testimony that the corporations had plugged up wells in Iraq because their bargaining position would have been weakened if the Iraqis knew the extent of their own oil wealth. Senator Stuart Symington commented toward the end of McCloy's appearance,

> So they waive the law, by agreement, in the interest of national security. All of a sudden, reports come out that their profits have jumped all over the place, which is sort of not the kind of reward you generally get, talking as a representative of the people, for service. Instead of that they got a great deal back and we got stuck with a bad oil shortage.

That last sentence might stand as an epitaph for a crisis.[3]

III

There are three other major instances of federal policy which exhibit the same pattern of subordinating the common good to private corporate interest in the name of national security, with the result of making America both wasteful and vulnerable: the highway program, the depletion allowance and the oil import quotas. Since the basic mechanisms have already been identified, there is no point in simply piling up the details. In what follows, then, there will be a brief outline and just a few high points.

Perhaps the most momentous social program of the past generation was the federalization of most of the cost of interstate highways. Initiated by the Republicans under Eisenhower, it poured tens of billions of public dollars into an effort that helped to destroy the railroads, deteriorate the central cities, isolate the poor and minorities, and pollute the air. All this was done without any particular thought for the consequences and on the unstated assumption that the values of the automobile companies should establish the priorities of government policy. As one perceptive observer described the outcome, "When we buy an automobile we no longer buy an object in the old sense of the word, but instead we purchase a three-to-five-year lease for participation in the state-recognized private transportation system, a highway system, a traffic safety [*sic*] system, an industrial parts-replacement system, a costly insurance system . . ."

All of these systems, it will be noted, were subsidized directly or indirectly by Washington. Then the private interests made the antisocial worst of the handouts they received. But, it might be objected, the companies were not the only ones to benefit from these programs. The public funds also provided hundreds of thousands, perhaps millions, of jobs and were for that reason enthusiastically supported by trade-unionists as well as by executives. That, it will be seen in a moment, is only a partial truth. First, the obvious will be acknowledged: America needed a vast new transportation system after World War II, and one important function of building it was to provide employment. It is also understandable that some workers and unions did not bother to ask about the long-range implications of a policy that was providing them with wages. But it is not at all obvious that this transportation system had to be designed in order to maximize profits, a point which was made repeatedly by the largest union in the field, the United Automobile Workers (U.A.W.).

In January 1949, the U.A.W. pointed out that there was a market for small cars and urged the companies to produce them. Detroit ignored this excellent advice and conceded the low-price, small-car sector to foreign imports. In 1959, the auto giants finally got around to building "compacts," which were not really competitive with a Volkswagen and thus amounted to only half a step in the direction the U.A.W. had recommended in 1949. It was not until 1970 that Ford and General Motors came up with the Pinto and the Vega, which were at least roughly comparable to the European and Japanese imports.

But why, then, did the industry behave in this way? In her brilliant study *Paradise Lost: The Decline of the Auto-Industrial Age,* Emma Rothschild demonstrated that one of the few enduring principles in the Detroit board room is that next year's car must cost more than last year's car. Nat Weinberg, for many years the research director of the U.A.W., put it this way:

All through this period [of the refusal to build cheap, small American cars] the auto industry's rates of return on investment persistently ran far higher than the average profit rate for all U.S. manufacturing industry, while imports continued to flood into the country. Where an industry obtains super-profits while simultaneously its domestic market is penetrated deeply by imports, the conclusion is inescapable. That industry is clearly refusing to engage in price competition with imports.

So, the industry opted for bigger and bigger cars, which is to say higher profits, which is to say increasing gas consumption and pollution. Ironically, the poor were the beneficiaries of one—but only one—unintended consequence of this disastrous misuse of the federal subsidy. It seems that their mileage per gallon in the late sixties and early seventies was better than that of any other social class. The reason is that the poor drive older cars and the average fuel economy of new cars declined every year between 1968 and 1974, partly because of the increase in average-car weight over the same period. Forced to drive less and in decaying autos, the poor did not suffer as much from Detroit's carefully planned inefficiency as everyone else. But that, of course, is small compensation for the enormous price that the entire society, the poor above all, paid for the misallocation of governmental transportation resources when they were used according to the design of the automobile industry.

The government's oil-import quota system was a similar misuse of public power for private purpose.

The mandatory import quotas were established by President Eisenhower's executive order in 1959. They sharply restricted the amount of foreign oil that could enter the United States. The ritual invocation was, of course, made: "The basis of the new program is the certified requirements of our national security, which make it necessary that we preserve to the greatest extent possible a vigorous, healthy petroleum industry in the United States." There were a number of things wrong with this piety. First of all, it motivated domestic producers to "drain America first," that is, to use up as much of the nation's reserves as possible, since they were guaranteed a monopoly profit for them. Conversely, cheap Arab oil without political strings was kept out of the American market. So it was that this country paid a rigged price for using up domestic oil, which then was not available in the 1970s, when the Arabs started exercising *their* monopoly power. (Every tactic used by OPEC was pioneered by the oil multinationals.)

Secondly, the quota program came at a significant moment. Until the 1950s, the companies had controlled supply by the state prorationing system backed up by the federal power. But now, the Middle Eastern oil was gushing into the world market and America —in part because of wasteful, or nonexistent transportation and energy planning—was increasingly dependent upon it. The controls, the Federal Trade Commission later reported, were "to the advantage of the existing petroleum oligopoly," since they provided it with a means of planning production for their own purposes, unaffected by market forces. "It is noteworthy," the Commission said, "that complaints of financial distress from independent refiners and marketers became more prevalent after the imposition of quotas and that many of those firms trace their difficulties to the international arrangement."

There is a particularly clever technique in all of this. It was in the interests of the multinationals, given the handsome depletion allowance, to produce high-priced crude since that tax break is a percentage of the price. This high price is, however, a cost to the refinery. Where an integrated multinational owns the refinery as well as the crude, it can still make big profits, because it is getting a tax subsidy on the cost of that crude. But an independent refinery simply has to pay the high price, getting no subsidy. So the majors reduced refinery profits to zero, and this policy, made economically feasible by government support, was one of the reasons a refinery shortage was an important element in the energy crisis of the seventies.

The quota system, which was at the base of much of this finagling, began in 1959. In 1970, President Nixon's Cabinet-level Task Force on Oil Import Quotas estimated that consumers had paid $5 billion more for oil products in 1969 than they would have paid on a free international market. The Commission proposed to abolish the program and, if the industry needed protection, to introduce tariffs instead (which would mean that the Treasury, not the cor-

porations, would get some of the differential between United States
and foreign prices). Mr. Nixon, who was to receive almost $5 mil-
lion in campaign contributions from the industry in 1972, refused
to follow the advice of his own Commissioners, and the quota system stayed in place until 1973—that is, until the emergent energy
crisis forced the President to follow his own, free-enterprise principles.

As the Federal Trade Commission summed up this sorry experience,

> it created, and leaves in its wake, a shortage of domestic refinery
> capacity which will last for three or four years. The program re-
> stricted crude oil imports and limited imports of refined gasoline
> nearly to zero. In conjunction with other barriers which prevented
> entry into refining, it created a near monopoly over refining for the
> huge integrated firms who control the industry.

Finally, a brief notation on a giveaway that has already been
mentioned, the depletion allowance. This is a work of the political
accountant's art. It does not simply allow the companies a tax
deduction for the costs incurred in developing a vanishing resource,
like oil. Rather, it permits them to take off a percentage of all the
income received by removing gas and oil from the property, and it
can be paid to a landowner who has nothing to do with production
as well as to the companies. This abstruse distinction resulted in
an additional federal payment of $1.7 billion in 1972; the overall
cost of this special tax treatment has been estimated at $3.6 billion
a year.

Indeed, the maze of privileges that had been provided to the oil
corporations is so complex that it is difficult to come up with any
precise total. There are the value of having the United States kick
open foreign doors, as in Saudi Arabia in the 1940s; the billions a
year in avoided taxes due to the special status of oil royalties; the
$5 billion a year in high prices extracted from the monopoly situa-
tion created by the oil import quota; the worth of the depletion
allowance and other accounting tricks (like the "expensing" rather
than the capitalizing of intangible drilling costs) which are worth
billions a year; the direct and indirect subsidies which come from the

tens of billions invested in highways and the whole infrastructure of the Civilization of the Car; and so on. One cannot be exact, yet it is clear that over the past generation this dole for some of the wealthiest corporations in the world has cost the American people hundreds of billions of dollars. In return, the nation was given a criminally wasteful, economically and militarily vulnerable, energy economy.[4]

IV

The energy crisis of the seventies resulted, therefore, from a generation of government policy that followed and subsidized corporate priorities. Most of the proposals to deal with the subsequent disasters urge government policy to follow and subsidize corporate priorities. Three cases in point should illustrate how powerful Americans propose to reward the industry that did so much to create the crisis by putting that industry in charge of solving the crisis. The first is a scheme of the Ford administration to guarantee the prices which the private sector will receive for new types of energy (which the federal government will pay to develop). The second is a research and development program put forward in 1973 by Senator Henry Jackson who, in the name of fighting the corporations, wanted to make them a handsome gift of subsidized technology. In 1975, the free market president, Gerald Ford, proposed even more federal subsidies to benefit private companies than Jackson had. The third is the insistence of impartial observers, like the Chase Manhattan Bank and the New York Stock Exchange, that oil profits (and indeed, capitalist profits in general) should be higher.

In early February 1975, Secretary of State Henry Kissinger made a significant announcement of official American energy policy in a Washington speech. In it he urged a controversial scheme that had many foes within the administration and was greeted with some skepticism in the Common Market countries. What is revealing about this document is not the detailed plan that it urges—which may, or may not, come to fruition—but the philosophy that permeates it. Whatever the fate of those details, it can be confidently said that the framework in which Kissinger developed his theme is shared by his critics at home and abroad. For he made a revealing formulation of a commonplace of the capitalist welfare state: that one deals with problems by putting the private sector on the public payroll.

Kissinger began with a standard evasion. "The energy crisis," he said, "burst upon our consciousness because of sudden, unsuspected events." A little later on, however, he made a slightly more candid admission when he spoke of "the normal—which is to say wasteful— growth of consumption." The Secretary of State did not, of course, explain how "normal" became "wasteful" through the expenditure of hundreds of billions of federal dollars, with some of the most spectacularly subsidized misallocations coming under an administration in which he was a major figure.

Kissinger then briefly sounded a pessimistic theme that had much fascinated him in this period. It implies a conservative's acceptance of a simplistic leftist view of the welfare state as a mere instrument for the avoidance of revolution. "Economic distress fuels social and political turmoil," he said; "it erodes the confidence of people in democratic government and the confidence of nations in international harmony. It is fertile ground for conflict, both domestic and international." In short, the government's power must be vigorously used in order to save the status quo.

Then came the substance of the address. The oil-consuming nations—that is, the leading Western capitalist powers—must unite to solve the crisis through collective financing, research and development and energy policies. If this effort could cut consumption and increase new sources of Western supply, OPEC members would break ranks and start cutting prices in order to keep up their revenues in a declining market. This, however, requires a major effort by the capitalist collective.

> The United States alone shall seek to generate capital investments in energy of $500 billion over the next 10 years. The Federal Government will by itself invest $10 billion in search into alternative energy sources over the next five years, a figure which is likely to be doubled when private investment in research is included.

The Ford Foundation project reported that the highest short-term research-and-development payoffs would come from cleaning up existing energy systems which are the product of "previous neglect."

But there is a problem in all of this. The production costs of the new Western sources cannot compete with the Middle Eastern costs. If the new supply would cause the OPEC prices to fall,

> inexpensive imported oil could then jeopardize the investment made in alternative energy sources; the lower oil prices would also restimulate demand, starting again the cycle of rising imports, increased dependence and vulnerability.

The answer is that the Western governments must guarantee that they will not allow imports to undercut domestic prices. So, a floor price must be established by government.

The problem posed by Kissinger is quite real. But what is revealing about his proposal is its unstated assumption that, in America at least, the government's mobilization, its subsidization of research and development, its solicitude for profits high enough to maintain high rates of private investment, and its promise of what amounts to a guaranteed profit to those corporations which develop new energy sources, should all function to benefit the private sector. The initiative and much of the brains and capital will come from Washington; but the design of the system and the rewards that accrue from it will go to corporations.

In Congressional hearings on the Kissinger proposal, Representative Reuss was particularly perceptive. He commented:

> To the extent that this administration proposal envisages guaranteeing the giants of the American oil industry, who also control a lot of our coal, uranium, oil shale and other sources of energy, that they can enjoy a price which is deliberately rigged and maintained high by their government, I just wonder what shall it profit the American consumer of oil if he is freed from the tyranny of the OPEC countries only to be ripped off by the U.S. oil companies?

Kissinger is a conservative figure in a conservative administration. On the issue of oil, Senator Henry Jackson presented himself as something of a Populist and hectored the executives about the terrible things they were doing. But when he came up with a program, it rested on the same premises as Kissinger's.

In 1973, Jackson proposed a "National Energy Research and Development Policy Act." It was based on recognition of the fact that the capitalist system on its own was utterly incapable of responding to the emergency. It was delicately noted that

> the potential opportunities for non-Federal institutions to recapture the investment in the undertaking through the normal commercial exploitation of proprietary knowledge appear inadequate to encourage timely results . . . the degree of risk of loss is high, and the availability of risk capital to the non-Federal entities which might otherwise engage in the field of research is limited.

Research in new energy technologies was too risky to attract the private sector.

So Jackson proposed to establish joint, public-private corporations to develop coal gasification, shale oil, advanced power-cycle development, geothermal energy and coal liquefaction. Each one of these corporations would have nine directors, five appointed directly by the President and four appointed by him from a list of nominees of the companies participating in the venture. By the standards of the past forty or so years, this would probably mean nine procorporate directors; it would certainly mean a procorporate majority. After these corporations had developed the technology and rendered it commercially profitable, it would go out of existence. The corporations would then privately enjoy the fruits of a socialized energy free. The government is seen as competent—and indeed necessary—for the financing, the risks, and the scientific know-how, but incapable of sharing the profits of a sure thing it helped create.

The very same idea, but with a higher federal price tag, was put forward in September, 1975, by Gerald Ford. Ford urged the creation of an Energy Independence Authority, which "will undertake only those projects private business cannot undertake alone." The Authority would have $100 billion in government funds, credits and loans to use as a "stimulant working through, not in place of, American industry." Thus, there was a remarkable bipartisanship in this area, arising because a centrist like Jackson follows the same corporate logic as Ford, the self-avowed conservative.

The companies, however, want more than massive federal assistance. They also demand that Washington insure their profits. This was the theme of an ideological offensive that was initiated by the Chase Manhattan Bank during the early phases of the energy crisis but which then spread throughout all of American capitalism—including, of course, the government.

The problem, *Forbes* Magazine, a business publication, explained to its readers in 1974, was that *profit* "has become a dirty word, a synonym for capitalist greed." Profits, *Forbes* went on to say, are "a form of enforced saving to insure the nation's economic health." One reason why business felt embattled on this count was that irate consumers who lined up for hours in order to get a few gallons of gas during the shortage of the winter of 1974 had time to read about how the oil companies were making billions out of their misery.

Indeed, the ideologists at *Forbes* were so distressed by this situation that they issued a gentle reprimand to an oil industry which was discrediting all businessmen:

> To defend profits is not the same thing as saying that corporations, in return for their own continued prosperity, do not owe society some accounting. This is something the oil companies seem to forget when they say "Give us profits and we'll give you the oil." The public cannot forget that these were the same oil companies that delivered us into the hands of the Arabs rather than develop coal and other alternate sources of energy.

This is frankly said, and the last admission is an accurate assignment of responsibility. All that *Forbes* fails to understand is that the companies' behavior was inevitable within the framework of the profit doctrine that the magazine defends.

The oil industry, however, did not simply defend its profits; it attacked the nation for keeping them too low. As a Gulf ad put it, "The fuel industry has been warning . . . for the past decade that if government regulations continued to keep oil and natural-gas prices at levels too low to generate capital needed to find more oil

and gas, our nation would eventually run short." The Chase Manhattan Bank, an institution soaked in Rockefeller oil, had sounded
the same theme a little earlier. The controls on natural gas, it had
said, "severely restricted the petroleum industry's ability to generate the capital funds required to finance a continuing search for
oil and natural gas."

The unsuspecting reader might have forgotten a few details that
illuminate this argument. Natural-gas controls were the direct result of an industry attempt to bribe a United States Senator during
the Eisenhower years. Secondly, there is evidence that the corporations have responded to the controls by "capping" wells and refusing to produce until all price restrictions are lifted. And thirdly,
two of the oil majors invested their funds in Montgomery Ward and
the Ringling Brothers Circus, thus making profitable use of money
which was supposed to finance the "continuing search for oil and
natural gas." For the capitalist fact of the matter is that the companies invest their surplus, not in meeting the social needs of America, but in the area of the highest yield.

In any case, Chase Manhattan, the *Wall Street Journal* and the
industry kept on insisting that the proper answer to the oil crisis
was to increase profits in order to finance new investment. Chase
argued that the oil companies would need $400 billion to maintain
their operations and $600 billion to expand them—that is, $1 tril-
lion total—between 1973 and 1985. The argument was then generalized and applied to all of American business. The New York
Stock Exchange reported in September 1974 that there would be a
shortfall of $650 billion in savings from all domestic sources in the
period ending in 1985. To deal with this problem, the Exchange
proposed that corporate tax rates be lowered, that the enormous
subsidy to stockholders in the capital gains exemption be raised,
that the dividend exclusion from Federal income taxes be increased,
that there be higher depreciation allowances, and that the government should provide industry with a permanent-investment tax
credit.

Every one of these proposals amounts to a "tax expenditure"—a
federal handout to the private sector and, above all, to the wealthiest people in America. It will, for instance, be remembered that

Senator Proxmire pointed out that the capital-gains section of the Internal Revenue Code "is the major tax provision redistributing income to the rich" and that people with $20,000 to $25,000 a year receive $100 in benefits from it while those with $1 million in annual income get $640,000 a year in subsidies from it. This is just one of the measures which the Stock Exchange wants to expand. In the name of profits, it is effectively calling for billions, and even tens of billions, of public subsidies.

But then the government itself obligingly picked up this theme. In 1975, Arthur Burns told the Congress that profits were "too low to permit capital investment." This was being said on a day when unemployment stood at 8.2 percent and the American people were experiencing a decline in their standard of living at a rate of more than 3 percent a year. However, Burns and Chase Manhattan and the *Wall Street Journal* would surely respond to such a comment that it was sentimental. If profit rates were higher, there would be more investment, more work and less unemployment.

The argument is both right and wrong. It is a modern restatement of the classic error of Adam Smith and David Ricardo: to identify the specifically capitalist mode of carrying out a necessary economic function with that function itself. And, as with Smith and Ricardo, the result of this confusion is to make the capitalist method eternal and inevitable.

There is no question that all dynamic societies require the deduction of a surplus from current output. If everything that was produced were consumed, there would be no resources for depreciation, for new investment or for reserves to deal with unforeseen events. Marx always insisted upon this point as against those leftists who simply called for giving labor the "full fruit" of its toil. Volume II of *Das Kapital* analyzes the necessity of such a surplus in great detail. But the general economic necessity of having such resources deducted from current output is not at all identical with accomplishing this function through private profits. That is how it is done under capitalism, but it is not in the least an eternal necessity.

When the surplus for depreciation and new investment takes the form of profits, it is indeed true that those moneys can be used for job-creating investments (though Nelson Rockefeller also spends his oil dividends on extra mansions, personal jet planes, and other luxuries). This is the element of truth in the industry's case. But these ideologists ignore two crucial propositions: the consequences of carrying out the investment function in this way; the alternatives to it. Profits do not simply create jobs; they reinforce the maldistribution of wealth which was documented in the last chapter. Moreover, this mighty engine of inequality also gives to private, profit-seeking citizens the right to make momentous social decisions. We have seen the use that the oil industry made of this power. It was scandalously antisocial to the point that even *Forbes* Magazine had to chide its capitalist comrades.

That behavior is programed into the system. Here is how M. A. Adelman describes the attitude of an industry leader who was asked about nonprofit considerations in corporate decision-making. The oil-company president replied, "his indifference lightly tinged with scorn, that there is nothing wrong with adding security and growth to profits as a corporate goal '. . . if you want three goals rather than one, but the latter two are largely implicit in [profits].' " The fact of the matter is that it is of the capitalist essence to invest funds according to profitability, not on a calculus of social usefulness; and, for all the talk about the "conscience" of the corporation, that is the observable rule of American society in every one of its departments.

So, there are antisocial results when the job-creating investment function is carried out by private profiteers. And there are alternatives to this mode of operation. The investment decision can be made by a public corporation, and the surplus can go to the national treasury. Further, this can be, and is, done in either a democratic or a totalitarian manner. If, for example, Senator Adlai Stevenson's proposal for the creation of a federal oil-and-gas corporation were passed into law, then an alternative could even begin to become real in the oil industry itself.

In essence, then, what the ideologists of "free enterprise" present in this case is an example of the corruption of late capitalist society. The New York Stock Exchange wants the government to provide industry with its risk capital through a series of subsidies that would, in an eleven year period, add over $600 billion to the tens of billions of annual gifts which are now in effect. The heroic age of capitalism is clearly over. The executives want the people of the United States to run all the risks, while they retain the right to make all the decisions and keep all the profits.

The oil industry, then, presents a documented case in point of trends which operate throughout the entire society. This evidence will be generalized in Chapter 12, when a summary theory of the welfare state will be outlined. For now, I take it as proved that, in one of the most important areas of American society, the production of energy, the government, in an honest, relatively open fashion followed the priorities of oil corporations with disastrously antisocial results, spending billions in public dollars to render the nation so vulnerable to the OPEC cartel of the seventies. This was not, we have seen, a conspiracy in which evil plutocrats utilized state power as an instrumentality of private purposes. It was and is a much more complex process, in which sincere men make choices that are implicit in the very structure of the economy. For so long as companies are conceded the power to make the basic investment decision of the society, just so long will government be their servant and the common good private property. This is one of the most important secrets of the secret history of the contemporary crisis.[5]

CHAPTER 11

ADAM SMITH'S SOCIOLOGY

THERE are enormous complexities in social life, a fact that has become one of the most fashionable oversimplifications of recent years. It is a central element in what might be called Adam Smith's sociology.

In the 1970s, this complexity theme was sounded by a group of neoconservative thinkers, most of them disillusioned liberals or socialists. (American conservatism has been intellectually rather barren, with a few exceptions like Calhoun, so it is not at all surprising that some of its most sophisticated exponents in recent years are refugees from the left.) These men argued that the failures of the welfare state in the sixties were the results of some inherent flaw in social policy as such. They universalized about government programs, equality, the professionalization of reform, and so on, when actually they were talking about what was done and not done, in a specific historical context, that of late-capitalist society. This is, of course, Adam Smith's classic error in twentieth-century guise: the limitations of the bourgeois order are seen as the dictates of an eternal necessity, and the failures of the welfare state derive from laying impious hands upon the laws of human nature.

I will challenge this thesis on three different levels. First, I differ as to at least some of the facts. The neoconservatives tend to exaggerate the amount of social innovation attempted in the sixties, mistaking promises for operational plans and ignoring the hidden agenda established by the priorities of power. So what they offer as *Realpolitik* is actually rooted in a certain naïveté. Second, their interpretations of the data, even when the latter are accurate, abstract from the unique historical setting—the late-capitalist welfare state—which largely determines how the data function. Third, their methodological errors have political significance leading them to counsel a national policy of timidity, which is the cause of, not the solution to, most of the problems they pose.

Three men can be taken as representative of this neoconservative trend: Nathan Glazer, Daniel Patrick Moynihan, and Daniel Bell. Two of them, Glazer and Moynihan, have sometimes spoken favorably of conservatism, but Bell, as far as I know, has not. Bell and Glazer were public supporters of McGovern in 1972; Moynihan was silent on his vote, saying that a Democrat who had been in a Republican administration should stay out of the campaign. All of them—and particularly Glazer—advocate various liberal reforms, and Bell may still consider himself a man of the left. Yet whatever their personal predilections, their ideas have a consistency and import which in the recent period have been conservative. I honor them when they contradict their own premises, but unfortunately they do not accompany their essays to explain to the reader their velleities to the contrary. I discuss them, then, as a social-intellectual phenomenon, not as individuals.

In thus criticizing these pessimistic thinkers, I do not suggest that there are "easy answers" to the issues of the seventies. There are, indeed, unintended consequences which sometimes overwhelm the best-intentioned plans. But there is also a subtle and obscure truth: that there *are* some solutions to some of our problems. The Adam Smith sociologists are so busy with the timeless verities that they find in the passing moments of the welfare state that they miss this dynamic fact, among many others.

I

To begin with, there is the neoconservative version of what actually happened in the sixties.

The government did too much. In *The Politics of the Guaranteed Income,* Moynihan offers a statement of this theme:

> A further argument which in retrospect may be adduced on behalf of the new conservatism is that diffusing social responsibility for social outcomes tends to retard the rise of social distrust when the promised or presumed outcome does not occur. The modern welfare state was getting into activities no one understood very well. It had not reached the point of picking every man a wife, but it was getting close enough to other such imponderables to find itself increasingly held to account for failures in areas where no government could reasonably promise success.
>
> The conservative argument had heft. This became even more evident in the course of the 1960s as the federal government undertook an unprecedented range of social initiatives designed to put an end to racial and ethnic discrimination, to poverty, and even also to unequal levels of achievement among groups variously defined by race, class, religion, national origin, and sex, primarily through the strategy of providing new, or "enriched," social services.

Moynihan, as will be seen shortly, turns out to be a most persuasive witness against his own case. Yet the notion of "too much government intervention," which he states here so straightforwardly, is crucial to the neoconservative approach. In vulgarized version it also appears in George Wallace's racist pseudo Populism with its attack on the "pointy-headed bureaucrats" in Washington; in Richard Nixon and Gerald Ford's reactionary charge that the sixties liberals (among whom some would count Moynihan himself) "threw money" at problems; and in the agitation of some advocates of "community control" on the left. In the middle seventies, it even became a fashionable assertion for liberal Democratic governors, like Brown of California. Here, however, I am concerned with its sophisticated variant.

The difficulty with this interpretation of the sixties is that the central event it describes—a pervasive government intrusion into the private sphere—never took place.

Moynihan lists three areas in his indictment of liberal ultrareformism: ending racial and ethnic discrimination, abolishing poverty, and promoting equal achievement by means of enriched social services. However, his case does not hold up. The Civil Rights Acts of 1964 and 1965 hardly deal with "imponderables." In this long-overdue legislation, the Congress provided some minimal guarantees of basic rights in public accommodations and voting. Racists regarded that as intolerable interference with the states' right to be Jim Crow. Moynihan and the rest of the neoconservatives did not, happily, share that assessment; they favored these laws. Moreover, the 1964 and 1965 measures must certainly be regarded as successful examples of government action: the "promised or presumed outcome" *did* occur. Blacks voted and, among other things, elected black officials; travel in the South became integrated.

Then there is the accusation of excessive federal involvement in the war on poverty and the related attempt to end "unequal levels of achievement among groups . . . through the strategy of providing new, or 'enriched' social services." This last point does not attack "affirmative action" programs or inveigh against quotas (a neoconservative criticism which will be taken up in due course). Rather, it opposes the "service strategy" that seeks to aid the poor, not simply with money, but with educational, community-action, and other programs which seek to shape new attitudes. As a Nixon counselor, Moynihan made this a major argument in persuading the President to adopt the "incomes strategy" of the Family Assistance Plan (F.A.P.). It would provide hard dollars and cents, Moynihan held; it would avoid the experimentation of the do-gooders. Right now, however, the question does not pose these refined problems. It simply asks, did the government in fact innovate extensively to end racism, poverty, and inequality in the sixties?

In the same book in which he charges overreaching federal involvement, Moynihan answers this question brilliantly.

The social reforms of mid-decade had been oversold, and, with the coming of the war, underfinanced to the degree that seeming failure could be ascribed almost to intent. There was indeed considerable social change going on, and much of it in the direction most desired by those who were discontented, but it was progress clearly linked to the economic book brought on by the war, which made it difficult to take much satisfaction in it.*

The government's own figures corroborate Moynihan's judgment that the reforms of the sixties were "oversold and underfinanced." Between 1955 and 1965, the Brookings Institution study of the 1973 budget shows, there was practically no change in federal civilian expenditures as a percentage of G.N.P. Then, between 1965 and 1970, that percentage almost doubled. But when one looks at where this quantum leap occurred, it does not support the thesis of widespread federal innovation in social policy.

Between 1960 and 1970, there was a $44.3 billion rise in the funds for Social Security and Medicare ($33.9 billion and $10.4 billion respectively). This was three times the increased expenditure of public assistance (welfare, Medicaid, food stamps, housing subsidies, student aid). Social Security is neither innovative nor intrusive for—as Nathan Glazer pointed out in the May 1973 *Commentary*—"the program's objectives are clear and simple, and thus it is easy to evaluate." Medicare can be criticized—primarily on the grounds that it is an utterly inadequate installment on national health insurance—but its difficulties certainly do not derive from too much federal experimentation with the "imponderables" of social policy.

In the budget of the United States government for 1974, these patterns of expenditures are projected up to 1975. In the 1955–75 period, that budget tells us, the "human resources" percentage of

* Why does Moynihan contradict himself? The answer is, I suspect, biographical and therefore beyond the bounds of this chapter. But let me simply note that Moynihan, the assistant secretary of labor for policy research under Kennedy and Johnson, knew that the "service strategy" was pathetically funded, while Moynihan, the counselor to President Nixon, felt that he could win the President over to the Family Assistance Plan (which was a real accomplishment) by attacking the "service strategy" as an example of liberal social engineering, a theme long dear to Nixon's heart.

the budget will have increased from 21.1 percent to 64.8 percent, or from $14.5 billion to $134.9 billion. But of that total, more than 70 percent, or over $93 billion, is accounted for by Medicare, Medicaid, Social Security, veterans' benefits, and aid to the blind, the aged and the handicapped. By contrast, the Office of Economic Opportunity, which was supposed to be the command post in Lyndon Johnson's "war" on poverty, received less than $10 billion in the nine years between its creation under Johnson and its dismemberment under Nixon, with a peak single-year appropriation of $1.9 billion in 1969. And even that figure overstates the federal largesse in this area, since by 1969 a significant portion of O.E.O. funds were going, directly or indirectly, to private business paid to hire hard-core unemployed—whom they probably would often have hired anyway in that boom period.

Thus, Edward Banfield, a conservative conservative who sometimes travels with the neoconservatives, is incorrect when he says that "it was not for lack of money that the Great Society programs failed. Some of the principal efforts—Model Cities, for example— had more of it than they could spend." In fact, as Nathan Glazer has remarked, in the "most original area" of Great Society innovation—such neighborhood-controlled programs as Model Cities and Community Action, which sought popular participation in urban planning and social services—there was "not very much" money. In 1972 (the 1974 federal budget tells us) Model Cities spent all of $500 million, and it is quite clear that one of the reasons this program did not live up to its expectations was and is "lack of money."

Why, then, if the funds for innovating programs were so scant, is there such a resonance to Moynihan's charge? Why did Nixon make such political mileage out of such allegations?

First of all, the frantic style of the Johnson administration convinced people that the government was intervening in every area of life. Moynihan, for instance, notes that the New Towns in Towns Program, which was to use surplus federal land to build homes for the poor, was given a major White House send-off in 1967, and by 1971 had only 300 units of housing under construction.

Second, there were two specific areas in which important constituencies felt that the federal government was indeed moving in on them. The antisegregation laws—and court opinions—attacked deeply entrenched customs and were viewed as unwarranted interference by many Southern racists. When Nixon talked of Washington doing "too much," the Dixiecrats, to whom the Southern strategy was designed to appeal, did not have to consult the budget or the Brookings Institution to know what he meant.

The question of school segregation and busing, however, went beyond the issues of public accommodations and voting rights. For one thing, this problem was posed in the *de facto* segregated districts of the North as well as in the *de jure* systems of the South. For another, it involved, as difficult cases almost always do, a conflict of rights rather than a right versus a wrong, as in the case of discriminatory voting and accommodation statutes. If minority demands for quality education through integration were, and should have been, the dominant consideration, still, ethnic and class concerns for the integrity of neighborhoods were not simply a mask for racism, they derived from an authentic emotion.

Moreover, the sweeping orders sometimes handed down in these cases came from the courts—that is, from the least representative, most insulated of democratic institutions. The reason for that unfortunate—but, to my mind, necessary—reality runs counter to neoconservative theory. If the executive and legislative branches, with their attendant planners and technocrats, had intervened vigorously on this count, the courts would not have acted. It was precisely the default of federal action, not its ubiquity, which turned the judiciary into an agency for the redress of long-overdue grievances.

Also, had there been a serious housing program in the sixties, with new cities and towns and new towns in towns, it could have furnished the basis for neighborhood and citywide integration. But because the urban struggle became more and more of a battle between have-nots among the minorities and the poor and have-littles from the white working class, with the prize coming to be scarce resources such as schools and housing, the courts were called in as arbiters. Here, as in so many recent events, it was the lack of a radical program, the absence of innovation, that was crucial, not, as the neoconservatives have it, our prodigality.

So, the evidence does not back up the first count of the neoconservative indictment of the welfare state in the sixties, that it did too much.[1]

II

In a way, the second neoconservative count is a refinement of the first. It asserts that

The government was too egalitarian in its policies. Nathan Glazer writes of "the revolution of equality": "Perhaps only a Tocqueville saw its awesome potency. For it not only expresses a demand for equality in political rights and in political power; it also represents a demand for equality in economic power, in social status, in authority in every sphere." Leaving for later the issue of the democratization of authority, what Glazer is doing is calling into question the traditional socialist demand for economic and social democracy. That is, of course, his civil liberty, but it puts him on the side of the status quo.

Second, there is no question that some movements in the sixties stood for the kind of radical, egalitarian redistribution of wealth and power that Glazer distrusts. But it must be quickly added that the egalitarians lost. There is no factual basis for the assertion that there was a massive trend toward equality in the sixties, particularly in income and status. Perhaps the most ambitious attempt to argue the contrary is to be found in Daniel Bell's article "Meritocracy and Equality," in *Public Interest* (Fall 1972); I will make a fairly close reading of some of its assertions, since they are a just illustration of the way the sixties are read by neoconservatism.

Bell writes:

. . . the university, which once merely reflected the status system of the society, has now become the arbiter of class position. As the gatekeeper, it has gained a quasi-monopoly in determining the future stratification of society.

And,

Any institution which gains a quasi-monopoly over the fate of individuals is likely, in a free society, to be subject to quick attack.

Thus, the Populist revolt which Michael Young foresaw several decades hence has already begun at the very outset of the post-industrial society. One sees this today in the derogation of the IQ and the denunciation of theories espousing a genetic basis of intelligence; in the demand for "open admissions" to universities; in the pressure for increased numbers of blacks, women and specific minority groups such as Puerto Ricans and Chicanos on the faculties of universities, by quotas if necessary; and in the attack on "credentials," and even schooling itself as the determinant of a man's position in society.

Is it true that the university "has now become the quasi arbiter of class position"? That it has a "quasi-monopoly over the fate of individuals"? That "schooling itself" has ever been the "determinant of a man's position in society"?

That is most questionable sociology. As Daniel Patrick Moynihan and Frederick Mosteller summarize the Coleman Report (the Equal Educational Opportunity Report, a massive, federally financed effort to identify the causes of, and barriers to, equal learning): ". . . studies do *not* find adult social achievement well predicted by academic achievement" and "family background, measured in social class terms—primarily education of parents, but including many other considerations, such as the presence of an encyclopedia in the house—is apparently a major determinant of educational achievement." This latter assertion, it should be noted, inverts Bell's cause and effect, making educational achievement a result of class position rather than the other way round. Christopher Jenck's study of inequality (which Bell cites in his essay) came to an even more pointed conclusion as to the lack of relationship between scholarly and economic success. And David K. Cohen reported in the April 1972 *Commentary* that high-school seniors in the bottom fifth both economically and in terms of I.Q. had a 10 percent chance of going to college, while seniors who were in the top income fifth and the bottom I.Q. fifth had a 40 percent chance.

The great Recession of the seventies provided a stunning refutation of Bell's thesis. Suddenly, there was an "oversupply" of educated labor, and college graduates were to be found driving taxis and working as secretaries, jobs which previously had been held by people with no more than high-school training. Moreover, as Richard Freeman pointed out, there was a permanent devaluation of the economic value of a higher education, one which would persist even in the period of economic recovery. Those students who, like Bell, believed the "meritocratic" myth about America discovered that the constraints of the capitalist class structure and the ups and downs of the capitalist economy were more important than all the universities put together. In saying this, I do not want to invert Bell's error by denying any meritocratic function to the education system. I only, but emphatically, insist that schooling does not have the egalitarian—indeed, the revolutionary—effect that Bell imputes to it.

So, the figures simply do not confirm the thesis that we are on the verge of a meritocracy in which I.Q. is the decisive determinant of class position. Rather, they back up Cohen's statement that "nowhere can we find any empirical support for the idea that brains are becoming increasingly more important to status in America." So, Bell's basic assertion of a trend is debatable. Equality of opportunity, Bell writes (and there is more than a hint of nostalgia in his tone),

> derives from a fundamental principle of classical liberalism that the individual—and not the family, the community or the state— is the basic unit of society, and that the purpose of social arrangements is to allow the individual the freedom to fulfill his own purposes—by his labor to gain property, by exchange to satisfy wants, by upward mobility to achieve a place commensurate with his talents.

Counterposed to this approach is the current idea of equality of result: "Today we have come to the end of classic liberalism. It is not individual satisfaction which is the measure of social good, but redress for the disadvantaged as a prior claim on the social conscience and on social policies." This theory of equality of opportunity is, Bell says, a socialist ethic.

It should be said in passing that classical liberalism was, in some part, a swindle. If it helped to liberate men from feudal relationships of personal dependence, the "individual" of whom it spoke was mostly the bourgeois, the affluent, the privileged individual. For him, the system worked; for the majority it did not, and one reason for the fading of classical liberalism is that people came to see its limitations.

But is it indeed true that "today . . . it is not individual satisfaction which is the measure of social good, but redress for the disadvantaged as a prior claim on the social conscience and social policies"? In part, Bell is here talking about theories, like the philosopher John Rawls's influential book on equality; but in part, he is making assertions about current practice. Witness his remark, "the Kennedy and Johnson Administrations have made equality the central theme of social policy." Is that true?

The sixties sometimes talked as if moved by egalitarian passions. Ironically, Moynihan himself might plausibly claim some credit— or, would he now himself say, bear some blame?—for introducing the idea of equality of result into the mainstream of political debate. In Moynihan's report on the Negro family in 1965 he wrote of a new period beginning after the victories over juridical segregation. Now, Moynihan said,

> the expectations of the Negro Americans will go beyond civil rights. Being American, they will now expect that in the near future equal opportunity for them as a group will produce roughly equal results, as compared with other groups. This is not going to happen. Nor will it happen for generations to come unless a new and special effort is made.

In Lyndon Johnson's Howard University speech, inspired and partly composed by Moynihan, the President said, "We seek not just freedom but opportunity, not just legal equality but human ability, not just equality as a right and a theory but equality as a fact and a result."

As a statement of moral obligation toward people who have suffered discrimination for centuries, the argument for equality of result seems compelling. As a political tactic, I have the same criticisms that Moynihan eventually formulated: that programs to deal with the special needs of blacks and other minorities must also be designed so as to raise the living standards of others, the white working class in particular. Real full employment, for example, betters the bargaining position of all workers, but it aids the relative position of the most vulnerable more than that of any other group. It compensates minorities even as it aids the majority.

But if the sixties sometimes spoke—and rightly so—of national obligations to the victims of discrimination who are not dreamed of in the philosophy of classical liberalism, it did not act radically on that premise. Whatever one might think of the philosophic questions,* the welfare state in the last decade was anything but egalitarian. Big business was encouraged, and sometimes paid, to become an "equal-opportunity employer." Colleges dramatically increased the number of minority students. The best-placed blacks made significant gains—that is, the young educated Negroes with stable marriages were able to take advantage of the new opportunities.

This progress was not negligible. Yet neither does it justify Bell's sweeping generalization: "A sticky fact of Western society over the past 200 years has been the steady decrease in income disparity among persons—not by distribution policies and judgments about fairness, but by technology, which has cheapened the cost of products and made more things available to more people." This presumed trend is then made the basis of what Bell calls the "Tocqueville effect," an explanation of the ingratitude of the new Populists who recently benefited from the progress toward equality.

For according to Tocqueville, Bell says, democratic institutions and equality "develop sentiments of envy in the human heart." So,

* Bell refers to "equality of result" as a socialist ethic. Since the most famous discussion of the equality issue in the history of socialist thought—Marx's brief but profound comments on the Gotha Program of the German Social Democracy—is an *attack* on the notion that equality of result is a socialist ideal, this is a surprising assertion from one as well-versed as Bell in the literature. The socialist aim, at least in its serious formulations, has never been the impossible goal of guaranteeing everyone the right to win in a competitive rat race; it has been the abolishing of the rat race altogether. The formula, "From each according to his ability, to each according to his need," insists upon, and even glories in, human differences—*inequalities,* if you will—once they no longer rationalize a system of invidious competition. Socialists want to move toward equality, in order then to transcend it.

paradoxically, it is our more and more egalitarian reality, in Bell's view, that is the cause of antiegalitarianism.

A few general words about Bell's "sticky fact" are needed before turning to specifics in the sixties. The extent to which there has been a *relative* change in income shares over the past two hundred years in the West is difficult to document and certainly open to debate. There has, of course, been an absolute increase in the standard of living of the masses, but that is something else again and not relevant to Bell's assertions about "disparities." Second, to the degree that some relative progress may have been achieved, it was the result not only of technology but also of a furious social conflict —a class war—over the distribution of the fruits of technology.

However, once one reduces the focus from two centuries to two decades—that is, to the period in which Bell perceives his "Tocqueville effect"—we can be somewhat more precise about the figures (but only somewhat; the dirty little secret of the rich in a democracy is the extent of their wealth). All the evidence shows that there has been no change in basic income distribution at least since 1947. (There are those who argue that there were some changes between 1929 and 1947, because of the Depression and the War— two rather unfortunate instruments of social policy—but even that proposition has been criticized by serious analysts.)

Lewis Mandell of the University of Michigan Survey Research Center has computed that the top 5 percent of the wealth holders in America own 40 percent of the wealth, and that the top 20 percent possess three times as much as the 80 percent below them. A 1972 *Business Week* summary of recent research pointed out that the bottom 50 percent of the income recipients received 23 percent of the total personal income in 1969 and represented only 3 percent of net worth. And James D. Smith of Penn State has concluded that the rich get richer because they start from a higher base. In stock ownership, as Letitia Upton and Nancy Lyons have documented, the disparities are severe: the top 1 percent of the wealth holders own 62 percent of all publicly held corporate stock; the top 5 percent have 86 percent, the top 20 percent have 97 percent. So much for our stockholder democracy.

These tendencies, it must be remembered, were reinforced, not reversed, by the Kennedy-Johnson administrations of the sixties (and, of course, by the Nixon administration). Because John Kennedy had such a narrow Presidential margin and a shaky position in Congress, he moved to stimulate the economy through investment credits, accelerated depreciation and tax cuts, all of which notoriously benefited the rich more than anyone else. During the sixties, as the AFL-CIO has documented on many occasions, unit labor costs were stable for the first half of the decade while profits soared (and also the much more significant figure of corporate cash flow, profit, plus depreciation allowances and internal financing). During the second half of the decade, workers were forced to strike simply to keep pace with the cost of living and some of them suffered a decline in real purchasing power. The U.A.W.'s bitter battle with General Motors in 1970, for instance, was in considerable measure necessary because the union had to catch up with inflation, running furiously just to stay in place.

As Chapter 8 documented on the basis of 1972 data from the Treasury and Joint Economic Committee there are billions (over $90 billion in the 1976 budget) of tax subsidies, and the corporate rich get the lion's share. Moreover, the government—under Kennedy and Johnson as well as Nixon—used its power to favor corporate investment in machines even at times of high unemployment. Lyndon Johnson refused to fund the public-service jobs advocated by the Automation Commission of 1966 and the Civil Disorders Commission of 1968. Instead, he paid private business a bonus for hiring hard-core unemployed workers.

Even those increases in Social Security that formed the bulk of new government expenditures in the sixties contributed somewhat to this antiegalitarian trend. For as the Social Security tax, one of the most regressive in the nation, was increased, so was the burden on working people. (The Social Security tax does not vary according to family size, responsibilities, et cetera; and it is charged against only the first $15,300 of income, which makes it a bargain for those with over $15,300 a year and regressive compared even to the federal income tax.)

Indeed, even if one takes a country that would seem much more likely to bear out the Bell thesis than the United States—Great Britain, where the Labour Party is committed to egalitarianism on socialist grounds and has exercised power on a number of occasions since World War II—the remarkable fact is the *persistence* of inequality despite all the reforms. A Royal Commission Report on the distribution of income and wealth appeared in 1975. It is much more detailed and precise than any of the American studies and it shows the impact of Labour Party policies. In 1938–39, the wealthiest 1 percent of the British had 17.1 percent of the before-tax income and 11.7 percent of the after-tax income. By 1949–50, toward the end of Attlee's first Labour government, the before-tax figure had fallen to 10.6 percent, after tax to 5.8 percent. And by 1972–73, the percentages were respectively 6 and 4. In other words, there is clear statistical evidence that egalitarian Labour policies had a very real effect on the distribution of income.

But when one turns to the distribution of wealth, that picture begins to change. For although the ownership of the top 1 percent registers a dramatic decline—from 69 percent in 1911–13 to a "mere" 42 percent in 1960—the significant figure, as the Commission itself suggests, is what happened to the top 10 percent. The figures all count individuals, not families, and one of the seeming redistributive effects only describes the rich making gifts and spreading the assets around the family. When one looks at the top 10 percent, i.e., the families of the rich, the decline from 1911 to 1913 to 1960 becomes much more modest: from 92 percent of Britain's wealth to 83 percent.

However, even these numbers understate the persistence of inequality. The "wealth" of the working people is in household appliances, insurance policies and government bonds; the wealth of the rich is in property and stocks. In the latter category, the maldistribution remained, in 1972, extreme. The bottom 60 percent of the wealth holders (which excluded, of course, those who owned nothing) had 2.2 percent of the property yielding dividends and interest subject to direct tax. Adding another quintile, 81.6 percent of the wealth holders had only 5.3 percent of that property, and 98.2 percent held 28.7 percent. The truly rich, the top 1.8 percent, owned 71.3 percent; the top four-tenths of one percent, 52.1 percent! This was the case in a nation that had been much more consciously egalitarian than the United States, and yet could only make the most modest progress in the course of several generations. In this country, we do not have even that rather cold comfort.

So the notion that our troubles are caused by the egalitarianism of the welfare state in the sixties, as suggested by both Glazer and Bell, is not true. Instead of talking of a "Tocqueville effect," perhaps it is necessary to speak of the "Sisyphus effect"; the anger felt by people when they intuit that, despite the fact that they have more money to spend, they have not advanced their relative position in a society which regards that as the supreme good.[2]

III

Since the neoconservatives wrongly think that the Kennedy-Johnson years were excessively idealistic and egalitarian but still promoted discontent, they conclude that

The consequences of government intervention are, more often than not, unintended and usually negative. The philosophy behind this theory goes back at least to Edmund Burke and his assertion of an organic development of society as an argument against state interferences with the providence of the natural order of things. Perhaps the best-known contemporary writer in this intellectual tradition is the British philosopher Michael Oakeshott. In his *Politics of a Guaranteed Income,* Moynihan cites Oakeshott in the course of analyzing the dispute over the Family Assistance Plan, saying that he "has defined the conservative temperament in terms which showed with great distinctiveness, and not a little advantage, in the debate . . ." In Oakeshott's view, innovation involves "certain loss and possible gain" and is best when it resembles the process of growth. Oakeshott concludes that "as the conservative understands it, modifications of the rules should always reflect, and never impose, a change in the activities and beliefs of those who are subject to them." (On this calculus, much cited by the Dixiecrats at the time, the Civil Rights Acts of 1964 and 1965 were clearly unwise.)

The now-famous "notch" is invoked by the American neoconservatives as an instance of Oakeshott's wisdom. The "notch" defines that point at which working, or increasing income, or even escaping from poverty, becomes irrational, because government policy turns a marginal increment into a substantial loss. Under the provisions of Aid for the Families of Dependent Children (Unemployed)—AFDC(U)—states were given the right to provide AFDC benefits even though there was an able-bodied, though unemployed, man in the house. However, if the man worked more than 30 or 35 hours, he and his family would lose all assistance. Similarly, in states with decent Medicaid programs, a person who raises his income by five dollars but thereby fails the means test for Medicaid, forfeits much more than five dollars in medical benefits. There is, consequently, a positive incentive to stay under the "notch"—that is, to remain, or at least appear to remain, poor.

These cases do meet Oakeshott's criteria for unintended consequences, since they are the result of good, reformist intentions. The AFDC(U) legislation was a victory for those liberals who were aghast because the requirement that no man could be in the house literally drove fathers to leave their families (or to pretend that they had done so). And Medicaid was, of course, a sleeper provision of the Medicare law which permitted the most advanced states —notably New York, Massachusetts and California—to provide a partial installment of socialized medicine. Yet both these efforts, laudable as their intent was, tended to provide inducements to poverty.

There can be no doubt that this "notch" effect took place. But does this prove, as Oakeshott, Moynihan and the neoconservatives assume, that such mishaps are inherent in the very process of reform and therefore are an argument for caution with regard to innovation? That would be true only if other factors did not contribute to the "notch" effect—which is precisely the case. The "notch" was the creation of timid governmental action, not of sweeping programs.

First of all, it must be emphasized that both AFDC(U) and Medicaid were palliatives, not radical departures. AFDC(U) recognized that the government's full-employment policy was unable to provide work for a significant number of able and willing family heads, that is, that even Keynesian capitalism was deeply flawed. It was extremely limited in its application, required the states to act and spend money, and therefore operated in a significant fashion only in a few areas. Had there been genuine full employment— through the mechanism of a federal guaranteed right to work— AFDC(U) would have been unnecessary. The "notch" in this case was, therefore, the result of an inadequate response to a problem that should not have been allowed to exist in the first place.

Similarly with Medicaid. The reason the "notch" arises in this area is that National Health Insurance, first vigorously advocated by Harry Truman in 1949, was rejected, and the nation decided, after wasting more than a decade in indecision, on a second-best: some medical care for the elderly; a states-rights Medicaid provision that was practically smuggled into the law. It is a notorious fact that Medicare and Medicaid have, along with their undeniable accomplishments, bid up the cost of medical care for those under sixty-five and not poor. This provides an enormous incentive for someone to keep his income below the Medicaid cut-off line. But if there were National Health Insurance—had we passed Truman's 1949 proposal or were we to pass the Kennedy-Corman bill before the Congress in the middle seventies, the "notch" would simply disappear. So it is not the result of the immemorial frailties of the human condition, but of our own conscious, perverse, and reversible political decisions.

In saying these things, I do not want to suggest for a moment that reform is a seamless, utterly predictable affair. Of course it isn't. Admitting that is one thing; overgeneralizing from it, as the neoconservatives have done, is another thing.

There is, however, one area where the complexities do more nearly accord to the neoconservative account of them: education. The Coleman Report—the Equal Educational Opportunity Survey and Report—is prime evidence in this regard. As Moynihan tells it, everyone assumed prior to the Report that an increase in educational inputs—money for schools, teachers, books, equipment, et cetera—would result in better outputs: academic achievement. Therefore, it was said, particularly after the 1954 Supreme Court decision against segregation in public education, that the disparity in intellectual performance between the poor and the nonpoor, or the minorities and the majority, was to be explained by the lack of school inputs in poor neighborhoods. And this was the rationale of the various federal education programs of the sixties: they were to close the academic gap by channeling new resources to those who had suffered discrimination and neglect.

Some of these propositions were indeed shared by almost all liberals and radicals. To the extent that the Coleman Report disproved them—and the Report itself, it must be understood, is still the subject of debate—it did expose an area of well-meaning ignorance. The Report did show that the objective disparities between black and white educational inputs were not as great as had been imagined by many; and that the academic outputs which could be won by money were lower than most had thought.

But Moynihan and company exaggerate the degree to which the assumptions subverted by Coleman had been shared by the left. The belief that schools could—apart from changes in class position, the labor market, housing, et cetera—transform life at the bottom of the society is not a radical thesis. Indeed, it does not even represent the best of liberalism. Coleman's findings, that family background measured in social-class terms is a more important determinant of educational achievement than school buildings or chemistry labs, confirms a traditional socialist analysis. (Indeed, I had made a comment along these lines—arguing that the finest school and best teachers would be overwhelmed by a slum—in *The Other America* in 1962.)

Second, thinking in terms of input and output assumes that education can, and should be, described as a production function appropriate in a factory: x dollars invested yields y increases in reading scores. That equation, however, utterly fails to take into account some of the most crucial variables. The schools do not simply develop cognitive skills; they are also a basic socializing institution for a democratic society. If such a formulation strikes one as sentimental, a nonquantifiable claim, then it can be translated into an economic projection. For there are serious experts who believe that it is not so much what a child learns in school, but the school experience taken as a whole, that is crucial for increasing intellectual productivity.

Third, part of our inability to deal with education relates to unprecedented changes that have taken place. Just before World War II, about a third of American youth went to high school. Now that figure is around three quarters of the available population. A generation ago, grade schools functioned to provide minimal literacy, and high schools were the preserve of the more fortunate and motivated students. Now there is a massive group in the high schools such as never existed before, and one of the reasons that "Johnny" is not doing better is that this is the first time he has been asked to go beyond that basic literacy. We have most certainly failed to respond adequately to this challenge, but our difficulties stem from a new and worthy problem.

Still, I would distinguish between two areas of unintended consequences in the recent history of the welfare state. First, there are the cases where our deficiencies are the result of timid, pinch-penny programs, which create unnecessary "notches." Second, there are areas—education and drug addiction, for instance—in which our ignorance plays a role and our good intentions may sometimes be counterproductive. But the first category is a refutation of the Oakeshott analysis, and the second by no means confirms it. Nevertheless, the neoconservatives build upon this faulty base and argue against a "service strategy" that is seen as an unwarranted intervention in the domain of social complexity. They persuaded the Nixon policy-makers on this count and provided them with a rationale for dismantling a number of Great Society programs—though they failed to win Nixon to a serious fight for the alternative of an income strategy.[3]

IV

The critique of the service strategy was basic to Nathan Glazer's enormously influential article "The Limits of Social Policy." Glazer wrote: "In its efforts to deal with the breakdown of these traditional structures (family, ethnic group, church, neighborhood), however, social policy tends to encourage their further weakening." Services become professionalized; our lack of knowledge creates new problems rather than solutions. So, Glazer concluded, one of the things to recommend the Nixon Family Assistance Plan (F.A.P.) is that it is not a service strategy. And in a later article Glazer praised another program based on an "income strategy": "Thus we know enough generally about Social Security to act (although there are plenty of complexities in that program, too). The same amount of money is sent out from a central point to everyone in the same status. The program's objectives are clear and simple, and thus it is easy to evaluate."

Moynihan carried the attack against the service strategy into the White House itself in 1969 and 1970, persuading—if only briefly—Richard Nixon to advocate a guaranteed annual income (which the President constantly asserted was not a guaranteed annual income). "The service strategy," Moynihan wrote in his retrospect on the battle for F.A.P., "has been quintessentially that of political liberalism in the middle third of the twentieth century. And yet the actual *effect* of service programs such as education is probably to reallocate resources *up* the social scale, taxing, as it were, factory workers to pay schoolteachers." An income strategy, Moynihan said, did not involve the intrusions and confrontations of a service strategy. And, he added in a somewhat radical mood, "The concept of an 'income strategy' entailed many risks—it could only in the end mean *income redistribution. . . .*"

This analysis contains both an interpretation of the recent history of the welfare state and policy conclusions to be derived from it. Moreover, it is typical of a strand of thought that is to be found in almost all of neoconservative writing. So it deserves rather careful attention.

First, it is *not* true that the service strategy has been "quintessentially that of political liberalism in the middle third of the twentieth century"—nor even in the decade of the sixties. There were probably some social workers who believed in such an approach, but they were relatively few in number and certainly not the arbiters of liberalism. The traditional New Deal liberals of the labor-liberal coalition always made full employment their demand, as Moynihan must remember from his days at the Department of Labor. A. Philip

Randolph's *Freedom Budget,* which was endorsed by John Kenneth Galbraith as well as by a good number of international union presidents, put this issue at the very heart of government policy.

The Freedom Budget would have required the President to estimate the number of jobs required to achieve full employment and then to outline government policies (fiscal, monetary, manpower, et cetera) which would guarantee that the needed work level would actually be achieved. This was the original concept of what became the Employment Act of 1946. Roosevelt's original proposal was gutted by the Congressional conservatives, who refused to make any binding commitment to full employment but were willing only to state that it was the government's pious hope that it be realized. The Rooseveltian idea surfaced again in 1975 in a proposal made by Leonard Woodcock of the Auto Workers and Wassily Leontief, the Nobel Laureate in economics from Harvard. A version of it was submitted to the Congress in a bill sponsored by Hubert Humphrey and Jacob Javits. For more than a generation, then, a job strategy, not a service strategy, was a critical demand of American labor and liberalism.

It is, of course, true that in the original infighting over the Economic Opportunity Act, the Department of Health, Education and Welfare (through Wilbur Cohen) and the Council of Economic Advisors (through Walter Heller) battled the Secretary of Labor (Willard Wirtz) and his associate (Moynihan) on this question. Cohen, Heller and their allies wanted to make the war on poverty into a community-action program that would help the poor to organize themselves for self-improvement. That, of course, is a service strategy. Wirtz and Moynihan were for a job emphasis. But even then, the community-action proponents never isolated that idea from the whole range of macroeconomic measures in which the government was engaging. Heller, as the chief architect of the full-employment planning then called "New Economics," could hardly have thought that the service strategy was "quintessential."*

I do not cite this history merely to demonstrate that Moynihan's

---

* I am certain of these matters, because I participated in the debate and sided with Wirtz and Moynihan.

memory is faulty. It relates to establishing the broader context of all the welfare-state debates of the sixties. The Kennedy-Johnson manpower policies did reduce joblessness from the Eisenhower levels down to less than 4 percent, and that was probably the most effective accomplishment in the "war" on poverty. But in 1966 and 1968 when, as I have already noted, Presidential commissions recommended a ranging federal program of funding public-service employment, Lyndon Johnson turned down that liberal proposal and took the conservative ("trickle-down") line of encouraging private hiring by subsidizing it. In this case, the realistic politicians were wrong, the liberal intellectuals right.

It is precisely Moynihan's amnesia on this count that flaws his analysis of the Family Assistance Plan. In explaining why the Nixon proposals set the minimum so low (in the neighborhood of $2,500 for a family), Moynihan says that this was necessary because the working poor were being included in the program. Since they were to be given the right to keep a portion of the earnings (in contrast to the hundred-percent tax on such income that used to prevail in most welfare systems), a $2,500 base for the dependent (nonworking) poor thus meant some support to the working poor up to $5,000 of income. If, therefore, the minimum were set at $6,500, as urged by Senator Eugene McCarthy and the National Welfare Rights Organization, that would have required supplementing the income of everyone with less than $13,000—that is, the majority of the people. So, Moynihan concludes, it was essential to peg the minimum low if there was any hope of passing the plan.

In other words, the undeniable needs of the working poor, who would gain from F.A.P., were counterposed to the undeniable needs of the dependent poor in states with relatively high benefits. The latter would not get any increases at all—they might even lose in the shuffle. But this was true only because of an enormous and intolerable fact that Moynihan ignores: that there were unconscionably high levels of unemployment and underemployment creating that scandalous category of the "working poor." If the Nixon administration, in which Moynihan served, had not systematically increased unemployment as part of a strategy for price stability in

1969 and 1970, the problem would have been much less difficult. If the liberal proposals for full employment had been adopted in the sixties, it would not have existed at all.

Second, there is Moynihan's assertion that the service strategy reallocates resources *"up* the social scale." That depends, not on the nature of the service strategy, but on the tax system. If, for example, one were to finance community-action programs in the next period out of those billions in loophole savings that would be realized if effective tax reform were adopted, Moynihan's regressive effect would not take place. It is true that in the sixties the burden of paying for social services—and for the war in Vietnam—fell discriminatorily upon working people. That, however, was a function of the antiegalitarianism of federal wealth and income policy, which has already been documented in the discussion of Daniel Bell's view on equality.

Similarly, Moynihan's assertion that F.A.P. had to mean *"income redistribution"*—and it is interesting that as a neoconservative he counts this as a point in its favor—is, in and of itself, not true in the least. If F.A.P. were accompanied by a tough tax-reform proposal, that might have been the case; but in fact it was debated at a time when Nixon, as the Joint Economic Committee showed, was increasing the tax relief of the rich substantially. (He reduced taxes by about $20 billion a year.)

Third, Moynihan is somewhat ambiguous—and somewhat wrong—in another aspect of his critique of the service strategy. In the introduction that he wrote (along with Frederick Mosteller) to the essays on the Coleman Report, which were produced by a Harvard seminar, he said:

> One of the patterns of the 1960s was that of middle-class persons, in large measure professionals, conceiving a great range of social programs, supported by tax monies, which undertook to assist the poor through a process of employing middle-class persons. Reform was becoming professionalized.

In this formulation, Moynihan seems to be giving sophisticated utterance to a popular myth: that welfare programs are a cheat designed by social workers. In the process, he overstates the class bias of the service strategy. Nathan Glazer is much closer to the truth when he writes:

> . . . we hired great numbers of social workers and consultants, increasing their income. Many of these—few at the beginning, more later—came from minority groups; we were providing the jobs through these programs for the barely college-trained that other programs were producing; and from the same communities.

In the case of teachers, whom Moynihan has attacked on this count, my own guess is that a very large number of them are the children of working-class families.

But, then, Moynihan himself is ambiguous in his critique. In the same essay in which he deprecated the middle-class beneficiaries who allegedly profiteer from poverty programs, he also wrote, "Increasingly the most relevant findings concerning the state of society are the work of elites and must simply be taken—or respected—by the public at large, at times even by the professional public involved, on . . . faith." Social reality, Moynihan argues in this mood, is often "counterintuitive" and therefore the society must accept the data from the experts. So Moynihan is—as is Bell, who is at least as anxious to defend the perquisites of expertise—of two minds about the professionals in charge of the service strategy.

In this, as in the entire critique of the service strategy, there is the imprecision of overgeneralizations. In a good many cases, the flaws which are said to be inherent in such programs turn out, on closer examination, to be the result of the limitations—usually the cheapness—of the welfare state itself. President Nixon did not, however, bother to make such discriminations. He allowed himself to be persuaded, or perhaps it would be more precise to say that he permitted his prejudices to be reinforced, by the blunderbuss blast against the service strategy. And after a brief infatuation with Family Assistance, he abandoned the income strategy, too.[4]

V

The neoconservatives cannot, of course, be held responsible for a reactionary misreading of their views. But they are accountable for a philosophy that begs for such a fate. This is particularly true of their largest and most conservative abstraction:

The preference for the unplanned, and even the irrational, as opposed to conscious government policy. This is a fundamental conservative theme, the nostalgia for the vanished *Gemeinschaft,* the suspicion of the contemporary *Gesellschaft.* From Burke to Dostoyevsky to Spengler it has been at the very center of conservative thought.

In the early pages of *Maximum Feasible Misunderstanding,* Moynihan indulges in some romantic medievalism which leans heavily upon Robert Nisbet. But then, Moynihan is partly a product of Catholic social thought, which has always idealized that period of the Church's dominance. In the writings of Chesterton, Belloc, Gill, and others, the Middle Ages were held up as a model of a society in which all participants—the lords as well as the serfs—recognized mutual obligations and thereby obviated the need for a class struggle. The mythic happiness of that organic period of history was contrasted to the violence and materialism of the contemporary age. So there are biographical reasons why Moynihan would be attracted by the lure of *Gemeinschaft.* But Nathan Glazer, who comes from a completely different, socialist tradition, provides the most striking example of this tendency.

"Social policy"—Glazer wrote in "The Limits of Social Policy"—"is an effort to deal with the breakdown of traditional ways of handling disasters." What the family, church, ethnic group, *Landsmannschaft,* et cetera, once did, the government now attempts to do. "In the effort to deal with the breakdown of these traditional structures, however, social policy tends to encourage their further weakening." Putting it that way is to confuse the effect for a cause and to overlook a revolution. The "traditional way of handling disasters" broke down, in good measure, because of unprecedented new problems and disasters. By focusing on the breakdown as the author of our woes, one holds out the hope that all can be well again if only it can be repaired; by stressing the cause of the breakdown, a revolutionary process that has been going on for some centuries, one knows that the revival of the old *Gemeinschaft* is impossible. Moreover, it should at least be noted that in the "good old days," most people's lives were short and brutish.

Glazer believes that Humpty Dumpty is going to be put together again: ". . . some important part of the solution to our social problems lies in the traditional practices and restraints." But when the economic and social conditions for those practices and restraints have been destroyed, how can they rise from the dead to solve our problems?

I suspect that Glazer's emphasis derives in part from a very real and understandable concern about the breakdown of "traditional practices and traditional restraints" in his own neighborhood: the university. So it is that the climactic charge in Glazer's indictment of the "revolution of equality" is that it seeks to create "equality in authority." And Daniel Bell defends the "authority represented in the superior competence of individuals" from the scorn of the New Populists.

In part, these neoconservative fears have substantial content. There has indeed been a decline of ethical standards accompanying the effective collapse of organized religion. The emancipation of the psyche from the restraints imposed upon it by the hierarchical authority of the past has not, as Marx and the socialist tradition hoped, led to the emergence of a new, humanist and rational code. For one thing, this cultural revolution has occurred, not within the context of a political and social revolution, but under the domination of conservative social structures. As a result, the revolution was marketed, vulgarized, co-opted. There are, then, reasons to be disturbed. But this upheaval has been going on for perhaps a century, and it is hardly the result of recent—Populist or New Left—trends in American life. Moreover, if there is any possibility that this cultural revolution can become a vehicle for social emancipation, what is required is a radical response, a reshaping of the social structures, and not, as in the neoconservative proposal, a retreat.

On a more prosaic level, Glazer deduces some very faulty policy from his attempt to revive *Gemeinschaft* past. He writes: "Ultimately, we are not kept healthy, I believe, by new scientific knowledge or more effective cures or even better-organized medical-care services. We are kept healthy by certain patterns of life." That, I submit, is not true. England and Sweden are beset by the same cultural convulsions as the United States. Their churches, family structure, et cetera, are no more secure than ours. Yet their health is. The reason is simple enough: they have better-organized medical care than we have.

In some ways, this celebration of the organic as against the rational is the most unfortunate aspect of neoconservatism. It takes that fledgling ideology back toward conservatism pure and simple, to the notion that the hope of the future lies in the past. But the data simply do not corroborate these sweeping reactionary conclusions; the failures of the welfare state in recent years are the result of its conservatism, not its excessive liberalism or, more preposterously, of its radicalism. They derive from the antiegalitarian and capitalist limitations of the system, not from the flawed human nature and perverse reality that one reads of in Adam Smith's sociology.[5]

CHAPTER 12

SOME DIALECTICAL COMPLICATIONS

THE welfare state follows capitalist priorities, as has been seen. Does this, then, mean that the corporate rich, who are undeniably its greatest beneficiaries, run it to suit their own purposes?

Yes and no.

Obviously such an ambiguous answer involves dialectical complications. Indeed, these sometimes become so intricate that they may seem theoretical in the worst sense of that word, as the needless compounding of paradox upon paradox. And yet, these apparently abstruse refinements are the basis of some very practical political choices. So one begins with the obvious, that wealth is political power in a capitalist society, and then proceeds to the not-so-obvious, that even if the corporate rich were deprived of all personal influence in the welfare state, it would still promote their class interest. And having thus demonstrated that this system tends to co-opt its reforms, one must still understand that those reforms also provide the only Archimedian point from which the system itself can be changed.

A case in point from Karl Marx should make these complexities more concrete. It is found in *Das Kapital,* in the analysis of the Ten Hours Law, which limited the working day in nineteenth-century Britain. That law, it will be remembered, was seen by Marx in all its convolutions. Some of the workers opposed it because they thought it responsible for a raise in unemployment; some of the capitalists eventually favored it on pragmatic grounds; and the reactionary landlords were enthusiastically for it since they regarded it as a means of punishing the bourgeois *parvenus* who had abolished agricultural protectionism. Moreover, Marx wrote, the net impact of the law was to make capitalism more rational and efficient, and the economists who had fought it now proclaimed it a triumph of their discipline. But the workers were strengthened, too. Their living standard improved and they had learned the practical value of solidarity in the process. The law, Marx said in full knowledge of the fact that the capitalists had profited from it along with the proletariat, was a "modest Magna Charta."

Unfortunately, a good many Marxists do not have Marx's tolerance for, and understanding of, such ambiguities of social life. For instance, the British writer John Saville argued in the 1950s that the welfare state assures "a reasonable degree of economic efficiency by the erection of social and political shock absorbers, whose function is to offset the gross inequities and natural insecurities of the capitalist order." That is only partly true. Another British New Leftist of that period, Dorothy Thompson, rightly responded to Saville that the trade-union struggles and the social services "are, objectively, victories for working-class values within capitalist society." That is in keeping with the dialectical spirit of Marx, who held that the Ten Hours Law, which he well knew had promoted capitalist efficiency, was nevertheless a victory of "the political economy of the working class."

In this chapter, I will follow Marx's lead and focus on the complexities, contradictions and ambiguities of the welfare state. In the process, it will be necessary to criticize some of the leftists who have concentrated too exclusively on the undeniable proposition that social reform within capitalism eventually tends to help capitalism. I should, however, note at the outset that I am in sympathy with their error. There has been so much claptrap written about the glories and egalitarianism of the welfare state that an overreaction to that idyllic and fraudulent sociology is most understandable. The mistake is a most honorable one.

But it is a mistake and it has serious consequences for the Marxist method and for political strategy. On the theoretical plane, by making the welfare state into a mere tool of the corporations, these theorists turn it into a conscious, almost conspiratorial, phenomenon. Marxism, to cite Christopher Lasch's brilliant insight again, does not analyze ideas "as 'rationalizations' in the narrow sense of conscious lies, but as elaborate structures of thought, permeating the consciousness of entire epochs, which are so closely related to the dominant structures of production that the relationship is no longer a matter for conscious reflection." The tendency to see social institutions as the intentional creation of economic classes with an omniscient and objective sense of their own interests is, Lasch rightly comments, more Populist than Marxist. It is, therefore, very American.

These issues are important for Marxist theory, of course; but they also relate to American politics. For if one regards the entire welfare state as purely and simply façade, then its most militant defenders, the organized workers, are a part of the capitalist apparatus. Therefore, all commitment to reform is illusory, or worse, a process whereby the left unwittingly shores up the status quo. So the strategy that arises out of this theory is one of confrontation, and it orients toward the underclass, the excluded, the marginal people in society, since it views practically everyone else as dupes of the established order. This attitude had a certain vogue among American radicals in the late sixties and early seventies, and the critique of its analytic underpinnings in this chapter thus also relates to practical considerations about the tactics of the left in contemporary America.

These theoretical and political issues will emerge, first in a brief historical survey of the welfare state, and then in a closer examination of its structure today.[1]

I

There is a thesis that sees the welfare state as a means of pacifying —of buying off—revolutionary discontent. There is a good deal of truth in this; only it is one-sided.

Frances Fox Piven and Richard A. Cloward, theorists of the welfare rights movement in the sixties, make a succinct statement of the theme:

> Historical evidence suggests that relief arrangements are initiated and expanded during the occasional outbreaks of civil disorder produced by mass unemployment and are then abolished or contracted when political stability is restored.

At times other motives for reform are acknowledged, but even then the emphasis is upon welfarism as a stratagem of the ruling class.

> The landed gentry [Piven and Cloward write] who ruled Britain until 1832, and the manufacturing classes who joined them as rulers afterwards, responded to popular unrest partly because they feared revolution, partly because they recoiled from the trouble and property losses caused by disorderly mobs, and perhaps even, on some occasions, because they shared with the populace a sense of what was right and just.

The sense of what is "right and just" plays a most subordinate role, among the ruled as among the rulers. The real dynamic arises out of revolution and violence on the one side and fear on the other.

In a good many cases, Piven and Cloward are quite right. The Preamble to the original welfare law in England, the statute of Elizabeth I in 1598, was explicit enough: ". . . of late years more than in times past there have been sundry towns, parishes and houses of husbandry destroyed and become desolate, whereof a great number of poor people are become wanderers, idle and loose, which is the cause of infinite inconvenience . . ." Clearly, the Elizabethans were responding to the upheavals caused by the dissolution of feudalism and the rise of capitalism; their "charity" was shrewd.

There is another important aspect of these events. The Elizabethan Poor Law is an example of what Richard Titmuss calls the "Diswelfare State." The society, in this case emergent English capitalism, imposes enormous social costs upon helpless individuals, destroying their traditional way of life in the name of a higher economic good. It then creates a welfare state, which it regards as an act of benevolence, but which is, in fact, a systematic underpayment to the people for suffering thrust upon them for the profit of others. That process continues to this day.

The English welfarism that arose at the time of the French Revolution is another example of manipulative compassion. In part, the motivation was economic. There had been a series of bad harvests during the 1790s, and prices went up because of the conflict with France. It was, Maurice Bruce notes, "England's first wartime inflation," and it led to disturbances. So, the Berkshire Justices at Speenhamland decided to subsidize wages on a sliding scale that varied with the price of bread. But, then, there was more involved in such measures than simply pacifying economic dissension. There was a political function too.

As Bruce describes the period, "It was widely believed in the early-nineteenth century that it was the poor law which had seen the country through the struggle with revolutionary France." John Stuart Mill put it this way in 1863: ". . . in spite of the aristocratic concentration of wealth and social life in England, the proletarian class is seldom hostile, either to the institution of private property or to the Classes who enjoy it." There is no question that a major function of reform was to achieve precisely this happy—from the point of view of the ruling class—situation.

And yet, even in the first half of the nineteenth century welfarism was not merely a ruling-class tactic. There was a huge Chartist movement composed of workers, and even during the severe deprivation of the "Hungry Forties" in England, it remained nonviolent and committed to democracy. It was, to be sure, wrongly perceived by the powers that be as much more revolutionary than it really was, which is in keeping with the Piven-Cloward theory. But it is also early evidence of the role of the masses in creating the welfare state for their own purposes.* This trend was to become much more explicit when socialist electoral gains in Germany motivated Bismarck to illegalize their party and steal a good part of their pro-

---

* There was, of course, a revolutionary wing to the Chartist movement, and Marx associated himself with it. And although the central demands of the Charter were for political rights, the class composition of the masses who marched behind them make it clear that they saw their enfranchisement as a means to changing their economic and social conditions.

gram. In the Piven-Cloward history, the focus is upon a dialectic of confrontation and response; in reality there was a much more complex political process, in which the people at the bottom of society played a creative and organized role and were much more than a source of civil disturbances that drove the rulers to frightened concessions.

And there were other factors at work which do not fit any neat pattern at all. The Boer War, Titmuss argues, "touched off the personal health movement which eventually led to the National Health Service in 1948." The public was aroused because of the poor health of the troops. There was a ferment of inquiry after that shameful war ended, and it led, in 1906, to the establishment "of the school medical service, the school feeding of children in elementary schools, a campaign to reduce infant mortality and many other measures."

There was a similar, and forgotten, event in the United States. World War I alarmed the populace about the state of the nation's health. Between 1915 and 1918, there was a drive for universal compulsory health insurance which won support from some people because they regarded the bodies of potential soldiers as a national resource. The American Medical Association, then under the control of academic doctors, was for the proposal, and legislation was introduced in sixteen states. But then came the peace, and the movement collapsed. That the similar impulse in Britain went so much further shows that more than the war and a patriotic fervor for health were involved.

About the same time as the Boer War consciousness about the weakness of the troops, the Fabian intellectuals began to "permeate" the society with their reformist ideas, the Labour Party was growing, and there was a powerful and imaginative feminist movement.

Labour's conquest of "Old Liberal" seats in the by-elections of 1907 had much to do with the pension schemes which Asquith proposed, and the Webbs had done much of the intellectual spadework on public assistance. Even Winston Churchill was talking in 1906 of defining "a line below which we will not allow persons to live and labor."

The causes of the British reforms in the first decade of the century were, to use a Freudian concept, "overdetermined." That is, there was no single reason for innovation, but a whole complex of reasons that reinforced one another: the impact of the Boer War, the political changes within both Liberal and Labour parties, the appearance of a middle-class Fabian reformism, working-class militancy, the feminist movement and so on. There was most certainly an element of ruling-class concession to popular pressures in all this, just as Piven and Cloward say; there was just as certainly much more involved, for history, as usual, was being rather sloppy.

In the United States, many of the forces that pushed successfully for reform in Britain were missing. The labor movement did not become socialist, and although many of the muckrakers after the turn of the century were radicals, a Fabian Society did not develop. At the same time, the struggle between labor and business was more violent and bloody in America than in any European country. It is clear that confrontation and unrest alone are not enough to provoke reform. Between 1890 and 1960, government domestic spending rose from 5 percent to 30 percent of the Gross National Product in England, from 10 percent to 40 percent in Germany— and only from 5 percent to 18 percent in the United States.

It took the Great Depression of the 1930s to bring the welfare state to America. When it arrived, under the Presidency of Franklin D. Roosevelt, it was a most contradictory phenomenon. On the one hand, it was an effort to save the old order by making concessions to new forces. "I want to save our system, the capitalist system," Roosevelt said. "To save it is to give some heed to world thought of today. I want to equalize the distribution of wealth." The emphasis on income redistribution derived from Roosevelt's fear of a number of "share-the-wealth" movements in the middle thirties. He talked of Huey Long's proposal that the government guarantee every family a "homestead allowance" of $5,000 and an annual income of $2,000. "To combat this and similar crackpot ideas," Roosevelt went on, "it may be necessary to throw to the wolves the forty-six men who are reported to have incomes in excess of one million dollars a year."

Roosevelt's cynicism in this exchange might be partly explained by the fact that he was talking to an emissary of the conservative publisher, William Randolph Hearst. As Arthur Schlesinger describes the conclusion of the scene:

> "The thinking men," [Roosevelt said] "the young men, who are disciples of this new world idea of fairer distribution of wealth, they are demanding that something be done to equalize this distribution. . . . We do not want Communism in this country and the only way to fight Communism is by—." The Hearst official interjected "neo-Communism." The President threw back his head and laughed.

So, there is no doubt that Roosevelt's New Deal was in part a conscious attempt to stave off radical change by accepting moderate change. This follows the Piven-Cloward scenario. But then the New Deal was also the product of a vast surge from below. As Richard Hofstadter put it, "The demands of a large and powerful labor movement, coupled with the institutions of the unemployed, gave the New Deal a social-democratic tinge that had never before been present in American reform movements." Thus, there was an anticapitalist, anticorporate aspect to the reforms that saved capitalism.

These dialectical complexities can even be seen in the consciousness of people at the time. When Roosevelt, acting on the strategy to outflank Huey Long on the left, actually did introduce a redistributionist tax bill in 1935, Hearst wired his editors, "President's taxation program is essentially Communism." He also told them that this "bastard" scheme should be ascribed to "a composite personality which might be labeled Stalin Delano Roosevelt." Thus did one of the men whom Roosevelt was saving respond to his rescuer. (It should be noted that Roosevelt's bold program was emasculated, particularly in the Senate.)

If businessmen were quite ungrateful toward a New Deal that was preparing the basis for the greatest capitalist prosperity the world was ever to know, the workers were also somewhat unpredictable in their attitudes. The nation was convinced by the Depression that the government had to intervene in the economy and the workers were, as Hofstadter pointed out, in a social-democratic mood. Yet the most popular reforms were the ones which took the form of social insurance—and they still are. Even though the Social Security program is financed through the most regressive of Federal taxes, there is less objection to paying this levy than to paying any other tax. The reason is that even while the nation was moving in a collectivist direction, the individualistic spirit asserted itself. Social security seems to be something that the individual pays for; it does not look like "welfare." In fact, as a Brookings Institution study noted, "Social security benefits . . . have been raised far beyond the levels that would be justified by the annual contribution of retirees, so that a large fraction of social security payments are in effect welfare benefits."

In other words, a strong capitalist consciousness persisted in the minds of those victims of capitalism who were helping the system to change. This kind of seemingly perverse complexity even attached itself to the very name of the welfare state.

In its current coinage, the term "welfare state" dates back to the late 1930s. It is part of the new vocabulary that the Great Depression made necessary. It was probably first employed, Maurice Bruce tells us,

> by the internationally known Oxford scholar Alfred Zimmern, who used it to point the contrast with the Power State of the Fascist dictators. The term is first found in print, in this sense, in Archbishop William Temple's book of 1941, and was soon to be given a wider connotation and circulation in Britain by the Beveridge Report of 1942 . . . From Britain it penetrated to the United States, where it first attained prominence in 1949, and soon came to be used principally in a pejorative sense by critics of the Fair Deal who were in fact still haunting the political battlefields of the 1930s.

This negative implication of the phrase existed also in England, where conservatives like Colin Clark called for dismantling the social services and turning them over to private charity. There was in the British fifties, Titmuss reports, the stereotype of "an all-pervasive Welfare State for the Working Classes."

So, the term "welfare state" is positive or negative, depending on one's political attitude toward it. It is a rationalization whereby the government claims to be doing something for the general welfare (but is usually doing most for the corporate rich, as has been seen); it is an insult that brands every beneficiary as being dependent and weak. And there are both poor people and rich on each side of the debate on whether the welfare state is a good or a bad thing.[2]

II

World War II was, of course, a watershed for the welfare state. In the United States the postwar period saw its old critics totally routed as the Republican Party effectively moved, under Eisenhower and under Nixon, to accept the innovations of the New Deal. The corporate rich finally understood, one generation behind the times, that Roosevelt had been saving them from more drastic change and that the institution that he fashioned could, under conservative control, be a bulwark of the status quo. The more important change occurred in Britain. In that country, World War II had required such a pervasive organization of the society that even the Establishment began to accept the inevitability of reform. In July of 1940, the august London *Times* called for the redistribution of wealth. More to the point, a great leftist tide swelled within the ranks of the armed forces (where socialists often led the discussions of war aims set up by their superior officers). So, in 1945 the Labour Party came to power and, in a much more systematic fashion than has ever been done in America, put through a sweeping reorganization of the country's social services and economic planning.*

So it was that in the period after World War II, the welfare state became a feature of capitalist society throughout the industrial West. It was composed of two elements that had developed independently of each other: a system of social services which in Europe had been developing since the end of the nineteenth cen-

---

* In 1946 there were the nationalization of coal, National Insurance for Industrial Injuries, New Towns legislation, National Health; in 1947, Industrial Organization and Development, the nationalization of transport and electrical production. Town and Country Planning; in 1948, National Assistance, the nationalization of gas production, electoral reform, and investigation of the plight of children and of monopoly.

tury; macroeconomic planning and intervention by the government in order to maintain full employment, a policy that dates only from the thirties. Before summing up the reasons for this development, it would be well to examine the most recent American case of welfare innovation. It took place in the New Frontier and Great Society programs of the Kennedy and Johnson administrations in the sixties. Here again, Piven and Cloward have an explanation that stresses force on the part of the underclass and chicanery on the part of the ruling class.

They write of the sixties and early seventies in the United States that "the contemporary relief explosion was a response to the civil disorders caused by rapid economic change—in this case the modernization of Southern agriculture." In other words, the enormous increase in welfare recipients during this period was the result of the great influx of rural blacks from the South into the cities of the nation, an event that prepared the way for the ghetto riots of 1964–68. And yet, Piven and Cloward admit that

> the relationship between increasing black power and the welfare rolls is not altogether obvious. Great masses of poor blacks did not rise up in anger against a welfare system that denied them sustenance (although some did). Nor did the increased flow of public aid result from demands made by the black political leaders; quite to the contrary, the expanding welfare rolls have often been as much a source of dismay to black elites as to white elites.

But how, then, can it be argued that the dialectic of civil disturbance and welfarist response was at work? Piven and Cloward answer that

> we think that the Great Society programs were promulgated by federal leaders in order to deal with the political problems created by a new and unstable electoral constituency, namely blacks—and to deal with this constituency not simply by responding to its expressed interests but by shaping and directing its political future. The Great Society programs, in short, reflected a distinctively managerial kind of politics.

This explanation, it seems to me, drastically revises the generalization with which Piven and Cloward began: "that relief arrangements are initiated and expanded during the occasional outbreaks of civil disorder, produced by mass unemployment, and are then abolished or contracted when political stability is restored." The Kennedy-Johnson years were a time of decreasing unemployment and the longest prosperity in American history. Events during this decade can hardly be explained by "civil disorders produced by mass unemployment." Indeed, as the studies of the National Commission on Civil Disorders rightly suggested, what accounts for riots is a sense of relative deprivation that arises when the economy is on the ascendancy. Moreover, as Piven and Cloward themselves admit, there was no tremendous pressure from below prior to the welfare reforms of the sixties.

Exact dates are important in this regard. The main innovations of the Great Society—Medicare, the Office of Economic Opportunity, the stimulation of full employment through tax cuts, and so on —were initiated (and in most cases passed into law) prior to the escalation of the American intervention in Indochina in 1965. They were not, therefore, a response to the most violent of the ghetto explosions in Watts (1965), Detroit, New Haven and Newark (1967) and Washington, D.C. (1968). And these reforms were not a political reaction to a mass movement of the poor. The black forces led by Martin Luther King, Jr., unquestionably played a major role in awakening the social conscience of America and helped enormously in creating the climate in which social change would take place. But King was not at the head of an army of the wretched of the earth, even though he rightly fought in their behalf. His base was the Southern black church and his allies included significant sections of the trade-union movement, a renascent college campus, and a good portion of the educated middle class.

But what about the political explanation? "Our main point, then," Piven and Cloward write, "is that to reach, placate and integrate a turbulent black constituency, the national Democratic administration of the 1960s acted to help blacks get more from local government." There is no question that Democrats understood that blacks were a strategically placed constituency, with large concentrations in key states like New York and Illinois. But politically speaking, the blacks were one of the least turbulent groups in the sixties. They supported Democrats with a consistency that no other element in the coalition could match. Where manual workers went from a 70 percent support of Johnson in 1964 to only 50 percent for Humphrey in 1968, blacks were 94 percent for Johnson and 85 percent for Humphrey.

So, the cause of the Great Society was not riots or even black politics, though both of these had a certain influence. Piven and Cloward recognize that the innovations actually came from the top down, although they try to account for that fact by seeing it as a political response to black turbulence. Their explanation fails, but the fact remains. One must take into account the impact of middle-class (and even upper-class) conscience, trade-union pressure, Martin King's liberating movement, political factors, for there is no single cause for what happened during the sixties. Indeed, as Piven and Cloward rightly point out, by mid-decade there was a "vast array of groups—social workers, churchmen, lawyers, civic organizations, public-welfare employees, private foundations, activist students, antipoverty employees, civil rights organizations, settlement houses and family agencies, not to speak of organizations of the poor themselves." But if they recognize this fact, they cannot integrate into a theory which monochromatically interprets the history of reform in terms of conflict from below and concession from above.

Indeed, a serious case can be argued for a proposition that is the exact opposite of the Piven-Cloward thesis: that reform from the top stimulates conflict at the bottom rather than the other way around. As Claus Offe, the brilliant German Marxist, has pointed out, the government often places on the agenda an issue that then becomes a source of bitter struggle. In the United States, for instance, the antipoverty program of the sixties was the cause, not the effect, of militant politics on the part of the poor and of struggles between racial and ethnic groupings within the world of poverty itself.

Moreover, Piven and Cloward omit one of the most important causes of the innovations of the American sixties. There were, as the last chapter documented, two programs which received the bulk of the new federal money: Medicare and social security benefits. Both of these measures are designed for the aging. As capitalism develops and living standards rise and medicine conquers some of the old scourges, more and more people live beyond sixty-five years of age. At the same time, the extended family, which was the traditional way of dealing with a much smaller population of the aging, was shattered. The typical American did not want to take personal responsibility for his or her parents, and thus there was a vast constituency—of the middle-aged as well as the old—that favored more spending in this area. In the 1930s, when the original breakthrough in social security was made, there was an organized and militant movement demanding even greater help. It was part of that redistributionist tendency to which Roosevelt responded.

That is in keeping with the Piven-Cloward thesis: action from below can be said to have forced concessions from on high. In the sixties, there were organizations of the aging. But there was nothing like the seething mass movement of the thirties, and the economy was prosperous, not in shambles. So, among the reasons for the rise of the welfare state one must include the demographic consequences of capitalist success. Aging is not, as Harold Wilensky comes close to suggesting, the only cause of increased spending for human needs, and it has to occur within a specific social context which gives it a political significance. But with these qualifications, the large proportion of older citizens is a major factor in welfare politics.

The history of the welfare state, then, is most dialectical. In considerable measure, writers like Piven and Cloward are right: it represents the reluctant concessions of the ruling class, the increments of reform that function to make basic change unnecessary. But it is also the product of conscience and consciousness, that of socialist workers and middle-class liberals, of militant blacks and students, and of the aging. As such, it has been the instrument of the oppressed as well as of the oppressors, a means of partial liberation as well as of partial pacification.

So, the history of the welfare state is much more intricate than is suggested in the theories which see it primarily as a structure of reluctant concessions wrung from the rulers by means of mass pressure from below. In Britain, an abomination like the Boer War can set off tendencies toward socialized medicine, and World War I briefly had the same effect in the United States. This country, with the bloodiest history of labor confrontation, was the last of the industrial democracies to create a welfare state. And the people and the intellectuals played their own, and often creative, roles in this process.

Given the unevenness and sometimes the downright sloppiness of its genesis, one might expect that the structure of the welfare state would be most complex and anything but straightforward. So it is.[3]

III

To begin with, if the welfare state is seen as effectuating capitalist priorities, but not necessarily as a result of a conscious capitalist plan, how does this providential result (from the point of view of the corporate rich) come to pass?

The fundamental answer to this question has been implicit throughout Part II of this book. The welfare-state government is not itself the initiator of most production within the economy. The corporations do that. However, that same government is increasingly charged with arranging the preconditions for profitable production. Its funds, its power, its political survival, depend on private-sector performance. So do the jobs of most workers. The state's interest in perpetuating its own rule is thus, in economic fact, identified with the health of the capitalist economy. Thus Claus Offe put the point with remarkable precision and deceptive simplicity. The essential is that the capitalist state is not itself a capitalist: It therefore depends on capitalists. It is that the most honest and incorruptible of public servants wants and works for the maximum happiness of General Motors and Ford.

In the New York City crisis of 1975 all of this became apparent on the very surface of social and political life—paradoxically, one might add, deceptively apparent.

When that crisis erupted, it suddenly became obvious that the fate of the second-most important government in the United States depended on the confidence of a handful of bankers and brokers. Those bankers and brokers lobbied in Washington, D.C., against federal aid to their own city, for that would obviate the need for the particular kind of "discipline" they craved. In effect, a general strike of capital was organized and the elected officials of New York were required, not only to balance the municipal budget, but to do so in a certain way. The city fathers had the theoretical right to deal with the situation by imposing taxes upon the rich, but they were at the mercy of the rich. The New York Stock Exchange, for instance, said that if any levies were voted against it, then it would pick up and move. So it was that the *Wall Street Journal* put forward its program: New York should declare itself bankrupt, fire more public employees, tear up existing labor contracts, abrogate pensions previously agreed to, and reduce services. Meanwhile, Arthur Burns of the Federal Reserve announced that if the City defaulted on its debt, the government would come to the aid of the banks—but not of the city.

But, then, couldn't it be said that this display of the power of money had been caused by the profligacy of the New Yorkers who spent beyond their means? There was—no question of it—bookkeeping with mirrors under the administrations of Robert F. Wagner, John V. Lindsay and Abraham Beame. And yet, devious as the politicians were, their fiscal sleight of hand was only a response to a deeper cause for which they were not responsible. Within the framework of an economy still dominated by private corporate forces where labor power was and is allocated by the market, even if that market has been modified by state intervention, the result was a massive shift of manufacturing and administrative jobs from New York City. This was not done conspiratorially by capitalists who detested Bagdad on the Hudson. It was simple "common sense"—the common sense historically specific to capitalism, that is—to move factories to low-wage areas in the South, or to Mexico, Taiwan, Singapore or South Korea. It was "good business" to shift the executive headquarters to the Connecticut suburbs, and to shop among the competing tax jurisdictions of the region for the best deal.

At the same time when all of these rationally anti-social decisions were being taken by the corporations, the problems of New York City were mounting. It became a center for the poor, and especially the black poor who had been driven out of the rural South, in considerable measure because federal farm subsidies to agricultural business had rendered them superfluous. It also absorbed a significant portion of the Puerto Rican population which could not find work even though that island was going through an investment boom. (The investment often took the form of new, capital-intensive technology which did not create employment at the same rate as output and profit.) So, all of the costs of a gigantic poverty-stricken and miseducated population—welfare, health, police and the rest—mounted, in the main because Washington had funded a vast internal migration, without thought of social consequence but in obedience to the logic of corporate priorities. The municipal leaders kept these enormous facts from the people—and from themselves—by acts of statistical legerdemain. Then, when the crisis erupted, Wall Street successfully concealed the real facts from the people—and from itself—by blaming the social prodigality of America's most left-wing city.

These events were also one more consequence of the energy crisis (which bid up municipal costs incredibly), of the recession (which had been consciously manufactured in the White House for policy reasons), and of the failure of Washington to act in areas like national health care. In each of these instances the governmental devotion to private corporate priorities was a prime cause of the trouble.

But when the bankers began to take over state and city institutions in their own name in New York in 1975, the link between capital and political power became a bit too obvious. There had been a secret agreement between the banks and the city government during the Great Depression, which had included New York's promise not to impose any new taxes on the wealthy. But in 1975, the reality was out in the open as big-businessmen formally took charge of running the city without being forced to the inconvenience of submitting themselves to an electorate. But that situation—which is *in medias res* as this book is readied for the printer—is dangerous to the bankers and they know it. The political genius of capitalism was and is indirect rule; it is a system of bourgeois democracy. When the crises become acute, as they did in Germany in the 1930s, sterner measures are adopted. Still, the basic bias of the system is toward concealed power, for that is a key factor making for the legitimation of that power. So the New York City crisis makes painfully obvious the underlying reality that all governments in America, no matter what the social composition of their personnel, must win the confidence of the economically dominant corporate sector. But it also invites a dangerous overgeneralization—that the leaders of that sector normally rule in their own name. On the contrary, it can be predicted that the New York financiers of the seventies will, like their predecessors of the thirties, seek to return to democratic procedures as soon as possible.

Once this point is understood, a series of important problems can be unraveled.* Capitalism developed three kinds of "compensatory mechanisms" to deal with its tendencies toward crisis. (And it should be noted that the very existence of a crisis-management bureaucracy in Washington is eloquent testimony to the destructive impulses of the system when left to itself.) Markets were organized by monopolies, oligopolies, cartels and multinationals which permitted managerial planning and the elimination of price competition; technological innovation was institutionalized to create new needs and markets; and the state intervened in the economy with countercyclical policies. Two of these tactics could be adopted by corporations on their own, but the third, and most crucial, that of state intervention, could not. Thus, the government took on a critical role in integrating and effectuating the capitalist priorities of the society.

Moreover, the capitalists remained fixed in individual, narrow, spheres. Even a giant like General Motors had a certain parochial point of view. And there were intracapitalist conflicts between the oligopolies and the medium-sized firms, between old (usually Eastern) money and the (often Southwestern) *parvenus*. There were also factional disputes within single industries, as when the international oil firms opposed import quotas that would benefit primarily the domestic producers. And then the actual, living capi-

---

* In what follows, I am much indebted to the German Marxist sociologist Claus Offe. As I indicated earlier, I am also indebted to the work of Nicos Poulantzas, whose analysis on this count parallels Offe's.

talists are often short-sighted, or even perverse, about their class interest. Most of them bitterly fought Franklin Roosevelt's attempt to save the system in the 1930s.

All these considerations, as well as the sloppiness of welfare-state history itself, provide good reasons for viewing this phenomenon as a structure, with a life of its own, rather than as an instrument of the capitalist class. The "instrument" theory, it will be noted, goes well with a base-superstructure model of society and is flawed for that reason. It metaphorically imagines the government as an inert thing that has no life of its own and is wielded by the "real" powers residing in the economic base. The concept of a structure, on the other hand, fits in with Marx's analysis of the organic whole.

Still, this explanation leaves unspecified the precise mechanism whereby the priorities of the capitalist economy are translated into politics. It is well known that the American governmental structure is fragmented, in part because the conservatives among the Founding Fathers wanted to inhibit any decisive and radical action by mere majorities. And groups as disparate as the Ford Foundation and the Soviet theorists agree that this diffuseness remains a major factor in American life to this very day. Take the nation's budget. As James O'Connor points out in a brilliant book, this critical aspect of federal policy involves the President, the House Ways and Means Committee, the Senate Finance Committee, the Appropriations Committees in both Houses, the Council of Economic Advisors, the Office of Management and Budget, the Treasury, the Internal Revenue Service, the Government Accounting Office, and the Federal Reserve Board.

One way to explain why this intricate process almost always comes up with corporate capitalist conclusions is to assert that there "is a social upper class which owns a disproportionate amount of a country's wealth, receives a disproportionate amount of a country's yearly income, and contributes a disproportionate number of its members to the controlling institutions and key decision-making groups of the country." There is much to be said for this theory, which has been well argued by G. William Domhoff. Yet I think it understates the degree to which government on its own,

312   THE TWILIGHT OF CAPITALISM

and even when it is not under the influence of the disproportionate number of members of that social class in its rank, acts as the representative of the capitalist class as a whole, something the individual capitalists cannot do.

Claus Offe makes a shrewd interpretation of a famous statement by Marx that bears very much on this point. The assertion that the democratic state under capitalism is "the executive committee of the bourgeoisie" is usually taken to mean that the government is a mere front for the capitalists, a reading that fits neatly into a simpleminded, base-superstructure version of Marxism. Offe suggests that Marx's words have another, almost contrary, thrust. The capitalists, unlike the feudal nobility or the slaveowners, do not rule in their own name. It is, after all, the functional illusion of this society that in it equals freely choose their work (their class) as well as their rulers. The upper class, therefore, must be more discreet than in other epochs. Moreover, that class is itself anarchic and competitive. It therefore requires an "executive committee" which is not simply the creature of the wealthy and their managers but the articulator of a unity, of a national point of view that transcends all business rivalries and that the corporate rich cannot themselves effect.

This is excellent sociology for today, but is it Marx? Unquestionably. In Marx's own political analyses of French, British and German politics, as Chapter 7 noted, it is made clear that during the rise of the capitalist system the capitalist class itself only rarely played the leading role. The revolutionary political work was carried out by landed aristocrats in Britain and, quite often, by governmental bureaucrats in both France and Germany. In Japan, the Meiji Restoration provides another example of the creation of a capitalist society by a noncapitalist class. In all of these cases, the non- and even anti-bourgeois forces promoted the objective class interest, if not the personal political power, of the bourgeoisie.

Nicos Poulantzas has generalized Marx's specific analyses brilliantly, pointing out that it is precisely the unique characteristic of capitalism that it separates political and economic power, and thus opens up the way for the *relative* autonomy of the former. Poulantzas rightly remarks that under capitalism "the state is not the instrument of a class . . . it is the state of a society divided into classes." That is to say, in the long-range and basic interests of capitalism, the capitalist state must be prepared to adopt measures which may infuriate a section, or even the near totality, of the capitalists. Again, the New Deal is an obvious example.

There is unquestionably an upper class in America, but that does not mean either in theory or in fact, that there is a ruling class. Andrew Hacker has shrewdly defined that upper class as the group which derives the majority of its income from property rather than work. Work income is transitory, lasting only for the life of the job, and it is subject to higher tax rates than property income. One reaches this upper class at the $200,000-a-year mark. It represents three one hundredths of one percent of all taxpaying units, its average income is $407,000 (or 42 times the national average) and its unearned income of $290,000 a year is 337 times that of the average household ($860 a year). Yet, as Hacker summarizes the evidence, the data do not show that these people actually run the corporations (that is done by people making a mere $50,000 to $200,000 a year) or the government. Sometimes individuals from it, like Henry Ford or John J. McCloy or Nelson Rockefeller, do, but that is not the prevailing pattern.

It is sometimes thought that the "ruling class" theme is quite radical and Marxist. In fact, not only is it incapable of explaining vast stretches of capitalist history, but it also tends to underestimate the class character of capitalism by making it dependent upon the political fate of a group of individuals rather than rooting it in the exigencies of economic structure. So long as private corporations remain the dominant production institution of society, no matter who is in power, the long-run trend in society will be to promote the corporate interest. In short, the factors upon which Marx focused in the conscious simplification of Chapter I of Volume I of *Das Kapital* remain crucial to the understanding of this system more than a hundred years later and of all the enormous changes that have taken place.

This is not to suggest that there is a single schedule of priorities that dominate in all capitalist societies. There are enormous differences between these societies, and even within them, depending on their stage of development. And a conservative government will act in one way, a liberal or social-democratic government in another. But even this obvious distinction does not necessarily operate in a straightforward manner. John F. Kennedy, anxious to placate the business sector, authorized some accounting practices that Dwight Eisenhower, sensitive to criticism that he was a pawn of the millionaires, rejected as too obviously procorporate. In foreign policy, Richard Nixon's trip to Peking is a dramatic case in point. A man from the anti-Communist right could more easily strike a bargain with Mao than any liberal advocate of recognition for mainland China.

And yet, for all the historical and political and cultural differences between and within capitalist societies, their capitalist character puts certain fundamental constraints on the actions of elected governments. Liberals might enact more redistributionist tax laws, but they cannot go so far as abolishing profits or even endangering the process of capital accumulation. They could adopt such measures only if they ceased to be liberal—that is, if they were willing to socialize the investment function, which is to say, to begin to transform the system itself.

The capitalist state does not, of course, explain these things, or even think about them, in the explicit language that I have used. It has an ideology—a sincere and honest false consciousness—which it propagates, and this reinforces the tendency of decisions to conform to the underlying necessities of corporate power. Chapter 10 presented a current and important example of this phenomenon. The oil corporations and then the business community in general are working hard to equate profits with saving for investment, emphasizing only the positive and socially necessary function of deducting a surplus from output in this way and carefully ignoring the maldistribution of wealth and the private arrogation of public decision-making power which also result from it. This is not to say that these gentlemen are lying; they deceive themselves along with the rest of the society.

But, then, the business ideologists sometimes become relatively frank. In late 1974, Felix Rohatyn, a partner in Lazard Freres, an international investment banking house, urged the government to become an "investor of last resort" in order to deal with the crisis. Rohatyn proposed a new Reconstruction Finance Corporation (R.F.C.), which would come to the aid of troubled companies by giving them an injection of federally subsidized equity capital. Then, when the corporation had once again become a profitable operation, the government would back out. The risks and losses would have been socialized; the profits would, however, remain private. "There could be no denying," Rohatyn said, "that such an organization, with the type of wide-ranging freedom described above, can be perceived as a first step toward the state planning of the economy."

About the same time, Henry Ford was arguing in favor of

> more central planning. Not the kind of central planning the Russians have, where they order the whole damned economy from a central plan. I'm talking about a federal planning organization that collects and disseminates information. I'd bring in the Council of Economic Advisors and others, and I'd give this group cabinet status so that it's not just stuck away in some back room.

Rohatyn and Ford thus come fairly close to openly advocating what my analysis would describe as the secret of the welfare state: national economic planning subordinated to corporate priorities.

In a remarkable book, which corroborates Offe's interpretation of Marx from an impeccably anti-Marxist point of view, George C. Lodge, a faculty member of the Harvard Business School, argues that America must give up its individualistic, competitive "free enterprise" ideology. In fact, the corporations acting on those assumptions lacked "a decisive, consistent and coherent vision of what the society ought to be"; therefore "the state has moved in without being either decisive, consistent or coherent." Now, this process must be completed, and a "new American ideology" must make our new situation conscious of itself, which is to say, decisive, consistent and coherent.

Yet just as Captain Nemo, in *Twenty Thousand Leagues Under the Sea,* played classical music on his futuristic submarine—Jules Verne could imagine a new technology, but not a new culture—so Lodge's ideology still facilitates the rule of managers, even if in a drastically revised context. The idea of democratic decision-making, of working people deciding on the job on how they should work, of the purposive dissolution of the old hierarchies associated with capitalism, eludes him. That way leads, after all, to socialism. And one thing that the prophets of postindustrial society and the business converts to planning do not propose is the erosion, or destruction, of the power of the managerial class for which they speak. Their radical departures are all intelligent defenses of the status quo, old music in new submarines.

Ideology then—even sophisticated, plan-oriented, late-capitalist ideology—plays an important role in translating (and disguising) capitalist priorities in politics, and it is refracted in the schools, the media and the common consciousness of the rulers themselves. Money is another transmission belt. The possession of great wealth allows one to buy political influence—and to do so legally through campaign contributions and other favors. The Watergate case is such an extreme instance of the subversive workings of money in politics that it might obscure the fact that it ordinarily operates in a much more mundane and "honest" fashion. When a top executive from a major company accepts a high post in Washington, he ostentatiously sells his stock, or puts it in a "blind" trust, so that there will be no conflict of interest. It is then incredibly assumed that he has also divested himself of his corporate values and outlook, that as long as there is no immediate and direct profit being made from his public decisions he is acting impartially. That is absurd, but it is, as Domhoff stresses, an indispensable mechanism in making the democratic state subservient to a minority interest. That such a myth can be widely believed is itself one more proof of the irrational character of the society.

Finally, there is a new kind of contradiction, which arises during this latest phase of capitalism. (The capitalist crisis in general will be discussed in the next chapter.) It has been shrewdly analyzed by James O'Connor. Under welfare capitalism, O'Connor argues, the state socializes more and more capital costs, but the private sector continues to appropriate the profits. This creates "a fiscal crisis, a 'structural gap' between state expenditures and revenues. The result is a tendency for state expenditures to increase more rapidly than the means of financing them." Inflation, then, is built into the system. Unfortunately, O'Connor's theory is marred by a flaw that is by no means essential to it. Like Piven and Cloward, he thinks that a good part of the society, including the organized working class, has been co-opted.

So O'Connor holds that monopoly capital (the advanced portion of the business community) and its workers cooperate smoothly to export their conflicts to the competitive (small business) and state sectors. This is done because the wage increases of unions in the monopoly sector are passed on to the society and because big business and big labor have a common stake in seeking more social investments, social consumption and defense outlays. O'Connor does recognize that the corporations are hostile to direct government production of goods and services, while the unions are not, but basically he assumes that they are in partnership. This happens on some occasions—joint business-labor opposition to environmental restrictions that will cut down production and jobs is common enough—but the long-range trend is not in this direction at all. For in the boom phase of the cycle, the union's bargaining position becomes stronger and wage increases cut into profits (which are menaced also by the problems of inflation). There is then a very real class conflict between labor and big capital, and it was and is very much in evidence in the crisis of the seventies.

On this question, theoretical positions have immediate political consequences. For if one thinks, as Piven, Cloward, O'Connor and a significant section of the American left do, that the organized working class has been thoroughly and permanently integrated into the society, then one abandons tactics based on the Marxist concept of class struggle. So it is that O'Connor looks for ". . . alliances between teachers, students, and office and maintenance personnel, between welfare workers and welfare recipients, between public-health workers and people who use public-health facilities, and between transport workers and the public served by public transit . . ." The auto workers, the steel workers, the coal miners are not included in this list, for in the O'Connor perspective, they have already made their alliance with monopoly capital.

Another aspect of this tactical issue has to do with how manipulative one thinks the welfare state is. If it is seen as merely, or primarily, a tool in the hands of the ruling class, then the struggles between Republicans and Democrats, conservatives and liberals, really don't matter very much. The policy conclusion that follows is that one adopts a "radical" perspective and sees confrontation, or even revolution, as the only hope. This, for example, was the perspective of Herbert Marcuse's *One Dimensional Man,* a book that had a great influence on the New Left in the sixties. But if one has the point of view of this chapter, seeing the welfare state as an arena of struggle that is normally and systematically biased in favor of the powers that be, but in which gains can be made by the left, another stance is indicated. In this perspective, the victories of the unions in the thirties—the political as well as the industrial victories —made a significant, and positive, change in the conditions of life of the American nation.

The welfare state, then, is a dialectical and complicated phenomenon. It is predominantly and unconsciously (ideologically) structured so as to help the corporations more than the people. But this is accomplished in a complex way in which the government takes on a life of its own and is not simply an "instrument" of capital. As a result, it is a battle ground in which the popular forces, if they are massively and effectively mobilized, can make incremental gains of considerable value. But then the long-range tendency reasserts itself, and the victories of the organized workers and/or of the poor, the minorities and the middle-class advocates of social change are taken over and turned to ruling-class purposes. However, the possibility of assembling the political forces that might make irreversible structural changes and eventually transform the system itself occurs precisely in the course of the "reformist" battles for modest increments of dignity.

Indeed, the analysis of this chapter explains, in part, why those battles will go on and on. The capitalist welfare state can, under the very best of conditions, provide only limited concessions to the needs of the vast majority. It can, as long as production is expanding, increase the absolute living standard of the masses; it cannot change the basic structure of inequality, for that is essential to the accumulation of capital—that is, to the survival and perpetuation of the system itself. The welfare state will, then, even when operating optimally, disappoint and discontent vast masses of people. Therefore, there will be the rebellions of good times, like the 1960s. But, then, there is a built-in tendency in such a society to destroy the very best of conditions; it produces crises as well as goods and services.[4]

CHAPTER 13

TWILIGHT OF AN EPOCH

CAPITALISM, it has been shown, is outrageously unjust; it requires a continuing maldistribution of wealth in order to exist. But more than that, it is also self-destructive. This is why we live in the twilight of an epoch, one that has lasted more than four centuries.

I do not want to suggest for a moment that the crisis of the 1970s is a final breakdown of the system, its *Götterdämmerung*. I fully expect it to recover from this cruel and unnecessary depression. The event is only a moment in a complex process of decline and fall that will certainly go on for some time to come and just as certainly will end with the collapse of the bourgeois order.

Marxists, someone might understandably object, have been announcing the demise of capitalism for over a century. Marx and Engels were wrong in 1848, when they thought that the final conflict was at hand. They were wrong in 1850, when they became more cautious and said that the death of the bourgeoisie might not take place for another fifty years. One hundred and twenty-five years later that same bourgeoisie was still very much alive, more wily than ever before, impudently using measures invented by the left to serve the purposes of the right. Under such circumstances, how can one dare to draft a funeral oration, and a disrespectful one at that?

Because capitalism has collectivized its contradictions but not abolished them. In the process, it has unquestionably won time, like a patient restored to health, but by a miracle drug whose side effects will eventually kill him. One cannot set a date, or even a decade when the last scene will be played out or specify how long it will last. And it would be foolish to suggest that our heirs will necessarily inherit a millennium that will be socialist and humane. The successor to capitalism will be collectivist, of course. That has already been settled, and conservative Republican Presidents unwittingly promote this trend. But there are many possibilities within this tendency, the totalitarian, the authoritarian and the democratic-socialist among them.

In this final chapter, I will try to capture these lines of possibility in motion. Capitalism "socializes" private priorities and is institutionally opposed to any redistribution of the relative shares of wealth. This is related to its propensity for crisis and, ultimately, its self-destruction. In this context, the welfare state is seen as an ambiguous and transitional phenomenon, the temporary salvation of the system, but also the portent of its end. Then I will suggest, in a tone of chastened assertiveness, that the future Karl Marx— which is to say, the Marxist methodology applied to situations that Marx himself never imagined—can help us to understand these things, if not perfectly, then better than any other thinker.

I

The crisis of the 1970s is really the confluence of two crises, both of them explicitly capitalist in nature. One of the crises expresses some long-run contradictions, and it prepares its calamities, not only in, but by means of, good times. The other crisis is a result of specific events of this decade, and particularly with an energy crisis that capitalism labored so mightily to make possible.

As he was about to relinquish the Presidency in early 1969, Lyndon Johnson made a proud (and typical) boast:

> No longer do we view our economic life as a relentless tide of ups and downs. No longer do we fear that automation and technical progress will rob workers of jobs rather than help us to achieve

greater abundance. No longer do we consider poverty and unemployment landmarks on our economic scene.

It was the best of all possible worlds and "bourgeois socialism" had been achieved in America—that is, a resolutely capitalist society had solved all of its fundamental contradictions in a planned and democratic manner.

Six years later, unemployment was higher than at any time since the Great Depression of the thirties, poverty was on the increase, and the real living standard of the American people was declining along with the Gross National Product. For many people these disasters were the result of the bad luck of history—above all, of the quadrupling of the price of Middle Eastern oil which came in the wake of the Yom Kippur War. That, as the evidence has already suggested, was a major factor in the crisis, yet it cannot be understood apart from the capitalist character of the welfare state. But before generalizing on that point, a more subtle observation has to be made: that even in prosperity, and indeed because of prosperity, the contradictions of this system are at work.

For the explosive fact of the matter is that capitalism cannot tolerate its own success. The system, for all its Keynesian transformations, is fundamentally hostile to full employment; it is wracked by its own booms.

The years of the Kennedy-Johnson administration represent the pinnacle of American welfare-state performance. There were economic growth, reduced unemployment, the functioning of countercyclical policies and built-in stabilizers. This idyll was, of course, accompanied by the most unconscionable and, eventually, most unpopular war in the nation's history, but that fact did not seem to call the domestic achievement into question. Indeed, the planners of the Johnson administration regularly—and wrongly—argued that the economy was so incredibly sound that it could simultaneously afford a multibillion-dollar intervention in Southeast Asia and the construction of the Great Society at home.

But even if one abstracts from the catastrophic impact of Vietnam on the home front, even if one confronts the Johnson claim on the terrain most favorable to it, the jubilation of the New Economics was not warranted. For in many ways the welfare-state cure was itself a new disease. This is not, obviously, to agree with the conservatives who thought that the Great Society went too far. I supported, and still support, its reforms. What needs to be explained is how they were vitiated and subverted by the capitalist context in which they were undertaken—which is a call to transform that context, not to abandon the reforms.

First of all, the welfare state was, to use Richard Titmuss' term, a necessary response to the diswelfare state. For example, millions of rural Southerners were forced off the land because of the government's program of subsidizing agribusiness. They were driven into cities, totally unprepared to cope with the urban labor market and the brutality of life in the lower depths. If they were black, as many of them were, they also encountered the political economy of racism that exists in the Northern states. This process helped to destroy many of the traditional, often stagnant, structures of the old agricultural society in which these people had lived. They could no longer turn to the family, church and community in time of distress. Bureaucratized government institutions, created to deal with what were supposed to be the temporary problems of the Great Depression, now took on an impressive life of their own. A program of Aid to the Families of Dependent Children, which had been an afterthought in the original Social Security law, enrolled millions.

Nathan Glazer, as we have seen, captured the irony of this process. He wrote, "In its efforts to deal with the breakdown of . . . traditional structures, social policy tends to encourage their further weakening." But what Glazer failed to note—I suggest because of a flawed methodology as described in Chapter 11—was why this dynamic had begun in the first place. If agricultural policy had not, like the rest of the welfare state, followed commercial priorities—if it had subsidized family farms, cooperatives and balanced rural developments rather than giant corporations—most of these problems would not have arisen. It was not "social policy" that set loose the forces which Glazer describes, but a social policy with a capitalist value system.

A second, and related, point has to do with the enormous escalation of social costs resulting from advanced capitalist production and occurring most dramatically precisely in periods of feverish expansion. The existence of these costs was integrated into economic theory by A. C. Pigou in the 1930s. They first appeared as a relatively small phenomenon, as the "uncompensated damage done to the surrounding woods by sparks from railway engines." Yet, as time went on and planned capitalism grew to an unprecedented scale, these costs mounted and mounted. Sometimes they were the direct result of corporate action, as in the case of a polluting factory. But they were also the result of conscious, governmental decisions. Thus, in an urbanized, interdependent society, the federally funded highways made great sense from the point of view of middle- and upper-class suburbia and the new plants and laboratories located on its fringes. Yet they were disastrous for the cities, the minorities, the poor, the mass-transportation system and the environment.

Michael Barret Brown described this trend:

> The attempt of the Welfare Economists to discover ways to bring social and interpersonal costs and benefits into the market system, if necessary by legislation, reminds one of nothing as much as Ptolemy's construction of epicycles to correct the failure of predictions based on an earth-centered model of the solar system.

Eventually, some mainstream economists, like Karl Kaysen, began to wonder aloud if these "externalities" were not inherent in the system itself. Perhaps the easiest way to see that this is indeed the case is to look at one of the basic concepts of Keynesian economics: the Gross National Product (G.N.P.).

The very definition of G.N.P. and the theory underlying it are a product of the thirties, when, under the influence of Keynes, governments came to realize that they had to analyze and manage the economy in terms of aggregates like national income, government spending, private investment and G.N.P. So it is that G.N.P. has become a commonplace of all political and policy discussion. Yet it has been rightly subjected to vigorous liberal and social-democratic criticism because it is so utterly gross. It does not, Gunnar Myrdal points out, take into account some crucial dimensions of life as pollution, the distribution of income and wealth, the depletion of resources. Myrdal wrote, "There is a lack of clarity about what is supposed to be growing—whether it is real growth in any sense or merely accounting for costs caused by various developments, some of which are undesirable."

Myrdal is absolutely right, of course, but his insight can be carried a few steps further. First, this flawed concept of the Gross National Product was and is inevitable within a capitalist society. It is one of the characteristics of this system, it will be remembered, to make exchange value, or salability, decisive and use value subordinate. On this calculus, a cancer-producing cigarette which can be sold for a given sum is "worth" just as much as that sum invested in anticancer research. This is not a matter of the statisticians' art; it is an essential element of capitalist discipline. If a corporation begins to build use values into its products which are not exchange values—if, let us say, it spends resources on making its goods more socially functional but not more profitable—then it will become less competitive vis-à-vis its unscrupulous rivals, and it will take its sense of social utility to bankruptcy court.

When the state planners adopt a concept based on this reality as their fundamental tool, they cannot help but socialize and subsidize antisocial results. To be sure, there are occasions when the social costs become so intolerable that they threaten the environment of the profit-making society as such and must be stopped. So it was that the government in the late sixties and early seventies placed some limitations on the right of automobile manufacturers to destroy the very air we breathe. But that was seen as an exception to the rule, it was bitterly resisted by the companies, and the energy crisis was seized upon as a pretext for ending, or moderating, this interference with the sovereign rights of the antisocial commodity. In most cases, this controversy did not even arise. Washington simply assumed, as a capitalist government must, that its job was to facilitate the workings of a corporate infrastructure that was sound and good.

So there is an inherent tendency for the united front of corporations and the state to produce in a planned fashion, which is superficially social, but without any basic regard for social values. The latter, from a corporate point of view, become imperative only when they yield a high-enough profit. And that corporate perspective dominates the theoretical concepts of state planners, like G.N.P., as well as their actions.

There is a brilliant misunderstanding of this trend, and it helps to illuminate another aspect of it. Sometimes when a thinker makes a vivid sketch of reality upside-down, its right-side-up is then easier to see. Such is the case with Edward Banfield's *The Unheavenly City.* (A similar, but less scholarly, error was committed by Ben Wattenberg in *The Real America.*) In arguing that social life is really getting better, Banfield comments that in 1900 only about one fifteenth of the children finished elementary school, while in the sixties most of them completed high school. But why, then, is there such a pervasive sense of urban crisis? Banfield answers that it is because ". . . improvements in performance, great as they have been, do not keep pace with rising expectations." Like racing dogs chasing a mechanical rabbit, the people never catch up with the object of their desire. Therefore their malaise "results largely from rising standards and expectations."

But what Banfield egregiously fails to note is that in 1900 it was possible to achieve a relatively stable working-class position in society without a high-school education, but that by 1970 a worker who lacked a high-school diploma (or even post-high-school education) would be at a considerable disadvantage. Capitalism had indeed raised the standard of living by means of the welfare state —but it had also enormously increased the requirements of living. People were eating better, living longer, but they had new needs, real or manipulated, and continued to exist on the very same margin even if at a higher level of consumption. So it was, for instance, that the working-class and lower-middle-class students who were guaranteed college entry by New York City's policy of open enrollment discovered that they had received the privilege of higher education at the precise moment when it was ceasing to be a privilege and becoming a necessity. Richard Nixon's Council of Economic Advisors recognized this reality in 1974—"The greater opportunities for schooling among persons at all income levels and the larger subsidies for training less-advantaged persons, might have been expected to reduce earnings inequality in the last 20 years . . ." Only, "it is striking that there has been no change in the relative inequality among adult males."

The Council's point corroborates a basic theme of this analysis: that this society, for all its reformist achievements, is antiegalitarian.

Sophisticated businessmen, the decisive though not always dominant class of welfare-state society, have learned that a Keynesian government following corporate priorities is their friend, not their enemy. Thus we saw in the last chapter that investment bankers and industrial magnates have become advocates of national economic planning on their own behalf. They have also accepted the establishment of social minimums of income, health care, et cetera. They came to this knowledge after having been tutored in it by militant labor, socialist and liberal movements. And they did so with all the grace exhibited by those English capitalists who, as Marx said, accepted restrictions on the working hours of factory labor for the same reason that they spread guano on their fields: because they did not want to exhaust a productive resource.

But even though the ruling powers can thus be driven and cajoled into a modicum of decency, they refuse to allow the welfare state to change the relative shares of wealth. Even in England, where the social minimums are much more comprehensive than in the United States, there has been no basic shift in distribution. In the United States there is the evidence just cited, as well as the more extensive documentation of Chapter 11. One reason for the persistence of this maldistribution is that the government showers privileges upon the rich because they are presumed to be the most "productive" citizens. Another is that, to the extent that national planning does promote economic growth in good times, the top 5 percent of income recipients who own 86 percent of all publicly held corporate stock thereby receive a disproportionate share of the socially induced increment of wealth. There is, as Harold Wilson noted in 1960, "a law of increasing returns to the rich."

So the welfare state promotes antisocial priorities and antiegalitarianism even in the best of times. Under those same optimum circumstances, it also manifests the traditional capitalist propensity to boom and bust in new ways. In developing this theme, an important aspect of the secret history of the contemporary crisis comes into focus: that there would have been a serious recession-inflation in the seventies even if the oil cartel had not bid up the price of energy on the world market. The "normal" capitalist mechanisms were preparing a breakdown and it had surfaced prior to the OPEC boycott and price rises of 1973–74. In short, Lyndon Johnson's claim that economic life is no longer "a relentless tide of ups and downs" is not true even under ordinary conditions.

During the post-World War II period there was not, of course, a depression on the scale of that of the 1930s. Between 1929 and 1933, the Gross National Product was cut in two, falling from $103 billion to $55.6 billion. In those years, private investment declined from $16.2 billion in 1929 to $1.4 billion in 1933. Unemployment was a catastrophic 25 percent of the labor force, and was still well over 10 percent in 1941, after eight years of the New Deal. Full employment, of course, did not come until the middle of World War II, when federal outlays took nearly half of Gross National Product ($91.2 billion in expenditures, $210.1 billion in G.N.P. and a deficit of over $47 billion in 1944).

By that standard of misery, the postwar period was indeed qualitatively different from the thirties. There were, however, some extenuating circumstances. Right after the war, the Marshall Plan was, as Chapter 10 showed, an enormous stimulus to American prosperity. In effect, the multibillion-dollar federal commitment to the reconstruction of European capitalism was also a subsidy to American industry, which filled the orders. During these years, the United States reigned supreme over the world market. Moreover, it may well be that the years between 1940 and 1960 were one of those "long waves" of capitalist expansion brilliantly described by Leon Trotsky (but more widely known in the version of the theory developed by N. Kondratiev). In times of capitalist expansion, like 1851 to 1873, Trotsky wrote, "the crises are brief, superficial in character, while the booms are long-lasting and far-reaching. In periods of capitalist decline, the crises are of a prolonged character, while the booms are fleeting, superficial and speculative." If this analysis holds in the present situation, then 1940–1960 may be seen as a secular boom, powered by innovations such as electronics, and 1960– as a secular slump.

In any case, there were many, many reasons why the relative prosperity after World War II was not a permanent condition of capitalist life. But then, even within that prosperity there were chronic unemployment and poverty. There were no fewer than three downturns in the fifties—1949–50; 1953; and 1959–60—and in each recovery phase, unemployment remained higher than in the previous prosperity. Then came the Kennedy-Johnson years, and they provided the objective basis for the euphoria of the New Economics. Between 1962 and 1969, unemployment declined from 5.5 percent to 3.5 percent, the latter being the lowest jobless figure since 1945. So, there was a certain surface plausibility to Johnson's boast that a fundamental breakthrough had been made.

It now turns out that this optimism was, to say the least, premature. One of the reasons for the economic performance during Johnson's later years as President was the Vietnam war. It had the effect of tremendously stimulating the economy—there was a 25-billion-dollar deficit in 1968—but that set inflationary tendencies in motion. Here one confronts the capitalist capacity for crisis in both old and new forms.[1]

II

In Marx's analysis, recessions and depressions almost always begin at the peak of the boom. As the expansion nears its culmination, there is relatively full employment, the workers' position is strengthened, and they may even retrieve a portion of the surplus value they have created. This is a pressure on profit margins. At the same time, the investment in new plant and equipment which had marked the recovery phase slows down. Moreover, interest rates have been driven up during the period when business was booming and there was a growing demand for capital. At this point, success breeds failure, and a crisis becomes a "rational" solution for the accumulated problems of prosperity. As unemployment increases, the workers are weakened, and discipline picks up in the plant. The marginal producers who had been an inefficient pressure on resources are put out of business, the interest rates fall, and after an appropriate time of human suffering, the system is once more ready to take off under new conditions of profitability.

In the early seventies, part of the scenario was taking place in Marxist fashion. Wages were up, profit margins were down, interest was high, and so on. And Richard Nixon quite consciously turned to the classic remedy. He announced that his 1970 budget would propose "a substantial reduction in claims against future tax dollars and future budgets" as a means of combatting inflation. The President was, in short, sponsoring a recession, that classic anti-inflation mechanism of the capitalist system. Unemployment rose steadily, from 3.5 percent in 1969 to 5.9 percent in 1971. In the process, the Republicans lost heavily in the 1970 Congressional elections, in part because of the high rate of joblessness.

In August 1971, Nixon responded. He imposed wage and price controls and adopted very expansionary fiscal and monetary policies. There was, for example, a deficit of more than $23 billion in 1972. Nixon, who may have lost the Presidency in 1960 because of the recession that preceded the election, was taking no chances. He heated up the economy—and with it the rate of inflation.

There are two important, new aspects of the classic capitalist tendency toward crisis in this brief history.

First of all, depression levels of unemployment are politically intolerable, even for a conservative government. Nixon's interests were adversely affected in 1970 by a rise in joblessness from 3.5 percent of the labor force to 4.9 percent. That last figure was only about a third of the rate in 1941—that is, at the end of Dr. New Deal and the beginning of Dr. Win the War (the phrases are Roosevelt's). But the 1941 figure represented a substantial reduction in unemployment, the 1970 figure a steady increase during the course of almost two years. Moreover, the attitude of workers in the early seventies was that unemployment was abnormal, whereas in the thirties it was considered by some to be a chronic fact of life.

Now all this is obvious enough. What is not so obvious is that it means that capitalism has been deprived of one of its most useful —and cruelly destructive—mechanisms. Crises, as Marx understood, performed the irrationally rational function of making a contradictory system once again workable. Only, a point has been reached where, for political reasons that apply to the right as well as the left, that method of restoring "equilibrium" can no longer be used. In tinkering with, but by no means abolishing, the machinery of capitalist crisis, governmental intervention has created structural tendencies toward inflation.

The sophisticated business press understood this dilemma. *Business Week* noted in 1974 that the most important reason for inflation was "the worldwide commitment to full employment and maximum production. Without exception, the governments of the world have consistently chosen to risk inflation rather than risk unemployment." Almost wistfully, nostalgically, the magazine added:

> An economy that never has serious recessions tends to become increasingly inflationary. Partly this is because the stimulating effects of government spending and easy money create more demand than the economy can satisfy at any given time. And partly it is because long periods without significant contraction create a general expectation of rising demand and rising prices.

This situation, it should be stressed, has a specifically capitalist content. The "fiscal crisis" arises in considerable measure, as James O'Connor rightly argues, because the social costs of capitalism are increasingly subsidized by the government, while the profits and the decisions remain private. If, for example, the Johnson administration had forthrightly argued in favor of its unconscionable war and financed it through progressive taxes on those most able to bear the burden, it might have avoided some of the inflationary consequences of an intervention that should never have been undertaken in the first place. But to do that would not simply have required that Johnson candidly describe his war as a war (which would have invited Congressional rejection of the policy). He would also have been approaching one of the limits which the capitalist character of the economy fixes for all governments, the liberal as well as the conservative. For as long as private profit is conceded to be the prime source of new investment, just so long are the elected representatives of the people required to defer to the privileges of money.

If Johnson had seriously taxed wealth as a progressive way of dealing with inflation, he would have been accused of interfering with the process of capital accumulation and therefore of job generation. If one concedes that there is an eternal necessity in granting control of accumulation and investment to private, and often antisocial, institutions, that argument has a certain persuasiveness. In other words, any concerted attack on the position of the corporate rich must be accompanied by rather radical proposals for new ways to carry out the functions which the rich perform in their reactionary fashion. But Lyndon Johnson, who was operating on a Great Society theory of the constructive harmony of business and government, was not about to move along those lines. So it was not merely the war, but the profound limitations of capitalist society as well, that set loose the inflationary demons in the late sixties.

The new political situation, then, created not only a new inflationary problem. It created also a problem that was difficult, if not impossible, to solve within the range of options which a capitalist economy permits its ostensible masters to adopt.

Secondly, the history of Nixon's egregious failure focuses upon the political dimension of the business cycle. The recession of 1969–70 was the result of a conscious policy choice. It was not, to be sure, manufactured out of thin air; it was a response to a very real inflationary problem. But now the timing and tempo of crises can be, within certain limits, manipulated by political leaders. Having failed with a recession in 1969–70, Nixon "succeeded" with an expansion that in 1971–72 helped to elect him and also led up to the worst recession in forty years and the worst inflation in twentieth-century American history. This tactic might be called his economic Watergate.

The event also focuses the dialectical aspect of economic management under welfare capitalism. On the one hand, the recession-inflations of the late sixties and early seventies in the United States demonstrate that the "spontaneous" market-induced tendencies toward crisis continue to exist, and quite forcefully. Thus, it is wrong for a Marxist like Samir Amin to suggest that the business cycle which functioned from 1825 to 1940 has ceased to operate and that entirely new contradictions are now at work. But it would also be wrong to think that transition from an unconscious, blind succession of boom and bust to recessions and inflations which governments try to manage and sometimes even initiate is a mere formality. One momentous consequence of this shift, as Jurgen Habermas has stressed, is that the political order undergoes a crisis of legitimacy. It is now seen, often wrongly, as the locus of economic power, and new demands are accordingly made upon it—demands it cannot fulfill as long as it leaves the corporate infrastructure and the corporate priorities intact.

The economic crises since 1969, then, bear out the basic Marxist analysis that capitalism—even welfare capitalism—must be fearful of prosperity and full employment. If the facts have, for some perverse reason, not been sufficiently persuasive, perhaps an impeccably Marxist interpretation of them will clinch the point. It comes from Arthur Burns, the conservative Chairman of the Federal Reserve Board. In a speech in May 1975, Burns told the Society of American Business Writers that the depression was performing "a painful but unavoidable function" of correcting "basic maladjustments" in the economy. It was, he said, "restoring the balance between production and sales, orders and inventories, spurring efficiency, improving the conditions of the financial markets and wringing inflation out of the system." That is a marvelously succinct statement of the Marxist case, a brilliant application of it to the events of recent years.

Thus the secret history of the crisis of the seventies reveals that, first of all, an antisocial socialization of the economy in behalf of the corporations perpetuates and aggravates, rather than resolves, the contradictions of capitalism. Secondly, it shows that the capitalist mechanism of boom and bust continues in a moderated, and sometimes politically exacerbated, form and that the system thus sickens from its own success. Thirdly, these new expressions of the intrinsic instability of bourgeois society have, since 1973, been magnified by the effect of an oil cartel whose effectiveness is, in considerable measure, a result of the fact that American energy planning followed capitalist priorities for a generation.

In short, a fundamental Marxist insight allows one to fathom dimensions of the events of the seventies that are not at all visible on their surface. It is not technology or industrialism or the "bad luck" created by oil-rich sheiks that has brought us to the incredible pass of this decade. Rather, it is the capitalist use—or, more precisely, inherent misuse—of resources that is responsible for our plight.[2]

III

Is the Karl Marx of this analysis, then, a Delphic oracle resurrected? Is *Das Kapital* a new Book of Revelations?

No serious Marxist has ever thought anything so preposterous. And yet, there were those who thought their method gave them privileged insight into the future. Trotsky, as I noted in Chapter 1, could say in 1938 that his Fourth International would, because of the correctness of its ideas, become "the guide of millions" at the end of World War II. Marx himself occasionally spoke of the "natural necessity" of the laws he had discovered, and Engels did so much more often. And yet, in their analytic work neither Marx nor Engels ever engaged in stereotyped or rigid thinking. Engels, as will be seen shortly, made wholesale revisions in the Marxian model of capitalism. Both of them, as Schumpeter was among the few to understand, carefully distinguished between the structural possibilities inherent in capitalism, the specific causes which would actualize a possibility, and the symptoms which accompanied it. In such a version of reality, there is no substitute for the empirical study of the particular case, even if it can only be deciphered as functioning within the larger capitalist context.

But, then, there is no need to confront this issue on the plane of theory alone. More than a century of history has answered it decisively. The Marxists understood many crucial facts about society long before others did, and oriented themselves accordingly. They saw in the working class a potential that few others recognized;

they analyzed the crisis tendencies of capitalism while the academicians composed idylls of equilibrium. Yet in terms of predicting the future in a politically meaningful way—of knowing that the capitalist tendency to crisis would explode in the United States in the year 1929 or in the early seventies—there is no evidence that the Marxists, of whatever persuasion, have a better record of foresight than their bourgeois rivals.

The reason for this failure has to do with the distinction Marx made between the over-all structure of a system and its specific functioning. Marx, for instance, was right: laissez-faire capitalism was so unstable and crisis-prone that it would provoke masses into struggle and require the conscious intervention of the state if disaster were to be avoided. Not only was he right, but his truth was rejected by practically all of the established thinkers of his day. But Marx, as we have seen, was utterly wrong when he thought, in 1848, that the climax of this process was at hand. He was even wrong in 1850, when he decided that the triumph of socialism might lie a mere fifty years in the distance. And he only had intimations that state planning would become a tool of capitalist stability, the dominant fact of capitalist society for the past generation.

The political future is the short and medium run. It functions as part of the longer and systemic movement of society, but it cannot be predicted simply because one knows the latter. Trotsky was incomparably more brilliant than Stalin, whom he rightly regarded as a Marxist mediocrity; only, the mediocrity made history and murdered the Marxist genius. A serious Marxist, then, should have a better grasp of the elemental forces of contemporary society than his bourgeois competitors; he or she knows about the unstable equilibrium and equilibrating crises that are usually ignored in the academy. But that, alas, does not confer the power to foretell specific events. It is a good reason for becoming a Marxist, but no reason at all for making exaggerated and oracular claims which cannot be fulfilled.

Trotsky had been cited earlier as a case in point for the excessive Marxist boast to prescience. Yet even here, there is complexity. For Trotsky was one of the few thinkers in the late twenties and early thirties who had any sense of the meaning of Nazism. His writings on the situation in Germany were, in the best sense of the word, prophetic. Even so, that knowledge did not permit Trotsky to intervene and to change the monstrous history that he so brilliantly predicted. So, the problem remains much as it was posed in the first chapter: the relatively few Marxists who were able to apply their theories to the anticipation of events were historically marginal in terms of affecting those events. The foreknowledge of necessity did not turn out to be, as Engels thought, freedom: it was sometimes an informed helplessness.

Clearly, then, the Marxist should be chastened, which has not always been the case. However, one must add immediately: Perhaps not quite so much as the anti-Marxists. For instance, the energy crisis was not anticipated by any Marxist I know of, but once the event happened it fitted easily into a Marxist scenario and could be subjected to a Marxist analysis with excellent results. The theorists of "postindustrial" society could not find such modest comfort. As Roger Gerard Schwartzenberg described "The End of the Technocrats" in *Le Monde,*

> It was yesterday. It was a time of expansion. It was the era of the technocrats. A new class of high functionaries had taken power. Forecasting, planning, technical causation were their key terms. They had science, knowledge; they were, we believed, specialists, experts who would master the economic mechanism. Henceforth governmental decisions would be taken rationally. By experts. Not by elected officials without technical competence. Only, this technostructure, so sure of itself, saw nothing coming. Not the energy crisis. Not the scarcity of raw materials. Not the exhaustion of natural resources. Nor the degradation of the environment. Nor the dangers of the "consumer society" for economic equilibrium.

The error made in all those "futurological" projections was classic. They, of course, took into account that there would be upheavals and surprises in the next generation, and they even tried to integrate them into their scenarios. But they did not consider that these breakdowns would come from within the system itself in the form of crises. What has already happened in the seventies was not really taken into consideration in the sixties, when predictions were made about the year 2000. The concept of systemic contradictions was omitted from the analysis. That, a Marxist might suggest, is no accident. It is a function of the (often tacit) assumption that capitalism has finally solved the dilemmas which Marx located at the very center of its existence. The futurists did not, for example, imagine that thirty years of careful, massive government intervention in energy policy would, because it was conducted according to corporate priorities, make the United States vulnerable to the pressure of countries with one tenth, of one hundredth, of its power.

But even though the anti-Marxists have been much more foolish —and it should be said, smug—on this count than the Marxists, that is no reason for the latter to make claims they cannot substantiate. Trotsky had previously been quoted as an arrogant example of how not to approach this problem. Another quotation from him gives a contrary, and excellent, illustration of the necessary Marxist sensitivity to the aleatory nature of history.

In 1921, Trotsky told the Third Congress of the Communist International:

> If we grant—and let us grant it for a moment—that the working class fails to rise in revolutionary struggle, but allows the bourgeoisie the opportunity to rule the world's destiny for a long number of years, say two or three decades, then assuredly some new sort of equilibrium will be established. Europe will be thrown violently into reverse gear. Millions of European workers will die from unemployment and malnutrition. The United States will be compelled to reorient itself on the world market, reconvert its industry and suffer curtailment for a considerable period. Afterwards, after a new world division of labor is thus established in agony for 15 or 20 or 25 years, a new epoch of capitalist upswing might ensue.

If one takes that as an anticipation of the years from 1921 to 1970, the details are wrong, but the underlying idea—that there would be a gigantic capitalist crisis followed, if the revolution fails, by a new capitalist upswing—is sound.

So, it is precisely a Marxist point of view that sees the possibility of the resolution of the crisis of the seventies and even of a new capitalist resurgence. That, to be sure, would be done at the price of enormous and needless suffering, and it would certainly entail further structural modifications of the system, a greater integration of the state and corporation in a national planning effort. But it could happen. In the long run, it would be one more instance, and a rather severe one, of the anticapitalist salvation of capitalism, of the glacial transformation of the system into one of the opposites which are possible within it. Exactly how these short and long runs intersect, however, is a matter for the most careful, even humble, empirical study. But that, in its turn, will be all the more rich if it is seen as suffused with the twilight of the bourgeois era.

In the process, one must be ready to abandon any of Marx's conclusions which turn out to be false or, as is much more often the case, which are no longer true. Marx himself noted less than ten years after the publication of Volume I of *Das Kapital* that the periodicity of the business cycle that he had described in that book seemed to be changing. And in a preface to Volume I written three years after Marx's death, in 1886, Engels noted that the crisis periods seemed to be slowing down. Then in the process of editing Volume III, which appeared in 1894, Engels made even more sweeping revisions of Marx's earlier assessments. Cartels, he commented, had altered some of the contradictions which Marx had described; the stock market had become much more important; the corporation had developed into an international instrument of the cartel; and so on.

In another addendum to Volume III Engels wrote:

Since the general crisis of 1867, great changes have taken place. The colossal expansion of the means of commerce . . . has for the first time really created a world market. . . . The investment of excess European capital has spread endlessly throughout the globe and opened up new areas, so that capital is now more widely dispersed and can overcome crises due to local speculations more easily.

Then Engels made this candid admission:

Through all these developments, the old crisis tendencies and the occasions for the buildup of the crisis have been greatly weakened or done away with. Competition yields in the domestic market in the face of cartels and trusts and is limited on the external market by protective tariffs with which all the great powers, except England, surround themselves. But these protective tariffs are only weapons for the final campaign, which will decide the domination of the world market. So, each element that works against the repetition of the old crisis conceals within itself the seeds of a much more widespread and powerful crisis in the future.

All the factors that Engels cited in these revisions impeded, or subverted, the workings of the law of value. And yet Engels did not for a moment propose to drop that part of Marx's analysis, for it provided insights into the basic nature of the system that were crucial for understanding its transformations. So, today one can hardly speak of the "anarchy of capitalist production" when there is welfare-state planning. But the incredible, fundamental and most Marxian paradox is that this anarchy has not been abolished, but only collectivized, that the antisocial priorities of private purpose as they permeate public action are the secret of calculated disorders in food, energy, transportation, in social life itself.

And Engels' remark that "each element that works against the old crisis conceals within itself the seeds of a much more widespread and powerful crisis in the future" might be taken as the motto of this analysis of the welfare state. Through this mechanism capitalism has done the most contradictory things in the most contradictory ways. It has reformed itself and created new problems; it has been forced to make significant concessions to militant mass movements, and it has co-opted them, but only in part. Inexorably now, for well over a century, it has been collectivizing itself, and in recent times this trend has become so profound that it has proceeded almost as fast under a conservative government, like the Nixon-Ford administrations, as under liberals like Kennedy and Johnson.

It is the twilight of the bourgeois epoch, because this process of collectivization will eventually lead to a transformation of the system itself. That will not happen automatically, and how it happens will make a crucial difference for millions of people. Whether the totalitarian or the authoritarian or the democratic-socialist variant of the collectivist future will prevail is a question that will be determined by political and social struggle.

The welfare state, as it emerges in this Marxist dissection of it, is indeed an organic whole of reciprocal causality, with a pervasive capitalist lighting and an atmosphere which bathes, but does not predetermine, every relationship within it. It is not, as some of the left think, a conspiracy, but a process filled with unintended consequences, surprising its rulers as well as the ruled. It is not, as the technocratic center imagines, a neutral, problem-solving apparatus that divvies up the proceeds of a crisis-free economy in a rational manner. It is a contradictory, crisis-prone, last stage of capitalism.

In developing this analysis, I have concentrated on the economic and political aspects of the domestic life of the welfare state. That is not to say that the cultural and international dimensions of this problem are unimportant. Far from it. But there are limitations of time and space, and in three other books—*The Accidental Century, Toward a Democratic Left* and *Socialism*—I examined these areas at some length. In the briefest of summaries, I would only add that it is now clear that the Western capitalist hegemony over the world market, which has its origins as far back as the thirteenth century, is beginning to come to an end. Neocolonialism has, to be sure, found effective mechanisms for perpetuating capitalist domination in the Third World even after national liberation movements have achieved political independence. And yet a momentous change has taken place. A generation ago, the OPEC cartel would not have been tolerated for long. It surely would have gone the way of Mossadegh in Iran. Now that is no longer possible.

That some of the powers in the Middle East exercising this new freedom are feudalist and others authoritarian, that most seek to exterminate the right of Jewish national self-determination in Israel, and that their cartel has had a fearful impact upon the masses who live in the Fourth World of starvation does not alter the basic point. These are some of the grim ambiguities and injustices which seem to accompany every transformation of modern life. The point made here is simply that they are also a portent of change, of the beginning of the end of a Western imperial system that for centuries has outrageously made the wretched of this earth into the hewers of its wood and the haulers of its water.

The cultural upheaval is just as marked. The bourgeoisie did not simply represent a new economy; it was the (often unwitting) agent of a new civilization. In its rise and triumph it won imperishable victories for the human spirit, bringing the values of freedom, of reason and individualism into a reality that, however flawed by its capitalist limitations, was a great advance for humankind. That civilization began to disintegrate a long time ago, a fact announced by Nietzsche in the nineteenth century. Now, however, that decadence has become the experience of everyday life rather than of prophetic geniuses.

In this twilight of the capitalist epoch, there is a decline in religious commitment, in moral conviction, indeed in almost any kind of belief. The old order has died in the realm of the spirit long before the new order has occurred in the realm of politics and the economy. The resulting dissonance should surprise no one who has understood Marx's brilliant analysis of that complex transition from feudalism to capitalism. It, too, was a centuries-long process of anomalies and contradictions.

That human life will be radically transformed in the medium range of the future cannot be questioned any longer, because that future has already begun. All that is in doubt is the most crucial of issues: Whether this collectivist society which is emerging even now will repress, or liberate, men and women. I conclude, then, with an "if"—but then, in this era to be even provisionally hopeful is to affirm—if the best of what humans have achieved is to prevail, which is to say, deepen, in the unprecedented environment that is already beginning—if all men and women are to be free in a just society—then, the spirit of the new Karl Marx must be our comrade in the struggle. So, this book has sought to liberate that spirit from the mausoleum in which an ironic history has imprisoned it.[3]

APPENDIX A

CHAPTER 1   Oracle in the Ruins

1. In defining the underground tradition of Marxism, two conclusions emerge in the course of description: that there is no necessary relationship between Marxist theory and political positions (that is, that those who agree as to methodology can utilize that method to reach contradictory political judgments); and that even though the Marxian underground was far distant from political power, it developed in response to historical events, and its ideas are suffused with the struggles of the times.

The underground is politically heterogeneous. At one time or another it included Social Democrats, Communists, Trotskyists, and nonparty academics. What binds this diverse group together is a rejection of the mechanistic, scientistic interpretation of Marx that dominated, for quite different reasons, both the Second International before World War I and the Stalinized Third International after it. It is precisely because all these thinkers recognized the importance of the "subjective" side of the dialectic, the reciprocal action of men and culture upon the economic determinants, that it was possible for them to differ politically on the basis of a common insight. They were all opposed to the "inevitablist" reading of Marx; they therefore allowed for much greater honest variations among Marxists.

The nature and history of this underground have been fairly well documented in the scholarly literature, and I need only summarize a few basic themes and cite leading names for a mere sketch of its historic development.

It is generally thought that the Marxian underground first appeared at the end of World War I as a response to the collapse of the "official" —schematic and evolutionist—Marxism of the Second International and to the triumph of the Bolsheviks, who made a successful socialist revolution in a country that had not gone through the required historical stages. That is not quite true, although reality would be a much more orderly affair if it were. Max Adler, a neo-Kantian Marxist and the philosopher of "Austro-Marxism," had developed a ranging critique of the inevitablist reading of Marx well before World War I.

Adler, for instance, was the first Marxist to reject the caricature that passed for a portrait of Hegel in the socialist camp; he insisted on the importance of Hegel in Marx's own development. He rejected Engels' attempt to create a Marxian *Weltanschauung*, complete with a materialist "philosophy"; he fought vigorously against the notion that Marxism "reduced" all reality to the economic factor, and he argued that the economic was permeated with spirit, with thought; and so on. Two comments about his achievements are particularly relevant to this brief evocation of the Marxist underground.

First, it was Adler's neo-Kantian perspective that motivated him to oppose all attempts to construct a "dialectical materialist" system of laws governing all reality, physical as well as social. He rightly and brilliantly criticized the epistemological naïveté of Engels' efforts in this area and was among the first to notice that Marx did not participate in them. Thus, the neo-Kantianism made him open to the humanism of Marx. Yet Adler's fellow Austrian, Rudolf Hilferding, took those same neo-Kantian and Marxist premises and used them to justify a "value-free," scientist vision of Marx. So not only is the relationship between philosophy and politics complex, but the very same philosophic principles can function in very different ways in the thinking of men who share political views. Secondly, Adler's rather lonely accomplishment demonstrates how an individual thinker can make a significant contribution to Marxism even though it does not become a factor in a mass movement. For, as Norbert Leser sadly chronicles, Adler left few intellectual heirs in the Austrian social-democracy he served so well.

A much more famous representative of the Marxists who rejected a mechanistic evolutionism even before 1917 was Rosa Luxemburg, that luminous figure of both the Polish and the German movements. The "leap" to socialism, she wrote in a typical passage, cannot take place unless "the spark of the will of the great mass of people ignites the stuff of the material preconditions which historical development has brought

together." Therefore, Rosa was not in the least afraid to admit that the
future was not inevitably socialist. It could be, she said in repeating a
remark of Engels, either socialist or barbaric. This political insight also
informed her scholarly work. She was one of the first Marxists to insist upon the notion of "Asiatic society," those despotically collectivist
formations which do not fit into any of the neat schemas. In 1900 she
noted that there was no such thing as an "iron law of wages," and she
commented that Marx had been the gravedigger of that theory. And she
understood a profound point, which is treated at length in Chapters 3
and 4, that bourgeois society was unlike any prior system of class rule
in that it, and it alone, dominated through economic rather than
through politics.

Rosa's most significant contribution as a Marxist theorist, however,
was her study of imperialism in *The Accumulation of Capital*. As a
Pole, she was particularly sensitive to the way in which capitalism
spread out to what we would now term its "periphery." More, she saw
that expansion as an inherent tendency of the capitalist economy and
documented that judgment in a study which, though clearly flawed in
some respects, was a much more complex and sophisticated account of
the imperialist phenomenon than Lenin's much more famous pamphlet.
"For all its confusions and exaggerations," Joan Robinson said of *The
Accumulation of Capital*, "this book shows more prescience than any
orthodox contemporary could claim."

So, there were Marxists like Adler and Luxemburg who rejected the
positivistic Marx long before the Russian Revolution. But it was unquestionably that revolution which helped to create an underground
that went back to the authentic Marx. Its members were, for the most
part dissidents within their own organizations and they were either ex-
pelled from them, like Karl Korsch, who was driven out of the German
party, or else concealed their own genius and opinions from them, like
George Lukacs. In addition to Korsch and Lukacs, the other prominent
name in this development is Antonio Gramsci, a man who escaped the
perils of Stalinization because he spent those years in one of Mussolini's jails.

What characterized these thinkers is their insistence on the importance of the dialectic (and usually of the Hegelian influence in Marxism) and their rejection of the "vulgar" Marxism that resulted from
neglecting this point. Karl Korsch's attack on the vulgar Marxists in a
seminal book of 1923 is typical of this attitude:

Instead of understanding the spiritual alongside the social, alongside social being and becoming, in the broadest sense of the words, and seeing that social consciousness is a real, even if ideal (or ideological) part of the over-all social reality, they explain all consciousness in an abstract, basically metaphysical and dualistic way, as a completely dependent or only relatively independent, and in the final analysis dependent, reflex of the actual process of development which is alone real.

Lukacs' *History and Class Consciousness* made a similar rediscovery of the role of subjectivity in Marxism. In this brilliant study of alienation in bourgeois thought, Lukacs, basing himself almost exclusively on Marx's statements in *Das Kapital,* developed the essential arguments of the *Economic and Philosophic Manuscripts of 1844* some years before he, or anyone else, had seen that posthumously published document. It was capitalism, Lukacs argued, that inevitably developed a rationalist, calculating view of the world and took mathematics as the paradigmatic science for all thought. But this bourgeois consciousness was mocked by the irrationality of the social totality that the bourgeoisie constructed with such great rationality (on this count, Lukacs was clearly influenced by a professor from his youth, Max Weber, as well as by Marx). So, it was eventually driven inward to subjectivism and irrationalism. Only Marxism offered the possibility of an unalienated, dialectical consciousness.

At the same time, Lukacs brilliantly attacked Engels' theory of a dialectical materialism that explained all of reality. The dialectic, he insisted, involved the reciprocal and very human relations of subject and object, and it was shocking that Engels took capitalist industrialism—an undialectical and antisocial rationalism—as a proof of the Marxist concept of "praxis." Since this assertion put Lukacs at odds with Lenin as well as with Engels, it was to provide the basis for a vicious attack upon him within the Communist International and the Hungarian Communist Party. In 1923, the Comintern was in the process of "Bolshevizing" itself under the leadership of Gregory Zinoviev—that is, setting up norms of uncritical obedience, norms that were to be taken over by Stalin (and, of course, then used against Zinoviev). Creative Marxists like Lukacs were not the kind of member the Communist leaders wanted in their "Marxist" parties.

Not that *History and Class Consciousness* is perfect. Its analysis of the bourgeois consciousness, and of German classical philosophy in particular, is brilliant and rich in insights to this day. But the account of proletarian consciousness is Hegelian—or Weberian—in the sense that it constructs an ideal type of what the worker's mind should be like, one which Lukacs himself admits does not correspond with the actual, empirical consciousness of the working class. But if the workers themselves deviated from the true proletarian consciousness, where was it to be found? In the Party, Lukacs answered. He made that fateful response in his youthful left-Marxist days, but it was to rationalize his lying to stay within the Communist movement. He repudiated his own theories on how to fight fascism in 1928 and 1929, even though he still thought them to be correct. (And, ironically, history proved them to be correct.) Paradoxically, then, it was Lukacs' Hegelian "deviation" that helped him become a Stalinist. But then, as George Lichtheim realized in his study of Lukacs, perhaps that is not such a paradox after all: "There is," Lichtheim wrote, "in Hegel's attitude toward Napoleon something that connects him with Lukacs' unconcealed admiration for Stalin: the captain who weathered the storm, even if he had to butcher half the crew and most of the officers."

Antonio Gramsci's case differs from that of Korsch and Lukacs, both of whom were Central European intellectuals, steeped in the tradition of classic German philosophy. Gramsci was a Sardinian, a founder of the Italian Communist Party, and a thinker who developed intellectually under the most difficult of circumstances. He had, to be sure, a very substantial Marxist tradition to draw upon—Antonio Labriola, Croce of his Marxist period, the challenging anti-Marxism of Vilfredo Pareto, and so on—but he first developed it under much more activist circumstances than Lukacs and Korsch were to know, and then, later on, in a fascist jail.

Gramsci's early writings were never vulgar and mechanistic. He was daring enough, for instance, to attack *Das Kapital* as a "book of the bourgeoisie" in less developed countries—that is, an argument for the evolutionary development of capitalism until it reached the maturity that socialism required. Moreover, he was influenced by a maximalist and ultraleftist tradition that had deep roots in the Italian left. Thus, he has the dubious distinction of being one of the first to formulate the theory of "social fascism"—the idea that social-democratic reformism is a form of fascism. Stalin was to take this notion from Zinoviev and to use it to turn the German Communists against the Socialists to the advantage of the Nazis. Gramsci, unfortunately, anticipated this dangerous, erroneous thesis.

But then, when Mussolini sent him to prison, Gramsci had the time to think and read (his books were paid for by Piero Sraffa, a path-finding genius of contemporary economics who is dealt with in Chapter 5). In his prison notebooks, there emerged a supple Marxist methodology that emphasized the complexities of working-class consciousness and stressed the changes that had taken place since Marx's day.

The influence of Gramsci's thinking was not felt until long after his death in Fascist Italy. But the Korsch-Lukacs interpretation was quite influential in Germany in the years before Hitler came to power. It helped prepare the way, among other things, for the famous Frankfurt Institute, which was founded in the 1920s, moved to America during the Hitler years and returned to Germany after World War II. Some of the members of the Frankfurt school were involved in the party politics of the left; others were not. Some were to break completely with the Marxist approach and almost all referred to their work as "critical theory" rather than as Marxism. But a good part of the work of these scholars belongs to the underground tradition of Marxism. The best-known among them are Max Horkheimer, Theodore Adorno, Herbert Marcuse, Erich Fromm, Walter Benjamin, Franz Borkenau, Franz Neumann. They were concerned with art and culture, particularly mass culture (Adorno, Horkheimer and Benjamin), with the encounter between Marx and Freud (Fromm and Marcuse), with the relationship of theory and practice (Borkenau's brilliant *Der Übergang vom feudalen zum bürglichen Weltbild*) and with fascism (Neumann). (For the history of the Frankfurt school, see Martin Jay, *The Dialectical Imagination.*)

The revived Frankfurt school after World War II produced a new generation of Marxist thinkers, including the most important contemporary theorist of Marxism, Jurgen Habermas. Habermas, as will be seen at some length in the Appendix to Chapter 3, developed a brilliant critique of scientism, systems theory and the technocratic approach to knowledge. His *oeuvre*, which is still very much in progress, is a living proof of the continued vitality of Marxist modes of thought in situations which Marx himself did not, and could not, anticipate. Even though Habermas and some of the young scholars who emerged out of the Frankfurt tradition (like Claus Offe) were politically involved in the German left, their work was primarily scholarly in character. The Trotskyists, on the other hand, were a political tendency called into existence by the Stalinization of the Russian Revolution, and their activism subjected them to physical attack and even murder.

Trotsky himself does not fit neatly into a history of underground

Marxism, not only because of his own work, but also because of the ambiguity of Lenin's philosophical heritage. In the first phase of the Marxist revival, associated with Korsch, Lukacs and the early Frankfurt school, Trotsky was a man of Soviet power, a "prophet armed," as Isaac Deutscher called him. As such, he took no part in the discussions of semiheretical Communists who were concerned basically with theory as theory rather than as a guide to practice. Then, when he was driven from power and exiled, Trotsky was constantly forced to rebut Stalin's charge that he had never really been a Leninist. This caused him to become an uncritical defender of Leninist orthodoxy, to be *plus royaliste que le roi.*

Lenin himself is difficult to define in terms of the issues which were basic to underground Marxism. His *Criticism and Empirio-Criticism* is a polemical and oversimplified book, which imputes to Marx a naïve materialism wherein ideas merely "reflect" reality. But his philosophical notebooks—significantly they were written at the beginning of World War I, when Lenin felt completely defeated and therefore had no ulterior political purpose in mind—comment on his reading of Hegel and are filled with a spirit very much like that of Korsch and the young Lukacs. Since they had not studied Hegel's *Logic,* Lenin said, "none of the Marxists understood Marx" for almost half a century. However, the Notebooks were not published until six years after Lenin's death, in 1929–30, and Trotsky did not take them seriously.

So Trotsky was "orthodox" in the pejorative sense of the term, and this even led him to the foolish assertion that workers, because of their experience in the factory, would instinctively understand the dialectic better than petty-bourgeois intellectuals. I nevertheless include him in this survey for a number of reasons. Some of his books, particularly the *History of the Russian Revolution* and his writings on literature, are anything but mechanistic and vulgar. Trotsky had an appreciation of the relative autonomy of art and of the value of modernist trends, including surrealism, that a man like Stalin could not abide. His applications of Marxism were superior to his generalizations of it. Secondly, even though I disagree with *The Revolution Betrayed,* Trotsky's last major theoretical statement on the nature of Stalinism, it shows him quite capable of thinking brilliantly with the Marxist methodology. Thirdly, some of the thinkers who were at one time a part of Trotsky's movement—who issue, so to speak, from his school—made significant contributions to Marxism.

Isaac Deutscher was a Polish Communist, and then a Trotskyist. His biography of Trotsky is a major intellectual achievement of Marxism (though I should indicate that I disagree with some of its basic premises). Pierre Naville was for a time a Trotskyist. His *Nouveau Leviathan,* of which three volumes have thus far appeared, is a serious work of theoretical Marxism. Ernest Mandel remains a Trotskyist, the leading theoretician of the Fourth International. His *Traité d'économie marxiste* is an important statement, particularly because it takes recent, non- and anti-Marxist scholarship into account. And finally, the late Max Shachtman, who broke with Trotsky in 1939, developed the theory of Communism as a "bureaucratic-collectivist" order, neither capitalist nor socialist, which I think is a major accomplishment of Marxism.

Shachtman reached his conclusions as a dissident Trotskyist. Around the same time, Lucien Laurat, a French socialist and colleague of Léon Blum, came up with a similar analysis. His political positions were quite different from Schachtman's at the time, and so were Milovan Djilas' when he wrote *The New Class,* another book based upon an idea very much like Shachtman's. The point is that there is no inevitable link between theoretical assumptions and actual political practice, that there is a personal element in the way in which various individuals translate the same methodological propositions into politics.

World War II did not allow the European Marxists much time for theorizing (though some of the exiles in the United States and some of the Americans could go on with their intellectual work). Then the Cold War broke out with the "peace," and the world was split into what seemed to be two irreconcilable camps. Marxist thinking, like international politics, was too often driven into a simplistic "either/or" as a result. Jean-Paul Sartre, to take a symbolic instance, had been led by his experience in the French resistance to consider his existentialism as an "enclave" of Marxism, "the only indispensable philosophy of our times." For a short period in 1947, he thought it possible to build a revolutionary alternative to both the Communist and the American camps. But he soon abandoned that enterprise and became a conscious, almost programmatic, fellow traveler of the Communist Party on the positivist grounds that, like it or not, the workers were Communist. It was only after the great upheavals of Poland and Hungary in the fifties that he changed this point of view.

The events that moved Sartre had, of course, an impact all around the world. With Stalin dead, Khrushchev's denunciations of his crimes public, and ferment in the satellite countries, new voices were heard in

Eastern Europe. To cite but a few familiar names, there were Kolakowski and Schaff in Poland; the impressive group of thinkers around
the review *Praxis* in Yugoslavia; Karl Kosic and Istvan Meszaros in
Czechoslovakia. The aging Lukacs even appeared briefly as a minister
in Imre Nagy's ill-fated revolutionary government in Hungary. Now it
turned out that the Marxist underground had been, in a literal sense of
the term, an underground. During the years of triumphant Stalinism in
Eastern Europe intellectuals had been formulating a Marxist critique of
a totalitarian regime claiming to be Marxist. The two versions of Marxism, the mechanistic and the dialectical, confronted each other from the
opposite sides of a barricade.

So, the Eastern European revival of authentic Marxist thought was
political and, on occasion, revolutionary. There was another, more
academic, source of underground Marxism. A number of important
Marxist texts were not published until long after Marx's death, particularly the *Economic Philosophic Manuscripts of 1844,* which the Russians issued in 1932, and the *Grundrisse,* the "raw outline" of *Das Kapital* from 1857 to 1858, which appeared in Moscow in 1939. It so happened that these two works, from quite different periods of Marx's life,
placed a special stress on the subjective, the "Hegelian" element in his
thought. At times, as Chapter 6 shows, this rediscovery led to a careless interpretation of Marx in the light of his youthful concerns alone.
But, on the whole, the diffusion of these texts—and the more widespread
awareness of Lenin's *Philosophical Notebooks*—unquestionably helped
in Eastern Europe to promote a new understanding of the meaning of
Marxism.

But, then, this development was not confined to Eastern Europe. On
the contrary, it was international. In England, for instance, the shattering of the Communist Party after the Khrushchev revelations of 1956
allowed former members of the Party, like the brilliant historian Edward Thompson, to join with the New Left intellectuals of *University
and Left Review,* a journal which approached socialism with a particular emphasis on the criticism of culture. In France, Sartre's *Temps
modernes* opened up to more vigorous discussion and *Arguments,* a
small but influential magazine of the independent Marxist left, carried
on discussions in the spirit of—and sometimes republished the classic
texts of—the Marxian underground. In Italy, there were similar developments around the Communist Party involving important thinkers like
Galvano Della Volpe and Lucio Colletti.

There are other cases which are either difficult, or even impossible, to classify. Paul Sweezy in the United States and Charles Bettelheim in France are one case in point. Both of them are knowledgeable Marxist scholars who have done extremely serious and useful work. Yet they were for many years critical supporters of Russian Communism, which gave at least an apologetic cast to some of their analyses. Then they broke with the Russians, seeing Soviet society as retrogressing toward capitalism, but shifted most of their illusions to Chinese Communism. They thus have an ambiguous relationship to the two Communist super-powers which made ideological use of Marxism—and yet they are very much worth reading.

More significantly, it will be noted that I have made no attempt in this brief outline to come to grips with Mao as a theorist. In the main that is because the subject is so vast and complex and my own research in it so limited that I do not want to hazard anything more than an intuition. Mao strikes me—say, in his famous essay, "On Contradiction" —as infinitely more subtle than Stalin, and therefore more interesting, but yet as a believer in that Hegelian Marx of Friedrich Engels' invention who had discovered universal laws of all reality. To say that the life cycle of a plant involves "contradictions" in a way that has any bearing upon the processes of society is, I think, to abuse metaphor and analogy in the extreme. But then, the "Great Helmsman," like Stalin, needs to justify the "scientific" rule of a dictatorial minority and I suspect that is one source of his attitude.

I have also omitted discussion of Third World Marxism even though I think some outstanding work—like Samir Amin's *Accumulation à l'échelle mondiale*—has been produced by these thinkers. Here again, the complexity bursts the bounds of this note. And I cut off this short historical outline without taking the sixties into account, even though they saw a revival of interest in Marx among students and intellectuals throughout the Western world. That decade is too close to serve, even provisionally, as a subject for intellectual history. Moreover, a good deal of the Marxism that it produced may turn out to have been more well-intentioned than profound. Finally, I make no claim to comprehensiveness in this brief outline. I have not been able, for instance, even to mention the work of some important Marxists—the Left Communists like Pannekoek, or brilliant, usually isolated, individuals like Arnold Hauser, Lucien Goldmann, Maximilien Rubel, Merleau-Ponty, Tom Bottomore, and many others. And I have not even touched on the fascinating story of Marxism's growing importance for religious thinkers. One of the best journals of the postwar era, *Marxismusstudien,* was edited on behalf of the German Protestants; a number of French priests made serious contributions to Marxian scholarship; and more recently, there has been a (mainly) Latin American "theology of liberation" that owes much to Marx.

But for all the brevity and inadequacy of this sketch, a few important points should have been established. First, there has been a serious Marxian underground and it has produced a small library of useful work. Secondly, the characteristic that unites the politically disparate figures of that underground is their vision of a dialectical Marxism in which "base" and "superstructure" are reciprocal moments of an organic whole. Thirdly, precisely because this genuine Marxism has been open to new ideas, it has been anything but politically monolithic. Finally, even though it developed largely on the outskirts of power or in the literal underground and has normally been the product of isolated thinkers, its rhythms are clearly those of the history that surrounded it. Indeed, on occasion in Eastern Europe, this Marxism has even had its rendezvous with the masses in whose name it thinks.[1]

2. The notion that a thinker can discover a fact without being aware of its meaning—because he lacks its concept—is central to Marx. It is, among other things, the main thrust of his criticism of Feuerbach, Ricardo and Hegel.

The analysis of Feuerbach in this mode is justly famous. In the Fourth Thesis on Feuerbach, Marx begins by acknowledging the realistic point of departure of his philosophy. "Feuerbach starts out from the fact of religious estrangement, of the duplication of the world into a religious and secular one. His work consists in resolving the religious world into its secular basis." So far, so good. Marx too "resolves" the religious world into its secular basis. Then the critique of what Feuerbach missed: "That the secular basis raises itself above itself and establishes for itself an independent realm in the clouds can be explained only through the cleavage and contradictions within this secular basis." What Feuerbach took for his answer—that the heavenly family of God is a projection of the earthly family of man—Marx regarded as a question: Why was this so? And his answer was that this was inevitable as long as the earthly family existed within a context of "cleavage and contradictions."

In a brilliant "translation," Hans-Georg Backhaus accurately put Marx's critique of Ricardo in terms of the *Theses on Feuerbach*. Backhaus' imaginary but believable Marx writes that

Ricardo starts out from the fact of economic estrangement, of the duplication of the product into a value thing, which is imaginary, and a real thing. His theory consists of resolving this value into labor. He ignores that the main thing still remains to be done. Namely, the fact that the product raises itself above itself and establishes for itself an independent realm of economic categories beyond consciousness, is only to be explained out of the cleavages and contradictions of social labor. These must first of all be understood in their contradiction and then revolutionized in practice.

And Marx's own youthful analysis of Hegel also credits that philosopher with articulating and defining a fact that he did not, however, understand. In Hegel, Marx wrote in the *Economic Philosophic Manuscripts,* "not that the human essence *objectifies* itself *inhumanly,* in contradiction to itself, but that it *objectifies* itself in difference from, and opposition to, abstract thought, is taken as the fixed essence of alienation which is to be transcended."

In each case, the thinker is seen as having rightly recognized a reality of "estrangement"—of the earthly family made into the heavenly; of the product turned into a value; of the human essence become an object. And in each case the thinker makes the same error, failing to ask why the fact he describes is a fact. Reality is accepted on its surface; it is not probed into its contradictory depths. This error is not, however, seen as a fault peculiar to Feuerbach, Ricardo or Hegel. Rather, the questions they failed to ask have a common quality: they did not investigate the contradictions of the status quo. So, these three men, for all of their enormous impact on history, unconsciously stood on the terrain of bourgeois society, taking its facts as facts rather than as invitations to further questions.

The contemporary Marxist who has most developed this aspect of Marx's thought is Louis Althusser. Since his name arises fairly often in this volume, and since he contains more than a few ambiguities, it might be well to place him in a broader context at the outset. Althusser asks many fascinating questions and reads his Marx with a Cartesian intellectuality. He has clearly been influenced by the "structuralist" ideas of Levi-Strauss and his school, with its emphasis on unconscious patterns which undergird all social institutions. The result is that he tends to stress the Marxian system—its particular structure, its "problematic"—and to ignore the individual facts. His study of *Das Kapital,* for instance, contains much philosophical speculation, very little economic theory and practically no economic data. So I have basic disagreements with him. Still, Althusser raises some extremely pertinent issues and he is provocative even when you do disagree with him.

In his study of *Das Kapital,* Althusser describes the phases of a "problematic" (or paradigm) that must accompany every science. For a science

> cannot pose a problem except upon the terrain of, and under the horizon of, a defined theoretical structure. . . . All objects or problems are visible that are situated on the terrain and under the horizon—that is to say, in the structured field defined by the theoretical problematic of a given discipline.

Thus,

> literally, it is no longer the eye (the eye of the spirit) which *sees* that which exists in the field defined by the theoretical problematic; it is the field itself which *sees itself* in the objects or the problems which it defines—vision being only the necessary reflection of the field upon its objects.

In the case of the ideologies, the problem is

> formulated on the basis of its response, as its exact reflection—that is to say, not as a real problem, but as the problem which it was necessary to pose so that the *ideological* solution one wanted to give it was indeed the solution of the problem.

All of this is said with typical convolutions; it stresses the problematic and plays down the evidence; and it also has a certain, quite important truth.

It is clear that the quotations just cited veer quite close to Kant and his focus on the *a prioris* that precede empirical investigation. Althusser does, however, qualify his position so that it does not describe a merely logical process:

> . . . the problematic is, *in itself,* a response, not merely to its own internal questions—problems—*but to objective problems posed by the times* to the ideology. It is in comparing the *problems* posed by the ideology to the *real problems* posed by the times to the ideology that it is possible to put into evidence the properly ideological elements of the ideology . . . It is not then the interiority of the problematic which constitutes its essence, but its relationship to real problems . . .

In his certitude that he knows the "real problems" on the basis of a Marxism that is the only scientific problematic of society, Althusser exhibits certain intellectual tendencies not unrelated to his long-time membership in the French Communist Party. The French Communists were, until quite recently, among the most orthodox of the pro-Moscow parties in the Communist world. (They did, finally, briefly and timidly, criticize the Russians on the issue of the invasion of Czechoslovakia in 1968.) Although Althusser has admitted that one could not do serious public intellectual work at the height of Stalinism in the Party, his philosophy is not without its Stalinist aspects. Its scientism, its emphasis on structures rather than subjectivities, its focus on the paradigm (the problematic) rather than on the data, are similar to the scientistic Marxism with which Stalin rationalized "saving" the Soviet working class over its prostrated body. But there is much in Althusser that does not fit this rigid, mechanistic pattern, and that is why he is of interest. He will, therefore, appear in this book as an ambivalent reference, and one would do well to examine the context quite carefully every time his name appears. In Chapter 6 there will be a critical evaluation of his Marxist "anti-humanism" and a further consideration of his concept of a "problematic."[2]

APPENDIX B

CHAPTER 2   Marxism Misunderstands Itself

1. The contrast described in the text between Marx's abstract statements about his method and his actual practice of it could be misleading. Therefore I want to expand just a bit on this very complex matter.

First of all, I am not applying to Marx Friedrich Engels' judgment of Hegel—that his method and the conclusions to which it led are in conflict with each other. For Engels, Hegel was simultaneously a child of the French Revolution and of the counterrevolutionary restoration. When he wrote explicitly about politics and religion, his conservative side predominated; when he spoke more generally, more abstractly, the progressive aspects of the age in which he lived came to the fore. "The principles," the young Engels wrote of Hegel, "are always independent and liberal [*freisinnig*], the conclusions . . . are truly illiberal." And much later on, in *Ludwig Feuerbach and the Close of the Classical German Philosophy,* Engels made much the same point. Hegel's approach, he wrote,

> has, to be sure, . . . a conservative side. It recognizes the legitimacy of specific stages of knowledge and society for their time and circumstances; but also, only for their time and place. The conservatism of this mode of viewing things is relative, its revolutionary character is absolute—the only absolute whose validity it concedes.

Now, I think Engels was wrong with regard to Hegel, as Lucio Colletti has suggested. It is most undialectical—be that dialectic Hegel's

357

or Marx's—to separate a thinker's content from his mode of reaching it. That, however, is not germane here. What is to be made clear is that I am not asserting a conflict between Marx's method and his conclusions, but only between certain poor, and even erroneous, statements of the method on the one hand and his real method and his conclusions on the other. But how, then, can one talk of two methods in Marx, the one made explicit in the *Forward* of 1859 and to be rejected, the other found elsewhere?

Louis Althusser's *Lire le capital* is quite helpful on this point, and I want to acknowledge my debt to it, even though I am critical of other aspects of the book (as Appendix A, § 2 details). Althusser makes Marx's analysis of Smith and Ricardo on the subject of the value of labor his point of departure. In it, Marx pointed out that Smith and Ricardo had answered a question that they did not ask and ignored the question that they actually put. In their theories, the value of a commodity was determined by the labor time it contained. But what, then, was the value of labor? The only possible response was a vicious circle: an hour of labor time has the value of . . . an hour of labor time. Unconsciously, Smith and Ricardo dropped their unanswerable question and answered a question they never asked. They said that the value of labor is determined by the cost of producing, and reproducing, the laborers. The question implicit in their answer was: What is the value of labor power?

Althusser proposes to "apply to the reading of Marx the 'symptomal' reading by which Marx read the unreadable in Smith . . ." He will not confine himself to the questions that Marx asked; he will also look for the questions that are implicit in his answers. In a daring assertion he writes that "Marx did not possess, during the time when he was living, and was not able to possess in his lifetime, the adequate concept with which to think about what he was producing: the concept of the efficacy of a structure upon its elements."

I disagree with this statement on at least two counts: that Marx could not have defined the method behind his scientific practice; and that Louis Althusser and the structuralist Marxists have done so. These differences do not, however, affect the central point. It is indeed true that a profound thinker may utilize a methodology which, for a variety of reasons, he never formulates or does not formulate adequately. And it is also true that it can be extremely rewarding to try to deduce the method imminent in a given application of it. So one must be sensitive to what Althusser calls the "symptomatic silence" in Marx, the moment when he acts on a principle that he does not first define. In this perspective, the methodology which is deducible from the four volumes of *Das Kapital* is much richer, much more authentic, than the assertions of the 1859 *Forward*.

But finally, another Marx scholar, Jurgen Habermas, has developed an analysis that, on this point, is much more critical of Marx than I am. On this count, Habermas, a democratic-socialist, and Althusser, a Communist are quite close together; and, with politics similar to Habermas', I am at odds with both. It is one more demonstration of the fact that there is no neat and schematic relationship between theory and political practice in Marxism.

Marx, Habermas writes in *Erkenntnis und Interesse,* takes up a position somewhere in between Kant and Hegel. He accepts the Hegelian position that labor—the active transformation of the world—is the way in which mankind produces itself and its nature. But, like Kant, he rejects the notion that thought and being become one. The problem is, Habermas continues, that the Marxian stress on labor omits, or understates, the role of consciousness and theory in human development—and conflicts with Marx's analyses which very much take these factors into account. "In its assessment," Habermas writes, "the Marxist theory of society considers the institutional structure, the relationships of production, along with the powers of production in which instrumental action incorporates itself." In short, the Marxist practice recognizes the importance of the world of symbols and of cultural tradition. "But this side of Marx's practice does not enter into his philosophic reference system."

As a result,

> there arises in the work of Marx a characteristic misrelationship between the praxis of analysis and the limited philosophic self-knowledge of this praxis. In his substantial analyses, Marx conceptualizes the history of the species under categories of material activity *and* of the critical transcending of ideologies, of instrumental action *and* of transforming praxis, of labor *and* of reflection. But Marx interprets what he does in a narrow concept of the self-constitution of the species through labor.

This is, it will be noted, the exact opposite of the contradiction that Engels located in Hegel. In that case, a revolutionary method was said to be at war with conservative conclusions; in this case, accurate conclusions are seen as insufficiently grounded in a defective method. I am not sure that Habermas is right in his assertion, but I cite his comments because of their relevance to the discussion of methodology and its application. However one decides the nuances, I think Engels, Althusser and Habermas show that it is possible for a thinker to misunderstand his own work, to badly state his own method, and that the actual theoretical practice of such a person—in Marx's case, the four volumes of *Das Kapital* above all else—is the best evidence of the method employed.[1]

2.   Engels' distortion of Marxism is a commonplace theme among serious students of the subject. As Maximilien Rubel put it,

> Engels used to attribute two fundamental discoveries to Marx:
> (1) the "law of evolution of human history" revealed by "historical materialism"; (2) the "special law of motion of the capitalist mode of production" and of its product, bourgeois society, symbolized by surplus value . . . [But] Marx did not have any metaphysical concept of "historical materialism"; and with regard to surplus value, he recognized that he had taken the concept from the classical economists . . . The judgment formulated by Engels on the significance of the scientific discoveries of his friend—whom he thought of in this regard as his master—cannot then be accepted without reserve. This is not to blame Engels, but to consider him as the inventor—perhaps involuntarily—of 'marxism' erected into a system of thought.

Similar judgments are to be found in George Lichtheim, *Marxism: An Historical and Cultural Study;* Iring Fetscher, *Karl Marx und der Marxismus;* Sidney Hook, *Towards the Understanding of Karl Marx;* and Louis Althusser, *Lenin and Philosophy.* I take the scholarly issue to be definitively settled, even though an Italian Marxist, Sebastiano Timpanaro, has recently attempted a partial rehabilitation of Engels. The only questions relate to why Engels acted in this way and why Marx permitted him to do so.[2]

3.   Alexandre Kojeve's brilliant (if idiosyncratic) reading of Hegel would suggest that I am unfair to that thinker in making him responsible for the idea of a universal dialectic in both nature and social life. In the *Encyclopedia,* Kojeve argues, Hegel did indeed say that all entities can overcome themselves and are therefore dialectical. But in the *Phenomenology* only humans are dialectic—they exist in *historic* time—and nature is forever identical with itself. In this view, the transition of the acorn to the oak is not dialectical; but making the oak into a table, which involves man's labor, is.

Lucio Colletti would disagree, seeing Hegel as the author of a theory in which all of reality, animate and inanimate, is ruled by a dialectical reason. Ultimately, I think Colletti is right and that Hegel is a source of Engels' ubiquitous dialectic. However, there is still much ambiguity. Hegel, for instance, makes the very same point that Colletti praises in Engels. *"Matter,"* he wrote in the *Phenomenology,* "is not an *existing thing,* but being as being in general or in the mode of the concept." So, perhaps the truth in his case is as complex as in that of Engels, and therefore both Kojeve and Colletti are right.[3]

4.   Popper's contemptuous dismissal of Hegel—and his ignorance of the philosophy that he thereby rejected—is key to his failure to understand Marx on this point and to attack him for "essentialism."

At first glance, it would seem that Popper is quite right. *Das Kapital* is literally strewn with references to "essence" and "appearance." To take a random example, the Volume III analysis of the production of surplus value talks of "the inner essence, the inner form of this process behind the appearance." If words only said exactly what they seem to mean in normal speech, then Popper would be vindicated. But that is not the case in this instance from Marx, and a knowledge of Hegel explains why.

In Hegel, the essential is also appearance and must be so. "The essence, arising out of [empirical, observable] being seems to be counterposed to it. Immediate being is first of all the nonessential. But it is, secondly, more than only nonessential, it is being without an essence, it is *appearance.* Thirdly, this appearance is not something external, foreign to the essence, but it is its own appearance." In his *Philosophical Notebooks,* Lenin understood the importance of this point and expressed it well: ". . . the movement of a river—the foam above and the deep currents below. *But even the foam* is an expression of the essence."

So it is that Marx criticizes the classical economists in Chapter I of *Das Kapital* for not having demonstrated the necessary connection between the form of the commodity and its essence. And, as Helmut Reichelt commented in a recent study,

> . . . an "antiessentialist critique" [of Marx] which oriented itself exclusively by taking over these categories expressly encumbered with their meaning in the metaphysical tradition would miss the mark. . . . Marx is much more oriented by the Hegelian philosophy in which the essence is not conceptualized as an absolute be-

yond, but as an essence which—as in the Hegelian conception—*must* appear. If it did not appear, then it would not be the essence.

Althusser has rightly said that it was unfortunate that Marx used a vocabulary that did not mean at all what it seemed to say on this point. He used words in a Hegelian fashion, which differs from normal usage. Popper, who professes a respect for Marx along with his dismissal of Hegel, makes a major error about the former because of his ignorance of the latter. But then this simply reinforces the Joycean point made in the text. All that serious Marxism demands of you is your lifetime.[4]

APPENDIX C

CHAPTER 3   The Pervasive Light, The
Special Atmosphere

1. One of the most brilliant statements of the Marxist method, one
with which my own analysis is in substantial agreement, is to be found
in Bertell Ollman's *Alienation: Marx's Conception of Man in Capitalist
Society*. I cite it, and some passages from Louis Althusser and Joseph
Schumpeter, not simply for their intrinsic worth, but to once again
stress the complex relationship between a person's perception of Marxism and his politics.

Ollman writes:

> Each entity with which Marx came into contact was viewed as
> internally related to numerous others in a setting that was forever
> fluctuating; it was seen as something which experiences qualitative
> change with an alteration, at some point, in quantity; as something
> which appears quite different, even the opposite of what it does
> now when looked at from another angle for another purpose; and
> as something which progresses through repeated conflicts between
> its parts, conflicts that are taken to constitute a series of reactions
> against what went before.

Ollman summarizes:

> Marx's subject matter comprises an organic whole; the various
> factors he treats are facets of the whole; internal relations exist
> between all such factors; reciprocal effect has replaced causality;
> laws are concerned with patterns of reciprocal effect; the concepts

Marx uses to refer to factors convey their internal relations; this makes it possible to speak of each factor as an "expression" of the whole (or some larger part of it) or as a "form" of some other factor; finally, Marx's view that factors are internally related, together with his practice of incorporating such relations as a part of the meanings of the covering concepts, allows him to transfer qualities which are associated in the popular mind with one factor to another to register some significant alteration in their reciprocal effect.

Ollman and I have similar, though not identical, political views on socialist strategy in the late-twentieth century. Louis Althusser, as a French Communist, comes from quite another camp. Yet, with the serious qualifications noted in the Appendix A, he has a very similar sense of what Marx is about:

> In Marx, [he writes] one sees . . . that the nature of the relations of production considered does not simply call forth, or not call forth, this or that form of the superstructure, but equally fixes *the degree of effectiveness* delegated to this or that level of the social totality. . . . One cannot then think through the relations of production in their concept by making abstraction of their specific superstructural conditions of existence. To take but one example, we easily see that the analysis of the purchase and sale of labor power where the capitalist mode of production exists (the separation of the proprietors of the means of production on the one hand and the wage workers on the other) directly presupposes, for the understanding of the object, the consideration of *formal juridical relations* which constitute the buyer (the capitalist) as well as the wage worker [*salarié*] as legal subjects. Thus, it presupposes a political and ideological superstructure that maintains and contains the economic agents in the distribution of roles, which makes of a minority of exploiters the proprietors of the means of production, and of the majority of the population producers of surplus value. Thus the entire superstructure of the society under consideration finds itself implied and present, in a specific way, in the relations of production—that is to say, in the fixed structure of the means of production. . . .

Joseph Schumpeter was not any kind of Marxist. Indeed, he was associated with the tradition of theoretical anti-Marxism in Austrian economics. Yet, Schumpeter maintained a high regard for Marx and though the account of Marxism in his *History of Economic Analysis* is not at all affected by the Marxian underground described in Chapter

1, it shows how an independent, non-Marxist thinker can grasp some of the same points. For instance, Schumpeter stresses a distinction in Marx that most Marxists ignore, to their detriment. Like the quotations from Ollman and Althusser, it illustrates the complexity of causation in Marx's work.

Schumpeter asserts that

> Marx attended carefully to the vital distinction between general institutional conditions that permit cyclical movements and "causes," or factors, that actually produce them. For instance, the famous "anarchy" of capitalist society, the intervention of money between "real" transactions and the vagaries of bank credit were for him facts to be taken account of, but as permissive—though necessary—conditions only, and not as "causes"; he perfectly realized the emptiness of any "theory" that contents itself with pointing to these and similar facts. Finally, he distinguished from both conditions and causes, another set of facts, the symptoms. It stands to reason that neglect of these distinctions must be a fertile source of error in analysis and of futile controversy and that this methodological contribution is itself sufficient to give Marx high rank among workers in this field.

Here, for example, is Marx in the *Theories of Surplus Value* talking about economic crises under capitalism:

> The general, abstract possibility of crisis means nothing more than the *abstractest form* of the crisis, without content or substantial motive. . . . However, how this possibility of a crisis becomes a crisis is not contained within this form itself; all that is contained in it is that the *form* of a crisis is there.

This critical distinction, which Schumpeter so rightly emphasizes, is regularly overlooked by a good number of Marxists. Paradoxically, another non-Marxist, Thomas Sowell, made one of the most succinct statements of it.

Jean-Paul Sartre makes a point similar to Schumpeter's, but it is as politically ambiguous as it is theoretically insightful. Sartre describes political intellectuals who do not understand Schumpeter's distinction between the general, permissive structural features of capitalism which allow an event to take place, and the immediate causes of the event. (That is, Sartre writes along the same lines as Schumpeter; he does not cite him.) These politicals, he says, operate from "Platonic ideas" of Marxism. In the case of the Communists responding to the Soviet intervention against the Hungarian Revolution of 1956, they simply relied on their *a priori:* the Soviet Union is a workers' state. It is clear that workers' states, by definition, crush only counterrevolutions, not revolutions. Therefore the Hungarian revolution must be a counterrevolution. At no point in this process did the "theorists" look at the facts: that the "counterrevolution" was made by the entire Hungarian working class in the name of socialism.

The anti-Communist left, Sartre continues, operated from a similar, but opposite *a priori:* the Soviet Union is not led by socialists. In much the same ways as the Communists, but with the contrary result, they concluded that the Soviets must have been counterrevolutionary. This methodological criticism is telling, and it applies to most of what calls itself Marxism (including some—very few, I hope—of my own analyses in the past). My objection to Sartre is that he made his comments some four years after the event. In the intervening period it had become quite clear that, however Platonic the method of the Trotskyist—or other left anti-Stalinist—ideologues in Paris in 1956, their charge of an imperialist attack on a workers' revolution had been amply corroborated. Sartre's sound perception is, unfortunately, encapsulated in a reprehensible context implying a plague on both houses in the Hungary of 1956, that of the revolutionary workers and that of the Soviet tanks.

However, the point of this note is not to argue the characterization of the Hungarian Revolution. Rather it is to stress again the fact that there are no political conclusions that necessarily follow from adopting a genuine Marxist methodology. Ollman, Althusser, Sartre and this writer have many differences in attitude on important theoretical questions, but we are all talking, I think, about the same Marx. Schumpeter, as an outsider, also recognizes the same Marx. Yet the four of us who are Marxists have quite different political orientations, and Schumpeter could be fairly described as the most brilliant conservative of the epoch.[1]

2.   Hegel's concept of the organic whole, like every other idea in his incredibly interdependent system, cannot be abstracted from his total vision without some harm being done. In order, however, to provide the setting of Marx's own—and quite different—development of this basic notion, I will run the risk of quoting, paraphrasing and briefly commenting upon a few isolated passages. They are taken from Part II of his *Encyclopedia,* a book in which Hegel took more pains than usual to render his thought accessible to the non-Hegelian reader.

The idea of the organic whole is, of course, counterposed to the mechanistic model. The solar system was, Hegel writes, the first organism, but it was not really organic, since its various parts were independent of one another. It is only when a system is self-contained in its movement, only when it has its purpose within itself, that one encounters the truly organic. It forms a totality. The most obvious case in point is a living body.

On this count, Hegel quotes the French naturalist Georges Cuvier, who wrote:

> Each organic being constitutes a whole, a single and closed system, whose various parts correspond to one another and contribute toward the same final activity through their reciprocal interaction upon one another. None of these parts can change itself without the others doing so, and consequently every one of them, taken for itself, shows and indicates all the others.

A number of things are obvious from this quotation. The concept of the organic whole was a scientific commonplace of the period, one which Hegel did not create, but which he borrowed and developed in his nature philosophy. One can, for example, find an extended discussion of the notion of reciprocal causality in Kant's *Critique of Pure Reason,* as well as a description of the world as a "dynamic totality [*Ganze*]," which is contrasted to a "mathematical totality." And the political metaphor of the organism was used, for quite conservative purposes, by thinkers who predate the rise of science, from Plato and Aristotle (the latter, a biologist himself), to Shakespeare in *Coriolanus.* So, secondly, in and of itself this idea is so general that almost everything depends on precisely how a thinker uses it. Hegel, as noted in the text, employed it for monarchist purposes in his analysis of society, as the Third Volume of the *Encyclopedia* demonstrates. Therefore, when I insist upon its importance for the understanding of Marx, that has to do with his basic and underlying concept, which is, in some ways, the least important part of his work even though it is, obviously, essential to all his specific analyses.

George Lichtheim is excellent on some of the complexities of intellectual history which surface in this concept. Organicism, Lichtheim wrote,

> was a reaction to the mechanism of the Enlightenment which increasingly—since Bacon and Locke, not to mention their eighteenth-century French followers—tended to see society in the image of a

machine. In rejecting this form of rationalism, Hegel fell in with the romantic current, whose political influence had already made itself felt in Burke's critique of the French Revolution. Yet Hegel's attitude on this point is equivocal, and the long-run effect of his thought has not worked out uniformly in favor of political and social conservatism. The truth is that organicism can be given a radical interpretation if it is seen in evolutionary terms. Cycles of change can be viewed pessimistically as suggesting that there is nothing new under the sun; there is a notorious line of thought to this effect which runs from the cosmological myths of antiquity and the Orient, via the established religions, to pre-Establishment thinkers like Vico and ultimately to Hegel in his more conservative moods. But the anthropomorphic model can also be used to legitimatize such terms as "growth," "development" and even "revolution."

Maurice Godelier and Jurgen Habermas have been among the relatively few contemporary Marxists who, from quite different points of view (Godelier is an Althusserian; Habermas is a critic of Althusser), stress the importance of the concept of the organic whole in Marxism. Habermas also points out that it ramifies throughout the social sciences, providing, for instance, a central image for Malinowski's anthropology.[2]

3.   It would, of course, be impossible to summarize in a brief note the *"Positivismusstreit"* in West Germany in the sixties, or even to outline the work of such a complex thinker as Jurgen Habermas. My aim in this Appendix is much more modest: simply to give some sense of the debate, and particularly of the ongoing relevance of the concept of the organic whole to contemporary social theory, primarily through a few comments on Habermas' involvement in these matters. The reader who wants to pursue the question at a greater length would be well advised to begin with two books, *Logik der Sozialwissenschaften* and *Des Positivismusstreit in der deutschen Soziologie.*

The pertinent aspect of Habermas' work focuses on positivism and scientism, the latter defined as the theory which takes the natural scientific method as the only mode of acquiring truth. There is, of course, a long intellectual history behind this preoccupation, which in German culture goes back at least to Kant's critique of a naïve empiricism. In the case of the Frankfurt school two political developments, the Stalinization of Communism and the rise of the fascist state in Germany itself, placed this issue most urgently upon the agenda. In both instances, reason itself had been enlisted in monstrous causes, and planning was made to serve, not human emancipation, but total domination. Max Horkheimer and T. W. Adorno asked in that near-despairing book of their World War II exile in America, if all this might not be the result of that Faustian—and scientistic—urge to subject the very universe itself to scientific control. And was not part of this process a result of the worship of "facts" in a scientific culture that disdained nonobjective values? This history will surface again in Chapter 9. For now, I cite it only as a prelude to a brief exposition of Habermas' critique of scientism and his assertion of the continuing relevance of the Marx (and Hegel) approach to the organic whole.

Deepening Horkheimer and Adorno's insight, Habermas described how the scientistic school in the social science claimed to follow the universally valid method that had been developed in the natural sciences. One makes hypotheses and corroborates or disproves them empirically just as in physics or chemistry. There is, Habermas argues, an entire philosophy underlying these seemingly simple, and even unexceptionable, assertions. For one thing, it makes the enormous assumption that human beings, acting purposively and on the basis of values and cultural traditions, can be treated in the same way as physically measurable things or events. For another, the individual subject disappears, his or her place is taken by the anonymous experimenter, and only those data are admitted which can be repeated in a predictable way according to the rules of scientific experiment. The "scientific process" becomes the knowing subject; the individual scientist is incidental to it.

Moreover, Habermas continues, this scientistic attitude fits into, and legitimatizes, the power structure of technocratic (capitalist or Communist) societies. Knowledge is now defined as that which is technologically useful, and science is oriented accordingly. Descriptions and prescriptions (facts and values) are rigorously counterposed, with the scientist providing the former without any concern about how the rulers will make the latter. Paradoxically, decisions thus become totally arbitrary and subjective, because they must not be allowed to encroach upon the sphere of scientific objectivity. This provides a rationale permitting scientists to serve any and all exploiting classes.

Given this scientistic theory of the social sciences, these thinkers then develop a characteristic concept of the "system." It is—whether in nature or in society—a whole in which there are functionally interrelated, empirical uniformities. In it, the different quantities which make it up vary reciprocally with one another. This abstraction can then be applied indiscriminately to all reality. (In the example cited in the text, taken from Daniel Bell, the systems concept is illustratively applied to the human body, the economy, a work group, a pattern of bombers and bases.) * All this requires the rather large assumption that somehow a providence has instilled a conformity with systems' equations into all of reality. The advocates of the scientistic theory, I would add, would be embarrassed to learn that they thereby follow in the methodological steps, not only of Friedrich Engels, but even of that great scientist Joseph Stalin.

For Habermas and for the Frankfurt school in general this method abstracts the data without considering either the influence upon them of the social (organic) whole or the position of the observer in relation to them. Sociology, Adorno commented during the debate over positivism, does "not dispose of unqualified data, but only of such data as are structured by the social totality."

One can, he commented in another study, do a careful empirical survey of tastes in classical and popular music without noticing that the distinction between "classical" and "popular" is itself a social product of a given totality at a historic point in time. These are, of course, contemporary restatements of the basic Marxist knowledge that the "facts" on the surface of most societies are rationales or concepts, not facts.

However, it should be noted that there are many aspects of the Frankfurt critique that the non-Marxist could accept. This, as Habermas notes, in the case with Niklas Luhman, a systems theorist who also rejects the scientistic version of his method. Indeed, Luhman is determined to find precisely a functionalist systems approach to values and decisions. He agrees with Habermas that the organic concept cannot be transposed from nature to society, chiefly because natural sys-

---

* Bell's definition of a system is only one of four general types identified by Niklas Luhman, Habermas' antagonist in a memorable discussion. There is, first of all, the Hegelian concept which, Luhman notes, is still very much in use today; then there is the equilibrium model, in which any external stimulus provokes a self-correcting response within the system; thirdly, there is the system that is open to the world and changes in interaction with its environment; and finally the cybernetic system that maintains itself in a world of infinite complexity by means of a selective, reduced, but adequate complexity of its own. I note the variety of meanings to forestall the objection that I am dealing with the systems concept in too narrow a compass (say, that of Bell's definition). The point is that the Habermas critique applies to all of these variants of the basic notion.

tems, like the human body, define their own limits whereas societies do not. The world, Luhman argues, is of such complexity that societies arise in order to reduce that complexity, and to stabilize the difference between the inside (the society) and the outside (the world). Therefore, *"Everything* that has been said about systems . . . can be functionally analyzed as the reduction of complexity."

This is a powerful idea, Habermas concedes; and I agree. Indeed, it can and should be incorporated into a Marxist analysis. But what it omits is a consideration of the elements *internal* to the system which account for its evolution; a consideration of how, for instance, the successful reduction of external complexity in a given mode of production by means of a certain development of the productive forces becomes problematic and contradictory, an incitement to change rather than a mechanism guaranteeing the stability of the system.

Luhman's ingenious analysis of society as a self-enclosed and functional reduction of complexity is, among other things, designed to show the continuity between systems theory in general and systems theory in the social sciences. This is so, even though Luhman clearly understands that one cannot simply transfer the methods appropriate to the study of the physical universe to social life. In criticizing him, Habermas does not simply question this or that part of his analysis. He challenges the basic, scientist assumption that persists in Luhman's sophisticated version of it, that only the methods of the physical sciences allow us to perceive truth. He sometimes calls his own, contrasting view—which concedes, of course, the validity of the scientific method but challenges its claim to be the exclusive mode of truth—hermeneutics. This insists upon the value of self-reflection, of practical and subjective concerns and other means of perception which the established wisdom regards as "unscientific." In a brilliant critique of Dilthey, Habermas shows how the colloquial speech of people in the real world must be understood within its context. Words cannot be isolated from the totality in which they function (which contains gestures, intonations or, at a higher level, all of the resonance and connotation of a culture). Here again, the social fact cannot be understood apart from the whole in which it acquires its meaning.

One of the best summary statements of these themes occurs in an essay in which Habermas explains and defends Adorno's use of this Marxist-Hegelian idea of the social totality. The scientist sociologists, Habermas charges, use those equations which do not arise out of the necessities of the subject matter itself, but are applied to it from the outside. Dialectical theory, he continues,

> doubts that science can proceed in this indifferent way in the consideration of the world made by men. . . . Social science must make a prior determination of the adequacy of its categories to its subject matter, because schema for the ordering of the data in which the co-varying quantities only accidentally relate to one another, do not satisfy our concern for society. Certainly the institutionally reified relationships enter as so many empirical uniformities in the social scientistic model. Certainly an analytic, experimental procedure of this type can enable us, in the knowledge of isolated interrelationships, to gain technical control over social quantities as over nature. But as soon as our concern for knowledge takes us beyond the domination of nature, i.e., beyond the manipulation of the natural sphere, the indifference of the system in relation to the area in which it is applied turns into a falsification of the object.
>
> Ignoring the structure of the object in the name of a universal methodology condemns theory . . . to irrelevance. In the sphere of nature, the triviality of true knowledge has no particular weight. In the social sciences, on the other hand, the object takes its revenge, since the disconcerted subject remains imprisoned by the constraints of the system which he will analyze. He only becomes free of these constraints to the degree that he conceptualizes the interconnections of social life as a totality which conditions the very exploration of itself. At the same time, the social sciences thereby lose their presumed freedom in the choice of categories and models. Now it knows that "it does not dispose of unqualified data, but only over such data which is structured by the interconnections of the societal totality."

Therefore, Habermas rejects the idea that the "controlled observation of physical relationships which are organized by arbitrarily interchangeable subjects in an isolated field under reproducible conditions" is the only assurance of truth. He even insists that, in the choice of initial categories, social science must refer to a "prescientific and accumulated experience from which the resonance of a living-historical and social environment . . . has not yet been excluded as a merely subjective element." In all of this, one notes, Habermas is making use of the Marxist insight that method must arise out of subject matter and that the method of the social sciences in particular is immersed in its object and can free itself from the errors of a false objectivity only if it candidly recognizes its own subjectivity.[3]

4. There are in Hegel many, many quotations that seem to prove that Althusser is right in arguing that Marx's predecessor asserted a doctrine of "expressive totality," according to which an entire age can be reduced, in all of its manifestations, to a single principle. Here, for example, is a not untypical passage from the *Encyclopedia of the Philosophical Sciences*. Hegel writes that

> worldly self-consciousness, the consciousness of that which is the highest determination in men, and with it the consciousness of the nature of the morality of people, the principle of its laws, of its actual freedom and constitution as well as its art and science, corresponds to the principle which constitutes the substance of religion. All these moments of the reality of a people make up *one* systematic totality, *one* spirit imagines and creates it . . .

This is clear enough and, one might think, authorizes Althusser to write Q.E.D. to his assertion that Hegel believed in "expressive totality."

But Hegel, like Marx and other gigantic thinkers, cannot be judged in terms of isolated quotations. I believe that the main thrust of his analysis on this count is not at all the one so apparent in the comments from the *Encyclopedia*. In the *Forward to the Philosophy of Right,* Hegel makes a statement which is much more representative of his considered judgment. It is just after he has remarked (as he did on several occasions) that "What is reasonable is real; and what is real is rational." He then goes on to define what he means by the rational, that which is eternal in time. The rational, he writes, "in so far as it enters into external existence, does so in an infinite richness of forms, appearances and shapes, and surrounds its kernel with the most variegated rinds . . ." Hegel, as a philosopher, concentrates on the kernel, on that which endures in the midst of change, and this could give the impression that he thinks that there is only that kernel and everything else is an expression of it.

But Hegel also insists on countless occasions that the oak is not the acorn—that is, that one cannot derive reality from its core, its seed. The rind is most variegated. Moreover, ideally things should correspond to their concept; in fact, they often do not. Therefore, in Hegel's special vocabulary, something can exist and yet be untrue, unreasonable, not "real." "A defective state or a sick body," he writes, "may . . . exist; but these objects are untrue, because their concept and their reality do not correspond to each other." All this is not quite so strained and bizarre as at first it might seem. In common speech one says that someone is not a "real" man or woman—that is, that they do not fulfill our ideal of manhood or womanhood. Hegel theorizes this insight.

If the real and the concept always corresponded in Hegel's analysis, or if when they corresponded they did so in a simple and predictable way, then Althusser would be quite right and the wily dialectician could be accused of harboring a vision of "expressive totality." But this, as we have seen is simply not the case.[4]

5.   Pierre Naville is particularly good in his emphasis upon wage labor as a, perhaps even *the,* critical Marxian category. I quote him at some length, because he reinforces two extremely important points made in the text: that the dominant economic factor is in reality how men and women work, their relationship to one another and to their boss; and that this relationship functions in a most complex way within capitalism.

> When Marx decided to give a dialectical explication of contemporary society [Naville writes] he confronted the problem of method and exposition. For a long time (up until 1863 at least) he thought it possible to analyse the different sectors of social life "successively," enumerating them in the following way in 1859: capital in general (commodities, money, capital in general), landed property, wage labor, the state, international commerce, the world market. This plan, outlined under the combined influence of Hegel and Ricardo, had the grave default of presenting some facts conceived, to be sure, as a whole, but without their unifying principle appearing clearly. *Wage labor,* that is to say, the general modern form of labor, did not immediately play the role of essential matrix of all social relationships; it intervened almost as a consequence of mercantilism and competition rather than as its cause. In the definitive plan, put to work in 1863, succession is replaced by an integration: the entire system deploys itself on the basis of the specific form of labor in contemporary society in order to know the form of production and of the appropriation of surplus value proper to this society.

Later on, in another volume of his *Nouveau Leviathan,* Naville emphasizes that this centrality of wage labor is far from simple. It is not the "essence" in the traditional philosophic sense. He does so in discussing two rules of dialectical analysis:

The first: a social or physical system cannot be constituted by *only one* opposition or contradiction which would be its principle. So, consequently one cannot consider *the* contradiction as a fundamental characteristic of the system. One will object to me that the capitalist system, in its formal analysis, is precisely constituted by a radical contradiction, that which opposes wage workers to capitalist owners. To which I respond . . . (1) that this contradiction . . . implies a series of other contradictions which determine it itself and which are determined by it; (2) that these contradictions can only manifest themselves because they are in contradiction with the principle of coordination which constitutes the system. The coordination between human groups and nonhuman nature, and between human groups, appears as the form where these oppositions manifest themselves. There is, then, a relation between these oppositions and the equilibrium which they suppose. The coordination appears as a mode of relationship simultaneously indispensable for the existence of the system and to the contradictions within the system.

All this must surely sound quite abstract in this general statement. And yet, Naville's point is crucial to a basic error of Marx interpretation (and reality interpretation) made by Raymond Aron, Daniel Bell, and other theorists of "industrial," or "post-industrial," society. They do not realize that Marx presents a social system as being *simultaneously* coordinated and self-contradictory and that this opens up the way for all kinds of divergences between "superstructure" and "base," for breakdowns and equilibriums alike. Chapter 4 makes this point more precisely.[5]

APPENDIX D

CHAPTER 4   The Mode of Life

1.   An extended statement of the Althusser school's version of the theory of the mode of production is found in Etienne Balibar's "On the Fundamental Concepts of Historical Materialism." Like Althusser's own work, it contains much of value, and much that is overly schematic, structuralist rather than Marxist. It is Marx as he might have been, were his influential predecessor Descartes, not Hegel.

Balibar writes, "We can . . . define a 'mode' as a system of forms which represents *a state of the variation* of the totality [*ensemble*] of elements that necessarily enter into *the process considered."* The similarity between this approach and the structuralism of Levi-Strauss is obvious. Here, too, there are persistent and unchanging elements (the "synchronic") and variations in them (the "diachronic"). At one point, Balibar even talks of the invariant elements of every mode of production. They are:

1. Worker.
2. Means of production.
   i. Object of labor.
   ii. Means of labor.
3. Nonworker.
   A. Relation of property.
   B. Relation of material, or real, appropriation.

It is certainly true that many of these relationships are to be found in *Das Kapital,* and that Marx considers them crucial. In Volume II, for instance, one finds this statement:

Whatever the societal form of production, worker and means of production always remain its factors. But the one and the other are only in a potential state so long as they remain separated. For production to take place with them, they must be combined. The particular manner and mode according to which this combination is accomplished differentiates the various economic epochs in their societal structure. In the case before us [capitalism] the separation of the free worker from his means of production is the given starting point, and we have seen how and under which circumstances both are united in the hands of the capitalist—namely, as the productive mode of existence of his capital. The actual process whereby the personal and material commodity elements are thus brought together, the production process, becomes itself thereby a function of capital—the capitalist production process, whose nature was developed at length in the first volume of this work.

This passage is quite precise, and it articulates the underlying methodology of the longer discussion of modes of production that takes place during Marx's analysis of labor rent under feudalism. And it emphasizes the crucial point that it is the relationship under which the worker and the means of production are brought together that is decisive. On the basis of these remarks (and many others in *Das Kapital*), Balibar is right to say that there are two processes of "appropriation," which take place simultaneously: the appropriation of nature by man, (that is, work transforming raw materials into goods and services); and the appropriation of the surplus labor by the capitalist. So, capital functions as an organizer of labor and as an exploiter of labor at the same time.

All this is true. Moreover, Balibar emphasizes the difference between the feudal and capitalist modes in excellent fashion. We know from Marx, he writes, that the forms of the feudal mode of production will not arise from the economic base alone, but will also be "master and serf"—relations which are *"not directly economic, but directly political and economic, indissolubly.* Which means, finally, that some different modes of production do not combine *homogeneous* elements and do not give rise to disparities [*découpages*] . . . between the 'economic,' and 'juridical' and the 'political.' "

I am obviously in agreement with these individual insights. Why, then, am I dissatisfied with the totality of Balibar's (and Althusser's) analysis? It is because their drive to systematize and categorize Marx robs him of one of his most important qualities, his constant insistence on the empirical, his suspicion of historical schema. The Marxian "structure" that Althusser, Balibar and friends thus define, becomes an entity in its own right—which is not the case in Marx, where method is a means to understanding a subject matter that arises out of that subject matter itself. Thus, I think Alfred Schmidt is quite right to analogize Althusser to the American functionalists, like Talcott Parsons. But I think it a bit superficial to see structuralism as a refraction of the bureaucratic world of organized capitalism, as Schmidt does. I would place a much greater stress on its French heritage; it is a very Parisian theory.[1]

2.   Helmut Reichelt succinctly summarizes the scholarly significance of the notion of "capital in general." He writes:

It is the service of two authors, Roman Rosdolsky and Witali Solomonowitsch Wygodksi to have offered detailed proof that Marx's entire *Kapital* is only the completion of the first section of the original conception from the year 1857, that is, the development of the "general concept of capital." The more Marx concerned himself with political economy, the more he structured the material into the primary and secondary. This "general concept of capital" became the dominating concept that motivated him not to write the originally planned books on wage labor, landed property, the state and foreign commerce, but only to take up portions of these unwritten books in his "general investigation," as he was later to call it on a number of occasions. That this was not a matter of a shortening of the materials, but was seen by Marx as a completely adequate mastering of all the materials, is apparent in a letter to Kugelman in which he writes that it is the quintessence of political economy and that "the development following, as well as other points, will be easily done on the basis of what is accomplished."

Rosdolsky himself has this to say:

Capital in *general,* as differentiated from the particular capital, appears, to be sure, (1) *only as an abstraction,* but as an abstraction that conceives the *differentia specifica* of capital as distinguished from all other forms of wealth. . . . (2) but capital in general, as differentiated from particular real capitals, is itself a real existence. This is recognized, if not understood by the ordinary economists and plays a very important role in their theory of equalization, etc. For example, capital in this general form, although belonging to individual capitalists . . . forms the capital that is accumulated through banks, or is distributed by them, so marvelously dividing itself up in relation to the needs of production. Through loans, etc., it reaches an equal level in different lands. . . .

This "capital in general" is contrasted by Rosdolsky to "many capitals"—that is, to the sphere of competition. He quotes Marx from Volume I:

The general and necessary tendency of capital must be differentiated from its phenomenal forms. The manner and mode whereby the imminent law of capitalist production appears in the external movement of capitals, asserts itself as the compulsory law of competition . . . It is not now to be observed, but rather to be illuminated by what goes before. The scientific analysis of competition is possible only so long as the inner nature of capitalism is conceptualized—much as the apparent movement of the heavenly bodies is understandable only when their actual movement, which is not perceptible to the senses, is known.

There is a certain ambiguity here, as Norman Geras has pointed out. Marx's claim for the scientific character of his method is analogized to astronomy and, through it, to the natural sciences in general. That implies that there is no basic difference in the methodology of the natural and social sciences. The more profound statement is made in Chapter I of the first volume, where the purposively deceptive nature of capitalist categories—which the data of the physical world do not share—is the unique reason why the observer of society must "go behind" them. This second explanation actually describes the method of *Das Kapital*. However, the imprecision in this particular quotation does not affect the point Rosdolsky is making. It is of the very nature of capitalism to seek insatiably after more and more surplus (unpaid) labor. This can be seen in the production process, which is where that surplus is created and acts as the driving force of the entire system. Competition then enforces this law, sometimes brutally, but it does not create it. Therefore, Marx abstracts from "many capitals," or competition, in Volume I; but then he brings these factors into play in his Volume III analysis.

Here again, it might seem that Marx is saying that the production relations are the "essence," and competition only "accidental" or the "appearance" of things. But one must be reminded that Marx uses these concepts in a Hegelian mode. As he put it in the *Grundrisse*, "conceptually, competition is nothing but the inner nature of capital, its essential determination, as it appears and is realized as the interaction of many capitals upon one another, the inner tendency as external necessity."

Moreover, the contrast between "many capitals" and "capital in general," Rosdolsky rightly insists, does not counterpose capital in its social interrelations (Volume II) to an individual capital (Volume I). Rosdolsky attributes this view to Rosa Luxemburg and rejects it. Volume I, he points out, deals with the total capital of the society, not with the individual capitalist. One capitalist may sell his product under its value, over it or at its value, but in Volume I the assumption is made that products exchange according to their value because the system is being treated globally, in its totality, even if in a very abstracted version of that totality.

I thus go into some detail with regard to Rosdolsky's analysis for a purpose: to emphasize the great care that must be taken in noting under what simplifying assumptions a particular passage by Marx operates. As I noted in the text, the myth of the Marxian theory of the subsistence wage is, in some considerable measure, the result of scholars ignoring the fact that it is a premise in part of Volume I only because it facilitates the examination of other issues, which must be taken up first. A carelessness on this same count is also at work in Daniel Bell's confused statement of the Marxist view of social class (it will be taken up in Note 4 of this Appendix).[2]

3. If Alexandre Kojeve's brilliant Marxist reading of Hegel is right (and I do not consider myself qualified to judge a matter that requires a thorough knowledge of the Hegelian *oeuvre*), the conception of the capitalist as a person whose authority is not personal but only economic and functional has its roots in his great predecessor. The bourgeois, Hegel says, works for himself. But, Kojeve remarks, "in the Hegelian conception, work can truly be work, a specifically *human* action, only on the condition that it be carried out in relation to an *idea* (a 'project') —that is, in relation to something other than the *given,* and in particular, other than the given that the worker himself is." But the bourgeois has no master and no community. He is an isolated private property holder.

Kojeve continues his summary of Hegel's critique of the bourgeois:

> The *Bourgeois* does not work for another. But he does not work for himself taken as a biological entity either. He works for himself taken as a "legal person," as a private Property *owner;* he works for Property as such—i.e., Property has now become money; he works for Capital.

In other words [Kojeve continues] the bourgeois Worker presupposes—and conditions—an *Entsagung,* an *alienation,* of human existence. Man transcends himself, surpasses himself, projects himself far away from himself onto the idea of Property, of Capital, which—while being the Property-owner's own product becomes independent of him and enslaves him just as the Master enslaved the Slave; with this difference, however, that the enslavement is now conscious and freely accepted by the Worker. (We see, by the way, that for Hegel, as for Marx, the critical phenomenon of the bourgeois world is not the enslavement of the workingman, of the *poor* bourgeois by the rich bourgeois, but the enslavement of both by capital.)

In his *History and Class Consciousness,* George Lukacs, then very much under the spell of the Hegelian interpretation of Marx, emphasized the victimization of the bourgeois under capitalism. In his *The Young Hegel,* Lukacs also stressed the degree to which Hegel was a precursor of Marx who had been profoundly influenced by British political economy and the French Revolution as well as by classical German philosophy. In this reading, what have traditionally been regarded as the "three sources" of Marxism are found in Hegel. (I generally agree with George Lichtheim on these matters, but I do not share his estimate of the Lukacs study of Hegel as a "dull tome.")[3]

4.   In *The Coming of Post-Industrial Society,* Daniel Bell argues that there are two different, and contradictory, schema in Marx, and that these affect his analysis of social class. In fact, Bell's own distinction is based on a misunderstanding of the model of capitalism in Volume I.
   Bell writes:

Marx's first scheme of social development, it should be emphasized, is not an empirical description, but is derived from his model of "pure capitalism." Yet "pure capitalism" itself was a theoretical simplification, and by the time Marx had begun to write the third volume of *Capital,* the growth of a large-scale investment-banking system had begun to transform the social structure of capitalist society. If in the first stages of capitalist society there had been an "old" middle class of farmers, artisans and industrial proprietors, what was one to say of the emerging "new" middle class of managers, technical employers, white-collar workers and the like. This is the basis of *schema two.* Marx observed this phenomenon with extraordinary acuity.

Before turning to Bell's confusion about the "pure capitalism" model, another error has to be cleared up. Bell writes as if the two schema in Marx were written successively—that is, as if experience had taught Marx by the time he came to Volume III that he must modify his over-simplifications in Volume I. This is supposed to apply to Marx's analysis of class structure, but the charge is identical with one that is traditionally made about the law of value, and it is just as mistaken. It was first made by Eugen von Boehm-Bawerk in 1898, when he said that Marx had changed his mind when he came to Volume III, realizing that commodities do not actually exchange according to the ratios of the socially necessary labor time that they contain. The Volume I labor-value theory, Boehm-Bawerk said, was abandoned when subsequent exerience taught that the cost-of-production theory of Volume III was closer to reality. Bell changes the terms of this argument and has Marx bowing to the new data and changing his sociology rather than his economics, but his central assumption is the same as Boehm-Bawerk: that Volume III was written after Volume I.

This was not the case, as even a critic of Marx like Paul Samuelson has now conceded. The bulk of Volume III, Friedrich Engels, who edited the manuscript, tells us, dates from 1861 to 1863 and from the late 1860s. The only portion that was written after Marx had the opportunity to correct Volume I (which he did in the course of the publication of the second edition in 1872 and in helping to prepare the Russian edition of 1872 and the French translation that appeared between 1872 and 1875) was a mathematical discussion of the relation between the rate of surplus value and profit in 1875 (and this was confined to a single notebook). Therefore, the more complex class analysis of Volume III (and of Volume IV, the *Theories of Surplus Value*) were written for the most part long before Marx completed Volume I. The two schema coexisted in Marx's mind.

Why? Here Bell's failure to comprehend the method of Volume I causes him to err. Of course "pure capitalism" was a simplification. It was explicitly presented as such. Moreover, it did not simply abstract from large-scale investment banking and other phenomena of the capitalist society of the time. It also put competition and the circulation process into parentheses, the better to isolate what Marx took to be fundamental: the production process. One can object that this simplification is illegitimate because it obscures what is really essential (although I, obviously, do not think this to be the case). But one cannot charge Marx with failing to include what he had decided to exclude, or claim that the class analysis of Volume III came as a surprise to its author.

But Bell is right that Marx observed the phenomena pointing toward a substantial modification of the capitalist class structure with "extraordinary acuity." He wrote about the separation of ownership and control in the modern corporation, the growth of new middle strata, et cetera. And he did so at the same time that he was still working on Volume I. Bell's confusion is an excellent case in point of how one must scrupulously observe Marx's own simplifying assumptions.[4]

APPENDIX E

CHAPTER 6   The Spiritual Materialist

1. For Althusser, there are three political sources for the interpretation of Marxism as a humanism: the Communist reaction to the scientistic reading of Marx in the pre-World War I Second International; the Social Democratic use of the young Marx as a weapon against Marxism-Leninism (read Stalinism); the disillusioned Communist response to Khrushchev's revelations about Stalin at the Twentieth Congress of the Soviet Communist Party in 1956.

He writes of the first—Communist—Marxian humanism:

> We know quite well in what circumstances this humanist, historicist interpretation of Marx was born. . . . It was born from a vital reaction against the mechanism and economism of the Second International in the years that preceded and, above all, in those that followed the Revolution of 1917. It possesses in this guise real historic merit, as the recent renaissance of this interpretation in the aftermath of the Twentieth Congress possesses it, though under a quite different form. . . . It was around the German left wing of Rosa Luxemburg and Mehring that the themes of revolutionary humanism and historicism were first put on the agenda. They were followed, after 1917, by a series of theoreticians, among whom some lost themselves, like Korsch, but others played important roles, like Lukacs, or very important roles, like Gramsci. We know the terms in which Lenin condemned this "ultraleftist-tending" [*gauchissant*] reaction against the mechanistic platitudes of the Second International, scoring its theoretical and political weakness but also recognizing that it contained something

authentically revolutionary, for example in the case of Rosa Luxemburg and Gramsci.

This is said with some balance and discernment and contains some truth. However, Althusser, like most French Communist intellectuals (but not the Italians) never came to grips with the phenomenon of Stalin, and he is therefore ambiguous—at best—about the post-1956 rediscovery of the young Marx. However, his reaction to the Social Democratic use of these texts is not at all ambivalent.

The debate over the works of Marx's youth [he writes] is first of all a *political* debate. We must recall that the works of Marx's youth, of which Mehring had, in sum, described the history and extracted the sense, were exhumed by the social-democrats and exploited by them against the theoretical positions of Marxism-Leninism. The great ancestors of the operation were named Landshut and Mayer (1931). . . . Everything is clear in their preface to these writings. *Das Kapital* is an *ethical* theory, whose silent philosophy speaks loudly in the works of Marx's youth. This thesis, whose meaning I have given in just a few words, has known a prodigious fortune. This took place not only in France and Italy, where we have been alerted to it for a long time, but also in contemporary Germany and Poland, as we learn in strange articles. Philosophers, ideologues, religious people have thrown themselves into a gigantic enterprise of criticism and *conversion:* so that Marx goes back to the sources of Marx, and it is said that the mature Marx is nothing but the young Marx in disguise.

It is certainly true, as Althusser says, that the debate over the young Marx is political. And it is good that he candidly states that his theories are directed at, among other persons and things, the opponents of existing Communist power. It is one more illustration of a major point in the text of this chapter: that theoretical ideas often have very serious practical and political consequences. In this part of his analysis, then, Althusser's Marx has been drafted to defend Communist totalitarianism. This can be done only by denying the humanism of the actual Marx. This political dimension is not always so obvious or even so real, as the cases of some other authors, discussed in Note 3 will show.[1]

2.   Althusser is at his most convoluted in describing Marx as the author of a theory of history as a *"process (process or processus) without a subject"* but his analysis is worth a brief examination. It shows, among

other things, how a Marxist can take an idealist and Hegelian position and call it "dialectical materialism." I owe this insight (but not its application to Althusser) to a brilliant book by Lucio Colletti, *Marxism and Hegel*. Colletti traces this confusion in the writings of Engels and of Lenin.

In his *Philosophic Notebooks,* Lenin had been profoundly impressed by how Hegel was almost a materialist. He wrote,

> Movement and "self-movement" . . . "change," "movement and vitality" . . . the opposite to "dead Being"—who would believe that this is the core of "Hegelianism," of abstract and *abstrusen* (ponderous, absurd) Hegelianism? This core had to be discovered, understood, *hinüberretten* (rescued). And a little earlier: "I am in general trying to read Hegel materialistically: Hegel is materialism which has been stood on its head (according to Engels) . . .

All of this involved, as Colletti points out, a rather spectacular mis-understanding. In the pages that Lenin greeted so enthusiastically Hegel was defending God! The finite world, he argued, was not the ground, the base, of the infinite. To translate the notion into common speech, one does not proceed from reality to the existence of God, for that would make God dependent upon the contingent, evanescent and ultimately meaningless flux of things and events. The finite, Hegel held, does not exist, it is nonbeing; the sole reality is the infinite, the absolute. Given such a position, it makes sense to assert that there is a "dialectic of matter," for matter is really spirit. But for a materialist to endow matter with such purposive, "spiritual" qualities is an absurdity—although one that escaped the notice of Engels, Plekhanov and Lenin when they did exactly that.

Althusser builds his own analysis upon Lenin's confusion of Hegel and materialism. Indeed he notes, without serious qualifying comment, that the concept of the process without a subject is to be found in the chapter on the Absolute Idea in Hegel's *Logic*. And he argues, with perfect consistency that his reading of *Das Kapital,* and indeed of all of Marxism, *requires* a "dialectic of nature." He notes, of course, that his notion of process is not dependent on God. But how, then, account for the providential character that Althusser ascribes to both nature and history? Hegel had an answer to this question: God. Althusser and Lenin accept the Hegelian vision of a teleological material world but do not confront the issue of how and why it came to be thus.

This gives Althusser a version of Marxism in which people are sociologically the puppets of their class position and philosophically the unwitting participants in a willful material process. He would, to be sure, explicitly deny this, and his own life as a Communist militant is a rejection of his philosophy in action. But his premises are clear, and his antihumanism, his structuralism, his Hegelian (not Marxist) sense of an almighty process are pertinent to his politics.[2]

3. The general attitude toward the young and old Marx outlined in this chapter has an intellectual history.

In the Introduction to the French edition of Marx's philosophic works, S. Landshut and J. P. Mayer made an excellent summary statement of some of the issues discussed in this chapter. It is this interpretation that Althusser excoriated as a social-democratic attack on Marxism-Leninism.

> It is obvious [Landshut and Mayer wrote] that at the base of
> . . . the analytic mode in *Das Kapital,* there are certain hypotheses which do not become thematic in the economic analyses but which are found there by implication. These tacit hypotheses can alone give an intrinsic justification to the entire general trend of Marx's masterpiece. These hypotheses which are not articulated in *Das Kapital* but which buttress its claim to universality and finally give a foundation to this universal, historical aspect that one usually calls "historical materialism," these hypotheses were precisely the *formal theme* of Marx before 1847. It was not that the Marx of *Das Kapital* was liberated from the errors of his youth to the degree that his knowledge gained in maturity and that he, in his personal purgation, abandoned those ideas as useless residues. Rather in his works of 1840–47, Marx opened himself bit by bit to the entire horizon of historical conditions and fashioned for himself the general human foundation without which all explication of economic relations would remain the simple intellectual work of a shrewd economist. Anyone who has not grasped this profound current, which emerges in the youthful works and flows throughout *all* the work of Marx, cannot succeed in understanding Marx.

This, I think, is basically accurate, though I would quarrel with two details. The philosophic foundations of *Das Kapital* are not quite as silent as Landshut and Mayer suggest; and what is usually known as "historical materialism" tends to be vulgar, mechanistic and catechetical. It deals more with the later Engels than with the young, and mature, Marx.

Bertell Ollman's discussion of the meaning of "species being" in his *Alienation: Marx's Conception of Man in Capitalist Society* is outstanding and has already been referred to in the text of Chapter 6. Istvan Meszaros, *Marx's Theory of Alienation* also proposes the idea that Marx had a theory of human nature (though not in that language). That Meszaros and I agree on this count is interesting, given the fact that we disagree on some important political issues; for example, he is quite sympathetic to Mao and I am not. Thus, even though there is a clear relationship between Althusser's Communist commitment and his interpretation of Marx's philosophy, it would be wrong to imply that there is always a one-to-one correspondence of this kind. Marxists, like Meszaros and myself, who are at odds on the application of Marx's analysis to a contemporary situation, can nevertheless agree on the principles behind that analysis.

There is, Meszaros writes, "the *ontologically fundamental* self-mediation of man with nature." This is the ground of the "species being," of that unique human relationship to nature. What Marx opposes as alienation "is not mediation in general, but a set of *second-order* mediations (PRIVATE PROPERTY–EXCHANGE–DIVISION OF LABOR), a 'mediation of the mediation', i.e., a historically specific mediation . . ." Before the 1844 *Manuscripts,* Meszaros continues, Marx did not really concern himself with economic and social issues; at least he did not make them central to his work. But in the *Manuscripts* he adopted the unifying concept that the history of man is his self-creation through work and this is a crucial turning point.

In terms of my own analysis I would read Meszaros' "ontologically fundamental" mediation of man with nature as man's human nature—that is, that substratum of humanity which persists throughout all of the "second-order" incarnations of man. And those second-order mediations are the stuff of the relativity of man in history. Thus I take Meszaros as documentation for the thesis that the theory of man, and of morality, in Marx is absolute (in the qualified sense explained in the text of the chapter) and relative at the same time. Paul Walton and Andrew Gamble make much the same point in their excellent *From Alienation to Surplus Value.* They talk of man, in the Marxist perspective, as characterized by *"teleological or purposive* consciousness" and cite his discussion of the difference between a bee and an architect as a case in point. Here again, as I read between the lines of the Walton-

Gamble book, I suspect that I have some political disagreements with the authors—they talk of revisionism in such a way as to imply that they think themselves orthodox, which is not a word I would use—yet we have a clear consensus about the character of the Marxian problematic itself.[3]

APPENDIX F

CHAPTER 9   Bourgeois "Socialism"

1.   The dangers inherent in the kind of sweeping historical generalizations that James Burnham learned during his years in the Trotskyist
movement (he broke with Trotskyism in 1940 and soon after became a
leading conservative) are apparent in *The Managerial Revolution*. For
instance, Burnham argues that capitalism is, in 1941, in the process of
disappearing, because it is unable to avoid continuous mass unemployment; the new boom will be at a lower level than the previous one; the
volume of public and private debt "has reached a part where it cannot
be managed much longer"; there is a permanent agricultural depression, and a surplus of capital; the colonial world has become unman-
ageable; technological possibilities cannot be utilized; and the bourgeois
ideology is dead. As it turned out, the next thirty or so years saw reality
turn out almost exactly contrary to this prediction.

Burnham developed his ideas in association with Joseph Carter and
Max Shachtman when all three were members of a faction that opposed Trotsky in the Socialist Workers Party of the United States.
Burnham broke with Carter and Shachtman soon after they had split
with the S.W.P. and formed the Workers Party. But Carter and Shachtman then went on to develop a theoretical analysis of the Soviet Union
as a "bureaucratic-collectivist" society, a work that was much more
serious than anything Burnham wrote. An account of this theory is to
be found in Chapter 8 of my book *Socialism*.

Another figure who played a role in the intellectual development of
these ideas was an Italian Trotskyist, Bruno Rizzi, who had published

a book called *La Bureaucratisation du monde* before World War II. It argued, like Burnham, that Nazism, Stalinism and the New Deal were part of the same phenomenon. There is no evidence that Burnham plagiarized his study from Rizzi.[1]

2.   Lucio Colletti has made a trenchant criticism of the philosophical basis of the analysis made by Adorno, Horkheimer and Marcuse. They confuse, he argues, Hegel's idealistic reaction against science itself with Marx's critique of the uses of capitalist science. The former, which has more in common with Bergson than with Marx, can lead to reactionary, obscurantist conclusions; the latter provides for the possibility and necessity of struggle.

> The consequence of Marcuse's argument [Colletti writes] is an indiscriminate indictment of science and technology, or, to use Marcuse's expression, of "industrial society." If we examine it closely, the argument is the same as that which had already formed the basis for Husserl's *Krisis* (not to mention Horkheimer and Adorno's attacks on Bacon and Galileo). It has also been the theme which in recent decades has nourished all the publicity about the so-called "crisis of civilization" (for example, Jaspers' *Vom Ursprung und Ziel der Geschichte*). The "evil" is not a determinate organization of society, a certain system of *social relations,* but rather industry, technology and science. It is not capital, but machinery as such. Marcuse, let no one be mistaken, is the product of that very tradition which today fears him so much.

Colletti is, I think, quite right in arguing that Marcuse makes Marx much too much of a Hegelian on this count in *Reason and Revolution.* And, as will be seen in a moment, I agree with his charge that the Frankfurt school sometimes inspired a fatalistic and antipolitical pessimism. It is indeed true that the struggle for a humane—socialist—use of science and technology is still on the agenda. But Colletti is—or rather, may be—wrong in not entertaining the *possibility* that science will turn out to be the enemy of freedom. That is to say, Hegel and Marx did indeed differ on this crucial score, and perhaps Hegel was right. I propose to act on the Marxian possibility, not the Hegelian, since it is still a question of possibilities which may be affected by political struggle. I do not, however, rule out the miserable, Hegelian eventuality.

It is true that some thinkers who based themselves on the Marcusian perspective were led astray in their dissection of social reality. One of these is Hannah Arendt. In her *Origins of Totalitarianism,* Arendt, who was on the periphery of the Frankfurt school, based herself on the theories of "mass society" developed by Adorno and Horkheimer in *Dialectic of the Enlightenment.* Totalitarianism, she argued, was a society built upon the isolation of atomized individuals, and characterized by the control of all aspects of life, not just politics. As such, it appeared to be without any internal sources of opposition, since the mass men could hardly be expected to rebel against the mass society. Shortly after the book appeared, the East German workers went out on the general strike of 1953, and the Hungarian Revolution and Polish October occurred in 1956. Arendt had seriously overestimated the seamlessness, the totality of administration, in totalitarian society, in part because she did not recognize the persistence of class structures and conflicts.

In a later book, *The Human Condition,* Arendt developed another Frankfurt theme: that Marx had a productionist, instrumental attitude toward social reality and was therefore part of the problem that gave rise to fascism, not an alternative to it. In order to come to this conclusion, she had to simplify and even misrepresent Marx. She commented, for example, that "despite occasional hesitations, Marx remained convinced that Milton produced *Paradise Lost* for the same reason as the silkworm produces silk." This remarkable thesis overlooks the numerous occasions on which Marx commented that the worst architect was superior to the most ingenious spider, in that the former built according to an idea in his head, the latter spun out of instinct. She also did not notice that the specific passage on Milton that she quoted was intended by Marx as part of a bitter, ironic attack on capitalist society for reducing a Milton and his work to the level of a mere wage worker.

What Arendt and the Frankfurt thinkers to whom she owed so much did was to commit James Burnham's error, only in a serious and even profound way. That is, they took the present—the Nazi present of the thirties, the Stalinist present of the late forties and early fifties—and turned it into the inevitable course of the future. Their mistake was, of course, infinitely more fecund than Burnham's in that, even though their basic theoretical structure was seriously flawed, their insights were, and are, of great brilliance and relevance. Still, their experience is a warning to those who fail to see the persistence of capitalism within the increasingly planned economies of the West or of the class struggle in the totalitarian societies of the East.[2]

APPENDIX G

CHAPTER 10   The Common Good as Private Property

1. Does the analysis in the text mean that America is imperialist in the neo-Leninist sense of the term? I have answered this question in the negative and at great length in two books, *Toward a Democratic Left* and *Socialism,* and I will simply summarize those documented analyses here. An excellent study by Barrington Moore, *Reflections on the Causes of Human Misery,* which appeared after my own volumes, has reinforced my convictions in this regard.

The neo-Leninist theory does not simply assert that government power follows the flag or that capitalist nations act on behalf of their corporations. That is obvious and can be observed on the very surface of contemporary history. The neo-Leninist thesis argues that capitalist governments behave in this way because the contradictions of the final stage of the system—above all, a surfeit of capital and a lack of investment outlets—force those governments to seek, and compete for, foreign sources of new investment and of raw materials in the formerly colonial world. In the period since World War II, however, it is precisely the emergence of the welfare state that significantly altered this pattern. With managed economies and an unprecedented expansion of production, it became possible for the advanced capitalisms to profiteer off one another. American investment in the Third World, therefore, declined drastically as a percentage of total foreign investment, and the funds exported to Europe, Australia and Japan increased accordingly. So it was that the loss of the single largest colonial market, China, hardly affected world capitalism in this case. So it is, as Gunnar Myrdal has commented, that the disappearance of the Indian subcontinent would not have a particularly grave impact upon the Western economies. The welfare state, then, is not *dependent* on the exploitation of the Third World.

But two important qualifications must be made at once. First, the oil industry is exceptional precisely in that it is much more oriented toward the Third World than the rest of American capital. In this perspective, the data of this chapter might give an erroneous impression if it is taken as typical of American business' relation to Asia and Latin America. Secondly, if the welfare state is not dependent on Third World exploitation, it enjoys it enormously. With the hindsight of the middle seventies, it is now clear that cheap Arab oil in the fifties and sixties not only provided enormous profits to the corporations but also fueled the economic expansion of all of Western society (though the quota system in the United States modified this effect). The same holds true for all of the Third World's raw materials and agricultural products that, in the years between 1945 and 1972, exchanged in an unfavorable ratio with the industrial products of the capitalist nations. There was, in short, a gigantic subsidy from the poorest people of the world, some of them starving, to the richest, some of them struggling with problems of obesity.

And, as has just been seen, the American government used its not inconsiderable power to promote this injustice. Here again, though, it is necessary to be sensitive to complexities. The fact that World War II solved the unemployment crisis of the thirties (which the New Deal did not) should not be taken to prove that America entered that war in order to deal with its economic problems. Or take another example. A remarkably candid Congressional study pointed out that the Marshall Plan was good business for American companies: "The infusion of capital goods (to Europe) was to be supplied by the United States thereby helping to hold up the postwar demand level in the U.S. domestic economy." But this is not to say that the only—or even the decisive—reason that America embarked on the Marshall Plan was to prop up the economy.

Similarly with the oil industry. The anti-Communist motives of Truman, Eisenhower, and all the rest can be conceded at the outset. They were genuinely frightened by a Soviet threat in the Middle East. What is at issue is not their sincerity, but the fact that they inevitably acted on that sincerity in a capitalist way—that is, by subsidizing reactionary governments and private corporations and cynically ignoring the misery of great masses of human beings. That is not a neo-Leninist indictment of American society; it is, I trust, nevertheless a stinging indictment of a nation forced by its economic system to act against its own interests and those of the poor of the world.

NOTES

CHAPTER 1

1. Nietzsche: *Werke,* Vol. XV (2), p. 2.

    Max Weber: *From Max Weber,* p. 155; and *The Protestant Ethic,* p. 182.

    For a bibliographic discussion on Weber's writings on "value-free" sociology: Christian von Ferber, "Der Werturteilsstreit 1909–1959," in *Logik der Sozialwissenschaften,* Ernest Topitsch, ed., p. 178, n. 3.

    For an interpretation of Weber's attitude: Jurgen Habermas, *Zur Logik der Sozialwissenschaften,* p. 89; and W. C. Runciman, *Social Science and Political Theory,* pp. 15 and 59.

    On Weber and American social theory in the fifties: Alvin W. Gouldner, "Anti-Minotaur: The Myth of Value-Free Sociology," in *For Sociology.*

    Marx on the factory system: *Marx-Engels Werke* (hereafter *MEW*), XXIII, p. 367. For an earlier statement of this theme, see his *Misère de la philosophie,* p. 45. (All citations of Marx's works written in German are to the *MEW;* where he wrote in other languages which the *Werke* translated into German, an original text is used.)

    Einstein: quoted in Daniel Bell, *The Coming of Post-Industrial Society,* p. 9.

    Aron: *Les Marxismes imaginaires,* p. 248.

    Kuhn: *The Structure of Scientific Revolutions,* pp. x, 79.

    Engels on Lavoisier: *MEW,* XXIV, pp. 17 ff.

    Sartre: *Critique de la raison dialectique,* p. 22.

2. Hegel on monarchy: *Grundlinien der Philosophie des Rechts,* pp. 245–46.

Hegel's *Logic: Wissenschaft der Logik,* Vol. II, pp. 423–24.

Theory and practice in Hegel: *Phenomenologie des Geistes,* pp. 549 ff.

Alexandre Kojeve: *Introduction to the Reading of Hegel.*

Hegel on Adam Smith: *Grundlinien,* p. 170; see also Jean Hippolyte, *Études sur Marx et Hegel.*

Lenin on three currents: *Collected Works* (hereafter *CW*), Vol. XXI, p. 50.

Hegel on immiseration of workers: *Jenaer Realphilosophie,* pp. 231 ff; *Grundlinien,* p. 200.

Recent scholarship on Hegel and Marx: Georg Lukacs, *Der junge Hegel;* Herbert Marcuse, *Reason and Revolution;* Shlomo Avineri, *Hegel's Theory of the Modern State.*

Hegel on theodicy: *Vorlesungen uber die Philosophie der Geschichte,* p. 440.

Marx on Hegel's positivism: *MEW,* Erg. Bd. I, p. 581.

Hegel on owl of Minerva: *Grundlinien,* p. 17.

Marxism's openness: Alfred Schmidt, *The Concept of Nature in Marx;* Schmidt, *Beitrage zur marxistischen Erkenntnistheorie,* Introduction; Jurgen Habermas, *Erkenntnis und Interesse,* pp. 36 ff.

Engels in *Anti-Duhring: MEW,* XX, p. 35.

Lukacs: *Geschichte und Klassenbewustssein,* p. 13.

Socialism: p. 78.

Samuelson on Marx: *Economics,* 9th ed., p. 510.

Marx on Petty: *MEW,* XXIII, p. 58.

Mills: *The Marxists,* p. 131.

3. Trotsky: *Writings, 1938–39,* p. 145.

Harold Rosenberg: "Marxism, Criticism and/or Action," pp. 50, 55.

Marx, *Critique of the Hegelian Philosophy of Right: MEW,* I, p. 391.

Marx on workers: *Ibid.,* p. 390.

Marcuse: *Reason and Revolution,* p. 435.

Engels on "eclectic socialism": *MEW,* XX, p. 19.

Engels' 1895 Introduction: *Ibid.,* XXII, pp. 644, 515, 433.

Lukacs: *Geschichte und Klassenbewustssein*, pp. 165, 215.
Gramsci: *Quaderni del Carcere*, Vol. I, pp. 84–87.
Lichtheim: *From Marx to Hegel*, p. 66.

CHAPTER 2

1. Auden: *The Dance of Death*, p. 38.
   Janik and Toulmin: *Wittgenstein's Vienna, passim.*
   Mills: *The Marxists*, p. 41.
   Stalin: *History of the CPSU(B)*, p. 130.
   Marx: 1859 *Forward, MEW*, XIII, pp. 8 ff.
   Hegel on civil society: *Grundlinien*, pp. 165 ff. Marx's commentary: *Ibid.*, I, pp. 8 ff.
   Marx on Roman society: *Grundrisse der Kritik der politischen Ökonomie*, pp. 405, 428 n.
   Marx re-reading Hegel: David McClellan, *Karl Marx, His Life and Thought*, p. 304.
   Habermas on *Grundrisse: Erkenntnis und Interesse*, p. 66.
   Engels on relation to Marx: *MEW*, XXXIV, p. 17.
   Lenin on Engels: Collected Works, Vol. XXXVIII, p. 359.
   Engels' simplistic statement: *MEW*, XX, p. 249.
   Engels to Kautsky: *Ibid.*, XXXVI, p. 168.
   Engels on dialectics of nature: *Ibid.*, XX, p. 529.
   Lucio Colletti: *From Rousseau to Lenin*, pp. 5–6.
   Engels' letters: *MEW*, XXVII, pp. 463, 465.
   Lichtheim on Engels: *From Marx to Hegel*, pp. 64–65.
   Afterword to Second Edition of *Das Kapital: MEW*, XXIII, p. 25.
   Raymond Aron: *Marxismes imaginaires*, p. 656.
   Engels at graveside: *MEW*, XIX, p. 335.

2. Gramsci: *Quaderni del Carcere*, Vol. I, p. 11.
   Theses on Feuerbach: MEW, III, pp. 5 ff.
   Great Depression: Maurice Dobb, *Studies in the Development of Capitalism*, pp. 300 ff.
   Colletti: *From Rousseau to Lenin*, p. 56.
   Living standards 1890–1914: Wolfgang Abendroth, *Sozialgeschichte der europäische Arbeiterbewegung*, pp. 68–69.
   Engels in 1895: *MEW*, XXII, p. 524.
   Lenin on Hegel: *CW*, XXXIII, p. 234.

Stalin's philosophy: Iring Fetscher, *Karl Marx und der Marxismus.*
Stalin: *Economic Problems of Socialism,* pp. 7 ff.

3. Edmund Wilson: *To the Finland Station,* p. 233.
Hegel and triads: Alexandre Kojeve, *Introduction to the Reading of Hegel,* p. 308, n. 14.
Marx on trichotomies: *MEW,* XXXII, p. 9; *Philosophie de la misère,* p. 410.
Marx on negation of negation: *Ibid.,* XXIII, p. 791; Engels' comment: *Ibid.,* XX, p. 125.
Brecht: quoted in Helmut Reichelt, *Zur logischen Struktur des Kapitalbegriffs bei Karl Marx,* p. 7.
Karl Popper: *The Open Society and Its Enemies,* Vol. II.
Karl Popper and dogmatic Marxism: *Conjectures and Refutations,* p. 334.
Popper on Marx's Hegelian upbringing: *Open Society,* Vol. II, p. 107.
Popper on Hegel: *Ibid.,* p. 32.
Walter Kaufmann: *From Shakespeare to Existentialism,* p. 98.
Marx on form and value: *MEW,* XXIII, Chapter I.
Popper on Marxism and state: *Open Society,* Vol. II, p. 119.
Engels on bourgeoisie and political power: *MEW,* XXII, p. 307.
Popper on starvation wages: *Open Society,* Vol. II, pp. 166, 169.
Marx on rising wages: *MEW,* XXIII, pp. 640 ff.
Leopold Schwartzschild, *The Red Prussian.*

CHAPTER 3

1. "Rich totality": *MEW,* XIII, p. 631.
Hand mill: *Philosophie de la misère,* pp. 414, 415.
The 1857 Introduction: *MEW,* XIII, pp. 615 ff.
Organic whole: *Ibid.,* p. 631.
Social articulation: *Ibid.,* p. 628.
Hegel on organic whole and democracy: *Enzyklopadie der philosophischen Wissenschaften,* Vol. II, pp. 343, 347.
System definition: Bell, The Coming of Post-Industrial Society, p. 10.
Alexander Gershenkron, *Continuity in History and Other Essays,* p. 47.

Bell: *The Coming of Post-Industrial Society,* p. 10.
Hegel: *Enzyklopadie,* Vol. I, pp. 303–4.
Marx on "specific production": *MEW,* XIII, p. 637.
Marx on feudalism and the ancient world: *Ibid.,* XXIII, p. 96, n. 33.
Marx on Kugelman: *Ibid.,* XXXII, pp. 552–53.
Morgenstern: "The Compressibility of Economic Systems," p. 193.
Marx on "wisdom" of classical economics: *MEW,* XIII, p. 617.

2. Marx on art: *Ibid.,* pp. 640-41.
Marx and Balzac: *Marx-Engels über Kunst und Literatur,* Vol. I, pp. 20–21; *Karl Marx, Friedrich Engels über Kunst und Literatur* (for English original of Engels quote), p. 104.
Althusser: *Lire le capital,* Vol. I, p. 124.
Volume II sequences: *MEW,* XXIV, pp. 43 ff.
Galbraith: *Economics and the Public Purpose,* p. 38.

3. Engels on economics: *MEW,* XIII, p. 476.
Engels on wage labor: *Ibid.,* XX, p. 252n.
Labor as phenomenal form: *Ibid.,* XXIII, p. 562.
Marx on feudalism: *Ibid.,* p. 91.
Worker and potatoes: *Philosophie de la misère,* p. 329.
Marx on Smith and Ricardo: *MEW,* XXIII, p. 95.

4. Marx on beginning the analysis of society: *Ibid.,* XIII, pp. 631–32.
Inca civilization: *Ibid.,* p. 634.
German Ideology: Ibid., III, p. 25.

CHAPTER 4

1. Nicos Poulantzas: *Pouvoir politique et classes sociales,* Vol. I, p. 9.
German Ideology: MEW, III, pp. 37–38.
Marx on precapitalist societies: *Grundrisse,* p. 438.
Helmut Reichelt, *Zur Logischen Struktur* . . . , pp. 73 ff.
Marx on labor rent: *MEW,* XXV, pp. 798 ff.
Marx on capitalism as unique: *Ibid.,* XXIV, p. 42.
Marx on tradition: *Ibid.,* XXV, p. 801.
German Ideology: Ibid., III, p. 54.
Universal tendency of capitalism: *Grundrisse,* p. 438.

402   NOTES

2. Roman Rosdolsky: *Zur Entstehungsgeschichte,* Vol. I, *passim.*
   Grundrisse: p. 945 (final emphasis added).
   Historical factors in capitalism: *MEW,* XXIII, p. 779, 453; world market: *Ibid.,* XXV, p. 346; agricultural revolution: *Ibid.,* XXIII, p. 454.
   Marx on usury: *Ibid.,* XXV, p. 608.
   Reichelt: *Zur logischen Struktur,* p. 262.
   Holland: *MEW,* XXV, p. 345; *Ibid.,* XXIII, p. 744, n. 189; *Ibid.,* XXV, p. 346.

3. Marx, capitalism and technology: *Grundrisse,* p. 480; *MEW,* XXIII, p. 533; *Ibid.,* XXV, p. 347.
   Weavers: *Ibid.*
   Workers and machines: *Ibid.,* XXIII, pp. 531 ff.
   Borkenau: *Der Übergang vom feudalen zum burgerlichen Weltbild,* pp. 1–2, 14; *see also* C. E. Ayres, *The Theory of Economic Progress,* pp. xviii–xix.
   Marx's definition of capitalism: *MEW,* XXV, p. 887.
   Personification of capital: *Ibid.,* p. 888.
   Surplus from workers: *Ibid.,* XXVI, Pt. 1, p. 265.
   German Ideology definition of mode: *MEW,* III, pp. 21, 29, 38.

4. Bell on Marx: *The Coming of Post-Industrial Society,* pp. 10, 12, 114, 476.
   Aron: *Marxismes imaginaires,* p. 239.
   Bell on three areas: *op. cit.,* pp. 12–13.
   Hobsbawm: "Karl Marx's Contribution to Historiography," p. 280; *see also* Maurice Godelier, "Structure and Contradiction in Capital."

CHAPTER 5

1. Marx on money functions: *MEW,* XXIV, p. 37.
   Joan Robinson: *The Second Crisis of Economic Theory,* p. 63.
   Hans Albert: "Modell-Platonism: Der neoklassische Stil des ökonomische Denken in kritischer Beleuchtung."
   Arthur M. Okun: *Equality and Efficiency,* p. 2.

2. Marx on Smith-Ricardo labor theory: *MEW*, XXVI, Pt. 2, p. 171.
    Schumpeter: *History of Economic Analysis*, p. 596.
    Joan Robinson: *Economic Philosophy*, p. 37.
    Marx on values and prices: *MEW*, XXVI, Pt. 2, pp. 170 ff.
    Price deviation from values: *Ibid.*, XXIII, p. 180, n. 37.
    Ronald Meek: *Studies in the Labor Theories of Value.*
    Thomas Sowell: "Marx's Capital after One Hundred Years," *Canadian Journal of Economic and Political Science*, Vol. XXXIII, No. 1 (Fall, 1967).
    Volume III, Chapter I, of *Das Kapital: MEW*, XXV, pp. 33 ff.
    Schumpeter on value theory: *History of Economic Analysis*, p. 598.
    Samuelson: "Understanding the Marxian Notion of Exploitation . . ." p. 400.
    Bronfenbrenner: "Samuelson, Marx and Their Latest Critics," p. 60.
    Value as labor: *MEW*, XXIII, p. 53.
    Air as wealth: *Ibid.*, p. 55.
    Stuff of wealth: *Ibid.*, XXVI, Pt. 3, p. 421.
    Proudhon: *Ibid.*, XXIII, p. 53.
    Craftsmen and just price: Rudolf Schlesinger, *Marx: His Time and Ours*, p. 122.
    Hilferding: *Das Finanzkapital*, p. xlv.
    Aron: *Marxismes imaginaires*, p. 308.

3. Andrew Ure: English original in *Capital*, Progress Publishers edition, pp. 394–95.
    Critique of political Economy: *MEW*, XIII, p. 18.
    Bell: *The End of Ideology*, p. 270.
    Civilizing aspects: *MEW*, XXV, p. 827.
    Nicholas Barbon: *Ibid.*, XXIII, p. 52.
    Grundrisse formula: *Grundrisse*, p. 74.
    Wages: *MEW*, XXVI, Pt. 2, p. 407.
    Braverman: *Labor and Monopoly Capital.*
    Poulantzas: *Les Classes sociales* . . . pp. 267 ff.
    Phenomenal form: *MEW*, XXIII, p. 562.
    Ricardian socialists: *Ibid.*, XXVI, Pt. 3, p. 256.
    Capitalism without capitalist: *Ibid.*, p. 315.
    Popper: *The Open Society*, Vol. II, p. 172.
    Samuelson: *Economics*, 7th ed., p. 516.

Myrdal: *Against the Stream*, p. 57.

Robinson: *Economic Philosophy*, p. 35.

Robinson on Marx's grandeur: *An Essay on Marxian Economics*, p. 2.

Demand for goods: *MEW*, XXV, p. 191.

Distribution of products: *Ibid.*, XIII, p. 628.

4. Bell: *The End of Ideology*, p. 221.

Marx on Ricardo: *MEW*, XXVI, Pt. 2, p. 408.

Marx on modern industry: *Grundrisse*, p. 592.

Bell: *End of Ideology*, p. 270.

5. Marx to Engels on subsistence: *MEW*, XXIX, pp. 312–13.

Soviets and revisionism: *Revisionism*, Leopold Labedz, ed., p. 25.

Engels on iron law: *MEW*, IV, p. 83, n.

Bronfenbrenner: "Samuelson, Marx and Their Latest Critics," p. 60, n. 5.

Schumpeter: *History of Economic Analysis*, pp. 664, 650.

Workers receiving part of surplus: *MEW*, XXIII, pp. 646, 669.

Absolute general law: *Ibid.*, XXIII, p. 674; ultimate cause: *Ibid.*, XXV, p. 501.

Lazarus stratum defined: *Ibid.*, XXIII, pp. 670 ff.

Proportionate wages: *Ibid.*, XXVI, Pt. 2, p. 421.

Marx cycle theory: *Ibid.*, XXIII, pp. 645 ff; *Ibid.*, XXV, p. 267.

Marx on nonfalling profit rate: *Ibid.*, XXV, p. 242.

6. Marx on metamorphosis: *Ibid.*, XXIII, p. 181.

Marx equations: *Ibid.*, pp. 161 ff.

Paul Samuelson: *Economics*, 7th ed., p. 863.

Marx's procapitalism: *MEW*, XXIII, p. 618.

Abstemious capitalist: *Ibid.*, p. 615.

Growth of middle class: *Ibid.*, p. 469; *Ibid.*, XXVI, Pt. 2, p. 576.

7. John Bates Clark: Quoted, Ben Seligman, *Main Currents in Economic Theory*, p. 316.

Samuelson: *Economics*, 7th Ed., p. 515.

Marx on capital: *MEW*, XXV, p. 839.

Monsieur le Capital: *Ibid.*, p. 938.

Marx on wages: *Ibid.*, p. 866.

Constant capital: *Ibid.*, XXIII, p. 411, n. 110.

Piero Sraffa: *Production of Commodities by Means of Com-
modities,* pp. 34 ff.
Wages of superintendence: *MEW,* XXIII, pp. 351 ff.
Trinitarian apologetic: *Ibid.,* XXVI, Pt. 3, pp. 493–94.

8. Joan Robinson: "Capital Theory Up to Date" in *A Critique of
    Economic Theory,* E. K. Hunt and Jesse G. Schwartz eds.,
    p. 233.
    Thurow, Lester: "Toward a Definition of Economic Justice," pp.
    71–72.
    Gunnar Myrdal: Quoted, Hunt and Schwartz, eds., *A Critique of
    Economic Theory,* p. 9.
    Joan Robinson on leets: *Ibid.,* p. 236.
    Veblen: *Ibid.,* pp. 182–83.
    Keynes on profit rate: Joan Robinson, *Economic Heresies,* p. ix.
    Sraffa: *Production of Commodities by Means of Commodities,
    passim.*

CHAPTER 6

1. Fromm: *Marx's Concept of Man,* p. 3.
    Engels on *German Ideology: MEW,* XXI, p. 263.

2. Althusser: *Lire le capital,* Vol. I, p. 150; *Pour Marx,* pp. 225 ff.
    Revisionism: Quoted in *Revisionism,* Leopold Labedz, ed., p. 19.
    Althusser on problematic: *Pour Marx,* p. 64, n. 30.
    Problem solution: *Lire le capital,* Vol. II, p. 18.
    Hegel: *Jenaer Realphilosophie,* p. 232.
    Althusser on Economic Philosophic Manuscripts: *Pour Marx,* pp.
    27 ff.
    1843 class analysis: *MEW,* I, pp. 283 ff.
    Marx as liberal: *Ibid.,* p. 104.
    Marx's second stage: *Pour Marx,* p. 232.
    The rupture: *Ibid.,* p. 233.
    Althusser on "concrete individuals": *Lire le capital,* Vol. II, p. 53.
    Process without a subject: Althusser, *Lenin and Philosophy,* p. 121.
    Althusser on *Grundrisse: Lenin and Philosophy,* p. 103.
    Althusser on 1857 Introduction: *Lire le capital,* Vol. I, p. 154;
    Pour Marx, pp. 201 ff.

Kolakowski: *Socialist Register, 1971*, p. 118.
Bell: *Revisionism*, p. 203; original quote in *MEW*, XXIII, p. 16.
Bell, "gnomic references": *Ibid.*, p. 205.
Marx and Freiligrath: *Freiligraths Briefwechsel* . . . Vol. I, p. 96.
Marx, January 1858: *MEW*, XXIX, p. 210.

3. Fromm on Bell: *Marx's Concept of Man*, p. 78.
   Fromm on individualism: *Ibid.*, p. 3, 13.
   Fromm on socialism and devotion: *Socialist Humanism*, p. 209.
   Marx on mankind: *MEW*, IV, p. 15.
   Marx on individualism: *Ibid.*, I, pp. 284–85.
   1857 Introduction: *Ibid.*, XIII, p. 616.

4. Marx's embarrassing position: *Ibid.*, p. 7.
   Marx and Hegel: Lucien Goldmann, *Recherches dialectiques*, p. 11.
   Species being: *MEW*, Erg. Bd. I, p. 516.
   Working up world: *Ibid.*, p. 517.
   Alienation: *Ibid.*, pp. 514 ff.
   Double sense of species being: Istvan Meszaros, *Marx's Theory of Alienation*, p. 80.
   Marx on senses: *MEW*, Erg. Bd. I, p. 542.
   Kolakowski: *Toward a Marxist Humanism*, p. 66.
   Ollman: *Alienation: Marx's Conception of Man in Capitalist Society*, p. 76.
   Volume I of *Das Kapital: MEW*, XXIII, p. 192.
   Marx in 1843: *Ibid.*, I, p. 231.
   Feuerbach on Hegel: *Zur Kritik der Hegelischen Philosophie*, p. 160.
   Marx on fetish in 1842: *MEW*, I, p. 147.
   Althusser on Chapter I of *Das Kapital: Lenin and Philosophy*, p. 95.

5. Christopher Lasch: *Agony of the American Left*, pp. 5, 7.
   Gramsci: *Prison Notebooks*, p. 408.
   Guevara and Communism: *Venceremos*, p. 293.
   Guevara and material incentives: *Ibid.*, p. 301.
   Cuba, force and incentives: *Socialism*, pp. 236 ff.

Horrowitz: *Cuban Communism,* p. 7.
Engels on German Revolution: *MEW,* VII, pp. 400–401.
Popper: *The Open Society,* Vol. II, p. 95.
Marx on rights: *MEW,* XIX, p. 21.
Slumbering powers: *Ibid.,* XXIII, p. 192.
Marcuse: in *Socialist Humanism,* Fromm, ed., pp. 99 ff.
Marcuse: *One Dimensional Man,* p. 256.

CHAPTER 7

1. T. B. Bottomore and Maximilien Rubel, *Karl Marx, Selected Writings in Sociology and Social Philosophy,* p. 48.
    Marx and the sociologists: *Ibid.,* pp. 29 ff.
    Weber against Marx: Martin Nicolaus in *Ideology and Social Science,* Robin Blackburn, ed., p. 48.
    Runciman: *Social Science and Political Theory.* p. 110 ff.
    Gouldner: *The Coming Crisis of Western Sociology,* p. 113.
    Talcott Parsons: *Ibid.,* p. 149; and Gouldner, *For Sociology,* pp. 139 ff.
    Gareth Stedman Jones: *Ideology and Social Science,* pp. 101–2.
    Samuelson: "Wages and Interest . . ." p. 911.
    Keynes on class war: quoted in *Ideology and Social Science,* p. 66.
    E. R. A. Seligman: *The Economic Interpretation of History.*
    Lefebvre: *La Pensée marxiste et la bille,* p. 151.

2. Gouldner on value judgments: *For Sociology,* p. 3.
    Kolakowski: *Toward a Marxist Humanism,* p. 173.
    Marvin Harris: *The Rise of Anthropological Theory,* p. 221.
    Ruling ideas: *MEW,* III, p. 46.
    Marx and simplified class contradictions: *Ibid.,* IV, p. 463.
    Factory girl: *Ibid.,* XXVI, Pt. 1, p. 171; new stratum: *Ibid.,* pp. 2, 576; *Ibid.,* XXV, p. 310.
    Poulantzas: *Pouvoir politique et classes sociales,* Vol. I, pp. 179 ff; Vol. II, pp. 75 ff.
    Engels and bourgeoisie: *MEW,* XXII, p. 307.
    Schachtman: *The Bureaucratic Revolution,* p. 230.
    Marx on credit and crisis: *MEW,* XXIII, p. 662.

CHAPTER 9

1. Bourgeois socialism: *MEW,* IV, pp. 488–89.
   Bell: *The Coming of Post-Industrial Society;* Aron, *Dix-huit leçons sur la societé industrielle.*
   Bell: *The End of Ideology,* pp. 397, 399.

2. *Wohlfahrtsstaat:* Schumpeter, *History of Economic Analysis,* pp. 171, 400, n. 3.
   Karl Kautsky: *Die neue Zeit,* p. 708.
   French schoolteachers: Norman Birnbaum, *The Crisis of Industrial Society,* p. 30.
   Churchill: quoted in Maurice Bruce, *The Coming of the Welfare State,* p. 213.
   William Appleman Williams: *The Contours of American History,* pp. 360–61.
   Kolko: *The Triumph of Conservatism.*
   Finanzkapital, pp. 318, 408; Hilferding, "State Capitalism or Totalitarian State Economy," in *Essential Works of Socialism,* Howe, ed., p. 274.
   Bukharin: *Imperialism and the World Economy,* pp. 155, 157.
   Bukharin in 1920s: Stephen Cohen, *Bukharin and the Bolshevik Revolution,* p. 255.
   Bukharin on new form of society: *op. cit.,* p. 157 n 2.
   Rudolf Goldschied: *Staatssozialismus oder Staatskapitalismus,* p. 7.
   Spengler: Franz Neumann, *Behemouth,* pp. 197–98.
   Albrecht Wellmer: *Critical Theory of Society,* Chapter 2.
   Goebbels: *Braunbuch über Reichstagbrand und Hitler Terror,* pp. 22–23.
   Burnham: *The Managerial Revolution,* pp. 105, 118, 257.

3. Adorno and Horkheimer: *Dialektik der Aufklarung,* pp. 20, 52.
   Marcuse: *Reason and Revolution,* p. 410.
   Marcuse in sixties: *One Dimensional Man,* p. 32.
   Frederick Pollock: "State Capitalism," pp. 201, 207.
   Neumann: *Behemouth,* pp. 221 ff, 227, 358, 359.
   Kalecki: *Selected Essays on the Dynamics of the Capitalist Economy,* p. 141.

Stuart Hughes: *The Sea Change, The Migration of Social Thought, 1930–1965,* Chapter III; *see also* Anson G. Rabinbach, "Toward a Marxist Theory of Fascism and National Socialism."
Poulantzas: *Fascisme et dictature.*

4. Bell: "The Public Household," pp. 32–33.
Bell: *The Coming of Post-Industrial Society,* pp. 14, 159, 344, 377, 398.
Engels on Proudhon: *MEW,* XXI, p. 185.
Keynes: quoted, Robert Lekachman, *The Age of Keynes,* p. 122.
Kennedy and balance of payments: Theodore Sorensen, *Kennedy,* p. 459.
Socialism: pp. 274 ff; Council of Economic Advisors, quoted, p. 276.
Fragments of the Century: p. 237.
Farm statistics: *Monthly Labor Review,* 1974; Cliff Connor, "Hunger," *International Socialist Review,* September 1974.
National Farmers Union: Report, October 28, 1974 (Mimeo).
1970 subsidies: Joint Economic Committee, *The Economics of Federal Subsidy Programs.*
Council of Economic Advisors: Report, 1974, p. 141.
Lester Thurow: "Toward a Definition of Economic Justice," p. 7.
Pechman and Okner: *Who Bears the Tax Burden?,* pp. 10, 64–65.
Tax expenditure figures: *Hearings,* Subcommittee on Priorities and Economy in Government, January, 1972, pp. 97, 84.
1975 tax expenditures: Bureau of the Budget, *Special Analyses,* pp. 101 ff; Joint Economic Committee, *Federal Subsidy Programs,* p. 88.
Mondale: News release, May 26, 1975.
Proxmire: News release, October 17, 1974.
Okner on external financing: *Hearings,* Subcommittee on Priorities and Economy in Government, 1972, p. 101.
Michael Kalecki: *Selected Essays,* pp. 139 ff, 142.
Seymour Melman: *The Permanent War Economy.*
Tax reductions, 1964–1973: Leon Keyserling, *Wages, Prices and Profits,* p. 79.
Harold Wilensky: *The Welfare State and Equality,* p. 91.
Medicaid: Edward R. Fried, *et al., Setting National Priorities; The 1974 Budget,* p. 114; and Barry M. Blechman, *et al., Setting National Priorities: The 1975 Budget,* pp. 58, 211, 214.

CHAPTER 10

1. Ford Foundation: *A Time to Choose*, p. 339.
    1975 State of the Union Message: *The New York Times*, January 16, 1975.
    Wall Street Journal: January 10, 1975.
    David Haberman: Subcommittee on Multinational Corporations, on Multinational Petroleum Companies and Foreign Policy, Pt. 7, p. 15.

2. Daniels: Subcommittee on Multinationals, *A Documentary History of the Petroleum Reserves Corporation*, p. 18.
    Post-World War II panic: Herbert Feis, *Three International Episodes Seen from E. A.*, p. 94 and n. 1; and Subcommittee on Multinationals, *Hearings*, Part 7, pp. 17 ff.
    Connally Act: *A Time to Choose*, pp. 242 ff.
    Teapot Dome: *Ibid.*, p. 270.
    Feis: *Three International Episodes*, p. 97.
    Bullitt letter: *A Documentary History of the Petroleum Reserves Corporation*, pp. 3, 5.
    P.R.C. powers: Robert Engler, *The Politics of Oil*, p. 250.
    Feis—cod and whale: *Three International Episodes*, p. 129.
    National Oil Policy Commission: *A Documentary History . . .* , p. 118.
    Colonel on companies: quoted in Engler, *The Politics of Oil*, p. 250.
    Feis on settlement of issue: *Three International Episodes*, p. 152.
    Roosevelt and Ickes: *Power Play*, by Leonard Mosley, pp. 151 and 154.

3. George McGhee: Subcommittee on Multinationals, *Hearings*, Pt. 4, p. 84.
    Background paper: *Ibid.*, Pt. 7, pp. 128, 129.
    Tax credit: *Ibid.*, Pt. 4, p. 88.
    Ford Foundation: *A Time to Choose*, p. 247 n. b.
    Government proposal: Subcommittee on Multinationals, Pt. 7, p. 141.
    McGhee on proposal: *Ibid.*, Pt. 4, p. 98.

Senator Percy: *Ibid.*, p. 98.

Income tax on oil: *Ibid.*, pp. 15, 23.

1971 tax rates: Philip Stern, *The Rape of the Taxpayer*, p. 229.

Oil holdings in other energy forms: *A Time to Choose*, p. 232.

Arnold Miller: statement, Internal and Insular Affairs Committee, U.S. Senate, June 6, 1973.

Senator Percy: Subcommittee on Multinationals, *Hearings*, Pt. 7, p. 35.

1952 Trade Commission: *Ibid.*, pp. 14 ff.

Government lawyer: *Ibid.*, p. 55B.

Justice Department and President Truman: *Ibid.*, pp. 108, 107.

Idris regime: *Ibid.*, Pt. 5, p. 1.

Church and Akins: *Ibid.*, p. 9.

Percy on McCloy: *Ibid.*, p. 68; Senator Case: *Ibid.*, p. 69.

McCloy: *Ibid.*, p. 65.

London Policy Group: *Ibid.*, pp. 14 ff.

Staff member and Akins: *Ibid.*, p. 23.

Rigged supply: *Ibid.*, p. 192.

Iraqi wells: *Ibid.*, Pt. 7, p. 310.

Senator Symington: *Ibid.*, Pt. 5, p. 276.

4. Buy a car: Bell, *The Coming of Post-Industrial Society*, p. 142.

Emma Rothschild: *Paradise Lost.*

Nat Weinberg: "U.S. International Economic Policies and Labor."

Cars of the poor: *A Time to Choose*, pp. 124–25.

Eisenhower order, 1959: *Toward a Rational Policy . . .* , Committee on Interior and Insular Affairs, p. 3, n. 6.

Federal Trade Commission on controls: *Investigation of the Petroleum Industry*, Permanent Subcommittee on Investigations, p. 15.

Refinery shortage: *Ibid.*, p. 17.

Nixon task force: *A Time to Choose*, p. 244.

Federal Trade Commission: *Investigation of the Petroleum Industry*, p. 38.

Cost of tax treatment: Subcommittee on the Multinationals, *Hearings*, Pt. 4, p. 19; *A Time to Choose*, p. 245.

5. Kissinger, 1975: Bureau of Public Affairs, Department of State.

Ford Foundation: *A Time to Choose*, p. 309.

Congressman Reuss: Joint Economic Committee, *Hearings,* November 25–29, 1974, p. 62.

Jackson proposal: Senate Document 1283, March 19, 1973.

Ford proposal: Remarks, September 22, 1975.

Forbes Magazine: May 15, 1974, "The Seven-Letter Dirty Word."

Gulf ad: Quoted, Jerry Landauer, "A Different Story," *Wall Street Journal,* March 27, 1974.

Chase Manhattan: Quoted, John A. Grimes, "Wanted: A Rational Energy Policy," p. 9.

Chase on $1 trillion: "Golden Age is Ending . . . ," *Washington Post,* November 19, 1973.

New York Stock Exchange: *The Capital Needs and Saving Potential of the U.S. Economy.*

Proxmire on capital gains: Subcommittee on Priorities . . . , *Hearings,* p. 97.

Arthur Burns: "Can U.S. Grow without Big Profits," *Christian Science Monitor,* February 13, 1975.

Marx on depreciation and new investment: *MEW,* XIX, pp. 18–19.

M. A. Adelman: *The World Petroleum Market,* p. 2.

CHAPTER 11

1. Moynihan: *The Politics of a Guaranteed Income,* p. 53.

   Reforms oversold: *Ibid.,* p. 66.

   Brookings Institution, 1973: Charles L. Schultze, *et al., Setting National Priorities,* Table 6-1.

   Glazer: *Commentary,* May, 1973.

   1974 *Budget of the U.S. Government:* pp. 68–69.

2. Glazer: "The Limits of Social Policy," p. 53.

   Bell: "Meritocracy and Equality," p. 31.

   Moynihan and Mosteller: *On Equality of Opportunity,* pp. 7, 22.

   David Cohen: "Does I.Q. Matter?" *Commentary,* April 1972.

   Bell: "Meritocracy and Equality," p. 40.

   Bell: *Ibid.,* pp. 48, 58.

   Moynihan Report, 1965: Rainwater and Yancey, *The Moynihan Report and the Politics of Controversy,* p. 43.

   L. B. Johnson speech: *Ibid.,* p. 24.

Bell and "sticky fact": "Meritocracy and Equality," p. 64.

Income distribution: "Who Has the Wealth in America," *Business Week,* August 5, 1972; Bernard Haley, "Changes in the Distribution of Income in the U.S."

Royal Commission on the Distribution of Income and Wealth: Vol. 1, pp. 36, 38, 97, 102 and 139; Vol. 2, p. 36.

3. Moynihan: *The Politics of a Guaranteed Income,* p. 144.
    Oakeshott, Michael: *Rationalism in Politics, passim.*
    Coleman Report: Moynihan and Mosteller, *op. cit.*

4. Glazer: "The Limits of Social Policy" p. 52.
    Moynihan on service strategy: *The Politics of a Guaranteed Annual Income,* p. 55.
    Nixon tax subsidies: Joint Economic Committee, *Hearings,* Nov. 1974.
    Moynihan and Mosteller: *op. cit.,* Introduction.

5. Glazer: "The Limits of Social Policy," p. 52.
    Moynihan: *Maximum Feasible Misunderstanding.*

CHAPTER 12

1. Marx on 10 hours law: *MEW,* XXIII, Chapter VIII; *see also MEW,* XVI, p. 110.
    "Magna Charta": *Ibid.,* XXIII, p. 320.
    John Saville, "The Welfare State," *New Reasoner,* Number 3, 1957–58.
    Dorothy Thompson: Quoted, Michael Barret Brown, "The Welfare State in Britain," *The Socialist Register,* 1971, p. 195.
    Christopher Lasch: *The Agony of the American Left,* p. 8.

2. Piven and Cloward: *Regulating the Poor,* pp. xiii, 8.
    Elizabeth I statute: Bruce, *The Coming of the Welfare State,* p. 36.
    Titmuss: *Commitment to Welfare,* p. 133.
    1790: Bruce, *op. cit.,* pp. 55, 35.
    Mill: quoted, Piven and Cloward, *op. cit.,* p. 22.

Boer War: Titmuss, *Essays on the Welfare State*, p. 80.

1890–1960 figures: James O'Connor, *The Fiscal Crisis of the State*, p. 97.

Roosevelt: Arthur Schlesinger, *The Politics of Upheaval*, pp. 325–26.

Hofstadter: *The Age of Reform*, p. 398.

Hearst and Roosevelt: Schlesinger, *op. cit.*, p. 329.

Social security popularity: Barry Blechman *et al.*, *Setting National Priorities: The 1975 Budget*, p. 58.

Social security as welfare: Edward Fried, *et al.*, *Setting National Priorities: The 1974 Budget*, p. 70.

Term "welfare state": Bruce, *The Coming of the Welfare State*," p. 31.

Titmuss: *Essays on the Welfare State*, p. 37.

3. London *Times: Essays on the Welfare State*, p. 82.

Labor party legislation: Bruce, *The Coming of the Welfare State*, p. 233.

Piven and Cloward: *Regulating the Poor*, pp. 196, 248 n. 1, xiii.

National Commission on Civil Disorders: *Violence in America*, Hugh Graham and Ted Gurr, eds., Vols. I, II.

Piven and Cloward on black constituency: *Regulating the Poor*, p. 281.

Electoral statistics: Richard Scammon and Ben Wattenberg, *The Real Majority*, p. 333.

Piven and Cloward on vast array: *Regulating the Poor*, p. 248.

Claus Offe: *Strukturprobleme des kapitalistischen Staates*, p. 125.

4. Offe: *Capitalist State, Berufsbildungsreform*, p. 24.

Offe: "The Theory of the Capitalist State and the Problem of Policy Formation."

Ford and Soviet Theorists: *A Time to Choose*, p. 239; Irina Osadchaya, *From Keynes to Neoclassical Synthesis*, p. 192.

O'Connor: *The Fiscal Crisis of the State*, p. 65.

Social upper class: G. William Domhoff, *Who Rules in America?* p. 5.

Offe on executive committee: *Strukturprobleme* . . . , p. 76.

Poulantzas: *Pouvoir politique*, Vol. II, pp. 7 ff, 10.

Hacker: "What Rules America," *New York Review of Books*, May 1, 1975.

NOTES 415

Rohatyn: "A New R.F.C. Proposed for Business," *New York Times* Dec. 1, 1974.

Henry Ford: "Henry Ford's Idea: 'More Planning,' " *Time* Magazine, Feb. 10, 1975.

Lodge: *The New American Ideology*, pp. 142–43 and passim.

O'Connor on fiscal crisis: *The Fiscal Crisis*, pp. 9, 42 ff, 251.

CHAPTER 13

1. Lyndon Johnson: *Economic Report of the President, 1969*, p. 4.
   Nathan Glazer: "The Limits of Social Policy," p. 52.
   Pigou: *The Economics of Welfare*, p. 134.
   Michael Barret Brown: *Socialist Register*, 1971, p. 193.
   Keysen: "Model Makers and Decision Makers," in *Economic Means and Social Ends*, Robert Heilbroner, ed., p. 149.
   Myrdal: *Against the Stream*, p. 91.
   Banfield: *The Unheavenly City*, pp. 19, 21.
   Council of Economic Advisors: *Report*, 1974, p. 141.
   English wealth distribution: Dorthy Wedderburn, "Facts and Theories of the Welfare State," p. 156 ff.
   Postwar recessions: Council of Economic Advisors, *Report*, 1975, pp. 249, 264, 324.
   Trotsky: *The First Five Years of the Communist International*, Vol. I, p. 202.
   Downturns in 1950s: Council of Economic Advisors, *Report*, 1975, p. 279.
   Employment 1962–69: *Ibid.*, p. 276.

2. Wages and profits in 1970s: Raford Boddy and James Crotty, "Class Conflict, Keynesian Politics and the Business Cycle."
   Nixon 1970 Budget: Nixon: *The First Year of His Presidency*, pp. 46 ff.
   Unemployment, 1969–71: Council of Economic Advisors, *Report* 1975, p. 279.
   Nixon 1971 economic policies: Barry M. Blechman, *Setting National Priorities: the 1975 Budget*, p. 44.
   Business Week: "Scenario for Survival," September 14, 1974, pp. 52–53.

Arthur Burns: "Burns Says Recession . . . ," *Wall Street Journal,*
   May 7, 1975.
Amin: Accumulation à l'échelle mondiale, p. 479.
Habermas: Legitimations Probleme im Spätkapitalismus, *passim.*

3. Trotsky: *Writings,* 1938–39, pp. 59, 145.
   Trotsky on Germany: *Ecrits,* vol. III.
   Schwartzenberg: *Le Monde hebdomadaire,* Nov. 21–27, 1974.
   Futurological projections: Herman Kahn and Anthony J. Wiener,
      The Year 2000, Chapters I, VI.
   Trotsky in 1921: *First Five Years of the Communist International,*
      Vol. I, p. 211.
   Marx on business cycle: *MEW,* XXIII, p. 662, n. 1.
   Engels in 1886: *Ibid.,* p. 40.
   Engels' revision: *Ibid.,* XXV, pp. 130, n. 16; 454, n.; 488, n. 3.
   Engel's addendum: *Ibid.,* p. 506 n.

Appendix A

1. Adler: *Marxistische Probleme, passim.* See also "Max Adler als
   Philosoph des Austromarxismus," in *Zwischen Reformismus and
   Bolshewismus* by Norbert Leser and *Karl Marx und der Marxis-
   mus,* by Iring Fetscher, pp. 13, 308.
   Rosa Luxemburg on Will of Masses: *Gesammelte Werke,* IV, pp.
   61–2; Oriental Despotism: *Ibid.,* V, p. 652 ff; Iron Law of Wages:
   Ibid., I, Pt. 1, p. 768; Bourgeois Society: *Ibid.,* I, Pt. 1, p. 429.
   Joan Robinson on Rosa Luxemburg: "Introduction," p. 28.
   Korsch in 1923: *Marxismus und philosophie,* p. 121.
   Lukacs 1967 Introduction: *History and Class Consciousness,* Rod-
   ney Livingstone, trans., p. xxx.
   Lichtheim: George Lukacs, *History and Class Consciousness,* p. 75.
   Gramsci on *Das Kapital: Scritti Politici,* pp. 80, 465.
   Lenin on Hegel: *CW,* Vol. XXVIII, p. 180.
   Trotsky and Lenin's Notebook: "Hegelian Leninism" by Rays
   Dunayevskaya, in *Towards a New Marxism,* Grahl and Piccone
   eds.
   Trotsky on workers: *In Defense of Marxism,* p. 45.
   Sartre: *Critique de la Raison Dialectique,* Vol. I, pp. 9, 10.
   Mao, "On Contradictions": *Selected Works,* Vol. I, p. 301.

2. *Theses on Feuerbach: MEW,* III, p. 6.
    Hans-Georg Backhaus: "Zur Dialektik der Wertform" in *Beitrage zur Marxistischen Erkenntnistheorie. Alfred Schmidt* ed., p. 141.
    Economic Philosophic Manuscripts: MEW, Erg., I, p. 572.
    Althusser on problematic: *Lire le capital,* Vol. I, pp. 25, 62.
    Problematic and history: *Pour Marx,* p. 64, n. 30.

Appendix B

1. Engels on Hegel: *MEW,* Erg. Bd II, p. 176.
    Engels from Ludwig Feuerbach: *Ibid.,* XXI, p. 268.
    Colletti: *From Rousseau to Lenin,* pp. 115 ff, 128.
    Symptomatic reading: *Lire le capital* Vol. I, pp. 29, 40.
    Habermas: *Erkenntnis und Interesse,* pp. 58, 59.

2. Rubel: *Pages de Karl Marx pour une Ethique socialiste,* Vol. I, p. 98.
    Lichtheim: *Marxism.* . . , p. 251.
    Fetscher: *Karl Marx und der Marxismus,* p. 134.
    Sidney Hook: *Towards the Understanding of Karl Marx,* p. 29.
    Althusser: *Lenin and Philosophy,* p. 58.

3. Kojeve: *Introduction to the Reading of Hegel,* pp. 199, n. 10, 212, n. 15.
    Hegel: *Phänomenologie des Geistes,* p. 192.

4. Volume III and inner essence: *MEW* XXV, p. 178.
    Hegel: *Wissenschaft der Logik,* Vol. II, p. 7.
    Lenin: *CW,* Vol. XXXVIII, p. 130.
    Reichelt: *Zur logischen Struktur.* . . , p. 86.
    Althusser on Marx's language: *Lire le capital,* Vol. I, p. 43.

Appendix C

1. Ollman: *Alienation: Marx's Conception of Man in Capitalist Society,* pp. 58, 131.
    Althusser: *Lire le capital,* Vol. II, pp. 49–50.
    Schumpeter: *History of Economic Analysis,* p. 748.

418   NOTES

Marx, Theories: *MEW*, XXVI, Pt. 2, p. 506.
Sowell: "Marx's Capital after One Hundred Years."
Sartre: *Critique de la raison dialectique*, pp. 26–27.

2. Hegel and organic whole: *Enzyklopädie*, Para. 337, Zusatz, p. 339.
Cuvier quote: *Ibid.*, Para. 368, Zusatz, p. 505.
Kant: *Kritik der reinen Vernunft*, pp. 219, 288 ff, 460–61, 657.
Lichtheim: *The Phenomenology of Mind*, Introduction, pp. xxvi–
xxvii.
Godelier: *Rationalité et irrationalité en économie*, Vol. II, pp. 63 ff.
Habermas: *Logik der Sozialwissenschaften*, pp. 168–69.

3. Adorno and Horkheimer: *Dialektik der Aufklarung.*
Habermas: *Theorie der Gesellschaft oder Sozialtechnologie*, p.
171; *Erkenntnis und Interesse*, pp. 88 ff, 166; *Protestbewegung
und Hochschulreform*, pp. 252–53.
Luhman: *Theorie der Gesellschaft*, p. 10.
Adorno on data: *Kölner Zeitschrift für Soziologie und Sozialpsy-
chologie*, Vol. 14 (1962), p. 250; on music, in *Logik der Sozial-
wissenschaften*, p. 516.
Luhman on organic whole: *Theorie der Gesellschaft*, pp. 147, 148,
163.
Habermas on Dilthey: *Erkenntnis und Interesse*, pp. 178 ff.
Habermas summary: *Logik der Sozialwissenschaften*, pp. 292–94.

4. Hegel: *Enzyklopädie*, Vol. III, Para 562, p. 370.
Hegel on the rational: *Grundlinien*, p. 15.
Hegel and "Real": *Enzyklopädie*, Vol. I, Para. 135, p. 264.

5. Naville: *Le Nouveau Leviathan*, Vol. I, p. 372; Vol. II, Pt. 2,
p. 127.

Appendix D

1. Balibar: *Lire le capital*, Vol. II, p. 98.
Marx on societal form: *MEW*, XXIV, p. 42.
Balibar on feudalism: *Lire le capital*, Vol. II, p. 110.
Schmidt: *Beitrage*, pp. 209, 264.

2. Reichelt: *Zur logischen Struktur*, pp. 73–74.
    Rosdolsky: *Entstehungsgeschichte*, Vol. I., p. 68.
    Marx from Volume I: *MEW*, XXIII, p. 335.
    Geras: "Marx and the Critique of Political Economy," in *Ideology and Social Science*, Robin Blackburn ed.
    Grundrisse: Grundrisse, p. 317.

3. Kojeve: *Introduction to the Reading of Hegel*, pp. 64–65.
    Lukacs: *Der junge Hegel.*
    Lichtheim on Lukacs: *From Marx to Hegel*, p. 44, n. 19.

4. Bell: *The Coming of Post-Industrial Society*, p. 32.
    Boehm-Bawerk: *Karl Marx and the Close of His System.*
    Samuelson: "Understanding the Marxian Notion of Exploitation," p. 399 n. 1.
    Composition dates of *Kapital: MEW*, XXIV, pp. 8 ff.
    Marx and corporation: *Ibid.*, XXV, pp. 452 ff.

Appendix E

1. First Communist humanism: *Lire le capital*, Vol. I, p. 151.
    Marx's youth: *Pour Marx*, pp. 47–48.

2. Colletti: *Marxism and Hegel.*
    Lenin: *CW*, XXXVIII, pp. 141, 104.
    Althusser: *Lenin and Philosophy*, pp. 121–22.

3. Landshut and Mayer: Preface, pp. xiv, xv.
    Ollman: *Alienation.*
    Meszaros: *Marx's Theory of Alienation*, pp. 272, 79.
    Walton and Gamble: *From Alienation to Surplus Value*, p. 17.

Appendix F

1. *The Managerial Revolution:* pp. 31–35.
    Rizzi: Bell, *The Coming of Post-Industrial Society*, p. 96 n. 69.

2. Colletti: *From Rousseau to Lenin,* pp. 131 ff, 135.
   Critique of Arendt: Michael Harrington, "Marx v. Marx."

Appendix G

Marshall Plan: Committee on Foreign Relations, *Report,* February 1974, p. 12.

BIBLIOGRAPHY

Abendroth, Wolfgang, *Sozialgeschichte der europäische Arbeiterbewegung*. Frankfurt: Suhrkamp Verlag, 1965.

Adelman, M. A., *The World Petroleum Market*. Baltimore: Johns Hopkins University Press, 1972.

Adler, Max, *Marxistische Probleme*. Berlin: Dietz Verlag, 1974 [1922].

Adorno, T. W., and Horkheimer, Max, *Dialektik der Aufklärung*. Amsterdam: Querido Verlag, 1947 [1944].

Adorno, T. W., *et al., Des positivismusstreit in der deutschen Soziologie*. Neuwied and Berlin: Luchterhand, 1970.

Albert, Hans, "Model-Platonism: Der neoklassische Stil des ökonomische Denken in kritischer Beleuchtung," *Logik der Sozialwissenschaften*, E. Topitsch, ed.

Althusser, Louis, *Lenin and Philosophy*. New York: Monthly Review Press, 1971.

————, *Lire le capital;* 2 vols. Paris: Maspero, 1971.

————, *Pour Marx*. Paris: Maspero, 1965.

Amin, Samir, *L'Accumulation à l'échelle mondiale*. Paris: Anthropos, 1971.

Aron, Raymond, *Dix-huit leçons sur la société industrielle*. Paris: Gallimard, 1963.

————, *Les Marxismes imaginaires*. Paris: Gallimard, 1970.

Auden, W. H. *The Dance of Death*. London: Faber and Faber, 1933.

Avineri, Shlomo, *Hegel's Theory of the Modern State*. Cambridge, England: Cambridge University Press, 1972.

Ayres, C. E., *The Theory of Economic Progress*. New York: Shocken Books, 1962.

Banfield, Edward, *The Unheavenly City*. Boston: Little, Brown, 1970.

Bell, Daniel, *The Coming of Post-Industrial Society*. New York: Basic Books, 1973.

——, *The End of Ideology;* revised edition. New York: Collier Books, 1961.

——, "Meritocracy and Equality," *Public Interest,* Fall, 1972.

——, "The Public Household," *Public Interest,* No. 37, Fall, 1974.

Birnbaum, Norman, *The Crisis of Industrial Society.* Oxford, England: Oxford University Press, 1969.

Blackburn, Robin, ed., *Ideology and Social Science.* New York: Vintage Books, 1973.

Blechman, Barry M., *et al., Setting National Priorities: The 1975 Budget.* Washington, D.C.: Brooklings Institution, 1974.

Boddy, Reford, and Crotty, James, "Class Conflict, Keynesian Politics and the Business Cycle," *Monthly Review,* October, 1974.

Boehm-Bawerk, Engen von, *Karl Marx and the Close of His System.* New York: Augustus Kelly, 1949.

Borkenau, Franz, *Der Übergang vom feudalen zum bürgerlichen Weltbild.* Paris: Librairie Félix Alcan, 1934.

Bottomore, T. D., and Rubel, Maximilien, *Karl Marx: Selected Writings in Sociology and Social Philosophy.* New York: McGraw-Hill, 1964.

Braunbuch über Reichstagbrand und Hitler Terror. Basel: Universum Bucherei, 1933.

Braverman, Harry, *Labor and Monopoly Capital.* New York: Monthly Review Press, 1975.

Bronfenbrenner, Martin, "Samuelson, Marx, and Their Latest Critics," *Journal of Economic Literature.*

Bruce, Maurice, *The Coming of the Welfare State;* 3d edition. London: B. F. Batsford, 1968.

Budget of the United States Government, 1974. Washington, D.C.: Government Printing Office (hereinafter, G.P.O.), 1973.

Bukharin, Nikolai, *Imperialism and the World Economy.* London: B. F. Batsford, 1968.

Bureau of the Budget, *Special Analyses, Budget of the United States Government, Fiscal Year 1976.* Washington, D.C.: G.P.O., 1975.

Burnham, James, *The Managerial Revolution.* Bloomington: Indiana University Press, 1966 [1941].

Cloward, Richard, and Piven, Frances Fox, *Regulating the Poor.* New York: Vintage Books, 1972.

Cohen, David, "Does I.Q. Matter?" *Commentary,* April, 1972.

Cohen, Stephen, *Bukharin and the Bolshevik Revolution.* New York: Alfred A. Knopf, 1973.

Colletti, Lucio, *From Rousseau to Lenin.* London: New Left Books, 1972.

——, *Marxism and Hegel.* London: New Left Books, 1973.

Council of Economic Advisors, *Report* (annually, from 1947). Washington, D.C.: G.P.O., 1947–. In progress.

Dobb, Maurice, *Studies in the Development of Capitalism.* London: New York: International Publishers, 1947.
Domhoff, G. William, *Who Rules in America?* Englewood Cliffs, N.J.: Prentice-Hall, 1967.

Engels, Friedrich, *Marx-Engels Werke (MEW):* 39 vols. and 2 supplementary (Ergbd.) vols. Berlin: Dietz Verlag, 1953–
Engler, Robert, *The Politics of Oil.* New York: Macmillan, 1961.

Feis, Herbert, *Three International Episodes Seen from E. A.* New York: W. W. Norton, 1966.
Fetscher, Iring, *Karl Marx und der Marxismus.* Munich: R. Piper Verlag, 1967.
Feuerbach, Ludwig, *Zur Kritik der Hegelischen Philosophie.* Berlin: Aufbau Verlag, 1955.
Ford, Gerald, State of the Union Message to Congress, 1975, *The New York Times,* January 16, 1975.
———, Remarks, September 22, 1975 (mimeo).
Ford Foundation, *A Time to Choose, Final Report of the Energy Policy Project.* Cambridge, Mass.: Ballinger, 1974.
Freiligrath, Ferdinand, *Freiligrath's Breifwechsel mit Marx und Engels;* 2 vols. Berlin: Akademie Verlag, 1968.
Fried, Edward R., *et al., Setting National Priorities: The 1974 Budget.* Washington: Brookings Institution, 1973.
Fromm, Erich, *Marx's Concept of Man.* New York: Frederick Ungar, 1961.
———, ed., *Socialist Humanism.* New York: Doubleday, 1965.

Galbraith, John Kenneth, *Economics and the Public Purpose.* Boston: Houghton Mifflin, 1973.
Gershenkron, Alexander, *Continuity in History and Other Essays,* Cambridge, Mass.: Belknap Press, 1968.
Glazer, Nathan, "The Limits of Social Policy." *Commentary,* September, 1971.
Godelier, Maurice, *Rationalité et irrationalité en économie;* 2 vols. Paris: Maspero, 1947.
———, "Structure and Contradiction in Capital," *Ideology and Social Science,* Robin Blackburn, ed.
Goldmann, Lucien, *Recherches dialectiques.* Paris: Gallimard, 1959.
Goldschied, Rudolf, *Staatssozialismus oder Staatskapitalismus.* Vienna, Leipzig: Anzengruber Verlag, 1917.

Gouldner, Alvin, *The Coming Crisis of Western Sociology.* New York: Basic Books, 1971.

————, *For Sociology.* New York: Basic Books, 1973.

Graham, Hugh, and Roberts, Ted, *Violence in America: Historical and Comparative Perspectives;* 2 vols. Washington: G.P.O., 1969.

Grahl, Bart, and Piccone, Paul, eds., *Towards a New Marxism.* St. Louis: Telos Press, 1973.

Gramsci, Antonio, *Quaderni del carcere;* 6 vols. Turin: Einaudi, 1966.

————, *Prison Notebooks.* New York: International Publishers, 1971.

————, *Scritti politici.* Roma: Editori Riuniti, 1971.

Grimes, John A. "Wanted: A Rational Energy Policy." *The Federationist,* Washington, D.C., April, 1973.

Guevara, Ernesto "Che," *Venceremos, The Speeches and Writings of Che Guevara,* John Gerassi, ed. New York: Macmillan, 1968.

Habermas, Jurgen, *Erkenntnis und Interesse.* Frankfurt: Suhrkamp Verlag, 1968.

————, *Legitimationsprobleme im Spätkapitalismus.* Frankfurt: Suhrkamp Verlag, 1975.

————, *Protestbewegung und Hochschulreform.* Frankfurt: Suhrkamp Verlag, 1969.

————, *Zur Logik der Sozialwissenschaften.* Frankfurt: Suhrkamp Verlag, 1970.

————, *Theorie und Praxis.* Neuwied and Berlin: Luchterhand, 1963.

————, and Luhman, Niklas, *Theorie der Gesellschaft oder Sozialtechnologie.* Frankfurt: Shurkamp Verlag, 1971.

Haley, Bernard, "Changes in the Distribution of Income in the U.S.," *Perspectives in Poverty and Income Distribution,* James G. Scoville, ed. Lexington, Mass.: D. C. Heath, 1971.

Harrington, Michael, *The Accidental Century.* New York: Macmillan, 1965.

————, *Fragments of the Century.* New York: Saturday Review, 1973.

————, "Marx v. Marx," *New Politics* (Fall, 1961), Vol. I, No. 1.

————, *Socialism.* New York: Saturday Review Press, 1972.

Harris, Marvin, *The Rise of Anthropological Theory.* New York: Thomas Y. Crowell, 1958.

Hegel, G. W. F., *Enzyklopädie der philosophischen Wissenschaften;* 3 vols. Frankfurt: Suhrkamp Verlag, 1970.

————, *Grundlinien der Philosophie des Rechts.* Hamburg: Felix Meiner Verlag, 1955.

————, *Jenaer Realphilosophie.* Hamburg: Felix Meiner Verlag, 1969.

————, *Phänomonologie des Geistes.* Hamburg: Felix Meiner Verlag, 1952.

————, *Vorlesungen über die Philosophie der Geschichte*. Frankfurt: Suhrkamp Verlag, 1970.

————, *Wissenschaft der Logik;* 2 vols. Hamburg: Felix Meiner Verlag, 1966.

Heilbroner, Robert, ed., *Economic Means and Social Ends*. Englewood Cliffs, N.J.: Prentice-Hall, 1969.

Hilferding, Rudolf, *Das Finanzkapital*. Berlin: Dietz Verlag, 1947 [1910].

Hippolyte, Jean, *Études sur Marx et Hegel*. Paris: Marcel Rivière, 1955.

Hobsbawm, E. J., "Karl Marx's Contribution to Historiography," *Ideology and Social Science,* Robin Blackburn, ed.

Hofstadter, Richard, *The Age of Reform*. New York: Vintage Books, n.d. [1955].

Hook, Sidney, *Towards the Understanding of Karl Marx*. New York: John Day, 1933.

Horrowitz, Irving Louis, ed., *Cuban Communism*, 2d ed. New Brunswick: Transaction Books, 1972.

Howard, Dick, and Klare, Karl E., eds., *The Unknown Dimension*. New York: Basic Books, 1972.

Howe, Irving, ed., *Essential Works of Socialism*. New York: Holt, Rinehart and Winston, 1970.

Hughes, Stuart, *The Sea Change: The Migration of Social Thought, 1930–1965*. New York: Harper and Row, 1974.

Hunt, E. K., and Schwartz, Jesse G., eds., *A Critique of Economic Theory*. New York: Penguin Books, 1972 (1973).

Jackson, Henry, "National Energy Research and Development Policy Act," Senate Document 1283. Washington: G.P.O., March 19, 1973.

Janik, Alan, and Toulmin, Stephen, *Wittgenstein's Vienna*. New York: Touchstone Edition, 1973.

Jay, Martin, *The Dialectical Imagination*. Boston: Little, Brown, 1973.

Johnson, Lyndon B., *Economic Report of the President, 1969*. Washington: G.P.O., 1969.

Joint Economic Committee, U.S. Congress, *The Economics of Federal Subsidy Programs*. Washington: G.P.O., 1972.

Joint Economic Committee, U. S. Congress, *Hearings,* November 25, 27 and 29, 1974. Washington: G.P.O., 1974.

Kahn, Herman, and Weiner, Anthony J., *The Year 2000*. New York: Macmillan, 1967.

Kalecki, Michael, *Selected Essays on the Dynamics of the Capitalist Economy*. Cambridge: Cambridge University Press, 1971.

Kant, Immanuel, *Kritik der reinen Vernunft*. Stuttgart: Reclamm, 1970.
Kaufmann, Walter, *From Shakespeare to Existentialism*. New York: Doubleday Anchor, 1960.
Kautsky, Karl, *Die Neue Zeit*, Vol. X, Bd. 2, 1891.
Keyserling, Leon, *Wages, Prices and Profits*. Washington: Conference on Economic Progress, 1971.
Kissinger, Henry, Speech, February 3, 1975. Washington: Bureau of Public Affairs, Department of State, 1975.
Kojeve, Alexandre, *Introduction to the Reading of Hegel*. Now York: Basic Books, 1969.
Kolakowski, Leszek, *Toward a Marxist Humanism*. New York: Grove Press, 1968.
Kolko, Gabriel, *The Triumph of Conservatism*. Chicago: Quadrangle Books, 1967.
Korsch, Karl, *Marxismus und Philosophie*. Europäische Verlagsanstalt, 1966 [1923].
Kuhn, Thomas, *The Structure of Scientific Revolution*. Chicago: University of Chicago Press, 1962.

Labedz, Leopold, ed., *Revisionism*. London: Allen and Unwin, 1962.
Landshut, S., and Mayer, J. P., "Preface," *Oeuvres philosophiques de Karl Marx,* Tome IV. Paris: Costes, 1948 [1931].
Lasch, Christopher, *The Agony of the American Left*. New York: Knopf, 1969.
Lefèbvre, Henri, *La Pensée marxiste et la ville*. Paris: Gasterman, 1972.
Lekachman, Robert, *The Age of Keynes*. New York: Random House, 1966.
Lenin, Vladimir Ilyich, *Collected Works;* 45 vols. Moscow: Foreign Languages Publishing House, 1960–. In progress.
Leser, Norbert, *Zwischen Reformismus und Bolshewismus*. Vienna: Europa Verlag, 1968.
Lichtheim, George, *George Lukacs*. New York: Viking Press, 1970.
————, *From Marx to Hegel*. New York: Seabury Press, 1974.
————, Introduction, G. W. F. Hegel, *The Phenomenology of Mind*. New York: Harper Torchbooks, 1967.
————, *Marxism: An Historical and Cultural Study*. New York: Praeger, 1961.
Lodge, George C., *The New American Ideology*. New York: Knopf, 1975.
Lukacs, Georg, *Der junge Hegel*. Berlin: Aufbau Verlag, 1954.
————, *Geschichte und Klassenbewustssein*. Berlin: Malik Verlag, 1923.
————, *History and Class Consciousness,* with a 1967 introduction by

the author; Rodney Livingstone, trans. Cambridge, Mass.: M.I.T. Press, 1971.

Luxemburg, Rosa, *Gesammelte Werke,* in 5 vols. Berlin: Dietz Verlag, 1974.

Mao Tse-tung, *Selected Works;* 4 vols. London: Lawrence and Wishart, 1954.

Marcuse, Herbert, *One Dimensional Man.* Boston: Beacon Press, 1964.

————, *Reason and Revolution,* 2d ed. New York: Humanities Press, 1955.

Marx, Karl, *Marx-Engels über Kunst und Literatur;* 2 vols. Berlin: Dietz Verlag, 1967.

————, *Grundrisse der Kritik der politischen Ökonomie.* Berlin: Dietz Verlag, 1953.

————, *Misère de la philosophie.* Paris: Éditions 10/18, 1964.

————, *Marx Engels Werke (MEW);* 39 vols. and 2 supplementary vols. Berlin: Dietz Verlag, 1953–.

————, *Karl Marx, Friedrich Engels über Kunst und Literatur.* Berlin: Henschelverlag, 1952.

————, *Capital;* 3 vols. Moscow: Progress Publishers, n.d.

McClellan, David, *Karl Marx, His Life and Thought.* New York: Harper and Row, 1973.

Meek, Ronald, *Studies in the Labor Theory of Value,* 2d ed. London: Lawrence and Wishart, 1973.

Melman, Seymour, *The Permanent War Economy.* New York: Simon and Schuster, 1974.

Meszaros, Istvan, *Marx's Theory of Alienation.* New York: Harper Torchbook, 1972.

Mills, C. Wright, *The Marxists.* New York: Dell, 1962.

Mondale, Senator Walter, News Release, Washington, May 26, 1975.

Morgenstern, Oskar, "The Compressibility of Economic Systems and the Problem of Economic Constants," *Zeitschrift für Nationalökonomie,* Vol. XXVI, pp. 1–3.

Mosley, Leonard, *Power Play.* Baltimore: Penguin Books, 1974.

Moynihan, Daniel P., *Maximum Feasible Misunderstanding.* New York: Random House, 1970.

————, *The Politics of a Guaranteed Income.* New York: Random House, 1973.

————, and Mosteller, Frederick, eds., *Equality of Educational Opportunity.* New York: Random House, 1972.

Myrdal, Gunnar, *Against the Stream.* New York: Pantheon, 1973.

National Farmers Union, *Report,* 1974. Washington, D.C.: N.F.U., 1974.

Naville, Pierre, *Le Nouveau Leviathan;* 3 vols. Paris: Éditions Anthropos, 1970–.
Neumann, Franz, *Behemouth.* New York: Harper and Row, 1963 [original, 1942 and 1944].
New York Stock Exchange, *The Capital Needs and Saving Potential of the U.S. Economy.* New York: N.Y.S.E., 1974.
Nietzsche, Friedrich, *Werke.* Leipzig: Alfred Kroner Verlag, 1911.
Nixon, Richard, *The First Year of His Presidency.* Washington: Congressional Quarterly, 1970.

Oakeshott, Michael, *Rationalism in Politics.* New York: Basic Books, 1962.
O'Connor, James, *The Fiscal Crisis of the State.* New York: St. Martin's Press, 1973.
Offe, Claus, *Berufsbilungsreform.* Frankfurt: Suhrkamp Verlag, 1975.
————, *Strukturprobleme des kapitalistischen Staates.* Frankfurt: Suhrkamp Verlag, 1973.
————, "The Theory of the Capitalist State and the Problem of Policy Formation," unpublished ms.
Okun, Arthur M., *Equality and Efficiency.* Washington: Brookings Institution, 1975.
Ollman, Bertel, *Alienation: Conception of Man in Capitalist Society.* London: Cambridge University Press, 1971.
Osadchaya, Irina, *From Keynes to Neoclassical Synthesis.* Moscow: Progress Publishers, 1974.

Pechman, Joseph, and Okner, Benjamin, *Who Bears the Tax Burden?* Washington: Brookings Institution, 1974.
Permanent Subcommittee on Investigations, U.S. Senate, *Investigation of the Petroleum Industry.* Washington: G.P.O., 1973.
Pigou, A. C., *The Economics of Welfare.* London: Macmillan, 1972.
Piven, Frances Fox, and Cloward, Richard, *Regulating the Poor.* New York: Vintage Books, 1972.
Pollock, Frederick, "State Capitalism," in *Studies in Philosophy and Social Science,* Vol. IX, No. 3, 1941.
Poulantzas, Nicos, *Fascisme et Dictature.* Paris: Maspero, 1970.
————, *Les Classes sociales dans le capitalisme aujourd'hui.* Paris: Seuil, 1974.
————, *Pouvoir politique et classes sociales.* Paris: Maspero, 1972.
Popper, Karl, *Conjectures and Refutations.* New York: Harper Torchbooks, 1963.

————, *The Open Society and Its Enemies;* 2 vols. Princeton: Princeton University Press, 1971.

Rabinach, Anton G., "Toward a Marxist Theory of Fascism and National Socialism," in *New German Critique,* Fall, 1974.

Rainwater, Lee, and Yancey, William L., *The Moynihan Report and the Politics of Controversy.* Cambridge: M.I.T. Press, 1967.

Reichelt, Helmut, *Zur logischen Struktur des Kapitalbegriff bei Karl Marx.* Frankfurt: Europäische Verlagsanstalt, 1970.

Robinson, Joan, *Economic Philosophy.* New York: Doubleday Anchor, 1964.

————, *An Essay on Marxian Economics.* London: Macmillan, 1949.

————, "Introduction," *The Accumulation of Capital,* by Rosa Luxemburg. New Haven: Yale Univ. Press, 1951.

————, "The Second Crisis of Economic Theory," *American Economic Review,* May, 1972, Vol. LXII, No. 2.

————, *Economic Heresies.* New York: Basic Books, 1971.

Rosenberg, Harold, "Marxism: Criticism and/or Action," in *Voices of Dissent.* New York: Grove Press, 1958.

Rosdolsky, Roman, *Zur Entstehungsgeschichte des marschen "Kapital,"* 2 vols. Frankfurt: Europäische Verlagsanstalt, 1968.

Rothschild, Emma, *Paradise Lost: The Decline of the Auto-Industrial Age.* New York: Random House, 1973.

Royal Commission on the Distribution of Income and Wealth, 2 vols. London: HMSO, 1975.

Rubel, Maximilien, *Pages de Karl Marx pour une éthique socialiste;* 2 vols. Paris: Payot, 1970.

Runciman, W. C., *Social Science and Political Theory.* Cambridge: Cambridge Univ. Press, 1969, 2d ed.

Samuelson, Paul, "Understanding the Marxian Notion of Exploitation: A Summary of the So-called Transformation Problem Between Marxian Values and Competitive Prices," *Journal of Economic Literature,* Vol. IX, No. 2, June, 1971.

————, *Economics,* 9th ed. New York: McGraw-Hill, 1973.

————, *Economics,* 7th ed. New York: McGraw-Hill, 1967.

————, "Wages and Interest: A Modern Dissection of Marxian Economic Models," *American Economic Review,* December, 1957.

Sartre, Jean-Paul, *Critique de la raison dialectique.* Paris: Gallimard, 1960.

Scammon, Richard, and Wattenberg, Ben, *The Real Majority.* New York: Coward-McCann, 1970.

Schlesinger, Arthur, Jr., *The Politics of Upheaval*. Boston: Houghton Mifflin, 1960.

Schlesinger, Rudolf, *Marx: His Time and Ours*. New York: Augustus Kelly, 1950.

Schmidt, Alfred, *The Concept of Nature in Marx*. London: New Left Books, 1971.

————, ed., *Beitrage zur marxistischen Erkenntnistheorie*. Frankfurt: Suhrkamp Verlag, 1969.

Schultze, Charles L., *et al., Setting National Priorities: The 1973 Budget*. Washington: Brookings Institution, 1972.

Schumpeter, Joseph A., *History of Economic Analysis*. Oxford: Oxford University Press, 1968.

Schwartzschild, Leopold, *The Red Prussian*. New York: Grosset and Dunlap, 1947.

Seligman, E. R. A., *The Economic Interpretation of History*. New York: Gordian Press, 1967 [1902].

Seligman, Ben, *Main Currents in Economic Theory*. New York: Free Press, 1963.

Senate Committee on Foreign Relations, *Report, The Overseas Private Investment Corporation Amendment Act*. Washington, D.C.: G.P.O., 1974.

Senate Committee on Internal and Insular Affairs, *Toward a Rational Policy for Oil and Gas Imports*. Washington, D.C.: G.P.O., 1973.

Shachtman, Max, *The Bureaucratic Revolution*. New York: Donald Press, 1958.

Socialist Register, 1971. London: Merlin Press, 1971.

Sorensen, Theodore, *Kennedy*. New York: Bantam Books, 1966.

Sraffa, Piero, *Production of Commodities by Means of Commodities*. Cambridge: Cambridge University Press, 1971.

Sowell, Thomas, "Marx's Capital after One Hundred Years," *Canadian Journal of Economic and Political Science,* Vol. XXXIII, No. 1, February, 1967.

Stalin, Joseph, *Economic Problems of Socialism*. New York: International Publishers, 1952.

————, *History of the CPSU (B)*. New York: International Publishers, 1939.

Stern, Philip M., *The Rape of the Taxpayer*. New York: Random House, 1973.

Subcommittee on Multinationals, U.S. Senate Foreign Relations Committee, *A Documentary History of the Petroleum Reserves Corporation, 1943–1944*. Washington: G.P.O., 1974.

Subcommittee on Multinational Corporations, *Hearings,* Part 1, Washington: G.P.O., 1974.

Subcommittee on Priorities and Economy in Government of the Joint Economic Committee, U.S. Congress, *Hearings,* January, 1972. Washington: G.P.O., 1972.

Thurow, Lester, "Toward a Definition of Economic Justice," *The Public Interest,* Number 31, Spring, 1973.

Timpanaro, Sebastiano, "Considerations on Materialism," *New Left Review,* No. 85 (May–June 1974).

Titmuss, Richard, *Commitment to Welfare.* New York: Pantheon, 1968.

———, *Essays on the Welfare State.*

Topitsch, Ernest, ed., *Logik der Sozialwissenschaften.* Cologne and Berlin: Kipenheuer und Witsch, 1967.

Trotsky, Leon, *The First Five Years of the Communist International;* 2 vols. New York: Pioneer Publishers, 1945.

———, *Ecrits;* 3 vols. Paris: Quatrième Internationale, n.d.

———, *In Defense of Marxism.* New York: Pioneer Publishers, 1942.

———, *Writings, 1938–1939;* George Breitman and Evelyn Reed, eds. New York: Merit, 1969.

Walton, Paul, and Gamble, Andrew, *From Alienation to Surplus Value.* London: Sheed and Ward, 1972.

Weber, Max, *From Max Weber;* Hans Gerth and C. Wright Mills, eds. London: Routledge and Kegan Paul, 1948.

———, *The Protestant Ethic;* trans. by Talcott Parsons. New York: Scribner, 1958.

Wedderburn, Dorothy, "Facts and Theories of the Welfare State," *What Should Be the Role of the Federal Government in Extending Public Assistance to All Americans Living in Poverty?* Senate Document 93-12. Washington, D.C.: G.P.O., 1973.

Weinberg, Nat, "U.S. International Economic Policies and Labor," Paper Presented to German-American Forum, Washington, April 30–May 2, 1972. (Mimeo)

Wellmer, Albrecht, *Critical Theory of Society.* New York: Seabury Press, 1974.

Wilensky, Harold, *The Welfare State and Equality.* Berkeley, Los Angeles and London: University of California Press, 1975.

Williams, William Appleman, *The Contours of American History.* Chicago: Quadrangle Press, 1966.

Wilson, Edmund, *To the Finland Station;* revised edition. New York: Farrar, Straus and Giroux, 1972.

INDEX

433